SARDONICUS

Copyright © 2022 Marc Russell, Amanda Russell, Tom Weaver

No part of this book may be reproduced in any form or by any means, electronic, mechanical, digital, photocopying, or recording, except for inclusion of a review, without permission in writing from the publisher or Author.

No copyright is claimed for the photos within this book. They are used for the purposes of publicity only.

 Published in the USA by:
BearManor Media
1317 Edgewater Dr #110
Orlando, FL 32804
www.bearmanormedia.com

Perfect ISBN 978-1-62933-846-0
Case ISBN 978-1-62933-847-7

BearManor Media, Orlando, Florida
Printed in the United States of America
Front cover artist: Kerry Gammill
Back cover artist: Mary Runser
Book design by Robbie Adkins, www.adkinsconsult.com

Table of Contents

Acknowledgments iv

"But first, a word from the baroness..." by Audrey Dalton. v

Introduction by Marc Russell and Amanda Russell. 1

"Sardonicus": the novella by Ray Russell 5

"Sardonicus Reincarnate": a sequel by Amanda Russell. 22

Mr. Sardonicus: **The Script** by Ray Russell 35

Mr. Sardonicus **Production History** by Tom Weaver. 154

Mr. Sardonicus: **Script-to-Screen Changes** by Tom Weaver. 204

Meet the Sardonicuses:. 209

    Guy Rolfe: career article by Laura Wagner. 209

    Audrey Dalton: career article by Laura Wagner 225

"The Sound of Smilence" by David Schecter 237

Mr. Sardonicus **Reviews** 246

Russell's Other Horrors by Tom Weaver 250

Two More Ray Russell Stories: 263

    "Put Them All Together, They Spell Monster" 263

    "The Devil Is a Tightwad" 266

Breaking the Fourth Wall and Opening Eyes: The Calling of a Castle Connoisseur 269
    Turned Film Archivist by Rachel Del Gaudio

Endnotes 276

But first, a word from the baroness

by Audrey Dalton, star of *Mr. Sardonicus*

My involvement with *Mr. Sardonicus* started when I met with William Castle to discuss working on the film with him. We were already well acquainted, having worked together a couple of years before on an episode of the TV series *Men of Annapolis*, filmed on location at Annapolis. He was the same William Castle I remembered, full of enthusiasm for the project, brimming over with his ideas for the film. Both the story and the screenplay by Ray Russell, the master of terrifying horror, was intriguing. Maude is the heroine, trapped in a strange and mostly unknown country because of her recent forced marriage to a titled landowner, Baron Sardonicus, whom she had never met. With a broken heart, she parted from her fiancé, a talented London physician, to travel to this very strange Central European land.

In response to a letter from her, urging him to visit, the physician decides to journey to the little-known country to reunite with Maude and meet Baron Sardonicus. All this just setting the stage for the almost unbelievable situation he encounters when he gets there.

I was immediately hooked on the possibilities of working on this film with a script by the brilliant Ray Russell, and with William Castle directing.

First came endless wardrobe fittings for the fabulous gowns Bill Castle, who along with associate producer Dona Holloway, insisted were a necessary part of the film. Then film tests of the wardrobe, with its myriad details, along with tests of appropriate hairstyles. I was in Heaven when I saw the kind of production Bill had in mind. Through all this, over days and weeks, Bill's concentration and vision on every detail of the production never faltered.

With all this going on, other actors – Guy Rolfe, Ronald Lewis and Oscar Homolka – were arriving

Top-billed in Mr. Sardonicus, *Oscar Homolka played a menacing character, the baron's "man of all work" Krull. But according to Audrey Dalton, behind the scenes the Austrian actor and his "great sense of humor" made moviemaking fun.*

from London and going through the same process. What a production!

Shooting started and the focus changed as we all became wrapped up in our parts. Bill was a considerate, thoughtful director, and only lost patience if he felt that an actor, crew member or technician was not fully on board. However, he could not have been more sympathetic to any actor who had to endure trying moments in a scene, enduring painless but ... revolt-

Ronald Lewis, William Castle and Audrey Dalton on Mr. Sardonicus' *Torture Chamber set. (Courtesy Ronald V. Borst/ Hollywood Movie Posters)*

While we were shooting, we all realized it was important to believe, as always, the roles we were playing, however far-fetched. Naturally, off-screen, we had some hilarious moments as we tried the various torture instruments that Sardonicus kept in his eerie cellars, including the Iron Maiden and the rack. Oscar Homolka was in fact a very funny man, a great sense of humor. Some days he stayed fully in character, spooking us all, operating these horrific machines, and delighted us by showing how they were used in olden days.

Bill Castle had his fun moments with us too, and had his picture taken as he was locked into the Iron Maiden. Of course, his delicious sense of humor shows up near the end of the film when he conducts the Thumbs Up-Thumbs Down poll. Above all, I remember Bill Castle's focus on every aspect of the production. No detail was too small to be overlooked. A trait he adopted from Hitchcock.

Now we have a book involving two masters of horror, Bill Castle and Ray Russell. Tom Weaver and his *Scripts from the Crypt* team have the same level of involvement when they write about *Mr. Sardonicus*, as they have done with all the other books on their favorite film genres, sci-fi and horror. *Mr. Sardonicus* was a film made to order for their in-depth attention, a great read for anyone interested in what really goes on before and during the making of a film. Settle down for hours of great reading.

ing icky things like the servant wench who actually had live leeches applied to her skin as a means of torture. They may be painless to the skin, but I am sure I could not have mustered up the courage.

Introduction

By Marc Russell, with major contributions by Amanda Russell

My father, Ray Russell, was a versatile writer of novels, short stories, satirical pieces, poetry, song lyrics and even comic strip continuities. Although it's not entirely fair that he should be remembered primarily as a writer of grim horror tales, his best known and most reprinted work is the novella "Sardonicus," which Stephen King called "perhaps the finest example of the modern Gothic ever written." The novella, of course, reached the screen as *Mr. Sardonicus*.

Born in Chicago in 1924, my father was an avid reader from early childhood. This was undoubtedly due to the influence of his own father, a man who, despite a lack of much formal

According to Marc Russell, this shot of Ray Russell (from the late 1950s) was his favorite photo of himself.

education, placed great importance on books, learning and ideas. Dad was also a lifelong movie fan, and on one enjoyable afternoon in 1933, he enthusiastically sat through *King Kong twice* at the Crawford Theater, a few blocks from his home in Chicago's West Garfield neighborhood. (I saw a few movies at the same theater in my own childhood.) That movie remained a permanent favorite of his, and he introduced me to it at age six, for which I am grateful.

After service in the Army Air Corps during World War II (spent mostly on the island of Espiritu Santo in the South Pacific), he enrolled at the Chicago Conservatory of Music. (Music, in fact, played a role in many of his stories.) Shortly after, at the Goodman Memorial Theater, he studied acting and directing, while making some early efforts at writing fiction.

In 1954, after submitting two stories to a new magazine called *Playboy*, he was swiftly hired as associate editor, and later became the magazine's first executive editor. As I recall, he was only the second or third employee hired by publisher Hugh Hefner. In addition to his editorial duties, over the years he had approximately 70 stories and humorous pieces in *Playboy*. On quite a few of them, the byline was one of several *noms de plume* he used, so that it would not look like he was monopolizing the magazine. (Which he almost was!) I believe this still stands as the *Playboy* record for any one writer.

Because of a slight similarity, some people have assumed that the basic idea of "Sardonicus" was inspired by Victor Hugo's novel *The Man Who Laughs*. Not so. Dad was not even aware of the existence of the story, or the 1928 movie based on it, until after "Sardonicus" was written. The main inspiration came from a true story told to him by his mother-in-law: A few generations earlier, an ancestor in Poland had been buried with a lottery ticket which turned out to be a winner. The deceased man's widow then firmly stood guard at the grave for a considerable time, to ensure that it would not be violated.

I suspect another inspiration may have been a strange incident related to my father by a friend of his. The friend had planned to take some kind of stay-awake pill in order to remain awake all night to finish some urgent work, even though he knew the pill could cause some temporary bad side effects. The pill did everything it was supposed to do,

Sardonicus must intend to quickly make up for a lot of lost time chow-wise, because he's got his dining hall table creaking under the weight of enough food for the entire 1960 National Boy Scout Jamboree. Scripter Ray Russell hopes the baron won't notice one missing turkey leg.

including the side effects. But he then realized that he had forgotten to take the pill! *Thinking* he had taken the pill had the same effect as actually taking it. This incident may have impressed Dad with the amazing power that the human mind can have over the body.

"Sardonicus" caught the attention of producer-director William Castle, who purchased the story and hired Dad to come to Hollywood to write the screenplay. He did so, and the rest of the family soon emigrated to California. (Well, to me at age nine, it felt like an emigration.)

Among the few names that were considered for the title role were Jack Palance, Hurd Hatfield and Tim O'Connor. (I suspect that Dad may have suggested O'Connor as a possibility, because I think Dad was acquainted with O'Connor in his Goodman Theater days. O'Connor was a fine actor but, in my opinion, just too American for the Sardonicus role.) The right choice was certainly made. I cannot imagine anyone being as good as Guy Rolfe was as Sardonicus. And I think the same is true of just about everyone else in the film.

Production took place over a period of three weeks in March and April 1961. I believe my father was on the set during the entire filming. My mother was also there at least once, and she even made a small but significant contribution. Sardonicus is capable of eating "only the thinnest stews and porridges," and Castle was unsure of what type of food to use in the relevant scene. Mom suggested baby food, specifically Gerber's Strained Peas, and that item was immediately purchased. (Only a mother…)

Minor footnote: I was never on the set myself, but Dad did take me to visit the sets of two later films he scripted, *The Premature Burial* and *Zotz!* On the former, I met Roger Corman, on the latter, William Castle and big, menacing-looking Mike Mazurki.

The basic structure of *Mr. Sardonicus* is the same as the novella. One important difference is that in the novella, Sardonicus does not wear a mask. He obviously had to be masked in the movie, as it would have been a bad idea to have the hideous face on screen for any more than a few brief moments at a time. Another difference is that in the novella, Marek's violating of his father's grave is his own idea. In the movie, he is pressured into the deed by his greedy wife. The character of the servant Krull was also added to the movie, and Oscar Homolka did a great job in the role. The torturing of the servant girl Anna with leeches grew out of a brief suggestion from Castle to "get some leeches into it." Which Dad did, in a very logical way.

The word *Mr.* was added to the movie's title because someone at the studio, possibly Castle, feared possible confusion with Stanley Kubrick's film *Spartacus*, which had been released very recently. That was probably a good idea, but it did not quite work. One Hollywood columnist referred to the movie as *Mr. Spartacus*!

The movie was released nationwide in December 1961. Notice the chronology. Within 12 months after the novella's appearance in *Playboy*, the script had been written and the movie had been filmed and released. This may not be an all-time speed record, but it must come pretty close. Could it happen that fast in 21st century Hollywood? I doubt it.

In addition to the actors, some of the crew have impressive pedigrees. The makeup artist was Maurice Seiderman, who Orson Welles described as the finest makeup artist in the world. The superb old age makeups he created for *Citizen Kane* (1941) confirm that opinion.

Oddly enough, some people who have seen the movie have completely forgotten the entire point of the big payoff scene. When Krull frantically rushes to the railroad station and tells Sir Robert that Sardonicus is unable to open his mouth, Sir Robert finally tells him the truth, that the curing fluid was only distilled water. The initial paralysis of Sardonicus' face, as well as the "cure" and the final inability to open his mouth, were *all psychosomatic*. I recently saw an online video review of the movie which completely misses this vital point. Even the synopsis in the American Film Institute Catalog gets it wrong, and simply says that Sir Robert "refuses to return."

An interesting sidelight: An episode of the TV series *Thriller,* "The Terror in Teakwood," has several coincidental similarities to *Mr. Sardonicus*. Both were made in the same year, both are in black and

Charlie Largent wrote in Video Watchdog: *"[T]he self-named Sardonicus ... comes by his catchy moniker the hard way: When greed compels him to defile his father's grave, he is dealt a shock that wrenches his face into a mocking and permanent reminder of his crime –* The Scarlet Letter *with a fright mask." (Courtesy Ronald V. Borst/Hollywood Movie Posters)*

white, and both star Guy Rolfe as a man who violates the grave of a recently deceased man in a European country for personal gain and suffers terrible consequences which indirectly lead to his death.

As most readers of this book probably know, the Punishment Poll gimmick was basically phony. No alternate ending ever existed, so no one should waste any effort searching the Columbia vaults for it.

Sixty years down the road, the movie has become a minor cult favorite and has resonated in peculiar ways. Twenty years after the fact, a co-worker of mine told me she had seen it in its original release and found it so scary that it disturbed her sleep. Her experience was not unusual, as demonstrated by these IMDb user reviews:

❝ I initially saw this film on TV when I was 20 years old and it *still* scared the crap out of me! Thank God I didn't see it when it was first released...

❦ It sticks with you; once you've seen it, you are hooked forever…

❦ Saw this movie as a child. For the next few months, there were times when I would awaken, feeling a hand on my chest. Upon opening my eyes, there would be Dr. [sic] Sardonicus standing over me with that smile locked on his face. Try as I might, the scream that I wanted to emit was locked in my brain. To this day, it is still one of the most vivid and absolutely the scariest dream in my life.

❦ There is not a Boomer out there that saw this movie in the theater that does not, could not, forget it. For the most part, it is an icon that they carry to this day.

❦ Saw it as a kid. Gave me nightmares ever since. When I think of "a horror film," this is the film I'm thinking of. Even today when I imagine "something" is lurking in the shadows somewhere, it's "something" out of this film! …It put me off horror films for life.

TV horror movie host Svengoolie has featured *Mr. Sardonicus* more than once on his show, presenting commentary about the movie and the cast during breaks before commercials. And the face of Sardonicus has been on at least two magazine covers.

My father did not consider himself primarily a screenwriter, as he felt his novels and short stories were of greater importance, and I am strongly inclined to agree. However, he did feel that of the handful of movies he scripted, *Mr. Sardonicus* was probably the best, and I am inclined to agree with that as well.

"Sardonicus"

the novella by Ray Russell

I AN "S" OF VULGAR PRETENSION

IN THE LATE SUMMER of the year 18—, a gratifying series of professional successes had brought me to a state of such fatigue that I had begun seriously to contemplate a long rest on the Continent. I had not enjoyed a proper holiday in nearly three years, for, in addition to my regular practise, I had been deeply involved in a program of research, and so rewarding had been my progress in this special work (it concerned the ligaments and muscles, and could, it was my hope, be beneficially applied to certain varieties of paralysis) that I was loath to leave the city for more than a week at a time. Being unmarried, I lacked a solicitous wife who might have expressed concern over my health; thus it was that I had overworked myself to a point that a holiday had become absolutely essential to my wellbeing; hence, the letter which was put in my hand one morning near the end of that summer was most welcome.

When it was first presented to me by my valet, at breakfast, I turned it over and over, feeling the weight of its fine paper which was almost of the heaviness and stiffness of parchment; pondering the large seal of scarlet wax upon which was imprinted a device of such complexity that it was difficult to decipher; examining finally the hand in which the address had been written: *Sir Robert Cargrave, Harley Street, London*. It was a feminine hand, that much was certain, and there was a curious touch of familiarity to its delicacy as well as to its clearness (this last an admirable quality far too uncommon in the handwriting of ladies). The fresh clarity of that hand — and where had I seen it before? — bespoke a directness that seemed contrary to the well-nigh unfathomable ornamentation of the seal, which, upon closer and more concentrated perusal, I at length concluded to be no more than a single "S," but an "S" whose writhing curls seemed almost to grin presumptuously at one, an "S" which seemed to be constructed of little else than these grins, an "S" of such vulgar pretension that I admit to having felt vexed for an instant, and then, in the next instant, foolish at my own vexation — for surely, I admonished myself, there are things a deal more vexing than a seal which you have encountered without distemper?

Smiling at my foible, I continued to weigh the letter in my hand, searching my mind for a friend or acquaintance whose name began with "S." There was old Shipley of the College of Surgeons; there was Lord Henry Stanton, my waggish and witty friend; and that was the extent of it. Was it Harry? He was seldom in one place for very long and was a faithful and gifted letter-writer. Yet Harry's bold hand was far from effeminate, and, moreover, he would not use such a seal — unless it were as a lark, as an antic jest between friends. My valet had told me, when he put the letter in my hand, that it had come not by the post but by special messenger, and although this intelligence had not struck me as remarkable at the time, it now fed my curiosity and I broke that vexing seal and unfolded the stiff, crackling paper.

The message within was written in the same clear, faintly familiar hand. My eye first travelled to the end to find the signature, but that signature — *Madam S.* — told me nothing, for I knew of no Madam S. among my circle.

I read the letter. It is before me now as I set down this account, and I shall copy it out verbatim:

My dear Sir Robert,

It has been close to seven years since we last met — indeed, at that time you were not yet Sir Robert at all, but plain Robert Cargrave (although some talk of imminent knighthood was in the air), and so I wonder if you will remember Maude Randall?

Remember Maude Randall! Dear Maude of the bell-like voice, of the chestnut hair and large brown eyes, of a temperament of such sweetness and vivacity that the young men of London had eyes for no one else. She was of good family, but during a stay in Paris there had been something about injudicious speculation by her father that had diminished the family fortunes to such an extent that the wretched man had taken his own life and the Randalls had vanished from London society, altogether. Maude, or so I had heard, had married a foreign gentleman and had remained in Europe. It had been sad news, for no young man of London had ever had more doting eyes for Maude than had I, and it had pleased my fancy to think that my feelings were, at least in part, reciprocated. Remember Maude Randall? Yes, yes, I almost said aloud. And now, seven years later, she was "Madam S.," writing in that same hand I had seen countless times on invitations. I continued to read:

I often think of you, for — although it may not be seemly to say it — the company of few gentlemen used to please me so much as yours, and the London soirees given by my dear mother, at which you were present, are among my most cherished recollections now. But there! Frankness was always my failing, as Mother used to remind me. She, dear kind lady, survived less than a year after my poor father died, but I suppose you know this.

I am quite well, and we live in great comfort here, although we receive but rarely and are content with our own company most of the time. Mr. S. is a gracious gentleman, but of quiet and retiring disposition, and throngs of people, parties, balls, &c., are retrograde to his temperament; thus it is a special joy to me that he has expressly asked me to invite you here to the castle for a fortnight — or, if I may give you his exact words: "For a fortnight at least, but howsoever long as it please Sir Robert to stay among such drab folk as he will think us." (You see, I told you he was gracious!)

I must have frowned while reading, for the words of Mr. S. were not so much gracious, I thought, as egregious, and as vulgar as his absurd seal. Still, I held these feelings in check, for I knew that my emotions towards this man were not a little coloured by jealousy. He, after all, had wooed and won Maude Randall, a young lady of discernment and fine sensibilities: could she have been capable of wedding an obsequious boor? I thought it not likely. And a castle! Such romantic grandeur! "…Invite you here to the castle…" she had written, but where was "here"? The letter's cover, since it had not come by the post, offered no clue; therefore I read on:

It was, indeed, only yesterday, in the course of conversation, that I was recalling my old life in London, and mentioned your name. Mr. S., I thought, was, of a sudden, interested. "Robert Cargrave?" he said. "There is a well-known physician of that name, but I do not imagine it is the same gentleman." I laughed and told him it was the same gentleman, and that I had known you before you had become so illustrious. "Did you know him well?" Mr. S. then asked me, and you will think me silly, but I must tell you that for a moment I assumed him to be jealous! Such was not the case, however, as further conversation proved. I told him you had been a friend of my family's and a frequent guest at our house. "This is a most happy coincidence," he said. "I have long desired to meet Sir Robert Cargrave, and your past friendship with him furnishes you with an excellent opportunity to invite him here for a holiday."

And so, Sir Robert, I am complying with his request — and at the same time obeying the dictates of my own inclination — by most cordially inviting you to visit us for as long as you choose. I entreat you to come, for we see so few people here and it would be a great pleasure to talk with someone from the old days and to hear the latest London gossip. Suffer me, then, to receive a letter from you at once. Mr. S. does not trust the post, hence I have sent this by a servant of ours who was to be in London on special business; please relay your answer by way of him—"

I rang for my man. "Is the messenger who delivered this letter waiting for a reply?" I asked.

"He is sitting in the vestibule, Sir Robert," he said.

"You should have told me."

"Yes, sir."

"At any rate, send him in now. I wish to see him."

My man left, and it took me but a minute to dash off a quick note of acceptance. It was ready for the messenger when he was ushered into the room. I addressed him: "You are in the employ of Madam—" I realized for the first time that I did not know her husband's name.

The servant — a taciturn fellow with Slavic features — spoke in a thick accent: "I am in the employ of Mr. Sardonicus, sir."

Sardonicus! A name as flamboyant as the seal, I thought to myself. "Then deliver this note, if you please, to Madam Sardonicus, immediately you return."

He bowed slightly and took the note from my hand. "I shall deliver it to my master straightaway, sir," he said.

His manner nettled me. I corrected him. "To your mistress," I said coldly.

"Madam Sardonicus will receive your message, sir," he said.

I dismissed him, and only then did it strike me that I had not the faintest idea where the castle of Mr. Sardonicus was located. I referred once again to Maude's letter:

"...Please relay your answer by way of him and pray make it affirmative, for I do hope to make your stay in _____ a pleasant one."

I consulted an atlas. The locality she mentioned, I discovered, was a district in a remote and mountainous region of Bohemia.

Filled with anticipation, I finished my breakfast with renewed appetite, and that very afternoon began to make arrangements for my journey.

II THE SIGHT OF A GIANT SKULL

I AM NOT — as my friend Harry Stanton is — fond of travel for its own sake. Harry has often chided me on this account, calling me a dry-as-dust academician and "an incorrigible Londoner" — which I suppose I am. For, in point of fact, few things are more tiresome to me than ships and trains and carriages; and although I have found deep enjoyment and spiritual profit in foreign cities, having arrived, the tedium of travel itself has often made me think twice before starting out on a long voyage.

Still, in less than a month after I had answered Maude's invitation, I found myself in her adopted homeland. Sojourning from London to Paris, thence to Berlin, finally to Bohemia, I was met at _____ by a coachman who spoke imperfect English but who managed, in his solemn fashion, to make known to me that he was a member of the staff at Castle Sardonicus. He placed at my disposal a coach drawn by two horses, and, after taking my bags, proceeded to drive me on the last leg of my journey.

Alone in the coach, I shivered, for the air was brisk and I was very tired. The road was full of ruts and stones, and the trip was far from smooth. Neither did I derive much pleasure by bending my glance to the view afforded by the windows, for the night was dark, and the country was, at any rate, wild and raw, not made for serene contemplation. The only sounds were the clatter of hooves and wheels, the creak of the coach, and the harsh, unmusical cries of unseen birds.

"We receive but rarely," Maude had written, and now I told myself — little wonder! in this ragged and, one might say, uninhabitable place, far from the graces of civilized society, who indeed is there to *be* received, or, for the matter of that, to receive one? I sighed, for the desolate landscape and the thought of what might prove a holiday devoid of refreshing incident, had combined to cloak my already wearied spirit in a melancholic humour.

It was when I was in this condition that Castle Sardonicus met my eye — a dense, hunched outline at first, then, with an instantaneous flicker of moonlight, a great gaping death's head, the sight of which made me inhale sharply. With the exhalation, I chuckled at myself. "Come, come, Sir Robert," I inwardly chided, "it is, after all, but a castle, and you are not a green girl who starts at shadows and quails at midnight stories!"

The castle is situated at the terminus of a long and upward-winding mountain road. It presents a somewhat forbidding aspect to the world, for there is little about it to suggest gaiety or warmth or any of those qualities that might assure the wayfarer of welcome. Rather, this vast edifice of stone exudes an austerity, cold and repellent, a hint of ancient mysteries long buried, an effluvium of medieval dankness and decay. At night, and most particularly on nights when the moon is slim or cloud-enshrouded, it is a heavy blot upon the horizon, a shadow only, without feature save for its many-turreted outline; and should the moon be temporarily released from her cloudy confinement, her fugitive rays lend scant comfort, for they but serve to throw the castle into sudden, startling chiaroscuro, its windows fleetingly assuming the appearance of sightless though all-seeing orbs, its portcullis becoming for an instant a gaping mouth, its entire form striking the physical and the mental eye as would the sight of a giant skull.

But, though the castle had revealed itself to my sight, it was a full quarter of an hour before the coach had creaked its way up the steep and tortuous road to the great gate that barred the castle grounds from intruders. Of iron the gate was wrought — black it seemed in the scant illumination — and composed of intricate twists that led, every one of them, to a central, huge device, of many curves, which in the infrequent glints of moonglow appeared to smile metallically down, but which, upon gathering my reason about me, I made out to be no more than an enlarged edition of that presumptuous seal: a massive single "S." Behind it, at the end of the rutted road, stood the castle itself — dark, save for lights in two of its many windows.

Some words in a foreign tongue passed between my coachman and a person behind the gate. The gate was unlocked from within and swung open slowly, with a long rising shriek of rusted hinges; and the coach passed through.

As we drew near, the door of the castle was flung open and cheery light spilled out upon the road. The portcullis, which I had previously marked, was evidently a remnant from older days and now inactive. The coach drew to a halt, and I was greeted with great gravity by a butler whom I saw to be he who had carried Maude's invitation to London. I proffered him a nod of recognition. He acknowledged this and said, "Sir Robert, Madam Sardonicus awaits you, and if you will be good enough to follow me, I will take you to her presence." The coachman took charge of my bags, and I followed the butler into the castle.

It dated, I thought, to the Twelfth or Thirteenth Century. Suits of armour — priceless relics, I ascertained them to be — stood about the vast halls; tapestries were in evidence throughout; strong, heavy, richly-carved furniture was everywhere. The walls were of time-defying stone, great grey blocks of it. I was led into a kind of salon, with comfortable chairs, a tea table, and a spinet. Maude rose to greet me.

"Sir Robert," she said softly, without smiling. "How good to see you at last."

I took her hand. "Dear lady," said I, "we meet again."

"You are looking well and prosperous," she said.

"I am in good health, but just now rather tired from the journey."

She gave me leave to sit, and did so herself, venturing the opinion that a meal and some wine would soon restore me. "Mr. Sardonicus will join us soon," she added.

I spoke of her appearance, saying that she looked not a day older than when I last saw her in London. This was true, in regard to her physical self, for her face bore not a line, her skin was of the same freshness, and her glorious chestnut hair was still rich in colour and gleaming with health. But what I did not speak of was the change in her spirit. She who had been so gay and vivacious, the delight of soirées, was now distant and aloof, of serious mien, unsmiling. I was sorry to see this, but attributed it to the seven years that had passed since her carefree girlhood, to the loss of her loved parents, and even to the secluded life she now spent in this place.

"I am eager to meet your husband," I said.

"And he, Sir Robert, is quite eager to meet you," Maude assured me. "He will be down presently. Meanwhile, do tell me how you have fared in the world."

I spoke, with some modesty, I hope, of my successes in my chosen field, of the knighthood I had received from the Crown; I described my London apartment, laboratory and office; I made mention of certain mutual friends, and generally gave her news of London life, speaking particularly of the theatre (for I knew Maude had loved it) and describing Mr. Macready's farewell appearance as Macbeth at The Haymarket. When Maude had last been in London, there had been rumours of making an opera house out of Covent Garden theatre, and I told her that those plans had been carried through. I spoke of the London premiere of Mr. Verdi's latest *oeuvre* at Her Majesty's. At my mention of these theatres and performances, her eyes lit up, but she was not moved to comment until I spoke of the opera.

"The opera!" she sighed. "Oh, Sir Robert, if you could but know how I miss it. The excitement of a première, the ladies and gentlemen in their finery, the thrilling sounds of the overture, and then the curtain rising—" She broke off, as if ashamed of her momentary transport. "But I receive all the latest scores, and derive great satisfaction from playing and singing them to myself. I must order the new Verdi from Rome. It is called *Ernani*, you say?"

I nodded, adding, "With your permission, I will

attempt to play some of the more distinctive airs."

"Oh, pray do, Sir Robert!" she said.

"You will find them, perhaps, excessively modern and dissonant." I sat down at the spinet and played — just passably, I fear, and with some improvisation when I could not remember the exact notes — a potpourri of melodies from the opera.

She applauded my playing. I urged her to play also, for she was an accomplished keyboard artist and possessed an agreeable voice, as well. She complied by playing the minuet from *Don Giovanni* and then singing the *Voi lo sapete* from *Le Nozze di Figaro*. As I stood over her, watching her delicate hands move over the keys, hearing the pure, clear tones of her voice, all my old feelings washed over me in a rush, and my eyes smarted at the unalloyed sweetness and goodness of this lady. When she asked me to join her in the duet, *Là ci darem la mano*, I agreed to do it, although my voice is less than ordinary. On the second singing of the word "*mano*" — "hand" — I was seized by a vagrant impulse and took her left hand in my own. Her playing was hampered, of course, and the music limped for a few measures; and then, my face burning, I released her hand and we finished out the duet. Wisely, she neither rebuked me for my action nor gave me encouragement; rather, she acted as if the rash gesture had never been committed.

To mask my embarrassment, I now embarked upon some light chatter, designed to ease whatever tension existed between us; I spoke of many things, foolish things, for the most part, and even asked if Mr. Sardonicus had later demonstrated any of the jealousy she had said, in her letter, that she had erroneously thought him to have exhibited. She laughed at this — and it brightened the room, for it was the first time her face had abandoned its grave expression; indeed, I was taken by the thought that this was the first display of human merriment I had marked since stepping into the coach — and she said, "Oh, no! To the contrary, Mr. Sardonicus said that the closer we had been in the old days, the more he would be pleased."

This seemed an odd and even coarse thing for a man to say to his wife, and I jovially replied: "I hope Mr. Sardonicus was smiling when he said that."

At once, Maude's own smile vanished from her face. She looked away from me and began to talk of other things. I was dumbfounded. Had my innocent remark given offence? It seemed not possible. A moment later, however, I knew the reason for her strange action, for a tall gentleman entered the room with a gliding step, and one look at him explained many things.

III HE WHO MUST SMILE FOREVER

"SIR ROBERT CARGRAVE?" he asked, but he spoke with difficulty, certain sounds — such as the *b* in Robert and the *v* in Cargrave — being almost impossible for him to utter. To shape these sounds, the lips must be used, and the gentleman before me was the victim of some terrible affliction that had caused his lips to be pulled perpetually apart from each other, baring his teeth in a continuous ghastly smile. It was the same humourless grin I had seen once before: on the face of a person in the last throes of lockjaw. We physicians have a name for that chilling grimace, a Latin name, and as it entered my mind, it seemed to dispel yet another mystery, for the term we use to describe the lockjaw smile is: *Risus sardonicus*. A pallor approaching phosphorescence completed his astonishing appearance.

"Yes," I replied, covering my shock at the sight of his face. "Do I have the pleasure of addressing Mr. Sardonicus?"

We shook hands. After an exchange of courtesies, he said, "I have ordered dinner to be served in the large dining hall one hour hence. In the meantime, my valet will show you to your rooms, for I am sure you will wish to refresh yourself after your journey."

"You are most kind." The valet appeared — a man of grave countenance, like the butler and the coachman — and I followed him up a long flight of stone stairs. As I walked behind him, I reflected on the unsmiling faces in this castle, and no longer were they things of wonder. For who would be disposed to smile under the same roof with him who must smile forever? The most spontaneous of smiles would seem a mockery in the presence of that afflicted face. I was filled with pity for Maude's husband: of all God's creatures, man alone is blest with the ability to smile; but for the master of Castle Sardonicus, God's great blessing had become a terrible curse. As a physician, my pity was tempered with professional curiosity. His smile resembled the *risus* of lockjaw, but lockjaw is a mortal disease, and Mr. Sardonicus, his skullish grin notwithstanding, was very much alive. I felt shame for some of my earlier uncharitable thoughts towards this gentleman, for surely such an unfortunate could be forgiven much. What bitterness must fester in his breast; what sharp despair gnaw at his inwards!

My rooms were spacious and certainly as comfortable as this dank stone housing could afford. A hot tub was prepared, for which my tired and dusty frame was most grateful. As I lay in it, I began to experience the pleasant pangs of appetite. I looked forward to dinner. After my bath, I put on fresh linen and a suit of evening clothes. Then, taking from my bag two small gifts for my host and hostess — a bottle of scent for Maude, a box of cigars for her husband — I left my rooms.

I was not so foolish as to expect to find my way, unaided, to the main dining hall; but since I was early, I intended to wander a bit and let the ancient magnificence of the castle impress itself upon me.

Tapestries bearing my host's "S" were frequently displayed. They were remarkably new, their colours fresh, unlike the faded grandeur of their fellow tapestries. From this — and from Mr. Sardonicus' lack of title — I deduced that the castle had not been inherited through a family line, but merely purchased by him, probably from an impoverished nobleman. Though not titled, Mr. Sardonicus evidently possessed enormous wealth. I pondered its source. My ponderings were interrupted by the sound of Maude's voice.

I looked up. The acoustical effects in old castles are often strangeI had marked them in our own English castles — and though I stood near neither room nor door of any kind, I could hear Maude speaking in a distressed tone. I was standing at an open window which overlooked a kind of courtyard. Across this court, a window was likewise open. I took this to be the window of Maude's room; her voice was in some way being amplified and transported by the circumstantial shape of the courtyard and the positions of the two windows. By listening very attentively, I could make out most of her words.

She was saying, "I shan't. You must not ask me. It is unseemly." And then the voice of her husband replied: "You shall and will, madam. In my castle, it is I who decide what is seemly or unseemly. Not you." I was embarrassed at overhearing this private discussion on what was obviously a painful subject, so I made to draw away from the window that I might hear no more, but was restrained by the sound of my own name on Maude's lips. "I have treated Sir Robert with courtesy," she said. "You must treat him with more than courtesy," Mr. Sardonicus responded. "You must treat him with warmth. You must rekindle in his breast those affections he felt for you in other days..."

I could listen no longer. The exchange was vile. I drew away from the window. What manner of creature was this Sardonicus who threw his wife into the arms of other men? As a practitioner of medicine, a man dedicated to healing the ills of humankind, I had brought myself to learn many things about the minds of men, as well as about their bodies. I fully believed that, in some future time, physicians would heal the body by way of the mind, for it is in that *terra incognita* that all secrets lie hidden. I knew that love has many masks; masks of submission and of oppression; and even more terrible masks that make Nature a stranger to herself and "turn the truth of God into a lie," as St. Paul wrote. There is even a kind of love, if it can be elevated by that name, that derives its keenest pleasure from the sight of the beloved in the arms of another. These are unpleasant observations, which may one day be codified and studied by healers, but which, until then, may not be thought on for too long, lest the mind grow morbid and stagger under its load of repugnance.

With a heavy heart, I sought out a servant and asked to be taken to the dining hall. It was some distance away, and by the time I arrived there, Sardonicus and his lady were already at table, awaiting me. He arose, and with that revolting smile, indicated a chair; she also arose, and took my arm, addressing me as "Dear Sir Robert" and leading me to my place. Her touch, which at any previous time would have gladdened me, I now found distinctly not to my liking.

A hollow joviality hung over the dinner table throughout the meal. Maude's laughter struck me as giddy and false; Sardonicus drank too much wine and his speech became even more indistinct. I contrived to talk on trivial subjects, repeating some anecdotes about the London theatre which I had hitherto related to Maude, and describing Mr. Macready's interpretation of Macbeth.

"Some actors," said Sardonicus, "interpret the Scottish chieftain as a creature compounded of pure evil, unmingled with good qualities of any kind. Such interpretations are often criticized by those who feel no human being can be so unremittingly evil. Do you agree, Sir Robert?"

"No," I said, evenly; then, looking Sardonicus full in the face, I added, "I believe it is entirely possible for a man to possess not a single one of the virtues, to be a daemon in human flesh." Quickly, I embarked upon a discussion of the character of Iago, who took ghoulish delight in tormenting his fellow man.

The dinner was, I suppose, first rate, and the wine an honorable vintage, but I confess to tasting little of what was placed before me. At the end of the meal, Maude left us for a time and Sardonicus escorted me into the library, whither he ordered brandy to be brought. He opened the box of cigars, expressed his admiration of them and gratitude for them, and offered them to me. I took one and we both smoked. The smoking of the cigar made Sardonicus look even more grotesque: being unable to hold it in his lips, he clenched it in his constantly visible teeth, creating a unique spectacle. Brandy was served; I partook of it freely, though I am not customarily given to heavy drinking, for I now deemed it to be beneficial to my dampened spirits.

"You used the word 'ghoulish' a few moments ago, Sir Robert," said Sardonicus. "It is one of those words one uses so easily in conversation — one utters it without stopping to think of its meaning. But, in my opinion, it is not a word to be used lightly. When one uses it, one should have in one's mind a firm, unwavering picture of a ghoul."

"Perhaps I did," I said.

"Perhaps," he admitted. "And perhaps not. Let us obtain a precise definition of the word." He arose and walked to one of the bookcases that lined the room's walls. He reached for a large two-volume dictionary. "Let me see," he murmured. "We desire Volume One, from A to M, do we not? Now then: 'ghee' ... 'gherkin' ... 'ghetto' ... 'ghoom' (an odd word, eh, Sir Robert? 'To search for game in the dark') ... 'ghost' ... ah, 'ghoul!' 'Among Eastern nations, an imaginary evil being who robs graves and feeds upon corpses.' One might say, then, that he ghooms?" Sardonicus chuckled. He returned to his chair and helped himself to more brandy. "When you described Iago's actions as 'ghoulish,'" he continued, "did you think of him as the inhabitant of an Eastern nation? Or an imaginary being as against the reality of Othello and Desdemona? And did you mean seriously to suggest that it was his custom to rob graves and then to feed upon the disgusting nourishment he found therein?"

"I used the word in a figurative sense," I replied.

"Ah," said Sardonicus. "That is because you are English and do not believe in ghouls. Were you a Middle-European, as am I, you would believe in their existence, and would not be tempted to use the word other than literally. In my country — I was born in Poland — we understood such things. I, in point of fact, have known a ghoul." He paused for a moment and looked at me, then said, "You English are so blasé. Nothing shocks you. I sit here and tell you a thing of dreadful import and you do not even blink your eyes. Can it be because you do not believe me?"

"It would be churlish to doubt the word of my host," I replied.

"And an Englishman may be many things, but never a churl, eh, Sir Robert? Let me refill your glass, my friend, and then let me tell you about ghouls — which, by the way, are by no means imaginary, as that stupid lexicon would have us think, and which are not restricted to Eastern nations. Neither do they — necessarily — feed upon carrion flesh, although they are interested, most interested, in the repellent contents of graves. Let me tell you a story from my own country, Sir Robert, a story that — if I have any gift at all as a spinner of tales — will create in you a profound belief in ghouls. You will be entertained, I hope, but I also hope you will add to your learning. You will learn, for example, how low a human being can sink, how truly monstrous a man can become."

IV THE MOON HIS UNDOING

"YOU MUST TRANSPORT your mind," said Sardonicus, "back a few years and to a rural region of my homeland. You must become acquainted with a family of country folk — hard-working, law-abiding, God-fearing, of moderate means — the head of which was a simple, good man named Tadeusz Boleslawski. He was an even-tempered personage, kindly disposed to all men, the loving husband of a devoted wife and father of five strong boys. He was also a firm churchman, seldom even taking the Lord's name in vain. The painted women who plied their trade in certain elaborate houses of the nearest large city, Warsaw, held no attraction for him, though several of his masculine neighbours, on their visits to the metropolis, succumbed to such blandishments with tidal regularity. Neither did he drink in excess: a glass of beer with his evening meal, a toast or two in wine on special occasions. No; hard liquor, strong language, fast women — these were not the weaknesses of Tadeusz Boleslawski. His weakness was gambling.

"Every month he would make the trip to Warsaw, to sell his produce at the markets and to buy certain necessaries for his home. While his comrades visited the drinking and wenching houses, Tadeusz would attend strictly to business affairs — except for one minor deviation. He would purchase a lottery ticket, place it securely in a small, tight pocket of his best waistcoat — which he wore only on Sundays and on his trips to the city — then put it completely out of his mind until the following month, when, on reaching the city, he would remove it from his pocket and closely scan the posted list of winners. Then, after methodically tearing the ticket to shreds (for Tadeusz never lived to win a lottery), he would purchase another. This was a ritual with him; he performed it every month for twenty-three years, and the fact that he never won did not discourage him. His wife knew of this habit, but since it was the good man's only flaw, she never remarked upon it."

Outside, I could hear the wind howling dismally. I took more brandy as Sardonicus continued:

"Years passed; three of the five sons married; two (Henryk and Marek, the youngest) were still living with their parents, when Tadeusz — who had been of sturdy health — collapsed one day in the fields and died. I will spare you an account of the family's grief; how the married sons returned with their wives to attend the obsequies; of the burial in the small graveyard of that community. The good man had left few possessions, but these few were divided, according to his written wish, among his survivors, with the largest share going, of course, to the eldest son. Though this was custom, the other sons could not help feeling a trifle disgruntled, but they held their peace for the most part — especially the youngest, Marek, who was perhaps the most amiable of them and a lad who was by nature quiet and interested in improving his lot through the learning he found in books.

"Imagine, sir, the amazement of the widow when, a full three weeks after the interment of her husband, she received word by men returning from Warsaw that the lottery ticket Tadeusz had purchased had now been selected as the winner. It was a remarkable irony, of course, but conditions had grown hard for the poor woman, and would grow harder with her husband dead, so she had no time to reflect upon that irony. She set about looking through her husband's possessions for the lottery ticket. Drawers were emptied upon the floor; boxes and cupboards were ransacked; the family Bible was shaken out; years before, Tadeusz had been in the habit of temporarily hiding money under a loose floorboard in the bedroom — this cavity was thoroughly but vainly plumbed. The sons were sent for: among the few personal effects they had been bequeathed, did the ticket languish there? In the snuff box? In any article of clothing?

"And at that, Sir Robert, the eldest son leapt up. 'An article of clothing!' he cried. 'Father always wore his Sunday waistcoat to the city when he purchased the lottery tickets — the very waistcoat in which he was buried!'

"'Yes, yes!' the other sons chorused, saving Marek, and plans began to be laid for the exhuming of the dead man. But the widow spoke firmly: 'Your father rests peacefully,' she said. 'He must not be disturbed. No amount of gold would soothe our hearts if we disturbed him.' The sons protested with vehemence, but the widow stood her ground. 'No son of mine will profane his father's grave — unless he first kills his mother!' Grumbling, the sons withdrew their plans. But that night, Marek awoke to find his mother gone from the house. He was frightened, for this was not like her. Intuition sent him to the graveyard, where he found her, keeping a lonely vigil over the grave of her husband, protecting him from the greed of grave robbers. Marek implored her to come out of the cold, to return home; she at first refused; only when Marek offered to keep vigil all night himself did she relent and return home, leaving her youngest son to guard the grave from profanation.

"Marek waited a full hour. Then he produced from under his shirt a small shovel. He was a strong boy, and the greed of a youngest son who has been deprived of inheritance lent added strength to his arms. He dug relentlessly, stopping seldom for rest, until finally the coffin was uncovered. He raised the creaking lid. An overpowering foetor filled his nostrils and nearly made him faint. Gathering courage, he searched the pockets of the mouldering waistcoat.

"The moon proved to be his undoing, Sir Robert. For suddenly its rays, hitherto hidden, struck the face of his father, and at the sight of that face, the boy recoiled and went reeling against the wall of the grave, the breath forced from his body. Now, you must know that the mere sight of his father — even in an advanced state of decomposition-he had steeled himself to withstand; but what he had *not* foreseen — "

Here, Sardonicus leaned close to me and his pallid, grinning head filled my vision. "What he had not foreseen, my dear sir, was that the face of his father, in the rigour of death, would look directly and hideously upon him." Sardonicus' voice became an ophidian hiss. "And, Sir Robert," he added, "most terrible and most unforeseen of all, the dead lips were drawn back from the teeth *in a constant and soul-shattering smile!*"

V THE REMEMBRANCE OF THAT NIGHT

I KNOW NOT WHETHER it was the ghastliness of his story, or the sight of his hideous face so close to mine, or the cheerless keening of the wind outside, or the brandy I had consumed, or all of these in combination; but when Sardonicus uttered those last words, my heart was clutched by a cold hand, and for a moment — a long moment ripped from the texture of time — I was convinced beyond doubt and beyond logic that the face I looked into was the face of that cadaver, reanimated by obscure arts, to walk among the living, dead though not dead.

The moment of horror passed, at length, and reason triumphed. Sardonicus, considerably affected by his own tale, sat back in his chair, trembling. Before too long, he spoke again:

"The remembrance of that night, Sir Robert, though it is now many years past, fills me still with dread. You will appreciate this when I tell you what you have perhaps already guessed — that *I* am that ghoulish son, Marek."

I had not guessed it; but since I had no wish to tell him that I had for an instant thought he was the dead father, I said nothing.

"When my senses returned," said Sardonicus, "I scrambled out of the grave and ran as swiftly as my limbs would carry me. I had reached the gate of the graveyard when I was smitten by the fact that I had not accomplished the purpose of my mission — the lottery ticket remained in my father's pocket!"

"But surely—" I started to say.

"Surely I ignored the fact and continued to run? No, Sir Robert. My terror notwithstanding, I halted, and forced myself to retrace those hasty steps. My fear notwithstanding, I descended once more into that noisome grave. My disgust notwithstanding, I reached into the pocket of my decaying father's waistcoat and extracted the ticket! I need hardly add that, this time, I averted my eyes from his face.

"But the horror was not behind me. Indeed, it had only begun. I reached my home at a late hour, and my family was asleep. For this I was grateful, since my clothes were covered with soil and I still trembled from my fearful experience. I quietly poured water into a basin and prepared to wash some of the graveyard dirt from my face and hands. In performing my ablutions, I looked up into a mirror — *and screamed so loudly as to wake the entire house!*

"My face was as you see it now, a replica of my dead father's: the lips drawn back in a perpetual, mocking grin. I tried to close my mouth. I could not. The muscles were immovable, as if held in the gelid rigour of death. I could hear my family stirring at my scream, and since I did not wish them to look upon me, I ran from the house — never, Sir Robert, to return.

"As I wandered the rural roads, my mind sought the cause of the affliction that had been visited upon me. Though but a country lad, I had read much and I had a blunt, rational mind that was not susceptible to the easy explanations of the supernatural. I would not believe that God had placed a malediction upon me to punish me for my act. I would not believe that some black force from beyond the grave had reached out to stamp my face. At length, I began to believe it was the massive shock that had forced my face to its present state, and that my great guilt had helped to shape it even as my father's dead face was shaped. Shock and guilt: strong powers not from God above or the Fiend below, but from within my own breast, my own brain, my own soul.

"Let me bring this history to a hasty close, Sir Robert. You need only know that, despite my blighted face, I redeemed the lottery ticket and thus gained an amount of money that will not seem large to you, but which was more than I had ever seen before that time. It was the fulcrum from which I plied the lever that was to make me, by dint of shrewd speculation, one of the richest men in Central Europe. Naturally, I sought out physicians and begged them to restore my face to its previous state. None succeeded, though I offered them vast sums. My face remained fixed in this damnable unceasing smile, and my heart knew the most profound despair imaginable. I could not even pronounce my own name! By a dreadful irony, the initial letters of my first and last names were impossible for my frozen lips to form. This seemed the final indignity. I will admit to you that, at this period, I was perilously near the brink of self-destruction. But the spirit of preservation prevailed, and I was saved from that course. I changed my name. I had read of the *Risus sardonicus*, and its horrible aptness appealed to my bitter mind, so I became Sardonicus — a name I can pronounce with no difficulty."

Sardonicus paused and sipped his brandy. "You are wondering," he then said, "in what way my story concerns you."

I could guess, but I said: "I am."

"Sir Robert," he said, "you are known throughout the medical world. Most laymen, perhaps, have not heard of you; but a layman such as I, a layman who avidly follows the medical journals for tidings of any recent discoveries in the curing of paralyzed muscles, has heard of you again and again. Your researches into these problems have earned you high professional regard; indeed, they have earned you a knighthood. For some time, it has been in my mind to visit London and seek you out. I have consulted many physicians, renowned men — Keller in Berlin, Morignac in Paris, Buonagente in Milan — and none have been able to help me. My despair has been utter. It prevented me from making the long journey to England. But when I heard-sublime coincidence! — that my own wife had been acquainted with you, I took heart. Sir Robert, I entreat you to heal me, to lift from me this curse, to make me look once more like a man, that I may walk in the sun again, among my fellow human beings, as one of them, rather than as a fearsome gargoyle to be shunned and feared and ridiculed. Surely you cannot, *will* not deny me?"

My feelings for Sardonicus, pendulum-like, again swung towards his favour. His story, his plight, had rent my heart, and I reverted to my earlier opinion that such a man should be forgiven much. The strange overheard conversation between Maude and him was momentarily forgotten. I said, "I will examine you, Mr. Sardonicus. You were right to ask me. We must never abandon hope."

He clasped his hands together. "Ah, sir! May you be blest forever!"

I performed the examination then and there. Although I did not tell him this, never had I encountered muscles as rigid as those of his face. They could only be compared to stone, so inflexible were they. Still, I said, "Tomorrow we will begin treatment. Heat and massage."

"These have been tried," he said, hopelessly.

"Massage differs from one pair of hands to another," I replied. "I have had success with my own techniques, and therefore place faith in them. Be comforted then, sir, and share my faith."

He seized my hand in his. "I do," he said. "I must. For if you — if even *you*, Sir Robert Cargrave, fail me..." He did not complete the sentence, but his eyes assumed an aspect so bitter, so full of hate, so strangely cold yet flaming, that they floated in my dreams that night.

VI AN ABYSS OF HUMILIATION AND SHAME

I SLEPT NOT WELL, AWAKENING MANY times in a fever compounded of drink and turbulent emotions. When the first rays of morning crept onto my pillow, I arose, little refreshed. After a cold tub and a light breakfast in my room, I went below to the salon whence music issued. Maude was already there, playing a pretty little piece upon the spinet. She looked up and greeted me. "Good morning, Sir Robert. Do you know the music of Mr. Gottschalk? He is an American pianist: this is his *Maiden's Blush*. Amiable, is it not?"

"Most amiable," I replied, dutifully although I was in no mood for the embroideries of *politesse*.

Maude soon finished the piece and closed the album. She turned to me and said, in a serious tone, "I have been told what you are going to do for my poor husband, Sir Robert. I can scarce express my gratitude."

"There is no need to express it," I assured her. "As a physician — as well as your old friend — I could not do less. I hope you understand, however, that a cure is not a certainty. I will try, and I will try to the limit of my powers, but beyond that I can promise nothing."

Her eyes shone with supplication: "Oh, cure him, Sir Robert! That I beg of you!"

"I understand your feelings, madam," I said. "It is fitting that you should hope so fervently for his recovery; a devoted wife could feel no other way."

"Oh, sir," she said, and into her voice crept now a harshness, "you misunderstand. My fervent hope springs from unalloyed selfishness."

"How may that be?" I asked.

"If you do not succeed in curing him," she told me, "I will suffer."

"I understand that, but—"

"No, you do not understand," she said. "But I can tell you little more without offending. Some things are better left unspoken. Suffice it to be said that, in order to urge you towards an ultimate effort, to the 'limit of your powers' as you have just said, my husband intends to hold over your head the threat of my punishment."

"This is monstrous!" I cried. "It cannot be tolerated. But in what manner, pray, would he punish you? Surely he would not beat you?"

"I wish he would be content with a mere beating," she groaned, "but his cleverness knows a keener torture. No, he holds over me — and over you, through me — a punishment far greater; a punishment (believe me!) so loathsome to the sensibilities, so unequivocably vile and degraded, that my mind shrinks from contemplating it. Spare me your further questions, sir, I enjoin you; for to describe it would plunge me into an abyss of humiliation and shame!"

She broke into sobbing, and tears coursed down her cheeks. No longer able to restrain my tender feelings for her, I flew to her side and took her hands in mine. "Maude," I said, "may I call you that? In the past I addressed you only as Miss Randall; at present I may only call you Madam Sardonicus; but in my heart — then as now — you are, you always have been, you always will be, simply Maude, my own dear Maude!"

"Robert," she sighed; "dearest Robert. I have yearned to hear my Christian name from your lips all these long years."

"The warmth we feel," I said, "may never, with honour, reach fulfillment. But — trust me, dearest Maude! — I will in some wise deliver you from the tyranny of that creature: this I vow!"

"I have no hope," she said, "save in you. Whether I go on as I am, or am subjected to an unspeakable horror, rests with you. My fate is in your hands — these strong, healing hands, Robert." Her voice dropped to a whisper: "Fail me not! oh fail me not!"

"Govern your fears," I said. "Return to your music. Be of good spirits; or, if you cannot, make a show of it. I go now to treat your husband, and also to confront him with what you have told me."

"Do not!" she cried. "Do not, I beseech you, Robert; lest, in the event of your failure, he devise foul embellishments upon the agonies into which he will cast me!"

"Very well," I said, "I will not speak of this to him. But my heart aches to learn the nature of the torments you fear."

"Ask no more, Robert," she said, turning away. "Go to my husband. Cure him. Then I will no longer fear those torments."

I pressed her dear hand and left the salon.

Sardonicus awaited me in his chambers. Thither, quantities of hot water and stacks of towels had been brought by the servants, upon my orders. Sardonicus was stripped to the waist, displaying a trunk strong and of good musculature, but with the same near-phosphorescent pallor of his face. It was, I now understood, the pallor of one who has avoided daylight for years. "As you see, sir," he greeted me, "I am ready for your ministrations."

I bade him recline upon his couch, and began the treatment.

Never have I worked so long with so little reward. After alternating applications of heat and of massage, over a period of three and a quarter hours, I had made no progress. The muscles of his face were still as stiff as marble; they had not relaxed for an instant. I was mortally tired. He ordered our luncheon brought to us in his chambers, and after a short respite, I began again. The clock tolled six when I at last sank into a chair, shaking with exhaustion and strain. His face was exactly as before.

"What remains to be done, sir?" he asked me.

"I will not deceive you," I said. "It is beyond my skill to alleviate your condition. I can do no more."

He rose swiftly from the couch. "You must do more!" he shrieked. "You are my last hope!"

"Sir," I said, "new medical discoveries are ever being made. Place your trust in Him who created you—"

"Cease that detestable gibberish at once!" he snapped. "Your puling sentiments sicken me! Resume the treatment."

I refused. "I have applied all my knowledge, and my art, to your affliction," I assured him. "To resume the treatment would be idle and foolish, for — as you have divined — the condition is a product of your own mind."

"At dinner last night," countered Sardonicus, "we spoke of the character of Macbeth. Do you not remember the words he addressed to his doctor? —

'Canst thou not minister to a mind diseas'd;
Pluck from the memory a rooted sorrow;
Raze out the written troubles of the brain;
And with some sweet oblivious antidote
Cleanse the stuff'd bosom of that perilous stuff
Which weighs upon the heart?'"

"I remember them," I said; "and I remember, as well, the doctor's reply: *'Therein the patient must minister to himself.'*" I arose and started for the door.

"One moment, Sir Robert," he said. I turned. "Forgive my precipitate outburst a moment ago. However, the mental nature of my affliction notwithstanding, and even though this mode of treatment has failed, surely there are other treatments?"

"None," I said, "that have been sufficiently tested. None I would venture to use upon a human body."

"Ah!" he cried. "Then other treatments *do* exist!"

I shrugged. "Think not of them, sir. They are at present unavailable to you." I pitied him, and added: "I am sorry."

"Doctor!" he said; "I implore you to use whatever treatments exist, be they ever so untried!"

"They are fraught with danger," I said.

"Danger?" He laughed. "Danger of what? Of disfigurement? Surely no man has ever been more disfigured than I! Of death? I am willing to gamble my life!"

"*I* am not willing to gamble your life," I said. "All lives are precious. Even yours."

"Sir Robert, I will pay you a thousand pounds."

"This is not a question of money."

"Five thousand pounds, Sir Robert, *ten* thousand!"

"No."

He sank onto the couch. "Very well," he said. "Then I will offer you the ultimate inducement."

"Were it a million pounds," I said, "you could not sway me."

"The inducement I speak of," he said, "is not money. Will you hear?"

I sat down. "Speak, sir," I said, "since that is your wish. But nothing will persuade me to use a treatment that might cost you your life."

"Sir Robert," he said, after a pause, "yestereve, when I came down to meet you for the first time, I heard happy sounds in the salon. You were singing a charming melody with my wife. Later, I could not help but notice the character of your glances towards her…"

"They were not reciprocated, sir," I told him, "and herewith I offer you a most abject apology for my unbecoming conduct."

"You obscure my point," he said. "You are a friend of hers, from the old days in London; at that period, you felt an ardent affection for her, I would guess. This is not surprising: for she is a lady whose face and form promise voluptuous delights and yet a lady whose manner is most decorous and correct. I would guess further: that your ardour has not diminished over the years; that, at the sight of her, the embers have burst into a flame. No, sir, hear me out. What would you say, Sir Robert, were I to tell you — that you may quench that flame?"

I frowned. "Your meaning, sir?—"

"Must I speak even more plainly? I am offering you a golden opportunity to requite the love that burns in your heart. To requite it in a single night, if that will suffice you, or over an extended period of weeks, months; a year, if you will; as long as you need—"

"Scoundrel!" I roared, leaping up.

He heeded me not, but went on speaking: "…As my guest, Sir Robert! I offer you a veritable Oriental paradise of unlimited raptures!" He laughed, then entered into a catalogue of his wife's excellences. "Consider, sir," he said, "that matchless bosom, like alabaster which has been imbued with the pink of the rose, those creamy limbs—"

"Enough!" I cried. "I will hear no more of your foulness." I strode to the door.

"Yes, you will, Sir Robert," he said immediately. "You will hear a good deal more of my foulness. You will hear what I plan to do to your beloved Maude, should you fail to relieve me of this deformity."

Again, I stopped and turned. I said nothing, but waited for him to speak further.

"I perceive that I have caught your interest," he said. "Hear me: for if you think I spoke foully before, you will soon be forced to agree that my earlier words were, by comparison, as blameless as The Book of Common Prayer. If rewards do not tempt you, then threats may coerce you. In fine, Maude will be punished if you fail, Sir Robert."

"She is an innocent."

"Just so. Hence, the more exquisite and insupportable to you should be the thought of her punishment."

My mind reeled. I could not believe such words were being uttered.

"Deep in the bowels of this old castle," said Sardonicus, "are dungeons. Suppose I were to tell you that my intention is to drag my wife thither and stretch her smooth body to unendurable length upon the rack—"

"You would not dare!" I cried.

"My daring or lack of it is not the issue here. I speak of the rack only that I may go on to assure you that Maude would *infinitely prefer* that dreadful machine to the punishment I have in truth designed for her. I will describe it to you. You will wish to be seated, I think."

VII ENTERTAINMENT FOR A MONSTER

"I WILL STAND," I said.

"As you please." Sardonicus himself sat down. "Perhaps you have marvelled at the very fact of Maude's marriage to me. When the world was so full of personable men — men like yourself, who adored her — why did she choose to wed a monster, a creature abhorrent to the eyes and who did not, moreover, have any redeeming grace of spiritual beauty, or kindness, or charm?

"I first met Maude Randall in Paris. I say 'met,' but it would be truer to simply say I saw her — from my hotel window, in fact. Even in Paris society, which abounds in ladies of remarkable pulchritude, she was to be remarked upon. You perhaps would say I fell in love with her, but I dislike that word 'love,' and will merely say that the sight of her smote my senses with most agreeable emphasis. I decided to make her mine. But how? By presenting my irresistibly handsome face to her view? Hardly. I began methodically: I hired secret operatives to find out everything about her and about her mother and father — both of whom were then alive. I discovered that her father was in the habit of speculating, so I saw to it that he received some supposedly trustworthy but very bad advice. He speculated heavily and was instantly ruined. I must admit I had not planned his consequent suicide, but when that melancholy event occurred, I rejoiced, for it worked to my advantage. I presented myself to the bereaved widow and daughter, telling them the excellent qualities of Mr. Randall were widely known in the world of affairs and that I considered myself almost a close friend. I offered to help them in any possible way. By dint of excessive humility and persuasiveness, I won their trust and succeeded in diminishing their aversion to my face. This, you must understand, from first to last, occupied a period of many months. I spoke nothing of marriage, made no sign of affection towards the daughter for at least six of these months; when I did — again, with great respect and restraint — she gently refused me. I retreated gracefully, saying only that I hoped I might remain her and her mother's friend. She replied that she sincerely shared that hope, for, although she could never look upon me as an object of love, she indeed considered me a true friend. The mother, who pined excessively after the death of the father, soon expired: another incident unplanned but welcomed by me. Now the lovely child was alone in the world in a foreign city, with no money, no one to guide her, no one to fall back upon — save kindly Mr. Sardonicus. I waited many weeks, then I proposed marriage again. For several days, she continued to decline the offer, but her declinations grew weaker and weaker until, at length, on one day, she said this to me:

"'Sir, I esteem you highly as a friend and benefactor, but my other feelings towards you have not changed. If you could be satisfied with such a singular condition; if you could agree to enter into marriage with a lady and yet look upon her as no more than a companion of kindred spirit; if the prospect of a dispassionate and childless marriage does not repulse you — as well it might — then, sir, my unhappy circumstances would compel me to accept your kind offer.'

"Instantly, I told her my regard for her was of the purest and most elevated variety; that the urgings of the flesh were unknown to me; that I lived on a spiritual plane and desired only her sweet and stimulating companionship through the years. All this, of course, was a lie. The diametric opposite was true. But I hoped, by this falsehood, to lure her into marriage; after which, by slow and strategic process, I could bring about her submission and my rapture. She still was hesitant; for, as she frankly told me, she believed that love was a noble and integral part of marriage; and that marriage without it could be only a hollow thing; and that though I knew not the urgings of the flesh, she could not with honesty say the same of herself. Yet she reiterated that, so far as my own person was concerned, a platonic relationship was all that could ever exist between us. I calmed her misgivings. We were married not long after.

"And now, Sir Robert, I will tell you a surprising thing. I have confessed myself partial to earthly pleasures; as a physician and as a man of the world, you are aware that a gentleman of strong appetites may not curb them for very long without fomenting turmoil and distress in his bosom. And yet, sir, not once in the years of our marriage — not once, I say — have I been able to persuade or cajole my wife into relenting and breaking the stringent terms of our marriage agreement. Each time I have attempted, she has recoiled from me with horror and disgust. This is not because of an abhorrence of all fleshly things — by her own admission — but because of my monstrous face.

"Perhaps now you will better understand the vital necessity for this cure. And perhaps also you will understand the full extent of Maude's suffering should you fail to effect that cure. For, mark me well: if you fail, my wife will be made to become a true wife to me — by main force, and not for one fleeting hour, but every day and every night of her life, whensoever I say, in whatsoever manner I choose to express my conjugal privilege!" As an afterthought, he added, "I am by nature imaginative."

I had been shocked into silence. I could only look upon him with disbelief. He spoke again:

"If you deem it a light punishment, Sir Robert, then you do not know the depth of her loathing for my person, you do not know the revulsion that wells up inside her when I but place my fingers upon her arm, you do not know what mastery of her very gorge is required of her when I kiss her hand. Think, then; think of the abomination she would feel were my attentions to grow more ardent, more demanding! It would unseat her mind, sir; of that I am sure, for she would as soon embrace a reptile."

Sardonicus arose and put on his shirt. "I suggest we both begin dressing for dinner," he said. "Whilst you are dressing, reflect. Ask yourself, Sir Robert: could you ever again look upon yourself with other than shame and loathing if you were to sacrifice the beautiful and blameless Maude Randall on an altar of the grossest depravity? Consider how ill you would sleep in your London bed, night after night, knowing what she was suffering at that very moment; suffering because you abandoned her, because you allowed her to become an entertainment for a monster."

VIII A TOKEN OF DETESTATION

THE DAYS THAT PASSED after that time were, in the main, tedious yet filled with anxiety. During them, certain supplies were being brought from London and other places; Sardonicus spared no expense in procuring for me everything I said was necessary to the treatment. I avoided his society as much as I could, shunning even his table, and instructing the servants to bring my meals to my rooms. On the other hand, I sought out the company of Maude, endeavouring to comfort her and allay her fears. In those hours when her husband was occupied with business affairs, we talked together in the salon, and played music. Thus, they were days spotted with small pleasures that seemed the greater for having been snatched in the shadow of wretchedness.

I grew to know Maude, in that time, better than I had ever known her in London. Adversity stripped the layers of ceremony from our congress, and we spoke directly. I came to know her warmth, but I came to know her strength, too. I spoke outright of my love, though in the next breath I assured her I was aware of the hopelessness of that love. I did not tell her of the "reward" her husband had offered me — and which I had refused — and I was gladdened to learn (as I did by indirection) that Sardonicus, though he had abjured her to be excessively cordial to me, had not revealed the ultimate and ignoble purpose of that cordiality.

"Robert," she said once, "is it likely that he will be cured?"

I did not tell her how unlikely it was. "For your sake, Maude," I said, "I will persevere more than I have ever done in my life."

At length, a day arrived when all the necessaries had been gathered: some plants from the New World, certain equipment from London, and a vital instrument from Scotland. I worked long and late, in complete solitude, distilling a needed liquor from the plants. The next day, dogs were brought to me alive, and carried out dead. Three days after that, a dog left my laboratory alive and my distilling labours came to an end.

I informed Sardonicus that I was ready to administer the treatment. He came to my laboratory, and I imagined there was almost a gloating triumph in his immobile smile. "Such are the fruits of concentrated effort," he said. "Man is an indolent creature, but light the fire of fear under him, and of what miracles is he not capable!"

"Speak not of miracles," I said, "though prayers would do you no harm now, for you will soon be in peril of your life." I motioned him towards a table and bade him lie upon it. He did so, and I commenced explaining the treatment to him. "The explorer Magellan," I said, "wrote of a substance used on darts by the savage inhabitants of the South American continent. It killed instantly, dropping large animals in their tracks. The substance was derived from certain plants, and is, in essence, the same substance I have been occupied in extracting these past days."

"A poison, Sir Robert?" he asked, wryly.

"When used full strength," I said, "it kills by bringing about a *total* relaxation of the muscles — particularly the muscles of the lungs and heart. I have long thought that a dilution of that poison might beneficially slacken the rigidly tensed muscles of paralyzed patients."

"Most ingenious, sir," he said.

"I must warn you," I went on, "that this distillment has never been used on a human subject. It may kill you. I must, perforce, urge you again not to insist upon its use; to accept your lot; and to remove the threat of punishment you now hold over your wife's head."

"You seek to frighten me, Doctor," chuckled Sardonicus; "to plant distrust in my bosom. But I fear you not — an English knight and a respected physician would never do a deed so dishonourable as to wittingly kill a patient under his care. You would be hamstrung by your gentleman's code as well as by your professional oath. Your virtues are, in short, my vices' best ally."

I bristled. "I am no murderer such as you," I said. "If you force me to use this treatment, I will do everything in my power to insure its success. But I cannot conceal from you the possibility of your death."

"See to it that I live," he said flatly, "for if I die, my men will kill both you and my wife. They will not kill you quickly. See to it, also, that I am cured — lest Maude be subjected to a fate she fears more than the slowest of tortures." I said nothing. "Then bring me this elixir straightway," he said, "and let me drink it off and make an end of this!"

"It is not to be drunk," I told him.

He laughed. "Is it your plan to smear it on darts, like the savages?"

"Your jest is most apposite," I said. "I indeed plan to introduce it into your body by means of a sharp instrument — a new instrument not yet widely known, that was sent me from Scotland. The original suggestion was put forth in the University of Oxford some two hundred years ago by Dr. Christopher Wren, but only recently, through development by my friend, Dr. Wood of Edinburgh, has it seemed practical. It is no more than a syringe—" I showed him the instrument—"attached to a needle; but the needle is hollow, so that, when it punctures the skin, it may carry healing drugs directly into the bloodstream."

"The medical arts will never cease earning my admiration," said Sardonicus.

I filled the syringe. My patient said, "Wait."

"Are you afraid?" I asked.

"Since that memorable night in my father's grave," he replied, "I have not known fear. I had a surfeit of it then; it will last out my lifetime. No: I simply wish to give instructions to one of my men." He arose from the table, and, going to the door, told one of his helots to bring Madam Sardonicus to the laboratory.

"Why must she be here?" I asked.

"The sight of her," he said, "may serve you as a remembrancer of what awaits her in the event of my death, or of that other punishment she may expect should your treatment prove ineffectual."

Maude was brought into our presence. She looked upon my equipment — the bubbling retorts and tubes, the pointed syringe — with amazement and fright. I began to explain the principle of the treatment to her, but Sardonicus interrupted: "Madam is not one of your students, Sir Robert; it is not necessary she know these details. Delay no longer; begin at once!"

He stretched out upon the table again, fixing his eyes upon me. I proffered Maude a comforting look, and walked over to my patient. He did not wince as I drove the needle of the syringe into the left, and then the right, side of his face. "Now, sir," I said — and the tremor in my voice surprised me — "we must wait a period of ten minutes." I joined Maude, and talked to her in low tones, keeping my eyes always upon my patient. He stared at the ceiling; his face remained solidified in that unholy grin. Precisely ten minutes later, a short gasp escaped him; I rushed to his side, and Maude followed close behind me.

We watched with consuming fascination as that clenched face slowly softened, relaxed, changed; the lips drawing closer and closer to each other, gradually covering those naked teeth and gums, the graven creases unfolding and becoming smooth. Before a minute had passed, we were looking down upon the face of a serenely handsome man. His eyes flashed with pleasure, and he made as if to speak.

"No," I said, "do not attempt speech yet. The muscles of your face are so slackened that it is beyond your power, at present, to move your lips. This condition will pass."

My voice rang with exultation, and for the moment our enmity was forgotten. He nodded, then leapt from the table and dashed to a mirror which hung on a wall nearby. Though his face could not yet express his joy, his whole body seemed to unfurl in a great gesture of triumph and a muffled cry of happiness burst in his throat.

He turned and seized my hand; then he looked full into Maude's face. After a moment, she said, "I am happy for you, sir," and looked away. A rasping laugh sounded in his throat, and he walked to my work bench, tore a leaf from one of my notebooks, and scribbled upon it. This he handed to Maude, who read it and passed it over to me. The writing said: *Fear not, lady. You will not be obliged to endure my embraces. I know full well that the restored beauty of my face will weigh not a jot in the balance of your attraction and repugnance. By this document, I dissolve our pristine marriage. You who have been a wife only in name are no longer even that. I give you your freedom.*

I looked up from my reading. Sardonicus had been writing again. He ripped another leaf from the notebook and handed it directly to me. It read: *This paper is your safe conduct out of the castle and into the Village. Gold is yours for the asking, but I doubt if your English scruples will countenance the accepting of my money. I will expect you to have quit these premises before morning, taking her with you.*

"We will be gone within the hour," I told him, and guided Maude towards the door. Before we left the room, I turned for the last time to Sardonicus.

"For your unclean threats," I said; "for the indirect but no less vicious murder of this lady's parents; for the defiling of your own father's grave; for the greed and inhumanity that moved you even before your blighted face provided you with an excuse for your conduct; for these and for what crimes unknown to me blacken your ledger — accept this token of my censure and detestation." I struck him forcibly on the face. He did not respond. He was standing there in the laboratory when I left the room with Maude.

IX NOT GOD ABOVE NOR THE FIEND BELOW

THIS STRANGE ACCOUNT should probably end here. No more can be said of its central character, for neither Maude nor I saw him or heard of him after that night. And of us two, nothing need be imparted other than the happy knowledge that we have been most contentedly married for the past twelve years and are the parents of a sturdy boy and two girls who are the lovely images of their mother.

However, I have mentioned my friend Lord Henry Stanton, the inveterate traveller and faithful letter-writer, and I must copy out now a portion of a missive I received from him only a week since, and which, in point of fact, has been the agent that has prompted me to unfold this whole history of Mr. Sardonicus:

"... But, my dear Bobbie," wrote Stanton, "in truth there is small pleasure to be found in this part of the world, and I shall be glad to see London again. The excitements and the drama have all departed (if, indeed, they ever existed) and one must content one's self with the stories told at the hearthstones of inns, with the flames crackling and the mulled wine agreeably stinging one's throat. The natives here are most fond of harrowing stories, tales of gore and grue, of ghosts and ghouls and ghastly events, and I must confess a partiality to such entertainments myself. They will show you a stain on a wall and tell you it is the blood of a murdered innocent who met her death there fifty years before: no amount of washing will ever remove that stain, they tell you in sepulchral tones, and indeed it deepens and darkens on a certain day of the year, the anniversary of her violent passing. One is expected to nod gravely, of course, and one does, if one wishes to encourage the telling of more stories. Back in the Eleventh Century, you will be apprised, a battalion of foreign invaders were vanquished by the skeletons of long-dead patriots who arose from their tombs to defend their homeland and then returned to the earth when the enemy had been driven from their borders. (And since they are able to show you the very graves of these lively bones, how can one disbelieve them, Bobbie?) Or they will point to a desolate skull of a castle (the country here abounds in such depressing piles) and tell you of the spectral tyrant who, a scant dozen years before, despaired and died alone there. Deserted by the minions who had always hated him, the frightening creature roamed the village, livid and emaciated, his mind shattered, mutely imploring the succour of even the lowliest beggars. I say *mutely*, and that is the best part of this tall tale: for, as they tell it around the fire, these inventive folk, this poor unfortunate could not speak, could not eat, and could not drink. You ask why? For the simple reason that, though he clawed most horribly at his own face, and though he enlisted the aid of strong men — he was absolutely unable to open his mouth. Cursed by Lucifer, they say, he thirsted and starved in the midst of plenty, surrounded by kegs of drink and tables full of the choicest viands, suffering the tortures of Tantalus, until he finally died. Ah, Bobbie! the efforts of our novelists are pale stuff compared to this! English littérateurs have not the shameless wild imaginations of these people! I will never again read Mrs. Radcliffe with pleasure. I assure you, and the ghost of King Hamlet will, from this day hence, strike no terror to my soul, and will fill my heart with but paltry pity. Still, I have journeyed in foreign climes quite enough for one trip, and I long for England and that good English dullness which is relieved only by you and your dear lady (to whom you must commend me most warmly). Until next month, I remain,

"Your wayward friend,
"*Harry Stanton*
"(Bohemia, March, 18—)"

Now, it would not be a difficult feat for the mind to instantly assume that the unfortunate man in that last tale was Sardonicus — indeed, it is for that reason that I have not yet shewn Stanton's letter to Maude: for she, albeit she deeply loathed Sardonicus, is of such a compassionate and susceptible nature that she would grieve to hear of him suffering a death so horrible. But I am a man of science, and I do not form conclusions on such gossamer evidence. Harry did not mention the province of Bohemia that is supposed to have been the stage of that terrible drama; and his letter, though written in Bohemia, was not mailed by Harry until he reached Berlin, so the postmark tells me nothing. Castles like that of Sardonicus are not singular in Bohemia — Harry himself says the country "abounds in such depressing piles" — so I plan to suspend conclusive thoughts on the matter until I welcome Harry home and can elicit from him details of the precise locality.

For if that "desolate skull of a castle" *is* Castle Sardonicus, and if the story of the starving man is to be believed, then I will be struck by an awesome and curious thing:

Five days I occupied myself in extracting a liquor from the South American plants. During those days, dogs were carried dead from my laboratory. I had deliberately killed the poor creatures with the undiluted poison, in order to impress Sardonicus with its deadliness. I never intended to — and, in fact, never did — prepare a safe dilution of that lethal drug, for its properties were too unknown, its potentiality too dangerous. The liquid I injected into Sardonicus was pure, distilled water — nothing more. This had always been my plan. The ordering of *materia medica* from far-flung lands was but an elaborate façade designed to work not upon the physical part of Sardonicus, but upon his mind; for after Keller, Morignac, Buonagente and my own massaging techniques had failed, I was convinced that it was only through his mind that his body could be cured. It was necessary to persuade him, however, that he was receiving a powerful medicament. His mind, I had hoped, would provide the rest — as, in truth, it did.

If the tale of the "spectral tyrant" proved true, then we must look upon the human mind with wonderment and terror. For, in that case, there was nothing — nothing corporeal — to prevent the wretched creature from opening his mouth and eating his fill. Alone in that castle, food aplenty at his fingertips, he had suffered a dire punishment which came upon him—to paraphrase Sardonicus' very words — *not from God above or the Fiend below, but from within his own breast, his own brain, his own soul.*

"Sardonicus Reincarnate"

by Amanda Russell

> The character of Sardonicus was created by my father, Ray Russell (1924 – 1999), in his novella "Sardonicus" (© 1960). In this story, Sardonicus makes an appearance in an unexpected way. Quotations are taken directly from the novella; some other portions of the story summarize the novella. "Sardonicus Reincarnate" is dedicated to our late friend Michael Schweitzer, who suggested that I write my own story featuring Sardonicus. – A.R.

Robert Cargrave, M.D., Ph.D.

September 4, 2020

Dear George,

    I hope you're well. I'm sorry I haven't written in so long - after looking in my files, I realized it's been almost a year! Since you don't have e-mail, your friends must turn to the vanishing art of letter-writing. Sometimes I envy the simple life you lead in your mountain cabin, with no computer, television, or other electronic gadgets.

    I had an experience recently with a patient that almost defies belief. I have told no one about it, not even fellow psychiatrists in private conversations. I fear that if anyone in the mainstream medical profession found out, the excellent reputation I've built up over the years would be jeopardized. I know that because of our close friendship that began during our undergraduate years at UCLA, and your open-minded interest in the paranormal, you will believe what happened. I trust you never to tell anyone about my experience. Please destroy this letter after you read it. I'm keeping only one copy of this patient's records in my locked filing cabinet.

    I don't think I've told you in detail about my method for treating patients, a method that has become nearly extinct in the world of psychiatry. Unlike most psychiatrists today, I'm "old school" in that I take a lot of time to listen to my patients talk about what is troubling them, and gradually guide their personal narrative so that they can work out their problems for themselves, helped by some key suggestions and advice from me. I only prescribe medication as a long-term treatment for people with the most serious types of mental conditions such as schizophrenia and bipolar disorder. My other patients, whose problems are emotional in nature, usually don't need medication, because they are able to take a lot of time working out their feelings in their sessions with me. In some cases, I'll prescribe an antidepressant, but only as a temporary measure, and will help the patient taper off the medication as soon as they feel ready.

Very few psychiatrists practice this way because the real cost would be prohibitive for billing insurance companies. I get around this obstacle by spending an hour with a patient, and billing their insurance company for a 20-minute appointment. My fees are high enough to cover my expenses and support my lifestyle with its modest comforts, but are lower than most psychiatrists' fees considering the amount of time I spend with my patients. I do this because I strongly believe that my method is the best, and I don't want to limit my services to the wealthy.

Last year, my assistant told me she answered an unusual phone call from a man who wanted to become a patient. Most people are referred to me by other psychiatrists, psychologists, or therapists, but this man said he got my name from the Internet, and was impressed by patient reviews. There's nothing unusual about that, but the man also said that somehow, he had a feeling that I was the best doctor to help him. He couldn't explain this feeling. My assistant said that he was anxious to make an appointment; to his relief, there was an opening the following week.

As soon as I met this new patient, I was struck by his acute symptoms - muscle tension, sweating, and trembling. He was a tall, slender, handsome man in his late 20s, with aquiline features, brown eyes, and a full head of thick, dark brown hair - a type who could instantly attract many women, were it not for his obvious anxiety.

He came into my office and we began the initial appointment, which takes two hours. I invited him to sit down in the comfortable recliner armchair I reserve for patients. Most people make use of the reclining feature, since it is so relaxing. But he sat almost at the edge of the chair. I suggested that it would help him relax if he sat further back, or used the reclining feature. Eventually he sat back and relaxed a little, but wouldn't recline. He said he had been suffering from terrible insomnia. He could not sleep at all if lying on his back, it created such feelings of panic. Only if lying on his side could he eventually fall asleep, awakening not refreshed, but exhausted.

Instead of asking him why he thought I was the best doctor to help him, I began by asking what was troubling him. He said that he was bewildered by his anxiety and despair. Until recently, he had led a normal, happy life, with a good career as an insurance company sales representative. He had been making a lot of sales and had even won an award the previous month as the top sales rep for that month, so he hadn't been anxious about his job. He had always enjoyed playing tennis and going hiking in the mountains on the weekends, which was sufficient for working out any tensions that had built up over the work week. He had stopped doing these outdoor activities due to his anxiety, because he couldn't concentrate well enough. Though he didn't have a steady girlfriend, he recently met a young woman he had really hit it off with, and felt their relationship had great potential.

I asked him if he had seen his regular physician, to rule out any physical causes for his symptoms. He said he'd just had a complete physical, which showed that he was in excellent health. But he had downplayed his anxiety to his doctor, who told him, "Maybe you're working too hard. Make sure you get enough sleep, and don't drink too much coffee."

Then I asked him to tell me when the feelings of anxiety began. He said, "This is going to sound crazy." I told him, "You're not 'crazy,' there is a rational explanation for the way you're feeling."

Looking reassured, he began his story. It began the day when, on a whim, he bought a ticket for the California Lottery, something he had never done before. He put it in his shirt pocket. Almost immediately, he started to experience feelings of anxiety, panic, and despair. He never heard of anyone in his family or any friends losing a lot of money due to gambling, so these feelings made no sense to him. Yet, that ticket in his pocket made him uncomfortable. When he got home, he put it in a drawer right away. He didn't go so far as to destroy the ticket; he kept it in the drawer until he found out the winning numbers for that week (he didn't win anything), then ripped it up. He thought that would solve his problem, but it didn't - his anxiety continued. His boss and co-workers had started to notice, so he knew he had to get help as soon as possible.

Since he never had any reason to see a mental health professional, he looked online for options. The name "Dr. Robert Cargrave" jumped out at him. He felt that he had heard this name before, and that a Dr. Robert Cargrave had helped him somehow, yet he didn't know why - another feeling that made no sense!

After he described this bizarre experience, I spent a lot of time asking him many questions about his life. I learned that he grew up as a member of a happy, supportive family; he didn't recall any frightening experiences in his childhood. He was a popular boy who was never bullied in school or maltreated by sadistic teachers. For these reasons, I didn't think there were any suppressed memories of trauma in his early life. I did not find any signs of a serious mental condition like schizophrenia, which can cause delusions. He had never used recreational drugs, had never even smoked pot in college, because of his dedication to good health and fitness. He said he only drank beer and wine once in a while on social occasions.

I gave him the most likely explanation of his feeling that I was the best doctor to help him. I said that he may have had a dream where he saw or heard the name "Dr. Robert Cargrave," but he didn't remember the whole dream, he only remembered my name after he saw it on the Internet. I told him this was not unusual; many people have premonitions that can take the form of dreams.

Baffled by this strange case, I told my new patient that I would need to study the psychiatric literature for similar cases, so that I would be better equipped to help him. I said I wanted to see him in two weeks, so he set up another appointment. For patients with insomnia, I usually recommend the hormone melatonin to regulate their sleep cycle, but since this man's insomnia was severe, I prescribed a mild sleeping pill. I also gave him a CD with a guided meditation accompanied by soothing music, and a booklet about relaxation techniques such as breathing exercises and easy yoga postures. Most of my patients have found these techniques highly effective. I also advised him to do some moderate walking, preferably on residential streets with lots of trees and other plants.

I began to study late into the night, every night, looking in the many books on psychiatry in my home library. I could not find even one case that was similar to this patient's. Then a thought occurred to me, something I found almost impossible to believe. Yet the thought kept coming back to me, because it seemed like the only answer. What if the man's fear came from a memory from a past life?

George, I recall our conversations about the many accounts of reincarnation, most of which have been either hoaxes, or accounts with no evidence to back them up, told by people who just "feel" that they lived in another time and place (usually a glamorous epoch like Egypt in the time of the Pharaohs). Remember that book we read back in the '90s, written by a psychiatrist who said that he used hypnosis to help his patients regress to their past lives? The book was somewhat convincing, until the author's account of a young woman who, while under hypnosis, specified the year she was living in as "B.C." This was a giveaway that the whole book was a hoax, because if the woman's mind was really back in that era, she wouldn't have said that the time period was "B.C."! We couldn't stop laughing!

I also remember your conviction that some reincarnation stories could be real, and I agreed. Although I believe that most of these stories are not real, my mind has remained open to the possibility.

Though the psychiatrist who wrote the bogus book obviously didn't help his patients regress to past lives, I thought if my patient's troubles originated in a past life, I had to find out somehow. Hypnotherapy (now the preferred term, to distinguish it from hypnosis used as a form of entertainment) is a treatment method used for many reasons, so I'm familiar with it. Though I usually don't use hypnotherapy in my practice, I was trained in the technique during my psychiatric residency, and have used it occasionally. To refresh my memory, I read up on the subject and spoke with a colleague who often uses hypnotherapy (without telling him why I was consulting him).

Thinking about past lives got me curious about my own family history. Taking a break from my study of hypnotherapy, I opened a large wooden chest containing many old family documents that I had never taken the time to read. I think I told you that one of my third great-grandfathers was also a physician named Robert Cargrave, actually Sir Robert Cargrave, an Englishman who was knighted by Queen Victoria for his pioneering research on the ligaments and muscles. He developed sophisticated massage techniques that he used to treat injuries and even some types of paralysis.

Most of my distinguished ancestor's papers were the usual sorts of medical records. I found them fascinating, but I couldn't take the time to read them in detail. Then I found a different type of book, bound in burgundy leather, that had been placed underneath all the others. It was a personal diary! I began to read and quickly became absorbed by it. It was not technically a diary in that it was not a daily record of a period in Sir Robert's life (the word "diary" is derived from the Latin "dies," meaning "day"). It was the spellbinding account of his encounter with Mr. Sardonicus, a mysterious character who lived in a remote castle in a part of Central Europe that was then called Bohemia.

I was impressed by my ancestor's mastery of the English language. Today, the only writing most physicians do is scribbling prescriptions and jotting down notes of patient consultations. Some write articles for medical journals, but these are written in professional jargon that is incomprehensible to the lay person. A few write health-related books aimed at the general public, which vary in quality but are seldom page-turners. Only an exceptional small group of physicians write accurate, insightful medical accounts that are not only accessible, but enjoyable, to the general public. The late Dr. Oliver Sacks comes to mind as one of these rare few.

The account begins when Sir Robert receives a letter signed "Madam S." (Sir Robert only learned of the name Sardonicus upon his arrival at their castle.) In the letter, Madam S. explains that she is the former Maude Randall, who had been a love interest of Sir Robert's years before. (After I read further, I learned her sad story, that she married the wealthy Sardonicus for money - not out of greed, but because her destitute father had killed himself and her mother died shortly afterwards, and she had no way to support herself).

Maude had heard of Sir Robert's achievements in medicine, and of his knighthood. She was nostalgic about her life in London. She wrote:

> It was indeed only yesterday, in the course of conversation, that I was recalling my old life in London, and mentioned your name. Mr. S., I thought, was, of a sudden, interested. "Robert Cargrave?" he said. "There is a well-known physician of the same name, but I do not imagine it is the same gentleman." I laughed and told him it <u>was</u> the same gentleman, and that I had known you before you became so illustrious…
>
> I told him you had been a friend of my family's and a frequent guest at our house. "That is a most happy coincidence," he said. "I have long desired to meet Sir Robert Cargrave, and your past friendship with him furnishes you with an excellent opportunity to invite him here for a holiday."
>
> And so, Sir Robert, I am complying with his request - and at the same time obeying the dictates of my own inclination - by most cordially inviting you to visit us for as long as you choose. I entreat you to come, for we see so few people here and it would be a great pleasure to talk with someone from the old days…

Eager to see Maude again, Sir Robert sailed to Europe and made his way across the continent, which was no easy trip in those days: "…few things are more tiresome to me than ships and trains and carriages…" The last part of his journey was in a horse-drawn carriage, up a bumpy mountain road to a forbidding-looking castle. After his happy reunion with Maude, he met Mr. Sardonicus. **His face was frozen into a horrible grin!** Sir Robert described his first meeting his host:

> "Sir Robert Cargrave?" he asked, but he spoke with difficulty, certain sounds - such as the *b* in Robert and the *v* in Cargrave - being almost impossible for him to utter. To shape these sounds, the lips must be used, and the gentleman before me was the victim of some terrible affliction that had caused his lips to be pulled perpetually apart from each other, baring his teeth in a continuous ghastly smile…a pallor approaching phosphorescence completed his astonishing appearance.

Sir Robert realized that Sardonicus' unusual name was not a family name, but was a name he gave himself, based on the medical term *risus sardonicus*, the "continuous ghastly smile" of a person in the terminal phase of lockjaw, what we now call tetanus.

Sardonicus had asked Maude to invite Sir Robert to visit them because he'd heard of his successful treatment of severe muscle spasms, and was hoping Sir Robert could cure his affliction. He told Sir Robert his tragic story, that began when he was a young Polish peasant named Marek Boleslawski. I was stunned to discover that his hideous disfigurement was brought on in his youth when he retrieved a winning **lottery ticket** from the **vest pocket** of his dead father's decomposing corpse!

There was a monthly lottery held in Warsaw. Every month for 23 years, Marek's father traveled to the city to sell produce and buy a few things for their home. Each month he bought one lottery ticket, always putting it in the vest pocket of his only good suit. He died suddenly and was buried in the suit; no one in the family thought of the lottery ticket, because he had been buying the tickets for so long and had never won. When the winners were announced, the family was anguished to discover that the winning ticket was their father's - and it was in his vest pocket! Marek's mother insisted that the grave of her husband must not be desecrated. She even went to the cemetery at night to guard it.

Marek could not resist the temptation of the lottery winnings, so near and yet so far. He went to the cemetery and told his mother that he would guard the grave so that she could go home, out of the cold. He waited an hour, then took a small shovel out of his pocket. He dug up the soil, then performed the grim task of opening the coffin. Suddenly, the clouds that had been covering the moon parted, bathing the cemetery in bright moonlight. The shock of seeing his father's grinning skull caused his own mouth to suddenly and violently mimic the grinning skull, and freeze in that position. As Sardonicus told Sir Robert,

> "I would not believe that God placed a malediction on me to punish me for my act. I would not believe that some black force from beyond the grave reached out to stamp my face. At length, I began to believe that it was the massive shock that had forced my face to its present state, and that my great guilt had shaped it even as my dead father's face was shaped. Shock and guilt: strong powers not from God above or the Fiend below, but from within my own breast, my own brain, my own soul."

Marek never returned home. He claimed the lottery winnings, renamed himself Mr. Sardonicus, and traveled through Europe, visiting distinguished physicians in futile search of a cure. While in Paris, he saw the beautiful Maude Randall, and married her. He bought the castle and its luxurious furnishings, and became a recluse because of his repulsive face.

My incredible hunch about a past life had to be correct: My new patient was the reincarnation of Mr. Sardonicus! Now I knew why he felt I was the best person to help him - in his past life, he had sought help from my ancestor, another Dr. Robert Cargrave.

Sardonicus' story about digging up his father's corpse also explained why lying on his back caused my patient to panic: He had an unconscious memory of the body lying in the coffin, on its back forever.

By now unable to put the book down, I read on to learn the rest of the story of Sir Robert's encounter with Sardonicus.

The next day, Sir Robert employed the method for treating muscle spasms that had been successful in his medical practice - repeated applications of heat followed by special massage techniques. Sir Robert wrote:

> Never have I worked so long with so little reward. After alternating applications of heat and of massage, over a period of three and a quarter hours, I had made no progress. The muscles of his face were still as stiff as marble; they had not relaxed for an instant.

After a short break, he tried again, for hours, but to no avail. Sardonicus asked Sir Robert what remained to be done; Sir Robert told him it was beyond his power to help him. He said there was an experimental treatment, using a dilution of a poison that brings about *total* relaxation of the muscles, but it was far too dangerous to try, as it could be fatal. Sardonicus was willing to risk it, but Sir Robert was not. Then Sardonicus began pleading with him to use the experimental treatment. First, he offered increasingly large sums of money; Sir Robert declined these offers, saying it was not a question of money.

It is only natural that Sardonicus' affliction would have turned him into a bitter man, but in his case, bitterness had degenerated into revolting cruelty. After Sir Robert turned down the offer of money, Sardonicus turned next to a perverse incentive, then to an unspeakable threat.

He explained to Sir Robert that when he persuaded Maude to marry him, he had assured her that the physical expression of love meant nothing to him, that he had no desire for it - he only wanted her companionship. This was a lie. He thought that he could gradually seduce Maude, but realized that she was repelled even by his light touch or kiss on her hand.

Sardonicus had noticed how Sir Robert and Maude looked at each other; though they behaved with proper Victorian manners, it was obvious that they were still in love. He told Sir Robert that he could fulfill his love and desire for Maude for as long as he wanted, if he would cure him. Outraged, Sir Robert refused. Then Sardonicus turned to the worst possible threat: If Sir Robert didn't cure him, he would satisfy his long-suppressed desire for Maude by forcing himself on her every day, in all sorts of appalling ways he didn't describe, except to say, "I am by nature imaginative."

Sir Robert had no choice but to try the experimental treatment. He ordered poisonous plants from the New World and medical equipment from England and Scotland. When everything arrived, he spent long hours in solitude, working on a distillation that was dilute enough to be safe. Every day, dogs were brought to his laboratory, but were carried out dead. Finally, a dog survived, and Sir Robert told Sardonicus that he was ready to try the treatment.

The distillation would not be administered orally, but directly into his face by means of a new invention, a syringe with a hollow needle attached - a *hypodermic needle*. Sir Robert warned Sardonicus one last time of the possible danger of the treatment, that it could be fatal, but Sardonicus told him to go ahead. Sir Robert injected both sides of Sardonicus' face.

> Precisely ten minutes later, a short gasp escaped him … We watched with consuming fascination as that clenched face slowly softened, relaxed, changed; the lips drawing closer and closer to each other, gradually covering those naked teeth and gums, the graven creases unfolding and becoming smooth. Before a minute had passed, we were looking down upon the face of a serenely handsome man.

Sir Robert warned Sardonicus not to try speaking yet, because his facial muscles were so slackened that it would be beyond his power to move his lips, but that condition would pass. Sardonicus picked up Sir Robert's notebook, tore out two pages, and scribbled two notes. The first was for Maude, disolving their marriage, which had been a marriage in name only. The second note was for Sir Robert, and was a safe conduct out of the castle and into the village. On this second note he wrote, "*I will have expected you to quit these premises before morning, taking her with you.*" Sir Robert replied, "We will be gone within the hour."

He and Maude never saw or heard from Sardonicus again. Reading on in his story, I learned that they married and had a son and two daughters, so I am the descendant of their son!

Near the end of the account, Sir Robert copied a portion of a letter from his friend Lord Henry Stanton, which he received twelve years after he and Maude fled the castle and returned to London. Stanton had been traveling for a long time in remote parts of Europe, where he heard many strange tales told by the local people:

> [T]hey will point to a desolate skull of a castle (the country here abounds in such depressing piles) and tell you of the spectral tyrant who, a scant dozen years before, despaired and died alone there. Deserted by the minions who had always hated him, the frightening creature roamed the village, livid and emaciated, his mind shattered, mutely imploring the succor of even the lowliest beggars. I say *mutely*, and that is the best part of this tall tale: for as they tell it around the fire, these inventive folk, this poor unfortunate could not speak, could not eat, and could not drink. You ask why? For the simple reason that, though he clawed most horribly at his own face, and though he enlisted the aid of strong men, he could not open his mouth. Cursed by Lucifer, they say,

> he thirsted and starved in the midst of plenty, surrounded
> by kegs of drink and tables full of the choicest viands,
> suffering the tortures of Tantalus, until he finally died.

Sir Robert wrote, "Now, it would not be a difficult feat for the mind to instantly assume that the unfortunate man in that last tale was Sardonicus … But I am a man of science, and I do not form conclusions on such gossamer evidence." He continued that he planned to ask his friend Stanton the precise location of the castle. "For if that 'desolate skull of a castle' *is* Castle Sardonicus, and if the story of the starving man is to be believed, then I will be struck by an awesome and curious thing."

Although Sir Robert ordered poisonous plants from South America, and spent days extracting an elixir from them and experimenting with dogs, "I had deliberately killed the poor creatures with the undiluted poison, in order to impress Sardonicus with its deadliness. I never intended to - and in fact, never did - prepare a safe dilution of that lethal drug, for its properties were too unknown, potentially too dangerous. The liquid I injected into Sardonicus was pure, distilled water - nothing more. This had always been my plan." The ordering of plants from South America had been an elaborate façade. Sir Robert knew that since no physician had been able to help Sardonicus by physical means, he was "convinced that it was only through his mind that his body could be cured. It was necessary to persuade him, however, that he was receiving a powerful medicament. His mind, I had hoped, would provide the rest - as, in truth, it did."

> If the tale of the "spectral tyrant" proved true, then we
> must look upon the human mind with wonderment and terror.
> For, in that case, there was nothing - nothing corporeal -
> to prevent the wretched creature from opening his mouth and
> eating his fill. Alone in that castle, food aplenty at his
> fingertips, he had suffered a dire punishment which came upon
> him - to paraphrase Sardonicus' very words - *not from God
> above or the Fiend below, but from within his own breast, his
> own brain, his own soul.*

I finished this astonishing story in one sitting. I was astounded to learn that Sir Robert worked on Sardonicus' <u>mind</u> for the cure, which reveals another link between me and my distinguished ancestor - knowledge of the power of the mind.

With less than a week left before my patient's next appointment, I returned with new hope and determination to my study of hypnotherapy, going online and to the library for new information. I was encouraged to learn that there are reputable hypnotherapists who practice Past Life Regression Therapy, which is particularly useful when someone has a problem with no known or "rational" cause. Several therapists have written about the success they've had in treating people with phobias. They've found that many phobias are rooted in traumas suffered in a past life. At last, I found that there have been many cases similar to my patient's!

Past Life Regression has much in common with standard hypnotherapy, but there are special considerations involved. Originally, I had not planned to tell my patient about my belief that his inexplicable anxiety could have its origin in a previous existence. I had only planned to tell him that hypnotherapy would be a good way to help him relax and reach his unconscious, so that the reason for his fear could be revealed. Through my research, I learned that it is important for the person going through this type of therapy to have a specific intention focusing on a past life. Intentions about what is troubling the person (such as a phobia, an illness, or a relationship problem) work well.

This meant that I would need to share with my patient my belief that his fear had its origin in a past life. I then planned a good explanation of Past Life Regression Therapy, which would include showing my patient the successful case studies I had read. Most people who go through Past Life Regression seek out this form of therapy, and so are already open to it; I could only hope that my patient would be open to it as well. Of course, I could tell him nothing about Marek Boleslawski; he would need to regress to that life through the process of hypnotherapy.

Some people who are considering Past Life Regression are concerned that it would be too upsetting or frightening. I learned that in cases where the past life experience was traumatic (most likely, if it is causing a current problem), the goal is to remember only a little bit of the experience each session, otherwise it would be overwhelming, and the therapy would do more harm than good. I was familiar with this concept, because the same method needs to be applied in cases of suppressed memories of child abuse and other early traumas in a person's life.

By now I was confident of how to approach the next session with my patient. Thinking of reincarnation in general, I remembered the traditional Hindu and Buddhist view on the subject - if someone commits great evil in their lifetime, they will be reborn in ill-fated circumstances, even as an animal. This concept didn't seem to fit the case of the evil Sardonicus being reborn as this young man, who until recently, had led a very fortunate life.

Then I thought of Lord Henry Stanton's letter, with its account of what he thought was a "tall tale" about a "spectral tyrant" who had died in agony because he could not open his mouth. Because a human being can only live from a few days to a week without water, this wretched man, who Sir Robert thought might have been Sardonicus, must have gone through the torments of Hell in the space of only a few days. I felt that this horrible retribution must have expiated many of Sardonicus' foul thoughts, words, and deeds. Then his soul floated in some limbo or purgatory for over a century, until it was reincarnated into the body of my young patient, whose personality was like the peasant Marek, not the evil Sardonicus. Marek must have been a decent youth, driven by poverty and hunger to commit the desperate act of digging up his father's body for the lottery ticket.

My patient came back for his second appointment. He looked better. He said the relaxation CD and the sleeping pills had helped. Though he hadn't resumed playing tennis or going on strenuous hikes, he had started walking on his lunch hours and on the weekends. I was greatly relieved that he was open to the possibility that his anxiety was caused by a trauma in a past life. "That's got to be it - there's no other explanation!" he said. Though he was not a practitioner of any Eastern religion, he had read a lot about Hinduism and Buddhism in college, and had been favorably impressed by the doctrines of *karma* and reincarnation.

To go into detail about what followed would fill a book, so I'll sum up what happened. I'm thrilled to report that the Past Life Regression was completely successful. As I had planned, the process of hypnotherapy took a long time, six months of weekly sessions, gradually peeling away the layers of unconscious memories so that my patient would not be overwhelmed. His anxiety became much less debilitating during this process, because he believed in what we were doing and knew we were making progress. His co-workers noticed that he was feeling better, and best of all, he now had a happy relationship with the young woman he had mentioned during his first visit.

In our sessions, he gradually regressed through his life as Marek, first as a boy, then as a young man, in a family so poor that some days they had nothing to eat.

When he finally reached the point during the hypnotic state when he remembered taking the lottery ticket out of his father's vest pocket, his mind protected him from the worst. This is one of the "prime directives" of the unconscious, to protect the mind from anything it cannot handle. In the hypnotic state, he did not see the bright moonlight shining on the corpse, so he did not see the hideous grinning skull that had caused the "continuous ghastly smile." Marek had brought a small lantern with him to the cemetery, but it didn't provide much light, just enough to be able to see the vague shape of the body. In the hypnotic state, my patient saw only the light from the lantern, so the worst thing he remembered was feeling around on the body to reach the vest pocket and retrieve the ticket.

According to Sardonicus' story as told by Sir Robert, Marek was so ashamed by what he'd done and so horrified about what happened to his face that he left his family, never to return. My patient's mind also protected him from this memory. He only remembered enough to experience the guilt of digging up his father's body and taking the ticket.

We stopped the hypnotherapy at this point - I wanted to be sure that no more shocking memories would begin to surface. After that, we had several months of sessions without hypnotherapy, focusing on my patient's processing of his guilt. He was eventually able to resolve these feelings and put them behind him, thinking that his desperate act must have been worth it, because he must have given the lottery winnings to his family, saving them from a life of poverty. As for my patient's feeling that I was the best doctor to help him, he was content with the belief that he may have met a Dr. Robert Cargrave in this past life, who had helped him in some way he couldn't recall. He was glad about what he felt must be a coincidence, because it led him to me.

Finally, he became relaxed and happy again, thinking about how he must have helped his family in his past life. Though it didn't really happen this way, that's not the point. My goal was to treat my patient, to help bring him back to the life he had before he bought the California Lottery ticket.

And who knows? Perhaps in an alternate universe, there was a new moon the night young Marek Boleslawski opened his father's coffin. I'd like to think so.

I hope to hear from you soon.
All the best,

Mr. Sardonicus

Script

WILLIAM CASTLE PRODUCTIONS

MR. SARDONICUS

(#8610)

Screen Play By

RAY RUSSELL

From his Playboy magazine novella, "Sardonicus"

Screenplay by
Ray Russell
FINAL DRAFT
February 15, 1961

from H. N. SWANSON, Inc.
8523 Sunset Blvd. : : OLympia 2-5385
Los Angeles, Calif. 90069

MR. SARDONICUS

(#8610)

FADE IN:

EXT. LONDON STREET - NIGHT

1   LONG SHOT   (STOCK)   1
    London of the late 1800's, densely enshrouded in fog.
    Big Ben faintly visible. Sound of carriages.

2   MEDIUM LONG SHOT   LAMP POST   MAN   2
    A foggy street corner, with a gas lamp post. The lamp's
    meagre light is haloed in fog. We hear footsteps approach-
    ing. Out of the fog, a Man is walking closer to us, slowly,
    deliberately. He is a tall, massive man, wearing a high
    silk hat of the period. We cannot yet see his face.

3   CLOSE SHOT   MAN   3
    Now he is large on the screen, but still a fog-swathed
    silhouette. A match is struck... he is lighting a long,
    expensive cigar...and now we recognize WILLIAM CASTLE.

                    CASTLE
                (between puffs,
                 lighting the cigar)
            Confounded fog...makes the
            matches so damp, you know...
            ah, there we are...
                (cigar is lit)
            This, of course, is London...
            and I am William Castle. It's
            good to see you again, my homicidal
            friends. This time, our story is
            of a different kind... It is an
            old-fashioned story, full of
            gallantry...and graciousness...
            and ghouls! You know about ghouls,
            don't you? They are...

    He fishes in his pocket and produces a small pocket dictionary.

                    CASTLE
                (continuing)
            ... Well, let me find you an
            exact definition.
                (running his
                 finger down a page)
            Let me see... 'ghoom' (an odd

3   CONTINUED: 3

                              CASTLE (cont'd)
                    word, that -- it means 'to
                    search for game in the dark')...
                    'ghost'... Ah, here we have it!
                    'Ghoul'! An evil being who robs
                    graves and..

        Shocked, he looks up at us and continues in a hoarse whisper:

                              CASTLE
                         (continuing)
                    '...and feeds on corpses!'
                         (puts dictionary
                         back in his pocket)
                    Yes... just an old-fashioned
                    story... I hope you enjoy it.
                         (tips his hat
                         to us)
                    So nice to have met you again...

        He turns and walks off into the fog... It weaves about him
        and envelops him... He is swallowed up in it, and the screen
        is now completely filled with fog. Out of this --

                              THE GIMMICK

OPENING TITLE:

S A R D O N I C U S

CREDITS FOLLOW.

4   MONTAGE: STOCK LONDON STREET SCENES - DAY   4
THRU   now greet us. We see carriages of the period --   THRU
8   well-dressed ladies and gentlemen strolling --   8
        Big Ben -- London Bridge -- Buskers, their coats bedecked
        with big white buttons -- etc. The last SHOT in this series
        is:

EXT. HOSPITAL (STOCK) - DAY

9   LONG SHOT KINGS COLLEGE HOSPITAL   9

                                                        DISSOLVE TO:

sgb-8610

INSERT: A small building plaque, bearing
the legend:

        KINGS COLLEGE HOSPITAL

                                      DISSOLVE TO:

INT. HOSPITAL - DAY

10   LONG SHOT HOSPITAL CORRIDOR   10
        Nurses, doctors walking, etc.

                                      DISSOLVE TO:

INT. HOSPITAL DISPENSARY - DAY

11   CLOSE SHOT PAIR OF STRONG MASCULINE HANDS   11
        They are gently massaging the leg of a little girl (age five
        or six) who is lying on a hospital table.

12   GROUP SHOT ROBERT WAINWRIGHT GIRL MOTHER   12
        CAMERA PULLS AWAY to show a small dispensary and a GROUP
        SHOT of SIR ROBERT CARGRAVE, who is doing the massaging;
        WAINWRIGHT, his young assistant; the girl on the table, and
        her MOTHER, a poor, ill-dressed woman, who is standing
        anxiously in the b.g. Robert is a good-looking, amiable
        man in his late thirties. He exudes an aura of profession-
        alism and authority, in addition to humanity and warmth.
        Robert stops massaging.

                      ROBERT
                (to Wainwright)
        Very well, Wainwright... apply
        the heat.

                      WAINWRIGHT
        Yes, Sir Robert.

Wainwright places a steaming towel on the girl's leg.

                      ROBERT
                (to girl)
        That doesn't hurt, does it,
        my dear?

sgb

12 CONTINUED: 12

                    GIRL
            Oh no, Doctor... it's nice
            and warm.

                    ROBERT
              (to Wainwright)
            Exactly thirty seconds,
            Wainwright... no more, no less.

                    WAINWRIGHT
            Quite, sir.

                    ROBERT
            And then we resume the massage.

INT. HOSPITAL ANTE ROOM

13   MEDIUM LONG SHOT   HEAD NURSE   13
        We see a Head Nurse -- middle-aged, officious, very British --
        at a desk. She is speaking to a short, heavy-set man who
        stands in front of the desk, and whose face we do not yet see.
        He holds a letter in his hand -- it is a large letter, on
        heavy, parchment-like paper, sealed with an enormous blob of
        wax.

                    HEAD NURSE
            That's all very well, my good
            man, but Sir Robert Cargrave
            cannot possibly see you now.

14   SUDDEN TIGHT CLOSEUP KRULL   14
        He is lumpish, uncouth; unpleasant to behold. He lacks an
        eye, and the empty socket is imperfectly sewn into a jagged,
        stitch-crossed scar. He is somewhat Neanderthal in appearance
        -- short but powerfully built, with a sloping forehead and
        stubbled, prognathous jaw. His voice is rough, thick, deep-
        pitched. A menacing type, he can sometimes break into
        flashes of ghoulish humor, then suddenly cool into a compact
        mass of smouldering evil.

                    KRULL
            But this letter. My master
            said I must place it in Sir
            Robert's hand and in no other's.

15   TWO SHOT   KRULL   HEAD NURSE   15
        Head Nurse reaches for the letter.

                    HEAD NURSE
            I will give it to...

sgb

15   CONTINUED: 15

                    KRULL
              (snatching it away)
         No! Only to Sir Robert!

                    HEAD NURSE
              (vexed, imperious)
         Sir, I assure you I will place
         it in Sir Robert's hand immediately
         he is available. If that does
         not please you, perhaps you would
         care to simply... leave?

                    KRULL
              (quickly)
         No, no... my master would...
         Listen... if I give you the
         letter... do you promise...

                    HEAD NURSE
         I promise I will hand it to
         Sir Robert.

    He hands her the letter.

INT. DISPENSARY

16   GROUP SHOT   ROBERT   WAINWRIGHT   MOTHER   GIRL   16
    The towel has been removed from the girl's leg, and Robert
    is just finishing another period of massages.

                    ROBERT
         There!
              (a pause; then,
              with a certain
              anxiety)
         Now...

    Robert takes the girl's leg in his hands and gently bends
    it at the knee, back and forth, several times. Then he
    speaks to the girl:

                    ROBERT
              (to girl)
         Young lady... I want you to
         try doing that yourself.

                    GIRL
         Oh, but Doctor, I couldn't...

                    MOTHER
         She's never been able to do
         that, Sir Robert...

sgb

16   CONTINUED: 16

                        ROBERT
                  (gentle, but firm)
            Come, come. You must try.

17   CAMERA MOVES IN CLOSE to the girl. There is a tense   17
      silence.

18   CLOSEUP GIRL'S FACE   18
      afraid, near tears.

19   CLOSEUP ROBERT   19
      giving her a smile of encouragement.

20   CLOSEUP WAINWRIGHT   20
      tense and expectant.

21   CLOSEUP MOTHER   21
      in an agony of anxiety.

22   CLOSE TWO SHOT GIRL AND ROBERT   22
      Slowly, the little leg begins to move, quiveringly at first.
      Then, as the girl gathers strength, the leg begins to bend,
      the knee rises -- just a little -- then more -- and still more.

23   CLOSEUP MOTHER   23
      Tears of happiness streaming down her face.

24   CLOSEUP ROBERT   24
      triumphant.

                        ROBERT
            Good girl!

25   CLOSEUP GIRL   25
      shaken but pleased.

                        GIRL
            I did it!... I did it!...

26   CLOSEUP WAINWRIGHT   26

                        WAINWRIGHT
            It worked, Sir Robert! Your
            treatment worked again!

sgb

27   GROUP SHOT   ALL FOUR   27

                         ROBERT
                Yes... thank God!

                         MOTHER
                Bless you, Sir Robert... Oh
                bless you for this!

                         ROBERT
                You can take her home now,
                Mrs. Higgins. Keep up the
                exercises, just as I told you
                ... and I will see you again
                Tuesday week.
                     (to Wainwright)
                Come, Wainwright... let's see
                if the post has arrived.

28   CLOSEUP   WAINWRIGHT   28

                         WAINWRIGHT
                The post, Sir Robert? Oh, yes!
                The new instrument from Scotland!

INT. PERSPECTIVE OF HOSPITAL CORRIDOR

29   LONG SHOT   ROBERT   WAINWRIGHT   29
       Through a door at the far end, Robert and Wainwright appear.
       As they walk toward the camera, they are talking.

                         WAINWRIGHT
                Sir Robert, in yesterday's class,
                just before you dismissed us, you
                said something rather odd...

                         ROBERT
                     (amused)
                About a poison that might cure
                certain forms of paralysis?

                         WAINWRIGHT
                Yes...

                         ROBERT
                Nothing odd about it, Wainwright
                ...frequently, the most deadly
                of poisons can also be the most
                beneficial of medicines.

                         WAINWRIGHT
                Such as belladonna?

sgb

29   CONTINUED: 29

                    ROBERT
          Quite right. Fatally toxic...
          but very useful in treating
          ailments of the optic nerve.

                    WAINWRIGHT
          But it was not belladonna to
          which you referred yesterday...

They have reached the ante-chamber of the Head Nurse, and
Robert opens the door. They enter.

INT. HOSPITAL ANTE-ROOM

30   GROUP SHOT HEAD NURSE ROBERT WAINWRIGHT   30
     Inside the room the Head Nurse is at the desk, Robert and
     Wainwright entering.

                    ROBERT
          No. It was...
               (he interrupts
                himself)
          Ah, Sister... has the post
          arrived?

                    HEAD NURSE
          Yes, Sir Robert... a number of...

                    ROBERT
          I'm expecting a package from
          Scotland...

                    HEAD NURSE
          I do believe there is a package
          from Edinburgh, sir. Also,
          there is...

31   NEW ANGLE TABLE   31
     Table loaded with mail in f.g. Robert walking toward it and
     "us." There is a package, several letters, rolled-up news-
     papers and medical journals, etc. There is also a silver
     salver on which Krull's letter rests. CAMERA MOVES IN upon
     this letter closely, making it a focal point of the shot.
     Meanwhile, Robert has been talking.

                    ROBERT
          Yes, Edinburgh, that's right.
          From Doctor Wood. Ah! Here
          it is.

sgb

32   NEW ANGLE   ROBERT   WAINWRIGHT   HEAD NURSE   32
        Robert and Wainwright at table, Head Nurse in b.g. Robert
        ignores the salver and picks up the package.

                        ROBERT
                Look at this, Wainwright.

        Robert begins opening the package -- string, paper, wooden
        slats, excelsior, etc. While he unwraps, he is speaking:

                        ROBERT
                The original theory was put
                forth two hundred years ago or
                more at Oxford by Doctor
                Christopher Wren. But only
                recently, through development
                by my friend, Doctor Wood of
                Edinburgh, it has seemed practical
                ... Ah! Isn't it beautiful!

        The unwrapping completed, Robert holds up a very primitive
        hypodermic needle. It should not be as small and streamlined
        as modern hypodermics -- it should appear somewhat clumsy and
        large.

                        WAINWRIGHT
                Yes... very beautiful!

                        ROBERT
                You see, Wainwright, it is
                nothing more than a syringe...
                attached to a needle...

                        WAINWRIGHT
                An ordinary needle?

                        ROBERT
                Not at all. A very extraordinary
                needle, indeed...a hollow needle
                ... a ..
                        (he savors the
                         strange new word)
                'hypo-dermic' needle!

                        WAINWRIGHT
                Hypo...dermic. In other words,
                it is meant to puncture the skin.

                        ROBERT
                Correct! And carry healing
                drugs directly and immediately
                into the bloodstream.

                        WAINWRIGHT
                Ingenious, sir!

32   CONTINUED:

>   HEAD NURSE
>   Er... Sir Robert...
>
>   ROBERT
>   Directly, Wainwright. Immediately.
>   Those are the key words.
>
>   HEAD NURSE
>   Sir Robert...may I call your
>   attention to a letter which...
>
>   ROBERT
>   (not hearing)
>   No more detours through the
>   digestive system, you see...
>
>   WAINWRIGHT
>   Yes, sir.

Head Nurse picks up the salver and hands it to Robert.

>   ROBERT
>   Eh? What's this?
>
>   HEAD NURSE
>   By special messenger, Sir Robert.
>   It appears to be from the Continent.
>
>   ROBERT
>   Well, it can wait.
>   (then noticing
>   something on the
>   letter)
>   No... I say...

INSERT: THE FACE OF THE LETTER
In flowing, feminine script
is written:

>   Sir Robert Cargrave
>   Queen's ~~Kings~~ College Hospital
>   London, England
>
>   ROBERT'S VOICE (O.S.)
>   That handwriting...

33   CLOSEUP ROBERT
     suddenly pensive.

33   CONTINUED: 33

                    ROBERT
            I wonder...if I might be left
            alone for a moment?...

34   GROUP SHOT ROBERT WAINWRIGHT HEAD NURSE   34

                    HEAD NURSE
            Of course, Sir Robert.

She starts to leave.

                    WAINWRIGHT
            I must be running along at
            any rate, sir. Goodbye.

                    ROBERT
              (gazing at the
               letter)
            Eh? Oh, goodbye, Wainwright...

Head Nurse and Wainwright leave the room.

35   TIGHT SHOT ROBERT   35
He sits down slowly, and pulls a large gold watch from his
pocket. He opens it.

INSERT: THE OPEN WATCH
         In it is a daguerreotype of a lovely
         young girl, Maude. Over this, we
         hear her voice, as it lives in Robert's
         memory.

                    MAUDE'S VOICE
              (echo chamber)
            But my father forbids our
            marriage, Robert. He says you
            will never amount to anything...
            I must marry a man of substance,
            he says...a certain wealthy
            widower... and so we leave for
            the Continent tomorrow...

Echo chamber out.

36   CLOSE SHOT ROBERT   36
He is seated, the letter in one hand, the open watch in the
other. He closes the watch and puts it back in his pocket.
He looks at the letter again.

sgb

INSERT: FACE OF THE LETTER
         (Same as in Scene 32)

37   CLOSE SHOT ROBERT
     He turns the letter over, and suddenly his eyes narrow in puzzlement.

INSERT: REVERSE OF THE LETTER
         which bears a huge, oversize
         waxen seal featuring an ornate,
         baroque "S".

BACK TO SCENE 37:

     Robert breaks the seal and opens the letter, to a sound of crackling parchment. Robert reads silently. After a few seconds, he closes the letter and stands up.

                    ROBERT
               (calling)
          Sister!

38   TWO SHOT ROBERT HEAD NURSE
     entering.

                    HEAD NURSE
          You called, Sir Robert?

                    ROBERT
          Yes. You can help me, if you
          will...

                    HEAD NURSE
          Of course...

                    ROBERT
          Cancel my appointments... all
          of them...

                    HEAD NURSE
          For how long, sir?

                    ROBERT
          I don't know. Indefinitely...
          Then -- I would appreciate it
          if you would arrange transport
          for me, to...
               (he consults
                the letter)
          ...Bohemia...the region of
          Gorslava.

sgb

38   CONTINUED: 38

                    HEAD NURSE
            Gor -- slava... yes, Sir
            Robert...but when do you wish
            to leave?

39   CLOSEUP ROBERT   39

                    ROBERT
            Soon. As soon as I possibly
            can.

                                            FADE OUT.

sat

FADE IN:

EXT. ENGLISH CHANNEL - NIGHT

40   LONG SHOT SHIP (STOCK)   40
crossing English Channel. Fog. The mournful sound of foghorns.

41   CLOSE SHOT ROBERT   41
standing at ship's rail, looking out over the water. He is wearing a greatcoat or Inverness cape, and a hat. Perhaps he is smoking a pipe. Fog swaths him. Again, the foghorns.

                                  DISSOLVE TO:

EXT. EUROPEAN RAILROAD TRAIN - DAY

42   LONG SHOT TRAIN OF THE PERIOD (STOCK)   42
snaking cross country, into a tunnel, etc.

                                  DISSOLVE TO:

INT. CORNER OF SHABBY CENTRAL EUROPEAN RAILROAD STATION WAITING ROOM - NIGHT

43   TWO SHOT ROBERT STATION MASTER   43
At the rear, a window, through which we see it is night. Prominent on the wall, a large station-sign (faded, peeling, decades old) which says:

                    GORSLAVA

Robert, weary and dusty from travel, is standing next to his baggage, talking to the Stationmaster, an elderly man of Slavic origin.

                    ROBERT
        Look here. This _is_ Gorslava,
        is it not?

                  STATIONMASTER
        Yes, Sir. But there is no coach
        that will take you in the direction
        you speak of. The terrain up
        there is wild and mountainous...
        the roads are bad... some places,
        there are no roads at all...

sat

43   CONTINUED: 43

                        ROBERT
            You don't understand. I was to
            be met by a private coach.

                        STATIONMASTER
            A private coach? From those
            parts? Nobody lives up there!

                        ROBERT
            I assure you somebody does. My
            host -- Baron Sardonicus.

44   CLOSEUP STATIONMASTER   44
        It is as if Robert had said, "My host -- Satan."

                        STATIONMASTER
            Sardonicus!

45   CLOSEUP ROBERT   45
        puzzled.

                        ROBERT
            Yes -- what do you know of him?

46   CLOSEUP STATIONMASTER   46
        frightened.

                        STATIONMASTER
            Nothing, Sir... I know nothing...
            I said nothing against the Baron,
            did I, Sir?...

47   CLOSEUP ROBERT   47

                        ROBERT
            Of course not. But the mention
            of his name frightened you.

48   CLOSEUP STATIONMASTER   48

                        STATIONMASTER
            No, no... not at all...

49   CLOSEUP ROBERT   49

                        ROBERT
            Come, come! Do not dissemble --
            why were you frightened?

sat

50   CLOSEUP   STATIONMASTER   50

                              STATIONMASTER
                         (sighing)
                    Ah, Sir... you would not under-
                    stand... you are young... you
                    do not yet have... daughters!

          A crash of the station door flying open.

51   TWO SHOT   ROBERT   STATIONMASTER   51
            They turn, surprised. Stationmaster backs off.

                              KRULL'S VOICE
                    Sir Robert Cargrave?

52   MEDIUM LONG SHOT   ROBERT   KRULL   52
            Robert, in foreground, is turned away from us to look at
            Krull standing in the doorway. (Stationmaster is not in
            this shot.) Slowly, Krull walks toward the camera, until he
            is face to face with Robert.

53   TWO SHOT   ROBERT   KRULL   53

                              KRULL
                    I repeat -- Sir Robert Cargrave?

                              ROBERT
                    Yes.

                              KRULL
                         (with a hint
                         of mockery)
                    I am called Krull. Your humble
                    servant. It was I who brought
                    you a certain letter... some
                    weeks ago.

                              ROBERT
                    Then you are in the service of
                    the Baroness?

                              KRULL
                    I am in the service of the Baron.
                    He is most eager to meet you,
                    Sir. Shall we go?

                              ROBERT
                    Please.

          Robert indicates his bags. Krull picks them up and heads for
          the door in background. Robert follows him. They leave.

sat

54   CLOSE SHOT   STATIONMASTER   54
       looking after them. Slowly, he crosses himself.

                                                        DISSOLVE TO:

EXT. MOUNTAIN ROAD   HORSEDRAWN COACH - NIGHT

55   LONG SHOT OR TRAVELLING SHOT   COACH (STOCK)   55
       Horsedrawn coach plunging wildly along a rocky winding
       mountain road.

INT. COACH - NIGHT

56   MEDIUM SHOT   ROBERT   56
       being jostled by the rough ride. He peers out the window
       into the night. Moonlight affords some illumination, and
       he takes the letter (now rather crumpled) from his pocket.

INSERT: THE FAMILIAR LETTER
         now rather crumpled,
         with the inscription as before.

BACK TO SCENE 56:
         Robert opens the letter and reads. We hear Maude's voice
         (not echo chamber).

                        MAUDE'S VOICE
                   My dear Sir Robert... It has
                   been a long time since last we
                   saw each other, and I wonder if
                   you will remember the former
                   Maude Randall?...

       Robert looks up briefly, to smile the sad, rueful smile of
       lost love. Then he continues reading.

                        MAUDE'S VOICE
                          (continuing)
                   I am married now, as you know,
                   and live in the region of Gorslava
                   in Bohemia, with my husband, the
                   Baron Sardonicus. I have often
                   told him of you and your re-
                   searches... and recently we
                   have read of your being knighted
                   by the Crown. The Baron has ex-
                   pressed a desire to meet you...
                   indeed, it is most urgent to my
                   well-being that he meet you...

sat

56   CONTINUED: 56

       Robert looks up, slightly frowning.

                         MAUDE'S VOICE
                    (continuing,
                     distorted now)
               Most urgent to my well-being...
               most urgent... most urgent...
               most...

                                                            FADE OUT.

                                                            Bill —
                                                            sudden
                                                            cut?

hec-8610

FADE IN:

EXT. CASTLE - NIGHT

57   In the background, a medieval castle of Central European 57
design. Somehow, because of the placement of the windows
and portcullis, it bears a faint, almost "subliminal"
resemblance to a giant, grinning skull. Sharp in the foreground is a forbidding iron gate, into which a huge, ornate
"S" of iron has been wrought.

(NOTE: This is the same "S" we have already seen on the
waxen seal. It will reoccur in the film, as a symbol,
and should be designed with an eye to massiveness, baroque
evil, overpowering dark majesty.)

A whinnying of the horses. We hold this shot for a second
or two, then:

58   KRULL   58
on top of the now stationary coach, the reins in his hands.
Krull calls down in the direction of the gate:

                  KRULL
      Open the gate! It is I -- Krull!

              GATEKEEPER'S VOICE (O.S.)
    One moment!

59   CLOSEUP "S" OF GATE   59
with castle in b.g. Clouds part for a moment and the moonlight briefly reveals the castle in greater detail. We are
aware of the small, shadowy figure of the gatekeeper. Now,
the gate begins to open, inward and away from us, with a
long, rising shriek of rusted iron hinges. When the gate is
fully open, the coach passes through on its way up the road
to the castle. The gate closes. We hold the shot until
the coach reaches the castle and stops.

60   THE COACH   60
with the castle's main door directly behind it. Krull jumps
down and opens the coach door for Robert, who steps out,
looking around him in fascination.

61   EXTREME CLOSEUP KRULL   61

                  KRULL
             (smugly, almost
             insultingly)
    After _you_, sir.

hec-8610

INT. OTHER SIDE OF CASTLE DOOR - NIGHT

62 ENTRANCE KRULL ROBERT   62
    We are aware of flickering torches set in huge sconces. The
    door is opened (by Krull), and Robert enters, slowly. Krull
    follows, with the baggage.

63 NEW ANGLE ROBERT KRULL   63
    We see a choice of two archways, left and right.

                        KRULL
                (gesturing vaguely
                 to the right)
            That way, Sir Robert...through
            the archway...

    But Krull's directions are unclear and Robert is preoccupied--
    so Robert, in error, walks through the left archway. Too
    late, Krull notices the mistake.

                        KRULL
                (sharply)
            No! The other archway!

                                                SUDDEN CUT TO:

64 EXTREME CLOSEUP ANNA THE SERVANT GIRL   64
    Anna, barely conscious, her face and neck covered with
    hideous, fat, swollen leeches.

65 CAMERA QUICKLY PULLS AWAY with a jolt, and we see she   65
    is tied to a chair.

66 CLOSEUP ROBERT   66

                        ROBERT
                (shocked)
            My God!

67 GROUP SHOT ANNA ROBERT KRULL   67
    Anna in chair; Robert approaching her; Krull in background.

                        ROBERT
                (in Krull's direction)
            What is the meaning of this?

hec-8610

67 CONTINUED:

Robert is plucking the leeches from Anna's face and throwing them to the floor as Krull speaks.

>
> KRULL
> They are only leeches, Sir Robert.
>
> ROBERT
> I know what they are! But *why*?
>
> KRULL
> Among our people, they are believed to cure certain afflictions...
>
> ROBERT
> Witch doctor's nonsense! She might have died or been disfigured... Thank God I saw her in time!

68 CLOSEUP ANNA

The leeches have now been removed. Her face is covered with spots of blood. She moans slightly.

69 GROUP SHOT ROBERT ANNA KRULL

> ROBERT
> (to Anna)
> There, now...It is all over... You will be all right.
> (to Krull)
> And what *is* her affliction?
>
> KRULL
> Her affliction? Oh, none, Sir Robert!
>
> ROBERT
> *None*??! Blast it, man -- explain yourself!
>
> KRULL
> (shrugging awkwardly)
> She is...what can I say...Do you not, in your own work, make use of what you call...

70 CLOSEUP KRULL

> KRULL
> Guinea pigs?

hec-8610

71   GROUP SHOT   ROBERT   ANNA   KRULL   71

                    ROBERT
              (livid with out-
              rage; quietly)
         At whose bidding was this done?

                    KRULL
         Why...the master's, of course.

                    ROBERT
         Baron Sardonicus?

                    KRULL
         There is no other master here,
         sir.

                    ROBERT
         I will take up the matter with
         him. Meanwhile, untie this poor
         girl...see that she rests...give
         her brandy and the juice of red
         meat...I will treat her face
         presently.

                    KRULL
         Just as you say, sir...and now,
         if you will be so kind as to pass
         through the other archway, the
         Baroness awaits you there...

     Robert leaves the scene as Krull begins to untie Anna.

INT. THE SALON - NIGHT

72   LONG SHOT   MAUDE   72
     seated. We see Spinet, escritoire, divans, etc. Maude is
     sitting on a divan in the b.g., leafing through a magazine.
     It is a copy of The Illustrated London News of the period.

73   TWO SHOT   MAUDE   ROBERT   73
     Robert enters, foreground, and Maude looks up, laying aside
     her magazine.

                    MAUDE
         Robert!

                    ROBERT
         Baroness.

     Maude rises and comes forward. They meet in the center of
     the room.

hec-8610

73   CONTINUED: 73

                    MAUDE
          No, please...call me Maude, as
          you did in the old days.

74   NEW ANGLE   CLOSER   74
       favoring Robert

                    ROBERT
          These are not the old days...
          Maude.

                    MAUDE
          That's much better! Now, then --
          come sit next to me and tell me
          all about yourself...

They sit on the divan, and Robert picks up the magazine.

INSERT: THE ILLUSTRATED LONDON NEWS
          in Robert's hand.

                    ROBERT (O.S.)
          Do you miss London?

75   TWO SHOT   MAUDE   ROBERT   75
       on divan.

                    MAUDE
              (too brightly)
          Oh, we are quite cozy here! We
          receive all the current journals
          and illustrated gazettes... I
          order the latest fashions from
          Paris, the most recent musical
          scores from Rome and Berlin...the
          most popular novels...Do you not
          find Mister Conan Doyle a fascina-
          ting writer?

                    ROBERT
              (not taken in)
          Then you do not miss London?

                    MAUDE
              (sincerely, this
               time)
          I did not say that.
              (bright again)
          But do tell me how you have
          fared the world!

hec-8610

75   CONTINUED: 75

                    ROBERT
                (modestly)
            I have fared well. Perhaps
            better than I deserve. My re-
            searches have been fruitful...
            My name is well known...I have
            been made a knight at a rather
            early age...

                    MAUDE
            And love?

                    ROBERT
                (it is his turn to
                 be too bright)
            Oh, that! I am busy night and
            day...the clinic...my classes...
            writing papers...experimenting...
            making speeches...

                    MAUDE
                (chiding him)
            Come, Robert...are you suggesting
            that you have no time for love?

Robert drops his masquerade and looks directly into her face.

76   CLOSEUP   ROBERT   76

                    ROBERT
                (simply)
            There have been -- no others.

77   CLOSEUP   MAUDE   77
      touched.

                    MAUDE
            Robert. Oh, Robert...

Tears form in her eyes, and she looks away.

78   TWO SHOT   MAUDE   ROBERT   78
      Maude "recovers."

                    MAUDE
            But you must be tired after
            your journey...

hec-8610

78   CONTINUED: 78

                    ROBERT
          Yes, and rather the worse for
          dust!...

                    MAUDE
          We will dine soon, but in the
          meantime Krull will show you to
          your chambers so you may refresh
          yourself.
                    (starts to rise, saying:)
          I will ring for --

                                                       SUDDEN CUT TO:

79   NEW ANGLE ROBERT MAUDE KRULL   79
     Krull is suddenly standing in the archway.

                    KRULL
          You wish something, my lady?

                    MAUDE
                    (surprised)
          Oh, Krull...there you are...
          Yes. Please show Sir Robert
          to his rooms.

                    KRULL
          At once, my lady.

                    MAUDE
                    (to Robert)
          Until dinner, then...

                    ROBERT
          Until dinner.

     Robert follows Krull out of the salon.

80   CLOSEUP MAUDE   80
     the tears forming in her eyes again. She covers her face
     with her hands.

INT. STAIRCASE - NIGHT

81   KRULL ROBERT   81
     CAMERA FOLLOWS Krull and Robert up a long staircase. They
     walk past a cryptic series of large, ornate, <u>empty</u> picture
     frames. Robert regards them wonderingly.

hec-8610

81   CONTINUED: 81

                    KRULL
          Perhaps you are puzzled by the
          empty frames, sir?

                    ROBERT
          They do seem rather strange...

                    KRULL
          The Baron is an unusual man, of
          unusual convictions. In such
          frames, ordinary men would honor
          the portraits of their forefathers.
          But the Baron has disowned his
          forefathers in one magnificent
          gesture!

He indicates the empty frames with a sweep of his hand.

INT. FIRST LANDING CORRIDOR - NIGHT

82   NEW ANGLE ROBERT KRULL   82
     They have reached the first landing. Krull stops before
     a door.

                    KRULL
          Here are your chambers, sir.
          Allow me...

He opens the door for Robert.

                    KRULL
               (continuing)
          I trust you will find things to
          your liking. If not --

                    ROBERT
          I'm sure I will.
               (a sudden thought)
          Oh... the maidservant...I must
          treat the leech punctures on
          her face...

                    KRULL
          She is resting, sir, as you ad-
          vised. I have taken the liberty
          of treating her face with hot
          compresses and a disinfectant
          tincture.

                    ROBERT
               (pleased)
          Excellent.

hec-8610

| 82 | CONTINUED: | 82 |

>   ROBERT (Cont'd.)
>   (amused)
>   You are a man of medicine, Krull?

| 83 | CLOSEUP KRULL | 83 |

>   KRULL
>   I am a man of all work, sir.
>   When my master says, 'Krull --
>   do this thing,' I do the thing...
>   whatever it may be.

| 84 | TWO SHOT ROBERT KRULL | 84 |

at the open door.

>   ROBERT
>   Most commendable.
>
>   KRULL
>   Thank you, sir. And now I will
>   leave you.

He bows and leaves. Robert enters the room and shuts the door.

INT. ROBERT'S CHAMBERS - NIGHT

| 85 | MEDIUM LONG SHOT ROBERT | 85 |

entering. His bags are in the room. An old-fashioned "hip-bath" tub stands in the center of the room. It is filled with steaming water. Robert looks at it gratefully and begins to remove his coat, as we do a:

                                        DISSOLVE TO:

| 86 | NEW ANGLE ROBERT | 86 |

in tub. His knees obtrude almost comically, and he is feeling in a comparitively merry mood. As he washes himself, he sings a popular air.

>   ROBERT
>   (singing)
>   In a tree by a willow
>   A little Tom-tit
>   Sang willow, tit-willow, tit-willow.
>   And I said to him,

hec-8610

86   CONTINUED: 86

                         ROBERT (Cont'd.)
               'Dicky Bird, why do you sit,
               Singing willow --

A soft knock at the door. Robert stops singing, not sure if
he has heard anything or not. He resumes singing.

                         ROBERT
                      (continuing to sing)
               ...tit-willow...

The knock again.

                         ROBERT
                      (continuing,
                       spoken, softly)
               Tit-willow.
                      (calling)
               Yes?

INT. HALLWAY OTHER SIDE OF DOOR - NIGHT

87   ANNA   87
       obviously surreptitious, glancing about. Her face appears
       somewhat improved, although there are still small patches
       of irritation on it.

                         ANNA
                      (stage whisper)
               Sir...I must speak to you...

                         ROBERT'S VOICE (O.S.)
               Just a moment.

O.S. sound of splashing water. Anna glances fearfully about.
In a moment, the door opens and Robert stands there in a robe.

88   TWO SHOT ANNA ROBERT   88

                         ROBERT
                      (continuing)
               Oh, it's you, girl. How are you
               feeling?

                         ANNA
               Please, sir...don't tell them I
               spoke to you...

                         ROBERT
               Very well, but --

hec-8610

88   CONTINUED: 88

                    ANNA
          They'd punish me, they would...

                    ROBERT
          Rubbish. But I won't tell them,
          all the same. What do you want?

                    ANNA
          Sir -- you won't let them do
          that to me again, will you?
          Please promise you won't let
          them!

                    ROBERT
               (simply)
          You have my word.

89   CLOSEUP ANNA   89

                    ANNA
               (relieved, grateful)
          Oh, thank you, sir, thank you!
          Now that you're here...

                    ROBERT'S VOICE (O.S.)
          Yes?

                    ANNA
               (darkly)
          Now that you're here, sir...
          maybe the...experimenting will
          stop!

90   TWO SHOT ANNA ROBERT   90

                    ROBERT
          What do you mean --

                    ANNA
          No more, sir! I must not be
          found here!

     She quickly skitters away.

                    ROBERT
          But...

hec-8610

91   ROBERT   91
     Troubled, he is about to close the door again when he seems
     to notice something across the hall.

92   THE OPPOSITE DOOR   92
     There is an immense, forbidding padlock on it.

93   MEDIUM CLOSE SHOT   KRULL   93
     He has suddenly "appeared", carrying a large wooden bowl
     of a thin, soup-like stew.

                         KRULL
               I hope the maidservant was not
               making a nuisance of herself, sir...

94   TWO SHOT   ROBERT   KRULL   94

                         ROBERT
               No, not at all. Er...Krull...
               what is that padlocked door
               across the way?

95   OPPOSITE DOOR   95
     CAMERA FLASHES back to show us the padlocked door again.

96   TWO SHOT   ROBERT   KRULL   96

                         KRULL
               I cannot tell you, sir, for no
               one but the master has ever been
               on the other side of that door.
               He has the only key. The servants
               call it --
                    (he chuckles
                     unconvincingly)
               The Chamber of Horrors. A jest,
               sir.

                         ROBERT
               Yes, of course.

     Robert returns to his room, leaving his door <u>slightly ajar</u>.
     CAMERA FOLLOWS Krull as he walks past Robert's door, carry-
     ing the bowl, approaches yet <u>another</u> door, and knocks. The
     door opens very slightly. Two masculine hands reach for the
     bowl, take it and withdraw. The door closes, Krull turns.

hec-8610

| 97 | CLOSE SHOT   ROBERT'S DOOR | 97 |

ajar, with Robert's eyes quickly retreating as Krull walks past. Krull's footsteps diminish.

| 98 | NEW ANGLE   ROBERT | 98 |

slowly, gingerly, leaves his room and walks softly over to that other door. He listens.

INT. ROOM ON OTHER SIDE OF DOOR - NIGHT

| 99 | MAN AT TABLE | 99 |

A man (Sardonicus, but we do not know this, for his back is to the CAMERA) sits at a plain table, in his shirtsleeves. Holding the wooden bowl in both hands, he dips his face into the bowl and begins to suck up the contents in a crude, repellent manner. Some of the stew splashes on the table and trickles down his hands.

INT. HALLWAY OUTSIDE DOOR - NIGHT

| 100 | CLOSEUP   ROBERT | 100 |

listening. He hears the slurping, sucking, chomping sound, like a wild beast feeding. It is gross and disgusting. Robert's distaste registers on his face. The sounds continue.

FADE OUT.

ar

FADE IN:

INT. DINING HALL - NIGHT

101   LONG SHOT   LARGE BANQUET TABLE   ROBERT   MAUDE   101
      Table set with three place settings -- two at either end,
      one in the middle. Robert and Maude enter, talking.

                    MAUDE
          ...and so you see, Robert, we
          do very little entertaining here.
          My husband does not like throngs
          of people...

                    ROBERT
          Maude...

                    MAUDE
          Yes?

102   TWO SHOT   MAUDE   ROBERT   102

                    ROBERT
          In your letter...that rather odd
          letter...you said my presence
          here was urgent...urgent to your
          well-being. What did you mean?

                    MAUDE
          Did I say that? How foolish of
          me! I suppose I simply meant
          that I longed to play the hostess
          again...to see a familiar face...

                    ROBERT
          No -- you meant more than that.
          But what?

                    MAUDE
              (evasively)
          Robert, I'm sure I don't know...

                    ROBERT
          Very well. But this is no
          ordinary castle. The townspeople
          fear your husband, and --

                    MAUDE
          Really, Robert! Don't you think
          you exaggerate?

ar

103   THREE SHOT   MAUDE   ROBERT   SARDONICUS   103
Unbeknownst to Maude and Robert, a figure has entered the
room. We see only his back.

>   ROBERT
>   (to Maude)
>   Perhaps. But I am very anxious
>   to meet the Baron face to --

On this, he turns and sees the figure.

104   EXTREME CLOSEUP   SARDONICUS   104
masked. The mask of Sardonicus is a pliant, rubbery affair
that covers his entire face. It should roughly resemble the
actor playing Sardonicus, although the mouth is drawn downward like that of a character from Greek tragedy.

(<u>IMPORTANT NOTE</u>: Through this script, it will always be
assumed Sardonicus is masked, <u>unless</u> otherwise indicated.)

105   CLOSEUP   ROBERT   105

>   ROBERT
>   (finishing lamely)
>   -- face.

106   EXTREME CLOSEUP   SARDONICUS   106

>   SARDONICUS
>   Sir Robert Cargrave?
>
>   ROBERT'S VOICE
>   Yes...
>
>   SARDONICUS
>   I am Baron Sardonicus.

107   GROUP SHOT   SARDONICUS   ROBERT   MAUDE   KRULL   107
The two men shake hands.

>   ROBERT
>   It is -- a pleasure to meet you
>   at last.
>
>   SARDONICUS
>   The pleasure is mine, sir. Shall
>   we be seated?

All three sit down, Maude and Sardonicus at opposite ends of
the table, Robert in the middle. Krull appears, bearing food,
which he serves only to Maude and Robert. During this,
Sardonicus speaks.

107 CONTINUED:

>   SARDONICUS
>   (continuing)
>   My mask disturbs you, Sir Robert.
>
>   ROBERT
>   It would be foolish of me to deny
>   it.
>
>   SARDONICUS
>   Quite so. An idiosyncracy of
>   mine -- but a necessary one, I
>   assure you. Later, I will tell
>   you the reason for it -- but now,
>   please sample our poor fare.
>
>   ROBERT
>   (tasting the food)
>   Not poor at all. It's delicious.
>   (he notices that
>   Sardonicus has
>   not been served)
>   But are you not joining us,
>   Baron?
>
>   SARDONICUS
>   (lifting his glass)
>   Only a little Tokay. I have
>   already dined.

He sips the wine through the mask's thin mouth slit.

>   KRULL
>   (to Sardonicus)
>   If that will be all for now, my
>   lord, I should attend to a little
>   -- servant problem.
>
>   SARDONICUS
>   Yes, that is all.

Krull leaves.

>   MAUDE
>   (to Robert, trying to
>   make conversation)
>   Robert...Sir Robert...do tell us
>   what is happening on the London
>   stage...
>
>   ROBERT
>   Well...let me see...there has
>   been a revival of 'Macbeth'...

ar

INT. HALLWAY OUTSIDE ANNA'S ROOM - NIGHT

108   MEDIUM LONG SHOT KRULL
approaches the door and opens it.

INT. ANNA'S ROOM - NIGHT

109   CLOSE SHOT ANNA'S HANDS
The straining thumbs are suspended from bits of rope that are tied to two metal rings in the ceiling.

CAMERA PANS slowly down her arms, which are stretched high above her head -- her face, tear-stained and near-hysterical -- down the length of her body until it comes to rest on her feet, from which the shoes and stockings have been removed and the great toes tied, much like her thumbs, to two metal rings in the floor.

110   MEDIUM LONG SHOT ANNA
suspended in this manner.

111   NEW ANGLE FROM BEHIND ANNA KRULL
in background, closes the door. As he advances upon her, he speaks.

>   KRULL
>   Ah, there you are, waiting for
>   me, like a good obedient girl.
>
>   ANNA
>   (sobbing)
>   Krull, please...
>
>   KRULL
>   (suddenly vicious)
>   But you are not _always_ so obedient,
>   are you?
>
>   ANNA
>   Please, Krull!
>
>   KRULL
>   (slapping her face)
>   _Are you!!!_

112   CLOSEUP ANNA
recoiling from the blow.

ar

113   KRULL   FROM BEHIND ANNA   113

                        KRULL
            We must have a little talk,
            Anna, you and I. You and I,
            and -- some friends of yours.

He walks to a table and picks up a large wooden box which
he brings back to Anna.

                        KRULL
            Some little friends of yours...

He opens the box.

INSERT: THE OPEN BOX
        It is filled almost to overflowing
        with the leeches.

                        ANNA'S VOICE
            No! Not the leeches! Not the
            leeches again, Krull!!

114   NEW ANGLE ANNA KRULL   114
Anna is seen fully, writhing, facing us. Krull's back to
camera.

                        KRULL
            Oh, let us hope not, my sweet.
            Let us hope not. But you see,
            you are a very naughty girl. I
            expressly forbade you to speak
            to Sir Robert...and yet you spoke
            to him! That is too bad of you,
            Anna.

                        ANNA
            I didn't! I didn't speak to him!

                        KRULL
            Lies, now? First disobedience,
            then lies? Come, Anna, you must
            tell me what you said to Sir Robert...

                        ANNA
            I said nothing!

                        KRULL
            You must tell me, Anna...or it
            will be the leeches again...

                        ANNA
            No! Please! No!

ar

115   REVERSE POV KRULL ANNA   115
      Krull is facing camera, Anna's back to camera. We can see
      the open box of leeches.

                          KRULL
                    (looking down
                     at them)
                Ah, they are so thirsty, the
                little ones...so thirsty for the
                sweet nectar that flows in your
                veins, Anna!

                          ANNA
                    (squirming)
                Krull, no!

                          KRULL
                But this time, Anna, they will
                sip that nectar not only from
                your face...

                          ANNA
                Krull!

116   REVERSE POV ANNA KRULL   116
      Anna facing camera.

                          KRULL
                ...No, Anna, this time the leeches
                will become better acquainted
                with you! There are so many of
                the little fellows, you see...
                all most anxious to know you
                better!... They will cover you,
                Anna! From your face...down
                the whole length of you...all
                the way down to your toes!

                          ANNA
                    (hysterical)
                You wouldn't, Krull! You wouldn't
                do that!

117   CLOSEUP KRULL   117
      teasing her.

                          KRULL
                Hmmm...perhaps it should be
                reversed...and we should begin
                with your toes...and work up!
                Yes...yes...

ar

117   CONTINUED: 117

                         ANNA'S VOICE
                  No! No! No!

118   CLOSE SHOT ANNA'S FEET   118
      Krull's hand places a single leech on one foot.

119   CLOSEUP ANNA   119

                              ANNA
                         (a shriek,
                          then --)
                  Stop, stop! I'll tell you!!!

INT. DINING HALL - NIGHT

120 GROUP SHOT PERSPECTIVE OF DINING TABLE favoring Sardonicus.   120

> SARDONICUS
> ...It sounds like a most interesting performance, Sir Robert. Macbeth is such a totally evil character, is he not?

> ROBERT
> I have never thought so, actually. A man pressed into evil by circumstances, let us say. On the other hand, there is Iago -- a creature of pure evil, with no redeeming qualities, who tormented Othello with ghoulish delight.

> SARDONICUS
> 'Ghoulish', you say -- it is not a word to be used lightly. A ghoul, as I am sure you know, is a disgusting creature who opens graves and _feeds_ on corpses. Do you mean to suggest Iago did _that_?

> MAUDE
> (to Sardonicus)
> My dear, I am sure Sir Robert used the word in a figurative sense.

> SARDONICUS
> Ah. Perhaps. That is because he is English, and does not really believe in ghouls -- do you, Sir Robert?

> ROBERT
> Well --

> SARDONICUS
> Ah, of course not! But in my country, we _do_ believe. In fact --
> (he sips his wine)
> In fact, I have _known_ a ghoul.

> ROBERT
> (diplomatically)
> Indeed.

120   CONTINUED: 120

                    SARDONICUS
                (chuckling)
            You English are so blasé! Nothing
            shocks you. Or -- can it be you
            do not believe me?

                    ROBERT
            It would be discourteous to doubt
            the word of my host.

                    SARDONICUS
            And an Englishman may be many
            things, but never discourteous --
            eh, Sir Robert? Let me tell you
            about this ghoul --

    But Krull reappears. He slides up to Sardonicus.

121   CLOSE UP KRULL   121
      whispering in Sardonicus' ear.

                    KRULL
                (whispering)
            They are here, master.

                    SARDONICUS
                (whispering)
            I will be there presently.

122   GROUP SHOT SARDONICUS ROBERT MAUDE   122
      as Krull leaves the room in the background.

                    SARDONICUS
                (to Robert)
            Perhaps we may finish our dis-
            cussion of ghouls another time,
            Sir Robert?

                    ROBERT
            Yes, of course.

                    SARDONICUS
            I have visitors - very important
            visitors --

                    ROBERT
            Certainly.

    Sardonicus leaves the room. Maude and Robert watch him go.

rs

INT. LARGE CELLAR CHAMBER - NIGHT

123 LONG SHOT ROOM 123

An attempt has been made to render it rather festive. That is, a table has been laid, with candles, food and wine, etc. A large couch is very much in evidence. Krull enters, ushering in SIX GIRLS. They are all rather pretty and shapely and young -- but they are obviously poor girls, from peasant families, and they are dressed simply. There is a variety among them -- some are dark, some fair; some slender, some buxom; some tall, some short; some shy, some bold.

124 CAMERA MOVES IN CLOSER to Krull and the girls. 124

KRULL

This way, ladies, this way. Ah, here we are, nice and cozy. The master will be with us presently.

1ST GIRL

(shy, virginal)

You said it was to be -- a party?

KRULL

That's right, miss. A little party. A little private party, with lots of choice food and wine --

2ND GIRL

(bold; has been around)

~~Bit of all right, if you ask me!~~

But didn't you say something about gold?

KRULL

That I did. There will be a gold piece for every single one of you -- and for the lucky one, even more gold!

2ND GIRL

(puzzled)

The lucky one?

125 CLOSEUP KRULL 125

KRULL

(with evil meaning)

Yes. The -- lucky one.

126   NEW ANGLE   SARDONICUS   KRULL   GIRLS   126
Sardonicus enters. He bows gracefully to the girls, then walks to the table and pours a glass of champagne. As he pours, he speaks.

                    SARDONICUS
            How charming to meet you, ladies.
            It was good of you to accept my
            invitation. I hope we will --
            enjoy one another's company tonight.

127   CAMERA MOVES IN for a CLOSE SHOT of Sardonicus,   127
as he continues to speak. He lifts the glass of champagne.

                    SARDONICUS
            Wine is a wondrous bounty. A
            blessing. There is a wine for
            every mood, for every menu.
            There is champagne -- gay --
            carefree!

He drains the glass in one long draught, then throws the empty glass carelessly to Krull, who catches it. Now Sardonicus pours a glass of a "still" red wine.

                    SARDONICUS
                    (continuing)
            Then there is claret, full-bodied
            and deeply satisfying.

Again he drains the glass and tosses it to Krull. Now he pours a dark, deep purple wine, a port.

                    SARDONICUS
                    (continuing)
            There is the wine of Portugal --
            dark and sensuous and thick as
            blood.
                    (drains glass, tosses
                     it to Krull)
            As with wine, so with women.

128   SARDONICUS   KRULL   GIRLS   128
As Sardonicus speaks, he walks past the girls, inspecting them like an officer inspecting his troops.

                    SARDONICUS
            Dark -- fair -- slender -- buxom --
            shy -- saucy -- For every mood,
            for every menu. And tonight?

128   CONTINUED: 128

                              SARDONICUS (cont'd)
                         (pauses a moment, then
                          points to first girl)
                    This one.
                         (desultorily, to Krull)
                    Pay the others and dismiss them.

                              KRULL
                    Yes, master. Come, ladies, this
                    way --

Krull starts to usher them out. First girl makes as if to
follow, but Krull admonishes her roughly.

                              KRULL
                    No, not you! You stay here!

Krull and the other girls pass through the doorway, and we
hear Krull saying --

                              KRULL
                         (continuing)
                    Gold, my beauties -- gold for
                    each and all!

They are gone. Sardonicus and the first girl are alone.

INT. DINING HALL - NIGHT

129   TWO SHOT ROBERT MAUDE   129
       at dining table.

                              ROBERT
                    I fear the long journey has
                    fatigued me more than I thought,
                    Maude. I think I should retire.

                              MAUDE
                    Of course, Robert. I understand.

Robert rises.

                              MAUDE
                         (continuing)
                    And Robert --

                              ROBERT
                    Yes?

                              MAUDE
                    You were right. Your presence here
                    is most urgent to my well-being.

rs

129   CONTINUED: 129

                              ROBERT
                    But what --

                              MAUDE
                    Not now. Good-night.

                              ROBERT
                    Good-night.

INT. CELLAR CHAMBER - NIGHT

130   TWO SHOT   SARDONICUS   1ST GIRL   130

                              SARDONICUS
                    You are a very pretty little
                    thing.

                              1ST GIRL
                    Th -- Thank you, sir --

                              SARDONICUS
                    And a very shy little thing.

                              1ST GIRL
                    Well, sir, I've never known a
                    fine gentleman like yourself,
                    sir --

        Sardonicus is "moving in".

                              SARDONICUS
                    Do you find me - pleasant?

                              1ST GIRL
                    Oh, yes, sir-- only --

                              SARDONICUS
                    Only what?

                              1ST GIRL
                    Well, sir -- you would be much
                    more pleasant -- without that
                    funny mask --

        She quickly lifts her hand to the mask, as we suddenly
        cut to:

INT. CORRIDOR OTHER SIDE OF DOOR - NIGHT

131   KRULL   GIRLS   131
        Krull is distributing a gold coin to each of the girls.

131   CONTINUED: 131

                          KRULL
                And perhaps there will be more --
                if you are nice little girls!

       Suddenly, there is the o.s. scream of the first girl.
       All the girls freeze and turn in the direction of the
       door. Krull alone is undisturbed.

                          KRULL
                       (continuing)
                Pay it no mind, pay it no mind --

                          1ST GIRL'S VOICE
                No! Oh my God! Oh Merciful God
                in Heaven! No...no...NO!!

       The last "No" is a long, rising shriek of despair, on
       which we cut to:

INT. ROBERT'S ROOM - NIGHT

132   CLOSE SHOT ROBERT   132
       removing his shirt. O.s., almost inaudible, is the last,
       despairing "No!" of the first girl. Robert, hearing it,
       is visibly disturbed.

                                                       DISSOLVE TO:

INT. ROBERT'S ROOM - NIGHT

133   ROBERT   133
       in bed, asleep. The room is dark. His sleep is troubled
       by dreams, and he tosses in his bed.

       Over this shot we SUPERIMPOSE a series of shimmering
       dissolves adapted from previous scenes. Dialogue is
       on echo chamber.

                                              SHIMMERING DISSOLVE TO:

rs

46

134   CLOSEUP   STATION MASTER   134

                        STATIONMASTER
                You do not understand -- you do
                not yet have -- daughters!

                                          SHIMMERING DISSOLVE TO:

135   CLOSEUP ANNA   135
       (without leeches)

                        ANNA
                Now that you're here, sir, maybe
                the experimenting will stop!

                                          SHIMMERING DISSOLVE TO:

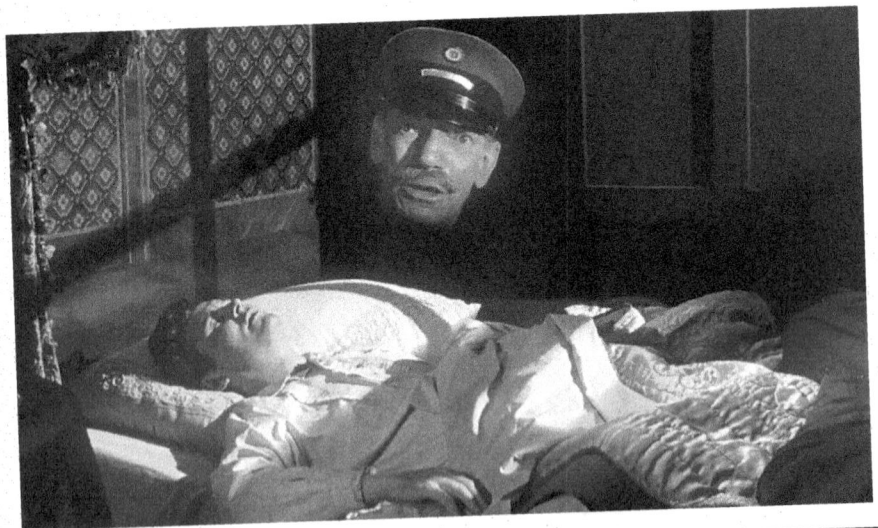

136   CLOSEUP KRULL   136

                    KRULL
           When my master says 'Krull --
           do this thing,' I do the
           thing, whatever it may be!

                                        SHIMMERING DISSOLVE TO:

137   CLOSEUP ANNA   137
      her face covered by leeches.

                                        SHIMMERING DISSOLVE TO:

138   CLOSEUP MAUDE   138

                    MAUDE
           Most urgent...most urgent...

                                        SHIMMERING DISSOLVE TO:

139   CLOSEUP SARDONICUS   139

                    SARDONICUS
           I have known a ghoul...a dis-
           gusting creature who opens
           graves and feeds on corpses...

      We HOLD this Sardonicus CLOSEUP. Over it, we now hear that
      sucking, slurping, chomping sound we heard before -- but now
      it grows louder and louder, deafening beyond all reality,
      infinitely hideous.

                                        SUDDEN CUT TO:

140   NEW ANGLE ROBERT   140
      in bed. (Slurping sounds out.) He sits bolt upright, crying
      out wordlessly in fright. Then, recovering -- shaken,
      sweating -- he returns to sleep.

                                        FADE OUT.

rr

FADE IN:

EXT. CASTLE - DAY

The sun shines cheerfully. Birdsong.

141   CLOSEUP BIRD (STOCK)   141
        on a leafy branch, singing.

INT. MAUDE'S BOUDOIR - DAY

142   MAUDE   142
        asleep in bed. Sunlight streams into the room.

143   BEDROOM   143
        CAMERA PANS over the very feminine, frilly bedroom, to an
        adjoining door. It is not only closed, it is barred -- a
        great oaken plank lies across it. CAMERA ZOOMS IN on the
        oaken plank.

INT. SARDONICUS' BEDROOM OTHER SIDE OF SAME DOOR - DAY

144   BEDROOM   144
        Sunlight. CAMERA PANS over another bedroom. This one is
        masculine in tone and appointments. We now see the massive
        bed. Sardonicus is asleep in it, and he is unmasked, but
        we do not see his face because it is buried in the pillow.
        Hanging on a bedpost within his reach is the mask. CAMERA
        ZOOMS IN on the mask.

INT. ROBERT'S BEDROOM - SUNLIGHT

145   ROBERT   145
        in bed, asleep. Slowly, he awakens. For a moment, he
        lies there. Then, resolutely, he arises and dons his robe.

146   NEW ANGLE ROBERT   146
        removing toilette articles from one of his bags. He takes
        shaving mug, brush and old-fashioned straight razor. CAMERA
        PANS with Robert as he walks over to a washstand on which
        rest a bowl and pitcher of water. (It is important that we
        do not clearly see the portion of wall above the washstand
        just yet.) He pours water into the bowl, wets his brush,
        and begins to work up a lather in the mug. When he has
        worked up a rich lather, he raises the brush to his face and
        looks upward to where the mirror should be. He frowns.

cp

147   NEW ANGLE   147
      showing Robert, brush in hand, staring at the wall above
      the washstand. Where a mirror would ordinarily hang, is
      a clearly defined, oval-shaped "clean" spot, as if a mirror
      had been removed. Robert glances about the room in mild
      annoyance. CAMERA PANS over the entire bedroom, describing
      a complete circle and coming back to Robert. There are no
      mirrors in the entire room. Robert is irked and puzzled.
      A knock at the door.

148   NEW ANGLE ROBERT   148
      brush still in hand, walks to the door and opens it.

149   ROBERT KRULL   149
      Krull is standing in doorway.

                          KRULL
                Good morning, Sir Robert.
                May I know your preference
                for breakfast?

                          ROBERT
                Oh... anything at all... but
                you can bring me a mirror,
                if you will.

                          KRULL
                A mirror, Sir Robert?

                          ROBERT
                Yes... so that I may shave.

                          KRULL
                I fear, sir, there _are_ no
                mirrors.

                          ROBERT
                No mirrors?

                          KRULL
                None in the entire castle,
                sir. The Baron's orders.

                          ROBERT
                But why not?

                          KRULL
                    (shrugging)
                It is not my place to question,
                sir... Will you be coming down
                to breakfast soon?

149   CONTINUED: 149

                        ROBERT
            Yes, presently.

                        KRULL
            Very good, sir.

Krull leaves, closing the door.

CAMERA FOLLOWS Robert as he returns to the washstand
and begins to shave "from memory," haltingly, uncertainly.

INT. SARDONICUS' BEDROOM - DAY

150   SARDONICUS   150
       in bed, stirring. We do not see his face. His hand
       reaches out to the bedpost for the mask. He puts it on.
       Only then, fully masked to the world, does he arise and
       turn to us.

INT. MAUDE'S BOUDOIR - DAY

151   MAUDE   151
       in a diaphonous peignoir, is sitting at her dressing table,
       brushing her hair, without the aid of a mirror. There is
       a knock on the adjoining door. She gets up, crosses to the
       door, and unbars it, admitting Sardonicus. He is dressed
       in a long, sumptuous, quilted robe.

152   MAUDE   SARDONICUS   152

                        SARDONICUS
            Good morning, madam.

                        MAUDE
                  (flatly)
            Good morning.

152   CONTINUED: 152

                    SARDONICUS
          May I come in?

                    MAUDE
          Why, I...

                    SARDONICUS
          Do not worry. I am not a man
          who is affectionate in the morning
          hours.

She lets him enter.

                    SARDONICUS
          This morning, I intend to tell
          him everything.

                    MAUDE
          Yes...last night you were inter-
          rupted, were you not? By your
          ...visitors...

                    SARDONICUS
          That is correct.

153   CLOSEUP MAUDE   153

                    MAUDE
                (shuddering)
          What was she like...the one who
          screamed?

154   TWO SHOT MAUDE SARDONICUS   154

                    SARDONICUS
          Let us not have a scene, madam.
          I merely wished to inform you
          that your precious Sir Robert
          will know all this morning. And
          he will make his decision this
          morning.
                (threateningly)
          If he decides wrongly...

                    MAUDE
                (afraid)
          No, Baron...

rr

155   CLOSEUP SARDONICUS   155

                    SARDONICUS
            If he decides wrongly, you
            know what to expect from me.

156   CLOSEUP MAUDE   156

                    MAUDE
              (pleading)
            No...you wouldn't...

157   NEW ANGLE MAUDE SARDONICUS   157
       Sardonicus returning casually to the door.

                    SARDONICUS
            Oh, but I would. I would, indeed.
            So, madam, perhaps it would be in
            your own best interests to...
            persuade Sir Robert to make the
            right decision.

                    MAUDE
            How persuade him?

                    SARDONICUS
              (shrugging)
            How do women usually persuade
            men?

                    MAUDE
              (infuriated)
            What exactly do you imply, sir?!

                    SARDONICUS
              (firm)
            Imply? Cowards imply. I
            command! And I command you to
            sway him by any and all means!
            Use your...I believe they are
            usually referred to as 'charms'...

       Maude raises her hand to strike him. He seizes her wrist,
       twists her arm behind her back until she gasps with pain.
       Then, roughly, he releases her, throwing her to the floor.

158   NEW ANGLE SHOOTING UP AT SARDONICUS   158
       As he towers over Maude on the floor.

rr

158   CONTINUED: 158

                    SARDONICUS
              That pain, madam...was only a
              sample!

159   LONG SHOT   SARDONICUS   159
      He stalks out of the room and slams the adjoining door.

160   CLOSE SHOT   MAUDE   160
      on the floor, weeping uncontrollably.

                                                        DISSOLVE TO:

EXT. GARDEN - DAY

161   LONG SHOT   SARDONICUS   ROBERT   161
      strolling along a garden path strangely devoid of flowers.
      Weeds and vines appear to be all that grows. We hear the
      voice of Sardonicus.

                    SARDONICUS
              I thought you might enjoy a
              stroll through my garden before
              breakfast, Sir Robert...

162   CLOSER SHOT   (TRAVELLING SHOT)   162
      CAMERA FOLLOWS them as they stroll.

                    ROBERT
              It is a strange garden...there
              are no flowers.

                    SARDONICUS
              Alas, no. Flowers grow poorly
              here. Only earth's ugly children
              flourish...the weeds. Here you
              will find those plants one hears
              about in romantic tales...wolf-
              bane...mandrake root...charlock...
              deadly nightshade...they are all
              here...

      They have reached a shaded arbor, with benches.

                    SARDONICUS
                   (continuing)
              Shall we be seated a moment?

162   CONTINUED: 162

They do so.

> SARDONICUS
> (continuing)
> Krull will be announcing breakfast soon, but in the interim, perhaps we might talk a bit?

> ROBERT
> I would like to talk to you about several matters.

> SARDONICUS
> Perhaps I might resume my little story of the ghoul?

> ROBERT
> Baron, there are other things I must speak of first. Strange things. Screams in the night, and other sounds...a young girl, tortured by leeches...

> SARDONICUS
> Ah, yes. You are right to question those things. But if you listen to my story, you will learn all. You will learn the answers to those mysteries. You will learn how low a human being can sink. And you will also learn about my first wife -- who died because of ... a ghoul!

CAMERA PANS OVER to a group of ugly weeds. Over this:

> SARDONICUS' (O.S.)
> (continuing)
> My name was not always Sardonicus... and I did not always wear a mask...

DISSOLVE TO:

cp

(FLASHBACK)

EXT. GRAVEYARD - SUNSET

163   CLOSE SHOT   GRAVE   163
        A bunch of lovely flowers strewn on a grave. CAMERA PULLS
        away.

164   LONG SHOT   TWO MEN AND GRAVEDIGGER AT GRAVE   164
        Two men stand over a grave. One is old, one is young. The
        old one places some flowers on the grave. Both cross them-
        selves. From the foreground, a hunchbacked gravedigger
        limps up to them. Over this:

                        SARDONICUS' VOICE (O.S.)
                    I was a simple peasant boy
                    named Marek... and my mother
                    had been dead only a year...

165   GROUP SHOT   GRAVEDIGGER   YOUNG SARDONICUS   FATHER   165
        Young Sardonicus is unmasked, and is a handsome youth. His
        father is a kindly, soft-spoken old man in his seventies.

                        GRAVEDIGGER
                        (to father)
                    Ah, Henryk... it is only you
                    and your boy...

                        FATHER
                    Yes. We have come to pay our
                    respects to my wife.

                        GRAVEDIGGER
                    She was a good woman.

                        YOUNG SARDONICUS
                    Her better never walked the
                    earth.

                        GRAVEDIGGER
                    My eyes are not what they
                    were... and when I saw two
                    men standing over a grave...
                    at sunset... well, as Grave-
                    digger, I have certain
                    responsibilities... and I
                    thought perhaps...

                        FATHER
                    You thought what, my friend?

165   CONTINUED: 165

                    GRAVEDIGGER
          You may have been... those
          lowest of men... if you can
          call them men...

                    FATHER
          You mean the --

166   CLOSEUP GRAVEDIGGER   166

                    GRAVEDIGGER
          Yes! The <u>ghouls</u>!

167   GROUP SHOT   167

                    YOUNG SARDONICUS
          But they are stories to scare
          children!

                    GRAVEDIGGER
          Ah no, young Marek... ask your
          father here... we old ones
          <u>know</u> that ghouls exist! We
          have seen them prowl by night...
          and open the graves of our
          loved ones... and we have
          <u>heard</u> them...

                    YOUNG SARDONICUS
          Heard them?

168   CLOSEUP GRAVEDIGGER   168

                    GRAVEDIGGER
          <u>Feeding</u>! Yes, my boy...
          creatures that once were men
          even as you and I... sunk so
          low that they do... <u>that</u>!

169   TWO SHOT FATHER YOUNG SARDONICUS   169

                    FATHER
          Come, you are upsetting the
          boy... Let us go home now,
          Marek. Your little wife
          Elenka will be waiting for
          us... and I have a gift for
          her!

     They turn to leave.

170   CLOSE SHOT   GRAVEDIGGER   170

                    GRAVEDIGGER
              Never fear, Marek! I will
              guard your mother well against
              the ghouls! They will not
              violate her grave.

                                                DISSOLVE TO:

EXT. HUMBLE PEASANT COTTAGE - SUNSET

171   LONG SHOT   YOUNG SARDONICUS   FATHER   171
      are approaching the cottage. We hear their voices.

                    YOUNG SARDONICUS
              But what kind of gift do you
              have for Elenka, Father?

                    FATHER
              Wait and see!

                    YOUNG SARDONICUS
              She is so fond of pretty
              clothes and trinkets...
              things I cannot afford to
              give her...

                    FATHER
              I know, I know. That is why --
              but, ah, here we are.

      They open the door and enter.

INT. THE PLAIN LIVING ROOM OF COTTAGE - SUNSET

172   MEDIUM LONG SHOT   YOUNG SARDONICUS   FATHER   172
      entering. Preening in a hand mirror is a very pretty but
      vain young girl, ELENKA.

                    ELENKA
              Oh, there you are. It took
              you long enough.

                    YOUNG SARDONICUS
              Is our meal ready, Elenka?

                    ELENKA
              I've eaten. You can heat up
              what's left.

172   CONTINUED: 172

                    YOUNG SARDONICUS
              It doesn't matter... I'm not
              hungry...

                    FATHER
              Elenka, my little one...

                    ELENKA
                  (obviously
                   bored by him)
              What?

                    FATHER
                  (puckishly)
              When I was in the city
              yesterday... I bought some-
              thing for you... something
              that might make you very
              happy...

                    ELENKA
                  (surprised)
              You did?

                    FATHER
              Yes... let me see...

He fishes in the pockets of his rough peasant's jacket,
frowning. Then his face lights up.

                    FATHER
                  (to Young Sardonicus)
              Ah, no, of course! I wore
              that lovely weskit your mother
              made for me before she died...
              it is in the pocket... I will
              get it...

Father turns and leaves room through his bedroom door.

                    ELENKA
                  (calling after him)
              But what is it?

                    FATHER'S VOICE
              Be patient!

INT. FATHER'S BEDROOM

173   CLOSE SHOT   WESKIT   173
        hanging on a peg. The old man's hand reaches into a pocket
        and extracts a pasteboard ticket.

cp

INT. LIVING ROOM

174   YOUNG SARDONICUS   FATHER   ELENKA   174

                    FATHER
            Here it is!

INSERT: A LOTTERY TICKET
    in Father's hand. It
    prominently bears the
    printed numbers:

        7 7 0 7

BACK TO SCENE 174:

                    YOUNG SARDONICUS
                (amused, indulgent)
            Father! A lottery ticket?
            Again??

                    FATHER
            Ah, but this one --

                    YOUNG SARDONICUS
            -- is different, I know!

                    FATHER
            Yes! It _is_ different!

                    ELENKA
                (nasty)
            You silly old man... How many
            lottery tickets have you bought
            in your life?

                    FATHER
            Many... perhaps hundreds...

                    ELENKA
            And how many times have you won?

                    FATHER
                (shamefacedly)
            Never...
                (brightening)
            But _this_ time --

                    ELENKA
            That is what you always say!
            'This time'...

174   CONTINUED: 174

                         FATHER
               I know. I know... but this
               time is truly different! I
               feel it -- here.
                    (touches his heart)
               Because this time... this time
               it is for you and Marek.

                         YOUNG SARDONICUS
                    (touched)
               Father...

                         ELENKA
               I've never heard of anything
               more ridiculous!

175   TWO SHOT YOUNG SARDONICUS FATHER   175
      The two men embrace.

                         YOUNG SARDONICUS
               Good night, Father.

                         FATHER
               Good night, Marek.

      The father goes back to his room.

176   CLOSE SHOT THE WESKIT   176
      The father's hand returns the ticket to the weskit pocket.

                         SARDONICUS' VOICE (O.S.)
               It was the last time I saw my
               father alive... for, that very
               night, peacefully, in his
               sleep... he left us...

                                                   DISSOLVE TO:

177   CLOSEUP FATHER IN COFFIN   177
      seen from neck up. It is a simple wooden coffin. The lid
      is slid into place and hands begin to hammer in the nails.

                                                   DISSOLVE TO:

sat

INT. COTTAGE - DAY

178 YOUNG SARDONICUS ELENKA   178
Young Sardonicus is at a table, adding up rows of figures.
Elenka is in a chair, sewing. Over this:

>   SARDONICUS' VOICE
> The weeks that followed were
> hard. Elenka and I continued
> to quarrel, and always over the
> same thing... money...

>   YOUNG SARDONICUS
>   (throwing down
>   his pen)
> What is the use? It always
> comes out the same! I sell our
> produce in the city, and then
> spend all the profits on feed...
> and seed grain... and...

>   ELENKA
> You could get a good price for
> the farm.

>   YOUNG SARDONICUS
> Sell my father's farm? No...
> but even if I did sell it, what
> then?

>   ELENKA
> We could go to the city, and
> rent a fine house...

>   YOUNG SARDONICUS
> And the money would be gone in
> half a year!

>   ELENKA
>   (blazing)
> Half a year of luxury, yes! Is
> it not better than this?

A knock at the door.

>   YOUNG SARDONICUS
>   (calling)
> Yes? Who is it?

>   JANKU'S VOICE
>   (slightly drunk)
> Marek! Open up, open up!

Young Sardonicus opens the door to admit JANKU (pronounced
"YON-koo"), a tipsy young peasant.

sat

178   CONTINUED: 178

                        YOUNG SARDONICUS
              Janku...

                        JANKU
              Marek, my ol' friend...!

Janku stumbles into the cottage, and bows deeply, drunkenly,
to Elenka.

                        ELENKA
                    (to Young Sardonicus)
              Your friend is drunk, Marek.

                        JANKU
              I? Drunk?? Jus' three, for
              glassesh... glashess...

                        YOUNG SARDONICUS
              You have been to the city, Janku?

                        JANKU
              I have been to 'a city....and
              I have brought you grea' news!
              Grea' news for my ol' friend --

                        YOUNG SARDONICUS
              What news, Janku?

                        JANKU
              News of money, Marek!

179   CLOSEUP   ELENKA   179

                        ELENKA
                    (looking up,
                     interested)
              Money?

180   GROUP SHOT   YOUNG SARDONICUS   JANKU   ELENKA   180

                        JANKU
              Money... losh and losh o' money!

                        YOUNG SARDONICUS
              For heaven's sake, man, what do
              you mean?

                        JANKU
                    (reaching into
                     his pocket)
              I mean... thish!

sat

180   CONTINUED: 180

Janku hands Young Sardonicus a printed sheet.

> YOUNG SARDONICUS
> (taking it)
> What is it?

> JANKU
> The winnersh!

> YOUNG SARDONICUS
> Winners?...

> JANKU
> (exasperated)
> The lo'rry, lot-ter-y winnersh!

> YOUNG SARDONICUS
> The lottery!

> JANKU
> See there?...
> (points to list)
> ... your father's name... and
> next to it... see?... a number!

INSERT: A huge printed number fills the screen:

    7 7 0 7

BACK TO SCENE 180:

> JANKU'S VOICE (O.S.)
> Sheven... sheven... zero...
> sheven!

181   CLOSEUP YOUNG SARDONICUS   181

> YOUNG SARDONICUS
> Seven seven zero seven... yes!
> That's right! That was it!

182   CLOSEUP ELENKA   182

> ELENKA
> Marek... you mean... your father's
> ticket...

sat

183   TWO SHOT   YOUNG SARDONICUS   ELENKA   183

                        YOUNG SARDONICUS
                            (joyously)
                    Yes, Elenka! It has won!
                    It has won hundreds, thousands!

                        ELENKA
                    Marek! Oh, Marek, how glorious!

184   CLOSEUP   YOUNG SARDONICUS   184

                        YOUNG SARDONICUS
                    The first thing tomorrow... at
                    dawn... I will go to the city
                    and redeem the --
                            (he is suddenly
                             fearful)
                    -- the ticket.

                        ELENKA'S VOICE
                    Marek... what is wrong?

                        YOUNG SARDONICUS
                    The ticket... where is the ticket???

185   GROUP SHOT   YOUNG SARDONICUS   ELENKA   JANKU   185
       Young Sardonicus rushes out of the picture, through the door
       of his father's bedroom.

INT. FATHER'S BEDROOM - DAY

186   YOUNG SARDONICUS   186
       He picks up a small box on top of a chest of drawers, and
       opens it.

INSERT: The open box in Young Sardonicus' hands.

                    We see a few cheap collar studs, some faded
                    Daguerreotypes, a pack of soiled playing
                    cards, a hunting knife, and other oddments,
                    but no lottery ticket.

BACK TO SCENE 186:

            Young Sardonicus empties the contents of the box on top of
            the chest of drawers. He finds nothing. He opens the drawers,
            now, one by one, and searches in them, throwing the shirts and
            other articles about him in a frenzy until they are all over
            the floor. Still, he finds nothing.

sat

187   CLOSEUP   YOUNG SARDONICUS   187

                        YOUNG SARDONICUS
                    (brightening;
                     softly)
                The money box...

188   NEW ANGLE   188
        Young Sardonicus pulls back a portion of the faded, rough
        carpet, kneels, and attacks a loose board. The board comes
        away. Young Sardonicus reaches under the floor and pulls out
        a metal box. He tries to open it. It is locked. Still hold-
        ing the box, he dashes to --

189   CHEST OF DRAWERS   189
        again. Young Sardonicus rummages in the odds and ends he
        dumped from the stud box -- finally finds a large, iron key.

INSERT: The key in his hand.

BACK TO SCENE 189:

        Young Sardonicus opens the metal money box. His face falls.

INSERT: Inside the money box are two small, dull coins,
        such as pennies.

190   CLOSEUP   YOUNG SARDONICUS   190
        infinitely chagrined. But a ray of hope crosses his face and
        he quickly turns his head to look at the weskit.

191   CLOSE SHOT   THE EMPTY PEG   191
        on which the weskit previously hung.

INT. LIVING ROOM   (AS IN SCENE 180)

192   GROUP SHOT   ELENKA   JANKU   192
        with Young Sardonicus slowly backing out of his father's room.

                        JANKU
                    (softly)
                Marek...

                        ELENKA
                Marek, what is it?...

sat

192   CONTINUED: 192

>   YOUNG SARDONICUS
>   (stunned, hoarse)
>   The weskit...
>
>   ELENKA
>   What weskit...
>
>   YOUNG SARDONICUS
>   My father's...
>
>   ELENKA
>   What about it?...
>
>   YOUNG SARDONICUS
>   The weskit... the one my mother
>   made for him...
>
>   ELENKA
>   (screaming)
>   What about the weskit, Marek???

193   CLOSEUP   YOUNG SARDONICUS 193

>   YOUNG SARDONICUS
>   (tonelessly)
>   He was buried in it.

194   GROUP SHOT   YOUNG SARDONICUS   ELENKA   JANKU 194

>   ELENKA
>   What of that? What difference
>   does it make?
>
>   YOUNG SARDONICUS
>   The ticket!
>
>   ELENKA
>   What?...
>
>   YOUNG SARDONICUS
>   The lottery ticket was in the
>   pocket!

Elenka, stunned, speechless, slowly sits down.

>   JANKU
>   Marek... I'm sorry...

Young Sardonicus does not answer him.

>   JANKU
>   (continuing)
>   I... I'll go now...

sat

194   CONTINUED: 194

Awkwardly, Janku turns and leaves.

                    ELENKA
              (softly)
          Marek...

                    YOUNG SARDONICUS
          Yes...

                    ELENKA
          You said... 'The lottery ticket
          was in the pocket'...

                    YOUNG SARDONICUS
          Yes...

195   CLOSEUP   ELENKA   195
      almost mad with greed.

                    ELENKA
          Not was, Marek! Is! The lot-
          tery ticket is in the pocket!

196   TWO SHOT   YOUNG SARDONICUS   ELENKA   196
      Young Sardonicus turns to her slowly.

                    YOUNG SARDONICUS
              (softly)
          What are you saying?

                    ELENKA
              (almost a whisper)
          It is clear as daylight, Marek...

                    YOUNG SARDONICUS
              (a shout)
          What are you saying!!!

                    ELENKA
          It is the only way, Marek!

                    YOUNG SARDONICUS
              (pityingly)
          May God forgive you.

197   CLOSEUP   ELENKA   197
      hard as steel.

                    ELENKA
          You have said that you loved me.
          This is your chance to prove it.

sat

197   CONTINUED: 197

                        YOUNG SARDONICUS' VOICE
                    Elenka, please don't put it that
                    way...

                              ELENKA
                    Prove it!

                                                        DISSOLVE TO:

EXT. CEMETERY (AS IN SCENE 178) - NIGHT

198   LONG SHOT   198
        The cemetery scene we previously saw. No people. Night
        sounds: the hooting of an owl, etc.

                           SARDONICUS' VOICE
                    And so that night, Sir Robert,
                    I became a profaner of the dead...
                    a robber of graves... a ghoul!

199   YOUNG SARDONICUS   199
        comes into sight, silhouetted against the moonlight. He
        carries a shovel. He stops at his father's grave.

200   CLOSEUP   YOUNG SARDONICUS   200

                           YOUNG SARDONICUS
                              (a whisper)
                    Father, forgive me.

201   LONG SHOT   YOUNG SARDONICUS   201
        begins digging.

                                                        DISSOLVE TO:

202   LONG SHOT   YOUNG SARDONICUS   202
        He has made considerable progress. He stands shoulder deep
        in the grave, and has created a small mountain of dirt. He
        stops, mops his brow, and resumes digging for a brief period.
        Then we hear the shovel strike something solid. Young Sardon-
        icus reacts. He digs with more fury now. Then, his digging
        completed, he kneels down, out of sight.

sat

203　　NEW ANGLE YOUNG SARDONICUS COFFIN　　　　　　　　203
CAMERA SHOOTING DOWN into the grave. Very scant moonlight now. Coffin is a plain wooden box with a nailed-down lid. Young Sardonicus uses the shovel as a crowbar, to pry off the lid. Slowly, one by one, the nails are wrenched out, the lid begins to lift -- and, finally, with a sharp sound of splitting wood, the lid falls away. We do not yet see the corpse clearly, for the moon is behind a cloud. Young Sardonicus begins to search in the four pockets of the weskit. He has tried two.

204　　THE SKY (STOCK)　　　　　　　　　　　　　　　　　　204
Clouds roll away from the moon, and the sky suddenly brightens.

205　　EXTREME CLOSEUP DEAD FATHER'S FACE　　　　　　　　207
The moonlight reveals the father's now hideously distorted face. The dead eyes are open and staring... strange rigor mortis has pulled back the muscles of his lips unnaturally, baring the teeth and gums in a terrible mockery of a smile, and the skin around the eyes is drawn horribly downward.

206　　LONG SHOT YOUNG SARDONICUS (AS IN SCENE 202)　　206
He is not visible yet. We hear his long drawn, soul-deep cry of horror. Now we see him scramble out of the grave and run in panic until he is a speck in the distance.

207　　CLOSE SHOT YOUNG SARDONICUS　　　　　　　　　　　　207
as he reaches the gate of the cemetery and leans against a pillar, breathing hard. (NOTE: From this point on, in the flashback sequence, we will not see Young Sardonicus' face. He will always be shot from the back or in deep shadow.)

> SARDONICUS' VOICE
> What I had not foreseen was that the face of my father, the muscles stretched by a terrible death-rigor, would look directly and hideously upon me... the dead lips drawn back in a constant and soul-shattering smile!

Young Sardonicus stiffens with a sudden thought.

> SARDONICUS' VOICE
> (continuing)
> Suddenly I realized... I had not performed my ghastly mission... the lottery ticket remained in my father's pocket.

Young Sardonicus turns and haltingly retraces his steps. CAMERA FOLLOWS him to the grave. He leaps into it.

sat

207   CONTINUED: 207

                              SARDONICUS' VOICE
                         (continuing)
                    This time, I avoided the sight
                    of my father's face.

INSERT: A pocket of the weskit.

         Young Sardonicus' fingers extract the
         lottery ticket. We can plainly read
         the number:

                            7 7 0 7

                                                              DISSOLVE TO:

(CHANGE FOR PAGES 71, 72)

INT. BEDROOM - NIGHT

209 MEDIUM CLOSE SHOT ELENKA 209
    awake in bed. Room is dark.

        ELENKA
    Marek ... is that you?

        YOUNG SARDONICUS (o.s.)
        (we hear him utter a strange,
        strangulated, wordless cry of
        frustration and fright.)

        ELENKA
    Did you -- get it?

        YOUNG SARDONICUS (o.s.)
        (again the cry, but closer)

210 TWO SHOT ELENKA YOUNG SARDONICUS 210
    She is in bed. He enters -- we see his silhouette
    move haltingly, almost as if in pain -- and he sits
    on the bed next to her. It is too dark for us to see
    his face.

        ELENKA
    Was it -- bad?

        YOUNG SARDONICUS
        (again he tries to speak;
        again he can utter only the
        strangulated animal sound)

        ELENKA
    Are you all right, my darling? Is
    something ... wrong? Wait ... I
    will light the candle ...

211 (PICK UP FROM PAGE 72 OF SCRIPT)

ar

EXT. COTTAGE - NIGHT

208   LONG SHOT (SAME AS SCENE 167)   208
        Young Sardonicus approaches it (we see only his back.)
        He opens the door and enters.

INT. BEDROOM - NIGHT

209   MEDIUM CLOSE SHOT ELENKA   209
        awake in bed. Room is dark.

                        ELENKA
                Marek...is that you?

                        YOUNG SARDONICUS' VOICE
                Yes.

                        ELENKA
                Did you -- get it?

                        YOUNG SARDONICUS' VOICE
                Yes.

                        ELENKA
                    (softening; offering
                    him his reward)
                I'm in here, Marek...come to me...

210   TWO SHOT ELENKA YOUNG SARDONICUS   210
        She is in bed. He enters, sits on the bed next to her.
        It is too dark for us to see his face.

                        ELENKA
                Was it -- bad?

                        YOUNG SARDONICUS
                It was horrible.

                        ELENKA
                Oh, my darling...my brave darling...

        She embraces him. He responds, and kisses her. Then she
        pulls away, slightly.

                        ELENKA
                    (puzzled)
                Does something amuse you?

                        YOUNG SARDONICUS
                    (equally puzzled)
                Amuse me? I have no reason to
                be amused...

ar

210   CONTINUED: 210

                        ELENKA
              But I could feel it when you
              kissed me.

211   CLOSE SHOT ELENKA ONLY   211
      Reaching out to a small bedside table, she strikes a match
      and lights a candle. Then she turns to "us" -- and suddenly
      her eyes widen, fear grips her, she looks straight into the
      camera and screams in wild, total terror!

                                              END OF FLASHBACK

EXT. GARDEN ARBOR - DAY (AS IN SCENE 166)

212   EXTREME CLOSEUP SARDONICUS   212
      unmasked. We see the present-day Sardonicus, without his
      mask. His face is distorted in exactly the same way as his
      dead father's -- the lips pulled unnaturally away from the
      teeth and gums in a ghastly perpetual smile, and the eyelids
      hideously pulled down.

213   GROUP SHOT SARDONICUS ROBERT   213
      CAMERA PULLS away and we see we are back in the arbor.
      Sardonicus is standing, his mask in his hand. Robert is
      seated. Robert is recoiling in shock.

                        ROBERT
              Merciful God...

214   NEW ANGLE SARDONICUS ROBERT   214
      Sardonicus is seen from the back, looking down upon Robert.
      He still holds the mask in his hand.

                        SARDONICUS
              Ever since that night, Sir Robert,
              my face has been as you see it now
              -- a replica of my dead father's...
              the lips drawn back in a perpetual
              mocking grin! I have never been
              able to close my mouth. The
              muscles are immovable, as if held
              in the rigor of death!

                        ROBERT
              Incredible! And yet your power
              of speech does not seem to have
              been impaired.

ar

214   CONTINUED: 214

                        SARDONICUS
                Ah, but it was, Sir Robert --
                very much impaired! For a long
                time I could hardly speak at all.
                Only through arduous training by
                the finest diction teachers did
                I master the art of utilizing
                dormant muscles of the throat and
                palate... I literally learned to
                speak all over again.

215   EXTREME CLOSEUP SARDONICUS (AS IN SCENE 214)   215
        unmasked.' He replaces the mask.

216   TWO SHOT SARDONICUS ROBERT   216
        Sardonicus sits down again.

                        SARDONICUS
                        (continuing)
                Through the years, I have evolved
                a kind of explanation for my
                strange affliction. At first, of
                course, my superstitious peasant
                mind believed that Heaven had
                placed a curse upon me to punish
                me for violating my father's rest --
                or that some devilish force from
                beyond the grave had reached out
                to stamp my face. But, at length,
                I began to believe it was the
                massive shock that forced my face
                to this state, and that my great
                guilt had also helped to shape it
                even as my dead father's face was
                shaped. Shock and guilt -- strong
                powers not from God above nor the
                Fiend below...but from within my
                own heart, my own brain, my own
                soul.

                        ROBERT
                But your wife...Elenka...

                        SARDONICUS
                She died. By her own hand.

217   NEW ANGLE ROBERT SARDONICUS   217
        favoring Robert.

                        ROBERT
                But you did redeem the lottery
                ticket.

217   CONTINUED: 217

>   SARDONICUS
>   (indicating, with a wave
>   of his hand, his present
>   grandeur)
>   Obviously. And bought for myself
>   the resounding title of Baron.
>
>   ROBERT
>   And your new name...?
>
>   SARDONICUS
>   Come, Sir Robert, you are a
>   medical man...surely you recognize
>   the word 'sardonicus'?
>
>   ROBERT
>   (slowly)
>   Yes...the Latin term for the
>   grimace on the faces of lockjaw
>   victims...<u>Risus sardonicus</u>...
>   'Sardonic smile'...
>
>   SARDONICUS
>   Of course. In my blighted con-
>   dition, I became interested in
>   the medical arts and began to
>   read a great deal...in the course
>   of my reading, I came across that
>   Latin term. The bitter irony
>   appealed to me, and I took
>   'Sardonicus' as my name.
>   (a pause)
>   Does my story answer your ques-
>   tions?
>
>   ROBERT
>   It answers many questions. The
>   'strange sounds of eating I heard...

218   REVERSE POV   218
      favoring Sardonicus.

>   SARDONICUS
>   (nodding)
>   I can eat only the thinnest stews
>   and porridges...sucking them up
>   like a beast...the sight is so
>   offensive that I always eat alone...
>
>   ROBERT
>   The leeches...

218   CONTINUED: 218

                    SARDONICUS
          I have tried everything...in my
          despair, I allowed Krull to test
          an ancient folk remedy on the girl.

                    ROBERT
          And the mirrors...

                    SARDONICUS
          If you had my face, your house
          would be devoid of mirrors, too.

                    ROBERT
          Yes, I understand now.

                    SARDONICUS
          And you understand why I have
          brought you here?

                    ROBERT
          Of course. You have read of my
          researches...

                    SARDONICUS
          And your <u>successes</u>. The successes
          that have earned you a knighthood.
          I have gone to many renowned
          physicians all over the world --
          Keller in Berlin, Morignac in
          Paris, Buonagente in Milan...

                    ROBERT
          They are great men.

                    SARDONICUS
          But none have been able to help
          me. <u>You</u>, Sir Robert, are my last
          hope. I entreat you to heal me...
          to lift this curse from me...to
          make me look once more like a man,
          that I may walk among my fellow
          human beings as one of them, rather
          than as a gargoyle to be shunned
          and feared and ridiculed.

219   CLOSEUP ROBERT   219

                    ROBERT
          You were right to ask me, Baron.
          We must never abandon hope. I
          can begin the treatment this
          afternoon.

                                                    DISSOLVE TO:

cp

INT. SARDONICUS' BEDROOM - DAY

220   MEDIUM LONG SHOT   ROOM   KRULL   ANNA   SARDONICUS   220
      Afternoon sun streams through the window. Stacks of snowy
      white towels are piled on a table. Krull enters, followed
      by Anna -- they both carry large copper basins of steaming
      water, which they place on a table next to a chaise lounge.
      Sardonicus enters the room. He removes his coat and shirt,
      baring a handsome torso. He lies down upon the couch.

INT. CORRIDOR OUTSIDE SARDONICUS' ROOM - DAY

221   ROBERT   MAUDE   221
      Robert approaches Sardonicus' door, but Maude appears and
      stops him. The following conversation is spoken quickly,
      furtively, in whispers:

                          MAUDE
                Robert.

                          ROBERT
                Yes, Maude?...

                          MAUDE
                Cure him! Oh, cure him, Robert!
                If you fail, I will suffer...

                          ROBERT
                A devoted wife could feel no
                other way.

                          MAUDE
                No, you do not understand! If
                you do not heal him... he will
                punish me.

                          ROBERT
                What! Surely he would not beat
                you?

222   CLOSEUP   MAUDE   222

                          MAUDE
                I wish he would be content
                with a mere beating. But his
                cleverness knows a more
                hideous torture.

223   TWO SHOT   ROBERT   MAUDE   223

                          ROBERT
                This is monstrous -- I will
                demand that he --

223   CONTINUED: 223

                         MAUDE
               No! Say nothing -- or he may...
               embellish the punishment!

                         ROBERT
               But what manner of --

                         MAUDE
                    (cutting in)
               Shh! No more! He waits for
               you...

She rushes away.

INT. SARDONICUS' BEDROOM (AS IN SCENE 220) - DAY

224   SARDONICUS KRULL ANNA ROBERT   224
       Sardonicus is on the couch. Krull and Anna in attendance.
       Robert enters.

                         ROBERT
                    (seeing Sardonicus)
               Ah, you are ready.

                         SARDONICUS
               Yes, Sir Robert.

                         ROBERT
                    (to Krull and Anna)
               Remain here. I will need your
               assistance.

                         KRULL
               Yes, sir.

Robert now stands over Sardonicus.

                         SARDONICUS
               What form will the treatment
               take?

                         ROBERT
               Repeated applications of heat,
               and special massage.

                         SARDONICUS
               But these have been tried...
               and they have failed...

                         ROBERT
               Massage differs from one pair
               of hands to another. I have

224   CONTINUED: 224

                              ROBERT (cont'd)
                    had success with my own
                    techniques, and I place faith
                    in them. Share my faith.

                              SARDONICUS
                    I do. I must.

                              ROBERT
                    Then let us begin.

          Robert sits down on a chair next to Sardonicus and removes
          the mask.

225   EXTREME CLOSEUP SARDONICUS   225
      unmasked.

226   LONG SHOT SARDONICUS ROBERT KRULL ANNA   226

                              ROBERT
                         (over his
                          shoulder,
                          to Krull)
                    Towel.

          Anna, who has been soaking towels in the basins of hot water,
          wrings out one and hands it to Krull, who in turn passes it
          to Robert. She then places another dry towel from the stack
          into the basin.

227   EXTREME CLOSEUP SARDONICUS   227
      unmasked. The towel is placed over his face.

228   CLOSEUP ROBERT   228

                              ROBERT
                    Exactly thirty seconds, Krull...
                    no more, no less...

                              KRULL'S VOICE
                    Yes, sir.

229   RAPID SERIES OF FLASH CLOSEUPS   229
thru Krull, followed by Anna, followed by Sardonicus with   thru
229C the towel over his face, followed by Robert, followed   229C
      by:

INT. MAUDE'S ROOM - DAY

230   LONG SHOT   MAUDE   230
       pacing up and down, with anxiety.

INT. SARDONICUS' ROOM (AS BEFORE) - DAY

231   LONG SHOT   GROUP   231

                        KRULL
                  (looking at a watch)
              It is thirty seconds, Sir Robert...

       Robert removes the towel.

232   EXTREME CLOSEUP   SARDONICUS   232
       unmasked.

233   TWO SHOT   ROBERT   SARDONICUS   233
       Robert begins to massage his patient's face.

                                              SLOW DISSOLVE TO:

INT. SARDONICUS' ROOM - NIGHT

234   LONG SHOT   234
       Same scene as before, but it is now night. The stack of
       snowy white towels is now a sodden heap. Krull and Anna
       are slumped in chairs, weary. Robert, finishing a bout of
       massage, leans back in his chair with a sigh. He seems
       almost dead with fatigue. CAMERA MOVES in very slowly
       until we have a:

235   CLOSEUP   SARDONICUS   235
       unmasked. There is no improvement.

                        SARDONICUS
                  (in despair)
              What remains to be done?

236   TWO SHOT   ROBERT   SARDONICUS   236

                        ROBERT
                  (infinitely tired)
              Nothing. I will not deceive
              you. I have done all I can...
              I can do no more.

236   CONTINUED: 236

Sardonicus rises swiftly from the chaise.

> SARDONICUS
> You *must* do more!

> ROBERT
> I am sorry.

> SARDONICUS
> Resume the treatment!

> ROBERT
> It would be futile... I have worked most of the day and into the night...

237   LONG SHOT GROUP   237

> SARDONICUS
> (to Krull
> and Anna)
> Leave us.

Anna and Krull leave. Sardonicus puts on his mask.

238   TWO SHOT ROBERT SARDONICUS   238

> SARDONICUS
> Surely there are other treatments?

> ROBERT
> None that have been sufficiently tested. None I would venture to use upon a human being.

> SARDONICUS
> Ah! Then other possibilities *do* exist!

> ROBERT
> Not really. They are still in the experimental stage...

> SARDONICUS
> Doctor! I *implore* you to use whatever treatments that remain -- no matter how untried they may be!

238   CONTINUED: 238

>   ROBERT
>   They are fraught with danger.
>
>   SARDONICUS
>   Danger of what? I am willing
>   to gamble my *life*!
>
>   ROBERT
>   *I* am not willing to gamble
>   *your* life.
>
>   SARDONICUS
>   Sir Robert, I will pay you a
>   thousand crowns.
>
>   ROBERT
>   This is not a question of
>   money.
>
>   SARDONICUS
>   Five thousand crowns... *ten*
>   thousand!
>
>   ROBERT
>   No.
>
>   SARDONICUS
>   (with a sigh)
>   Very well. Then I must ask
>   you to come with me...

                                                          DISSOLVE TO:

sat

INT. DANK NARROW SPIRAL STAIRWELL OF STONE - NIGHT

239   MEDIUM SHOT   SARDONICUS   ROBERT
      Descending the stairs are Sardonicus (holding a lantern),
      followed by Robert. They walk in silence for a moment.

240   TWO SHOT   SARDONICUS   ROBERT

                     ROBERT
            Where are you taking me?

                     SARDONICUS
            Patience, Sir Robert, patience.
            All will be made clear to you
            soon.

241   BOTTOM OF THE STAIRWELL
      We see a huge door, ancient, reinforced with iron bands and
      a monstrous lock. Sardonicus appears, followed by Robert.

                     SARDONICUS
            This castle is old, Sir Robert...
            very old. It was built in a
            dim age of fearful barbarity...

      From his pocket, Sardonicus produces a giant key ring and
      inserts one key into the lock. He pushes open the heavy
      door. It moves slowly, creaking, and a web of dust falls.
      When it is open, he gestures Robert inside. They enter.

INT. OTHER SIDE OF DOOR   TORTURE CHAMBER - NIGHT

242   TWO SHOT   SARDONICUS   ROBERT
      entering.

                     SARDONICUS
                  (with a sweeping
                   gesture)
            The torture chamber of the
            castle.

243   CAMERA PANS across the chamber. In addition to the
      usual chains, cages, manacles, etc., we see a whipping
      post with cat o' nine tails hanging on a hook, the Spanish
      boot, a branding iron lying in a brazier of long-dead coals,
      the iron maiden, the rack. They are all rusty and covered
      with web. CAMERA STOPS on a kind of alcove containing a
      massive iron chair. Maude is seated in it. Her wrists and
      ankles are secured by iron manacles, and her neck is held
      fast to the back of the chair by an iron collar.

sat

244 CLOSEUP MAUDE
terrified.

245 TWO SHOT ROBERT SARDONICUS

> ROBERT
> Maude!
> (to Sardonicus)
> What have you done to her?
>
> SARDONICUS
> Nothing... yet. You must know, first of all, that I am the victim of a little... domestic tragedy. My wife does not love me, Sir Robert. She has always been a wife in name only. She is revolted, you see. Revolted by my face.

246 CLOSEUP MAUDE
in chair.

> MAUDE
> It is not only that... it is --

247 NEW ANGLE SARDONICUS MAUDE
Sardonicus walks over to Maude.

> SARDONICUS
> Oh, come, Madam! My crudeness, my cruelty, my arrogance? This is what you tell yourself in your womanish way, is it not? But it is my _face_ you bar your door against -- not my... character flaws!

248 GROUP SHOT
Robert joins them.

> SARDONICUS
> (to Robert)
> If I am pushed to the limit of my endurance, Sir Robert... if you do not cure me... then I will be forced to make myself acceptable to my wife by an extreme measure...
>
> ROBERT
> You would torture her???

sat

248   CONTINUED: 248

                        SARDONICUS
                That would gain me nothing. I
                will simply detain my wife in
                this chair while she undergoes
                a bit of minor surgery.

                        ROBERT
                Surgery!!

249   CLOSEUP MAUDE   249
        in tears.

250   TWO SHOT SARDONICUS ROBERT   250

                        SARDONICUS
                Yes, Sir Robert. Surgery which
                will make her... sympathetic to
                my plight! And for this purpose,
                I have enlisted the services of
                a man who excels at simple surgery...

                        ROBERT
                You mean -- me??

                        SARDONICUS
                Oh, no. A man of quite different
                talents. In point of fact --
                he is standing behind you.

251   NEW ANGLE   251
        showing Sardonicus, Robert, Maude, and now Krull.

                        ROBERT
                Krull! But he is not a man of
                medicine.

252   CLOSEUP KRULL   252

                        KRULL
                    (satirically echoing
                     his earlier words)
                I am a man of all work, Sir.
                When my master says, 'Krull --
                do this thing', I do the thing...
                whatever it may be!
                    (smiling)
                I seem to remember you saying,
                Sir Robert, that this was...
                'most commendable'...

sat

253	GROUP SHOT ALL	253

      ROBERT
     (to Sardonicus)
   What devilish 'surgery' do you
   plan?

      SARDONICUS
   Something quite simple, really...
   The risorius muscle, Sir Robert...
   that which controls the act of
   smiling... a few deft incisions
   with a sharp knife... and Maude...

254	EXTREME CLOSEUP SARDONICUS	254

      SARDONICUS
     (rips off mask)
   ... <u>will look like me!</u>

255	EXTREME CLOSEUP MAUDE	255

horrified.

      MAUDE
   No...

      SARDONICUS' VOICE
   That lovely face...

256	EXTREME CLOSEUP SARDONICUS	256

still unmasked.

      SARDONICUS
   ... will resemble <u>mine</u>! And
   when her own beauty is transformed into hideousness... when
   she herself is a monster shunned
   by humankind... how can she <u>then</u>
   bar her door to me?

257	GROUP SHOT ALL FOUR	257

      SARDONICUS
   Krull! Begin!

Robert leaps at Sardonicus. Robert and Sardonicus struggle.
Krull picks a bludgeon from the wall... waits for his moment...
then clubs Robert into unconsciousness. Robert sinks to the
floor, as we:

            FADE OUT.

sat

FADE IN:

INT. TORTURE CHAMBER

258 STONE CEILING ROBERT'S POV
     As he regains consciousness.

259 CAMERA SWINGS DOWN to Robert, tied to the rack. He is unharmed, although thoroughly trussed up, hand and foot. Blinking and wincing, he turns to look about the chamber.

260 ROBERT'S POV
     CAMERA PANS. We see Sardonicus (masked again) looking at "us"... then Krull, also looking at "us"... and then we see the lower part of the iron chair with Maude's ankles still firmly manacled. Now the CAMERA PANS slowly up her body, building suspense. Just before we see her face:

261 CLOSEUP ROBERT
     apprehensive. A very BRIEF SHOT.

262 CLOSEUP MAUDE
     still held in the iron collar. Her face is tear-stained -- but unharmed.

263 CLOSEUP ROBERT
     A sigh of relief.

264 TWO SHOT ROBERT SARDONICUS
     Robert, on the rack, is approached by Sardonicus.

                    SARDONICUS
          Forgive me for tying you to The
          Rack, Sir Robert, but I assure
          you I do not intend to break
          your bones. I simply felt this
          was the best vantage point for
          you to watch the operation. I
          did not wish to proceed while
          you were still unconscious...
          it would have been most impolite.

                    ROBERT
          Sardonicus... don't do it... I
          beg of you!

                    SARDONICUS
          Ah, you beg. Just as I begged,
          above in my chambers. Do you

sat

264   CONTINUED: 264

                        SARDONICUS (cont'd)
                recall? I begged you to test
                the new treatment on me... and
                you refused.
                        (over his shoulder)
                Krull! You may begin!

265   TWO SHOT KRULL MAUDE   265

                        KRULL
                    (to the o.s.
                     Sardonicus)
                Master...

                        SARDONICUS' VOICE
                Yes, yes?

                        KRULL
                I have done many things for
                you... things out of nightmares...
                but her face...

266   GROUP SHOT MAUDE KRULL SARDONICUS   266
        Sardonicus enters the picture.

                        SARDONICUS
                What about her face, Krull?

                        KRULL
                It is so beautiful... are you
                quite certain...

                        SARDONICUS
                Yes, I am quite certain. Don't
                tell me, Krull, that you **object**?

                        KRULL
                    (confused)
                I... I only meant...

                        SARDONICUS
                Because you **know** what happens
                to people who raise objections
                to my acts... and what happened
                to **you** that single time you
                questioned my authority, many
                years ago... or have you for-
                gotten, Krull?

267   CLOSEUP KRULL   267
        Recalling, he draws one hand over his dead eye.

267 CONTINUED: 267

                    KRULL
              (low-pitched, with
               smouldering hatred)
         I have not forgotten.

268 GROUP SHOT SARDONICUS KRULL MAUDE   268
                    SARDONICUS
         Then begin!

269 CLOSE SHOT ROBERT   269
     on rack.

                    ROBERT
         Don't do it, Baron! Don't de-
         stroy her face!

270 TWO SHOT KRULL MAUDE   270
     Krull produces a gleaming surgical knife. He turns to Maude.

271 MAUDE'S POV KRULL   271
     knife in hand, approaches camera.

272 CLOSEUP MAUDE   272
     The knife approaches slowly... her eyes are fixed upon it in
     terror... then the cold metal actually touches her cheek.
     She screams.

273 CLOSEUP ROBERT   273

                    ROBERT
         Stop it! Stop it, Sardonicus!
         I'll do whatever you say!

274 CLOSEUP MAUDE   274
     Knife is removed from her face. It has not cut her.

275 GROUP SHOT ALL FOUR   275
     Maude is seized by hysterical weeping. Krull puts away the
     knife.

                    SARDONICUS
              (to Krull)
         Release the Baroness. And then
         release our honored guest here.

276   CLOSEUP   SARDONICUS   276

                         SARDONICUS
                    (looking down in
                      Robert's direction)
                You have made a wise decision,
                Sir Robert.

                                                         DISSOLVE TO:

sgb

90

INT. ROBERT'S ROOM - DAY

277 MEDIUM LONG SHOT ROBERT MAUDE   277
He at desk, writing a letter. Maude is sitting nearby.

                    MAUDE
        Robert...

                    ROBERT
            (preoccupied)
        Yes?...

                    MAUDE
        Can you really cure him?

                    ROBERT
        I do not know. It is a danger-
        ous, untried treatment. And I
        will require equipment and
        materia medica from far-off
        places...

278 MAP
A map of the world, circa late 1800's. CAMERA PANS   278
from Bohemia to South America, and over the PAN is SUPERIM-
POSED:

EXT. SOUTH AMERICAN JUNGLE (STOCK) - DAY

279 MEDIUM LONG SHOT SOUTH AMERICAN NATIVE   279
chopping off pieces of a tropical vine or "climber" with
a machete.

                                              DISSOLVE TO:

EXT. KINGS COLLEGE HOSPITAL LONDON (STOCK) - DAY

280 LONG SHOT (SAME AS SCENE 9)   280

                                              DISSOLVE TO:

INT. LABORATORY OF HOSPITAL - DAY

281 CLOSE SHOT WAINWRIGHT HEAD NURSE   281
Wainwright, Robert's letter in his hand, is supervising the
packing of equipment. Head Nurse is placing retorts, demi-

sgb

281 CONTINUED: 281

johns, test tubes, etc., in excelsior-packed crates.
Wainwright picks up the hypodermic we saw previously.

INSERT: THE HYPODERMIC IN WAINWRIGHT'S
         HAND
         He begins to swath it in layers
         of tissue paper.

                                                              DISSOLVE TO:

EXT. DESERTED ROAD IN GORSLAVA - DAY

282 MEDIUM LONG SHOT KRULL DOG   282
     Krull is coaxing a mongrel dog into a wooden crate, using a
     piece of meat as bait. The dog enters the crate, Krull
     quickly nails it shut, then he lifts the crate. CAMERA
     FOLLOWS him as he carries it to a nearby donkey-drawn cart
     where he places it among three or four other crates also
     containing dogs. He then climbs upon the cart and drives it
     off.

                                                              DISSOLVE TO:

INT. ROBERT'S ROOM - NIGHT

283 PANNING SHOT   283
     We hear several whining dogs. CAMERA PANS past a long lab
     bench bearing an impressive series of retorts, demijohns,
     test tubes, distilling apparatus, Bunsen burners, bottles.
     Liquids of various colors bubble. Some retorts give off
     festoons of steam. Here and there we see sprigs of the
     tropical plant, and dogs in crates. Finally... CAMERA COMES
     to REST ON:

284 ROBERT WITH KRULL IN B.G.   284
     Robert, clad in a white smock, is pouring a clear liquid from
     one test tube into another. Then he lays down one test tube,
     picks up the hypodermic needle, and draws off a syringeful
     of the liquid into the hypo.

sgb

285   MEDIUM CLOSEUP   ROBERT   285
      Needle in hand, he approaches the camera, as we hear o.s.,
      whimpering of a dog.

INT. CORRIDOR OUTSIDE ROBERT'S ROOM - NIGHT

286   SARDONICUS   286
      appears, just as the door to Robert's room opens. Krull
      emerges from the room, dragging an inert dog. Krull leaves
      the scene as Sardonicus -- who has reacted dubiously to this
      sight -- enters the room.

INT. ROBERT'S ROOM

287   ROBERT   WITH SARDONICUS ENTERING   287

                    ROBERT
          I have asked not to be disturbed.

                    SARDONICUS
          Are you making progress?

                    ROBERT
          Perhaps.

                    SARDONICUS
          I saw Krull.. and a dog.

                    ROBERT
          You will see many such dogs
          before I am through.

                    SARDONICUS
          Doctor! Are you preparing a
          cure -- or a poison?!

                    ROBERT
          Sometimes, they are one and the
          same thing.

                    SARDONICUS
          I warn you --

                    ROBERT
          Your warnings have ceased to
          frighten me, Baron.

                    SARDONICUS
          I demand an explanation!...

                    ROBERT
          Very well.

sgb

287   CONTINUED: 287

                    ROBERT (cont'd)
              (picks up a sprig
               of the plant)
          This tropical plant is known
          as Strychnos toxifera.

INSERT: STRYCHNOS TOXIFERA
          in Robert's hand.

288   TWO SHOT   ROBERT   SARDONICUS   288
      Favoring Robert.

                    ROBERT
          Centuries ago, the explorer
          Magellan wrote of a substance
          used on darts by the savages
          of South America. It killed
          instantly, dropping large animals
          in their tracks. The poison was
          extracted from this plant.

                    SARDONICUS
              (infuriated)
          And this is your so-called treat-
          ment???

                    ROBERT
              (ignoring him)
          There are many varieties of
          poisons. Some kill by corrosive
          action. But this -- this kills
          by bringing about a total relaxation
          of the muscles...particularly the
          muscles of the lungs and heart.
          And when they stop, life stops.
          However --

                    SARDONICUS
          Yes?

                    ROBERT
          Of recent months, I have asked my-
          self if a dilution of this deadly
          poison might not beneficially
          slacken the rigidly tensed muscles
          of paralyzed patients. It was only
          a theory, and a flimsy one at that
          ... much too dangerous to test on
          a human being.

sgb

288	CONTINUED:	288

                      SARDONICUS
    I see...

                      ROBERT
    I'm afraid a long program of
    research lies ahead of me... I
    would not want to fail.

                      SARDONICUS
    That is correct, Sir Robert.

289   CLOSEUP SARDONICUS   289

                      SARDONICUS
    See to it that you succeed!

                                          DISSOLVE TO:

hec-8610

INT. THE SALON - NIGHT

290 LONG SHOT   MAUDE   ROBERT 290
Maude in foreground at the spinet, playing something serene
and stately, perhaps the "Moonlight Sonata" of Beethoven.
Robert, in background, is relaxing in a chair, smoking his
pipe. This scene should be played for quietude and calm,
contrasting with the previous shocking events. For a
few moments there is no conversation, only music. Then
over the music Maude speaks.

              MAUDE
    I love this music...

             ROBERT
    It's exquisite -- but sad.

              MAUDE
    Yes. But there is strength
    under the sadness.

She plays for a moment more, and brings the piece to a soft
close.

291 MEDIUM CLOSE SHOT 291

              ROBERT
    That was very beautiful, Maude.
        (he rises and comes
         forward)
    You and your music are the only
    beautiful things in this place.

Now he sits next to her on the spinet bench.

              MAUDE
       (turning to him;
        softly)
    Robert...

Her face is flooded with tenderness and yielding. Slowly,
their lips meet in a gentle kiss. Then, embarrassed, they
turn away from each other.

              ROBERT
    Maude...I have never asked you...
    why --

              MAUDE
    Why did I marry him?

              ROBERT
    Yes.

291   CONTINUED: 291

>   MAUDE
>   It is not a pretty story. My
>   father had arranged the marriage
>   through letters...without having
>   met the Baron face to face...
>   and then, as you know, we sailed
>   for the Continent to seal the
>   agreement.
>
>   ROBERT
>   But surely, after meeting this
>   brute --
>
>   MAUDE
>   Oh yes...even my father, who
>   worshipped money, changed his
>   mind upon meeting the Baron.
>   But my father had gambled heavily,
>   and was sunken in debt...he had
>   even misused certain funds en-
>   trusted to him...and the Baron
>   offered him both a reward and a
>   threat.
>
>   ROBERT
>   (bitterly)
>   The Baron is fond of threats.
>
>   MAUDE
>   He offered to pay my father's
>   debts...and he also threatened
>   to expose him as an embezzler.
>
>   ROBERT
>   And so your father forced you
>   into this unsavory alliance?
>
>   MAUDE
>   No...the choice was mine. I did
>   it to save him.
>
>   ROBERT
>   (taking her hand)
>   My dear...

292   LONG SHOT OF SALON   292
      showing door. Maude and Robert seated at spinet. Sardonicus
      enters.

>   SARDONICUS
>   (seeing them; sarcastically)
>   Ah, what a charming tableau.
>   Sir Robert --

293   GROUP SHOT OF THREE   293

                    ROBERT
              (rising)
        Yes?

                    SARDONICUS
        Krull informs me that today a
        dog seemed to survive your in-
        jection.

                    ROBERT
        Krull is a reliable informant.

                    SARDONICUS
        Then the extract of the poisonous
        plant has been made safe?

                    ROBERT
        Apparantly. But I wish a few
        more days to --

                    SARDONICUS
        A few more days! Why? If the
        dog --

                    ROBERT
        Men are not dogs, Baron. I
        must be certain.

                    SARDONICUS
        I am certain enough for both of
        us. Doctor, I insist you per-
        form the treatment upon me tonight.

                    ROBERT
        But the risk is too great, Baron!

     Sardonicus produces the key ring and detaches one key. He
     hands it to Maude.

                    SARDONICUS
        Take this, madam.

INSERT: THE KEY
        passing from Sardonicus' hand to Maude's.

294   TWO SHOT SARDONICUS MAUDE   294

                    MAUDE
        But why?

                    SARDONICUS
        The room upstairs. Open it.

hec-8610

294 CONTINUED: 294

>   MAUDE
>   But you allow no one to open
>   that door except yourself...
>
>   SARDONICUS
>   Tonight I make an exception.
>   There is someone in that room...
>
>   MAUDE
>   Someone? There? Who?
>
>   SARDONICUS
>   A good and almost saintly man
>   who may be able to convince Sir
>   Robert he should perform the
>   treatment. Will you go? We
>   will follow.

295 GROUP SHOT 295
Maude looks at Robert; Robert is indecisive, finally nods affirmatively.

>   MAUDE
>   (to Sardonicus)
>   Very well.

296 LONG SHOT SARDONICUS ROBERT MAUDE 296
Maude leaves the room, and the two men follow her.

INT. HALLWAY - NIGHT

297 TRAVELING SHOT GROUP 297
CAMERA FOLLOWS them as they climb the stairs, walking past the empty picture frames. They reach the top of the stairs.

298 GROUP SHOT PADLOCKED DOOR (as in Scene 92) 298
Maude and the two men enter the picture. She inserts the key into the huge padlock, then turns questioningly to Sardonicus.

>   SARDONICUS
>   (graciously)
>   After you, madam -- do not be
>   afraid.

INT. ROOM ON OTHER SIDE OF DOOR - NIGHT

299 Utter darkness. Slowly, a crack of light appears as 299

hec-8610

299   CONTINUED: 299

        the door creakingly opens. We see Maude enter.

300   CLOSEUP MAUDE   300
        in semi-darkness. She glances about fearfully. Over this,
        we hear the door suddenly slam shut. Maude gasps.

301   Now the screen is completely black. We hear the floor-   301
        boards creak as Maude walks. Suddenly we hear her stop.
        Silence, then...

                        MAUDE'S VOICE
                Who is there?
                    (a pause)
                Someone is in here...I feel it...
                Krull, is it you?
                    (a pause)
                Anna? Is it Anna?...
                    (suddenly)
                Someone is in here!
                    (a pause)
                Why do you just stand there?
                Who are you?

302   A sudden sharp clink of metal, and a shaft of light   302
        falls upon:

303   EXTREME CLOSEUP DEAD FATHER'S FACE   303
        In the sudden shaft of light, we see the now dessicated,
        leathery face of Sardonicus' dead father. The hideous ex-
        pression is the same as we saw it in the grave, but the
        sight is now even more horrible, since the man has been dead
        for years. Over this, Maude's hysterical screams rise higher
        and higher.

INT. CORRIDOR OUTSIDE DOOR - NIGHT

304   SARDONICUS ROBERT   304
        Sardonicus' hand is on a "Judas window" of the door, which
        he has obviously just opened to admit the shaft of light.
        Maude's o.s. screams pierce our eardrums.

                        ROBERT
                What is happening to her? What
                have you --

        The scream stops.

hec-8610

304   CONTINUED: 304

                    ROBERT
            Why has she stopped?...Who is
            in there with her?

                    SARDONICUS
            Shall we see?

He opens the door wide, and the two men enter.

INT. ROOM - NIGHT

305   SARDONICUS ROBERT MAUDE   305
        Inside the room light from the open door streams in. Maude
        has fainted and lies on the floor. Robert bends over her.

                    SARDONICUS
            Poor lady. Perhaps it was a
            shock to meet him for the first
            time.

                    ROBERT
            Meet who?

                    SARDONICUS
            Why...her father-in-law!

306   CLOSE SHOT DEAD FATHER FULL FIGURE   306
        The corpse stands upright in a kind of open mummy case.
        CAMERA MOVES IN slowly to a:

307   CLOSEUP FACE   307
        Over this --

                    SARDONICUS' VOICE
            He is with me always...my reminder
            of mortality and human greed...
            My Nemesis...my demon...my _father_,
            whose grave I defiled!

308   GROUP SHOT ROBERT SARDONICUS MAUDE   308
        She is unconscious on floor. Robert rises and seizes
        Sardonicus' lapels.

                    ROBERT
                    (seething)
            Damn you, Sardonicus! Damn you
            to eternal hell! There is no
            decency in you...no human feeling!

hec-8610

308   CONTINUED: 308

                        SARDONICUS
              As always, Sir Robert, you speak
              with unwavering accuracy. Life
              has erased all decency and human
              feeling from my heart...and it
              is you who must restore it...
              tonight in your laboratory.

                        ROBERT
              If I refuse?

                        SARDONICUS
              Then Maude remains here. All
              night. With him.

309   EXTREME CLOSEUP   DEAD FATHER'S FACE   309

310   GROUP SHOT   310

                        ROBERT
                      (reluctantly)
              Very well. Tonight.
                      (with private
                       meaning)
              But not in my laboratory...

                                                            DISSOLVE TO:

INT. ROBERT'S ROOM - NIGHT

311   CLOSEUP   BUBBLING RETORT   311
        CAMERA PULLS AWAY and we watch a small amount of diamond-
        clear fluid travel from the retort through a length of glass
        distilling pipe and then fall, drop by drop, into a waiting
        test tube. The test tube is half full. Robert's hand
        enters the picture and picks up the test tube.

312   PERSPECTIVE SHOT   ROBERT'S FACE   312
        large in foreground as he holds the test tube up to the
        light and scrutinizes it. In background, Maude, Sardonicus
        and Krull stand by. A small table bears the hypodermic,
        cotton, etc. Robert reaches for the hypo.

INSERT: HYPODERMIC ON TABLE.
        Robert's hand picks it up.

313 CLOSE SHOT ROBERT   313
He inserts the needle into the test tube and draws off a
syringeful of the fluid.

                    SARDONICUS (O.S.)
              What is that strange instrument?

                    ROBERT
                (intent on what he
                is doing)
              A new invention, called a hypo-
              dermic needle. The South American
              natives, as I mentioned before,
              use the Strychnos toxifera extract
              to poison their darts. You might
              say this instrument...is my dart.

314 GROUP SHOT ROBERT SARDONICUS MAUDE KRULL   314

                    ROBERT
                (continuing)
              I must warn you again, Baron.
              This distillment has never been
              used on a human subject. It may
              kill you. I urge you for the
              last time -- do not insist upon
              its use.

                    SARDONICUS
              You seek to frighten me, Doctor...
              to plant distrust in my heart.

                    ROBERT
              No. But -- theoretically
              speaking -- what is to prevent
              me from injecting the undiluted
              poison into your blood and
              killing you here and now?

                    SARDONICUS
                (laughs; then)
              Three things. First, your
              silly code of ethics as an
              English knight. Second, the
              sanctimonious oath of your pro-
              fession. And third --

                    ROBERT
              Yes?

                    SARDONICUS
              Third -- the knowledge that, if
              I die, Krull has orders to put
              both you and my wife to the slowest

hec-8610

314   CONTINUED: 314

             SARDONICUS (Cont'd)
         and most hideous of deaths in
         the torture chamber below!

315   CLOSEUP KRULL 315
      nodding.

316   TWO SHOT SARDONICUS ROBERT 316

             ROBERT
         I accept your terms, Baron.
         And now please come with me.

      Robert turns to go.

             SARDONICUS
         Where are we going?

317   CLOSEUP ROBERT 317

             ROBERT
            (teasingly)
         Into the past, Baron...into
         your youth...

INT. PERSPECTIVE OF CORRIDOR - NIGHT

318   Showing Robert's room and the padlocked room. Robert 318
      appears, and walks over to the padlocked room. He is
      followed by Sardonicus, Krull and Maude.

INT. OTHER SIDE OF LOCKED DOOR - (Same as Scene 299)

319   Utter darkness. Slowly a crack of light appears as the 319
      door creakingly opens. We see Robert enter, followed by
      the others.

             ROBERT
            (to Krull)
         May we have some light, please?

      Krull lights a candle.

320   EXTREME CLOSEUP DEAD FATHER'S FACE 320

321   CLOSE SHOT MAUDE 321
      turning away from the sight.

hec-8610

322   TWO SHOT ROBERT SARDONICUS   322

                    ROBERT
          And now, Baron, if you will be
          good enough to sit in this chair.

He refers to a massive, carved chair of dark wood.
Sardonicus sits.

                    SARDONICUS
          I do not understand all this,
          Doctor...

                    ROBERT
          Then I will explain...while Krull
          ties you to the chair.

                    SARDONICUS
          What???

                    ROBERT
          For your own good. There may
          be...a violent reaction. Krull?

323   GROUP SHOT SARDONICUS ROBERT KRULL   323
Krull looks questioningly at Sardonicus. Sardonicus, with
a nod, gives him permission to tie him up. Krull produces
a rope and begins.

                    ROBERT
          There is a healing of the flesh...
          and there is a healing of the
          spirit. You have said, Baron,
          that shock was the factor that
          brought your face to its present
          condition. Do you remember?

                    SARDONICUS
          Yes...

                    ROBERT
          Then perhaps shock may be your
          cure. Shock combined with medical
          science.

                    SARDONICUS
          You speak in riddles...

                    ROBERT
               (holds up hypo)
          Medical science.

He points in the direction of the dead father.

hec-8610

324   EXTREME CLOSEUP   DEAD FATHER'S FACE   324

                    ROBERT'S VOICE
            Shock!

325   TWO SHOT   SARDONICUS   ROBERT   325
       Sardonicus is now securely tied to the chair.

                    SARDONICUS
                 (scoffingly)
            Do you think that dead thing
            can shock me now? I have lived
            with it for years.

                    ROBERT
            We shall see.

       Robert removes Sardonicus' mask.

326   CLOSEUP   SARDONICUS   326
       unmasked.

327   CLOSEUP   DEAD FATHER'S FACE   327

INSERT: HYPODERMIC
       in Robert's hand.

328   SILHOUETTE SHOT   328
       Against a bare wall, the flickering candle casts the gigantic,
       wavering shadows of Robert and Sardonicus in the chair. In
       silhouette, we see Robert bring the needle close to Sardonicus'
       face and plunge it into the flesh. Sardonicus stiffins
       visibly in the chair.

329   CLOSEUP   ROBERT   329

                    ROBERT
            And now...we will leave you
            alone...just as you were alone
            in that grave years ago.

330   GROUP SHOT   ALL FOUR   330
       Robert, Krull and Maude move toward the door.

                    SARDONICUS
            How long?

                    ROBERT
            As long as is necessary.

hec-8610

330 CONTINUED: 330

Robert, Krull and Maude leave the room. Just as the door is about to click shut,

331 CLOSEUP SARDONICUS 331
unmasked. Over this, the loud o.s. slam of the door.

INSERT: CANDLE BLOWING OUT
and leaving the screen in total darkness.

BACK TO SCENE 331:

There is a pregnant silence for a few seconds. Then we hear Sardonicus' voice.

> SARDONICUS' VOICE (O.S.)
> No...not like this...not like this...
> not in the dark...

INT. CORRIDOR - NIGHT

332 ROBERT MAUDE KRULL 332
listening at the door, they hear Sardonicus' screams.

> SARDONICUS' VOICE (O.S.)
> Not...in...the...dark!

Sardonicus' screams rise wordlessly, higher and higher.

> KRULL
> (to Robert)
> Let him out! Let him out!

He reaches for the doorknob.

> ROBERT
> No! Would you mar all my work?

> KRULL
> But he is suffering!
> (a sudden thought)
> That needle...you poisoned him!
> You are killing him!

Krull moves menacingly toward Robert, but now Robert suddenly throws open the little "Judas window."

INT. ROOM - NIGHT

333 EXTREME CLOSEUP DEAD FATHER'S FACE 333
in a sudden shaft of light.

hec-8610

107

INT. CORRIDOR - NIGHT

334   GROUP SHOT   ALL THREE   334
        O.S. there is a high, long, piercing shriek from Sardonicus --
        then total silence.

                        KRULL
                  (an awed whisper)
              He is dead...he is dead...

        Krull throws open the door and rushes in, followed by
        Robert and Maude.

INT. ROOM - NIGHT

335   GROUP SHOT   ALL FOUR   335
        Sardonicus is slumped in the chair, held up only by the
        ropes. He seems dead. We cannot see his face, for it is
        buried in his chest. Krull rushes to his side.

                        KRULL
              Master...

                        ROBERT
              Do not touch him!

                        MAUDE
              Robert, is he...?

336   CLOSEUP   SARDONICUS   336
        unmasked, his face buried in his chest. Slowly he raises
        his head and we see his face. He is cured. His face is
        now relaxed and serene. He is an older version of the hand-
        some youth we saw in the flashback. We think he is going
        to say something, but Robert stops him.

337   GROUP SHOT   337

                        ROBERT
              No, Baron. Do not try to speak
              yet. The muscles of your face
              are so relaxed it is beyond your
              power to move your lips -- it
              would destroy all our good work
              if you were to attempt it now.
              This condition will pass in a
              few minutes.

        Krull unties the ropes. Sardonicus leaps from the chair
        and dashes from the room. The others follow him.

hec-8610

INT. CORRIDOR - NIGHT

338   SARDONICUS   338
        approaches a section of wall. He begins to claw at its
        magnificently flocked wallcovering. The wallcovering comes
        away in strips and we begin to see that underneath it is a
        huge wall mirror.

339   GROUP SHOT   339
        Robert, Maude and Krull watching in fascination. O.S. the
        sounds of ripping continue.

340   SARDONICUS   340
        He has uncovered a large section of the mirror. The wall-
        covering lies in shreds about his feet. He looks at his
        handsome face with wonder and awe.

341   CLOSEUP   SARDONICUS' REFLECTION   341
        His fingers stroke his newly smooth cheeks. Whimpering
        sounds of joy issue from his closed mouth. Tears form in
        his eyes and run down his face. Then, he gains control of
        himself and some of the old arrogance and coldness returns.

342   PERSPECTIVE SHOT   342
        Sardonicus at mirror in background. Robert, Maude and Krull
        large in foreground, looking at him. Sardonicus turns to
        them suddenly and seems to regard them with mockery. Almost
        with a swagger, he leaves the mirror and walks up to them.

343   CLOSEUP   SARDONICUS   MAUDE   343
        Sardonicus regards her contemptuously. Maude, confused,
        turns away. Sardonicus emits a muffled, closemouthed laugh.

INT. SARDONICUS' ROOM

344   LONG SHOT   SARDONICUS   344
        enters, walking in the direction of the desk.

345   MEDIUM CLOSE SHOT   DESK   345
        Sardonicus sits down and begins to scribble a quick note.

346   NEW ANGLE   346
        Sardonicus at desk. Robert, Maude and Krull entering to
        watch him.

hec-8610

347 DESK   347
     Sardonicus finishes the note, signs it with a flourish, melts
     a stick of sealing wax at the candle and lets it drip upon
     the bottom of the note. Then he presses his massive signet
     ring into the wax.

INSERT: THE NOTE
     We see only the bottom of the note, with the single name
     "Sardonicus" in flowing bold script and the waxen seal
     with the familiar "S" insignia.

348 TWO SHOT   MAUDE   SARDONICUS   348
     Sardonicus walks up to her and hands her the paper.

349 CLOSEUP   MAUDE   349
     reading aloud.

                         MAUDE
                       (reading)
                 'By this document, and by the
                 power invested in me as a baronial
                 lord of this land, I do irrevocably
                 and forever annul my marriage with
                 one who was no wife to me and for
                 whom I now have neither need nor
                 use...Sardonicus.'

350 TWO SHOT   MAUDE   ROBERT   350
     Maude smiles at Robert, who places his arm about her
     shoulders.

351 DESK   351
     Sardonicus has been writing again. Finishing now, he does
     not affix a seal to this note but merely rises and walks over
     to Robert. CAMERA FOLLOWS him.

352 GROUP SHOT   352
     Robert takes the note and reads aloud.

                         ROBERT
                       (reading)
                 'You have fulfilled your part
                 of the bargain. Name your fee,
                 for I owe you much.'

     Robert crumples the note savagely and throws it to the floor.

hec-8610

352 CONTINUED: 352

                        ROBERT
            No, Baron. You owe me nothing.
            But I owe you much. In payment
            for forcing Maude into marriage...
            for terrorizing her...for threaten-
            ing to mutilate her...for your
            unfeeling cruelty and repacity...
            I owe you this!

Robert strikes Sardonicus. Sardonicus is thrown to the floor
by the blow. Krull moves in to wreak vengeance on Robert,
but Sardonicus waves him away.

353 NEW ANGLE   353
Sardonicus picks himself up off the floor and walks to the
fireplace, where he takes a large chunk of charcoal. With
this hand, he crosses to a plain wall and, with broad, sweep-
ing, savage strokes, writes a single huge word:

                        B E G O N E

Robert and Maude leave the room.

                                                        FADE OUT.

FADE IN:

EXT. MOUNTAIN ROAD (STOCK) - NIGHT

354   HORSEDRAWN COACH
      Similar to Scene 55, but the coach is traveling in the
      opposite direction.

355   TOP OF COACH ROBERT
      He is driving.

INT. COACH - NIGHT

356   MAUDE ANNA
      They are seated next to each other.

                    ANNA
          Oh, I'm so happy you let me come
          with you, Baroness!

                    MAUDE
          I couldn't let you stay there,
          Anna...and you must not call me
          Baroness any more, or I shall be
          very angry!

                                              DISSOLVE TO:

INT. CORNER OF RAILROAD STATION WAITING ROOM - NIGHT (Same as Sc 43)

357   ROBERT MAUDE ANNA STATIONMASTER
      Their bags stand on the floor.

                    STATIONMASTER
                    (to Robert)
          You are in luck, sir. The last
          train leaves in less than an hour.
          Please sit down, ladies.

      A crash of the station door flying open.

358   MEDIUM LONG SHOT ROBERT KRULL (Same angle as Sc.52)
      Robert, in foreground, is turned away from us to look at
      Krull standing in the doorway. Krull is obviously disturbed.

                    KRULL
                    (disturbed)
          Sir Robert --

358   CONTINUED: 358

                    ROBERT
            I thought we had seen the last
            of you.

    Krull walks quickly into the foreground until he is
    face to face with Robert.

                    KRULL
            You must return, Sir Robert!
            He needs you!

                    ROBERT
            Impossible. We would miss the
            train.

                    KRULL
            But you don't understand -- <u>he
            cannot open his mouth!</u>

359   REVERSE POV ROBERT KRULL   359
       Others in the background.

                    ROBERT
            Nonsense!

                    KRULL
            It is true! He cannot speak --
            he cannot eat or drink! I am a
            strong man - with my own hands I
            tried to pry his jaws apart -
            but I could not! He will starve,
            Sir Robert! He will die - horribly!

                    ROBERT
            He will not die. You must simply
            tell him that he can open his
            mouth, himself.

                    KRULL
            But you are his healer!

                    ROBERT
            I never healed him. The fluid
            I injected into his face was
            nothing more than distilled
            water!

rs

360   CLOSEUP   KRULL   360

                    KRULL
              Water! But the tropical plant --
              and the experiments -- and the
              dogs --!

361   CLOSEUP   ROBERT   361

                    ROBERT
              An elaborate show, nothing more.
              And the dogs did not die - they
              were merely drugged. I had to
              make the Baron think I was prepar-
              ing a new and powerful medication.

                    KRULL'S VOICE
              I still do not understand --

                    ROBERT
              Go to him, Krull. Remind him of
              something he said to me...that
              his affliction came not from God
              above nor the Fiend below, but
              from within his own heart, his
              own brain, his own soul. His cure
              came from within, too. I did not
              help him, nor can I help him now.

                    KRULL'S VOICE
              But he needs --

                    ROBERT
              All he needs is the knowledge that
              he was his own healer.
                    (with emphasis)
              Without that knowledge, he is
              doomed.

362   TWO SHOT ROBERT KRULL   362

                    KRULL
              Yes...yes...I see now --

                    ROBERT
              Go at once and tell him.

                    KRULL
              Yes...I will --

        Krull turns and leaves the scene.

363   NEW ANGLE TWO SHOT ROBERT MAUDE   363
       They are looking after the departing o.s. Krull. We hear
       the station door open and close as Krull leaves.

                           MAUDE
                      (turning to Robert)
                 But Robert...is that true? Was
                 your medication really nothing
                 more than water?

                           ROBERT
                 Nothing more. You see, I knew
                 that after all the best messaging
                 techniques of the world's foremost
                 physicians had failed, I would
                 have to work not on the Baron's
                 physical self, but on his mental
                 self.

                           MAUDE
                 Then the South American plant was
                 not acutally poisonous?

                           ROBERT
                 Oh, yes. Very poisonous. Too
                 poisonous to use. Some day, per-
                 haps, its powers may be harnessed
                 for the good of mankind, but that day
                 is not yet. And so I did not use
                 an extract of the plant at all.

                           MAUDE
                 Only water --

                           ROBERT
                 Only water -- and his own mind.

                                              DISSOLVE TO:

INT. DINING-ROOM OF CASTLE - NIGHT

364   CLOSEUP SARDONICUS   364
       unmasked. Handsome, but tormented, he is clawing at his
       face in a vain effort to pry open his mouth. He utters
       pitiful whimpering noises. O.S., we hear a door open and
       close. Sardonicus turns at the sound.

365   TWO SHOT SARDONICUS KRULL   365
       entering. Sardonicus mutely pantomimes a despairing
       question. Krull says nothing.

366 CLOSEUP   KRULL   366
Fleetingly, his face hardens in hatred as he draws a hand over his dead eye, repeating the gesture we saw in Scene 267. But this is only a flash, and his face quickly returns to its usual subservient cast.

367 TWO SHOT   SARDONICUS   KRULL   367
Sardonicus walks up to Krull and seizes the lapels of his coat, imploringly.

> KRULL
> (obsequiously)
> I am very sorry, master...but I missed them. The train has already left --

Crushed, Sardonicus stumbles away and sinks into a chair at the head of the long dining table.

368 CLOSEUP   SARDONICUS   368
at table. His head is in his hands. Now we hear the o.s. sound of wine being poured. Sardonicus looks up, tortured by the sound.   CAMERA PULLS AWAY to:

369 LONG SHOT   DINING TABLE   369
In sharp perspective, we see the long dining table, heavy with a dazzling variety of food and drink..meat..cheeses..fruit..bread..wine... In the background, seated at the head of the table, is Sardonicus, who regards with horror the sight of Krull, who is seated at the other end of the table, (near us, in foreground), calmly eating and drinking.

Sardonicus rises. He begins to wend his way toward the camera, picking up items of food from the table as he walks. He tries to cram them into his mouth, but each time he fails and throws the food to the floor in impotent rage. He tries to drink a goblet of wine, but it floods his face and drips upon his neck, and shirt. He flings away the goblet and it falls with a clang. By the time he has reached the foreground he is a mass of food and wine stains.

370 NEW ANGLE   LONG SHOT   DINING ROOM   370
We shoot down at a bird's-eye-view of the dining room. Sardonicus, a broken, defeated giant, stumbles away and leans against a wall with his head upturned, clawing at his mouth, in despair. Krull, unconcernedly, continues to eat a hearty meal.

rs

116

EXT. GATE OF CASTLE - NIGHT

371   CLOSEUP "S" OF GATE   371
      with castle in background (same as Scene 59). Out of this
      "S" looms the end title.

          END TITLE: THE END

                                    FADE OUT.

THE END

Mr. Sardonicus Production History

by Tom Weaver

He's one of the great "Horatio Alger figures" in horror film history: Marek Toleslawski. A Central European peasant, born with bleak prospects in Gorslava, circa 1830. On the one-year anniversary of the death of his mother Maria, his father Henryk died, and Marek inherited the family farm. He worked hard, but every time he sold his produce in the city, all moneys went toward the purchase of more feed and seed grain. This led to quarrels between Marek and his wife Elenka, who wanted more from life than the meager existence Marek could eke out for them.

When the gods at last smiled upon Marek, it was a cruel "skeleton smile": He suddenly came into wealth, and bought himself the title of baron.

And, legend has it, he became one of Gorslava's most feared men — with a new face more dreadful than his deeds.

This rags-to-wretched tale is, of course, fiction, the plot of a movie. But the story of the origin of the *character* of Marek, aka Mr. Sardonicus, is also interesting. He was born in the Chicago office of the young executive editor of *Playboy* magazine.

> It was mainly due to Ray Russell that [*Playboy*] became one of the finest showcases for imaginative fiction (principally SF and horror) during the 1950s and 1960s....
>
> — Jack Adrian in the English newspaper *The Independent*, 1999

A product of Chicago, Ray Robert Russell was the son of William and Margaret Russell. When Ray was born in 1924, his dad was working for the Chicago Transit Authority as a conductor on the "L" (elevated trains), a job he held from 1920 until 1961. Margaret was always a homemaker, or "Happy Housewife," as she proudly entered her occupation on their income tax return.

A kissing cousin to Baron Sardonicus (as if either one could kiss): Conrad Veidt's Gwynplaine in the 1928 silent The Man Who Laughs. *Makeup pro Michael F. Blake's considered opinion is that Veidt wore "a fake set of teeth over his own teeth, and just smiled a broad smile which was accentuated with a liner color around the lips. He may or may not have had a device that held the corners of his mouth in that grin."*

Right from boyhood, Ray was an avid moviegoer and saw some of the classic horror films on their original release. According to his son Marc Russell, one of this book's co-authors:

> In 1932, his parents took him to see *Frankenstein* [1931] at the Forest Theater in Forest Park, a Chicago suburb where they briefly lived. He sat through the first 20 minutes

calmly, but when the Monster's hand started to move, he simply got up and briskly walked out! (Give him a break, he was only seven.) He finally saw the entire film several years later, when it had that very successful re-release on a double bill with the 1931 *Dracula*.

In those days, Dad and his parents almost never attended movies at the big downtown Chicago theaters, but waited until they came to the nearby neighborhood theaters, of which there were several. This was during the Depression, and the neighborhood theaters were cheaper. But there was at least one exception: *King Kong* [1933]. Dad's mother took him to see it at a downtown theater in its original release. Later that year, when it showed up at the nearby Crawford, he went to see it alone and sat through it twice.

Ray also loved the science fiction serials *Flash Gordon* (1936) and *Flash Gordon's Trip to Mars* (1938) with Buster Crabbe and, still a kid, wrote short stories that were an homage to them. After evil Dr. Shard is killed at the end of Russell's "Captain Clark of the Space Patrol – On the Trail of Dr. Shard," Clark says, "A fitting end for a heartless rat."[1]

Russell lived in the Windy City for the first half of his adult life, save for the WWII years when he served in the South Pacific theater of war. In September 1950, he married Ada Sepanski, and in 1951 Baby made three ("Baby" being Marc Russell). Ray worked at an assortment of jobs to pay the bills and support the family. Writing-wise, he received many rejection slips before he finally made his first sale.

About a year after that first sale, Russell became associate editor of a new magazine called *Playboy*. He got the job principally on the strength of stories submitted to the magazine – stories that had been repeatedly rejected by others. It isn't now known when he started at *Playboy* as for eight issues (starting with #1, December 1953), no editorial staff members, not even publisher-editor Hugh M. Hefner, were credited within. At last, in *Playboy* #9, August 1954, there was a masthead, with Russell listed as associate editor, right underneath "Hef." The September 1955 issue was his first as executive editor.

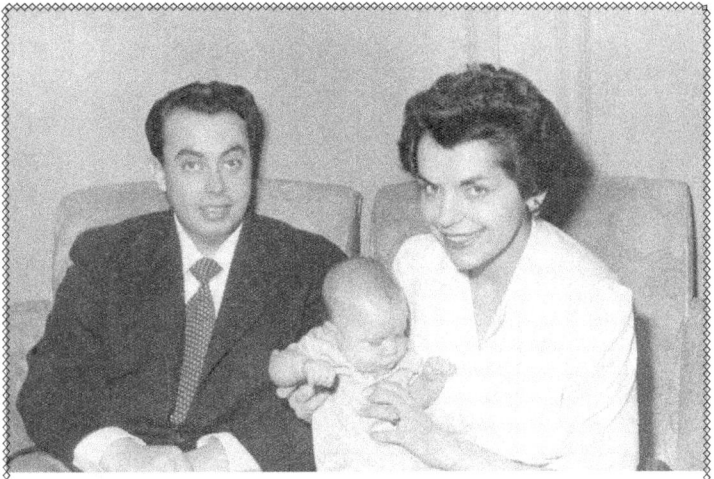

Ray Russell and wife Ada in January 1952 with their first present from the stork, son Marc. According to their daughter Amanda, Ada was a stage actress when she and Ray met: "She had received a B.A. degree from the University of Chicago and completed the acting program at the Kenneth Sawyer Goodman Memorial Theater, the city's oldest and largest non-profit theater. Dad was still a student at the Goodman, studying acting, with the goal of being a director. They didn't meet at the Goodman; they met in 1950 when one of the teachers organized a summer stock company in Seaside, Oregon. Actors and student actors carpooled across the country and met up in Seaside. According to Dad, Mom saw him in a small walk-on part in a production of Hamlet *and fell in love with him immediately, because he was so dynamic. Dad wrote a poem called 'Hamlet 1950' about the event."*

As mentioned above, Russell's time at *Playboy* was marked by the number of genre writers he published in its pages. "I suppose it was my early fondness for SF that made me receptive, as an editor, to story submissions from Arthur C. Clarke, Bob Sheckley, Avram Davidson, Dick Matheson, Bob Bloch, Chuck Beaumont and so many more," Russell told interviewer Roger Anker in the March 1987 *Starlog*. (He could also have name-dropped Ray Bradbury.) Another story bought by Russell for *Playboy*: George Langelaan's "The Fly,"

> **So You Want to Be a Writer**
>
> Ray Russell offers words of advice in the essay "The Devil Is a Tightwad," written in the late 1950s and never published until now. It starts on page 266.

Men who actually did *buy* Playboy *for its articles got a pretty good bang for their buck (actually just 60 cents) with the January 1961 issue, which included two previously unpublished works by Anton Chekhov, a story by Fritz Leiber, and Russell's novelette "Sardonicus." (Courtesy Jon Jashni)*

"after it had been turned down by the SF magazines. In fact, a rejection slip from [the magazine] *Fantasy and Science Fiction* fluttered out of the manuscript while I was reading it! Bad agenting. The story appeared in our June 1957 issue, and was immediately popular with our readers. Then, somebody at 20th Century-Fox read it in *Playboy*, and they made quite a successful movie out of it the following year."

After years of the Russells living in low-budget apartments, *Playboy*'s success enabled the family to start movin' on up – not to the East Side, à la the Jeffersons, but to Chicago's Near North Side. Beginning in early 1956, the Russells' new address was 1318 Astor Street, part of a fancy neighborhood known as the Gold Coast – a big step up for Russell, he of the working-class upbringing. 1318 Astor was a four-story building with one apartment per floor; the ground floor tenant was a Mrs. Hipple, mother of actor Hugh Hipple aka Hugh Marlowe (*The Day the World Stood Still*, *World Without End*, *Earth vs. the Flying Saucers*, etc.). Presumably Russell walked to and from work, as his Astor Street home was just blocks from *Playboy*'s office. In the back of the Russell apartment was a small room which he used as an office of sorts, but Marc and his sister Amanda (born in 1957 and another of this book's writers) agree that he probably did very little or none of his writing there. Instead, circa 1959, he rented a small office or tiny studio apartment on Cedar Street, about three blocks from home, and he did his work there, free from distractions. That is where "Sardonicus" would have been written.

Russell once said of the "architects" of *Playboy* magazine, "We were young men very much like our readers – educated, but not over-educated, hip, fond of money and material things like snazzy cars, plush apartments, and dressing well."

"Actually, Dad was never into snazzy cars," says Amanda Russell. "In fact, he never drove until we moved to California. But yes, in the '50s when he got the *Playboy* job, he was able for the first time to enjoy a prosperous lifestyle: dining out at fine restaurants, having suits tailor-made, bigger apartment in a good neighborhood, etc. Dad's life revolved around working at the magazine and spending time with his family and friends."

By the time Russell's "Sardonicus" appeared in the January 1961 *Playboy*, the process of turning it into a motion picture was already underway.

Here's Bill Castle, one of the great Hollywood "characters"! He was a wonder to work with, outrageously witty, and wise to what the public wanted. ...Castle's films don't date, they just become more fun as the years go by.

— Vincent Price's back-cover blurb for William Castle's autobiography *Step Right Up! I'm Gonna Scare the Pants Off America*

Monster Kids' favorite King of the Gimmicks, Hollywood's first interactive filmmaker, William Castle was just 29 in the summer of 1943 when, after several years as a bit player and dialogue coach, he made his directing debut via the aptly titled *The Chance of a Lifetime*, an entry in Columbia's low-level Boston Blackie mystery movie series.[2] And for the next 14 years, Castle charted a downhill course.

When "Sardonicus" crossed over into the paperback world, the cover featured a Richard Powers painting in which Sardonicus holds his mask out in front of his face. But in the tale published therein, the baron wears no mask.

"Sardonicus" has been translated into Japanese, German and Swedish. Guess which two are seen here.

At Columbia, he followed his Boston Blackie with Whistler and Crime Doctor movies that had their points of interest, although this may have been more due to their writers than their director. Columbia was a mini-major studio and so was Castle's next roost, Universal-International, where he made a handful of pictures that instantly dropped down the Memory Hole.

Then back to Columbia ... kinda: He ground out 17 cheapies for producer "Jungle" Sam Katzman at Columbia Sunset, the hole-in-the-wall studio where Columbia's B-picture units were kept stashed. Castle's next step down was into TV, shooting episodes of the Ziv series *Men of Annapolis* in three days each. If Hollywood was a circus troupe, Castle was fast approaching the level of the man who follows the elephants.

According to *Step Right Up!*, the turning point in his career came one thunder-and-lightning night when he convinced his wife Ellen to go to the movies with him. The attraction was the suspense-filled *Diabolique* (1955) and, despite the wicked weather, there was a line of hundreds of young people anxious to see a movie that "really scares the shit out of you," according to the boy ahead of them in line. Born in Castle that night was the desire to make movies that would scare the pants off America.

Is that really how it happened? Considering Castle's long record of infidelity to truth, how can we ever know?[3] The French-made *Diabolique* was a box office hit in America, but that was *long* before Castle's first chiller, *Macabre* (1958), was a twinkle in his eye. But perhaps he did stand in a *Diabolique* line in late 1955 or early 1956, and it took him a year or more to find the right story for *his* first foray into fright flicks. At last he found that story: Theo Durrant's 1950 novel *The Marble Forest*,[4] which he brought to the screen as *Macabre*.

To make a program of five feature films starting with *Macabre*, Castle and Robb White, a Navy veteran and *Men of Annapolis* scripter, formed a production company, Susina Associates, named for the Georgia plantation where White once lived. Their initial plans also included movie versions of White's recent novels *Jungle Fury* and *Up Periscope*.

Even before *Macabre* cameras rolled, Castle already had ideas about its distribution. From the July 3, 1957, *Variety*:

> [The Castle-White movies are] to be marketed via the old-type of film salesmanship ... when producers got out and sold their own product. "Showmanship today has gone down the drain," [Castle] said. In the belief, he added, that present methods are obsolete, he plans to take *Macabre*, following up with each successive picture, and go out on a "barnstorming tour" to personally sell the film. Feature will be set in selected smaller houses for anticipated longer runs. After these pre-releases, film may then be released generally through a regular distributor, he added....

From the collection of Ron Borst, a Macabre *Beneficiary Agreement, signed back in the day by Monster Kid Walter "Wes" Shank.*

Castle brought from New York William Prince and Jacqueline Scott to play *Macabre*'s top roles, a much-hated small-town doctor and his nurse, both searching for the doctor's young daughter who, a laughing telephone terrorist has hinted, has been abducted and buried alive. *Macabre* was shot on closed sets beginning on July 29, 1957.

Soon after the final day of principal photography, Castle and White were part of a group getting their first look at the finished film in a projection room. Castle saw what he had wrought ... and it was wrought-en. Well, perhaps not rotten, but he knew right away that *Macabre* did not have the blood-curdling quality he'd tried to achieve. An ingredient was missing and, again according to *Step Right Up!*, he realized what it was that night, while lying in

In 1952, Columbia gave director William Castle a one-picture-a-year contract starting with producer Sam Katzman's Serpent of the Nile. *Four and a half months later, Castle had already directed* three *Katzmans! Here's a pic of Castle and the boss sitting on their asps on the* Serpent of the Nile *set. (Courtesy John Antosiewicz)*

The poster for Castle's first horror picture proclaimed, "MACABRE MEANS HORROR!" Merriam-Webster may disagree but what does she know? Here's a behind-the-scenes photo of Castle on the funeral parlor set.

Castle told Variety *that he made* House on Haunted Hill *to try to capture the "untapped audience for classic ghost stories." Pictured: Castle and the terrifying Mrs. Slydes (Leona Anderson, sister of "Broncho Billy" Anderson).*

Visiting San Antonio in 1959 to promote The Tingler, *Castle gets the Skeleton Key to the City from a werewolf (Bob Burns) and Miss Shock (Kathy Burns).*

William Castle, at a New York City theater promoting 13 Ghosts *in 1960, poses with young fan Stephen Jochsberger, later the publisher of the fandom newsletter* Horrors. *(Courtesy John Antosiewicz)*

In Corpus Christi, Texas, an exhibitor showed Castle's Macabre *to radio, TV and newspaper people in an abandoned graveyard, to generate buzz, before the movie's Friday the 13th midnight showing at the Center Theatre. When an army of ticket buyers descended on the theater, another movie house two blocks away was opened to accommodate the overflow.* Boxoffice *magazine reported, "A police riot squad was sent out but was unable to organize the rush of teenagers from the Center to the Ritz." Business was brisk in theaters throughout the country as moviegoers risked their lives – in theory, anyway – to see this new attraction.*

bed: a publicity stunt. "I'm going to insure the entire world against death by fright during the showing of *Macabre*!" he ranted at his sleepy wife.

One phone call to Lloyd's of London later, his plan was in action – although the venerable English firm very conservatively and skeptically specified that the name "Lloyd's of London" could *not* be used in any paid advertising! Every moviegoer entering a theater to see *Macabre* was given a Beneficiary Agreement on which to write the name of the person who would receive $1000 if the moviegoer died of fright during the running of the movie. Castle and Lloyd's were certain that no one would expire from fright, but even with that confidence, the form specified that people with heart conditions or nervous conditions were ineligible. Castle dangled *Macabre* and his Lloyd's gimmick idea before distributors, without a nibble, until at last Allied Artists sensed their potential and made a deal. This despite the fact that four years earlier, Allied Artists' *The Maze did* scare a theater patron to death!⁵

Macabre got the reviews it deserved, *The Los Angeles Times* scoffing, "Well, you can throw away those Lloyd's of London policies – they don't cover death from boredom...." *The Hollywood Reporter*'s Jack Moffitt agreed: "I doubt if the film kills anyone who wouldn't have departed this vale of tears anyway...." Ronald Johnson of the *Toronto Globe & Mail*: "One attends this film only at one's own risk — of complete boredom. We rather suspect the only person ever frightened by it was producer William Castle when he sat through the first screening." (Johnson's review is priceless because, unknowingly, he did perfectly describe Castle's first reaction to the picture!) But *Macabre* drew the kinds of crowds that Castle craved — and, as promised, the director was present at many theaters to greet them.

Several months later, when *Variety* published its list of the most $uccessful movies of 1958, *Macabre* was the one Allied Artists release *on* it (albeit quite a ways down from the top). Also on the list for 1958, the year in which The Experts had forecast that the horror cycle would most certainly end: *The Fly*, *The Blob* and *Horror of Dracula*. The list ran on January 7, 1959, and a week later, January 14, the second Castle–Robb White production, *House on Haunted Hill* with Vincent Price, world-screamiered at the RKO Golden Gate in San Francisco.

Unlike the poky, depressing *Macabre*, *Haunted Hill* was a lapel-grabbing 75 minutes of goose pimples, jolts and campy fun.

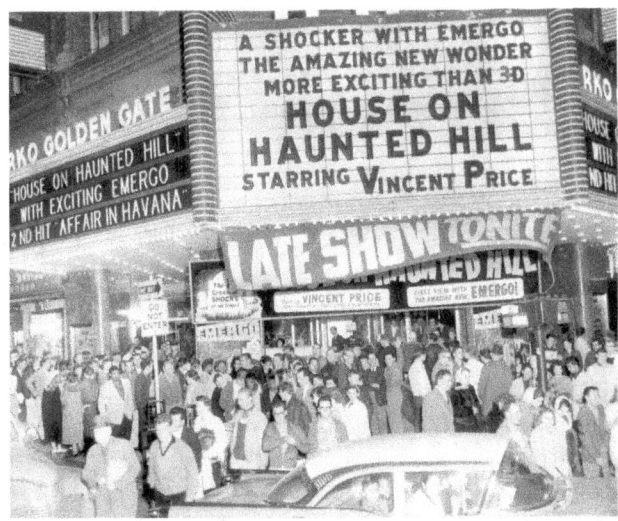

In San Francisco, a crowd of fun lovers enjoys the excitement of the House on Haunted Hill *premiere. William Castle told* Variety *that* Haunted Hill *was "the first ghost picture in many years. It's really scary and that's fine. It'll bring people in. What's wrong with that?"*

Gimmick-wise, the original plan for *Haunted Hill* was a repeat of *Macabre*'s Lloyd's of London "Death by Fright" stunt. But then a new and far more outrageous idea was hatched (and dubbed Emergo): At a key moment near the end of the movie, a box near the movie screen would open and a luminous prop skeleton would emerge(-o); it would travel out along a wire, bobbing over the heads of audience members, then retreat back to the box.⁶

The combination of *House on Haunted Hill*'s potent shocks and a party-crashing skeleton resulted in another top-grosser for Allied Artists, one of that company's *three* movies on *Variety*'s list that year (alongside *The Big Circus*, also with Vincent Price, and *Al Capone*).

Robb White:

The only thing I didn't like about *House on Haunted Hill* was that it made enough noise around town to attract Columbia Pictures, who, when I didn't want to be bought, swallowed us like a shark. ...Columbia offered us fabulous things. Bill was very impressed with Columbia: We had a corner office, we had a bar, we had two secretaries.... But it upgraded Bill, it gave him character. Years before, he had been fired from Columbia for some sort of dereliction of morals or something — he never talked to me about it.

Once the indie producers hung their shingle at Columbia, the first new Castle-White movie was *The*

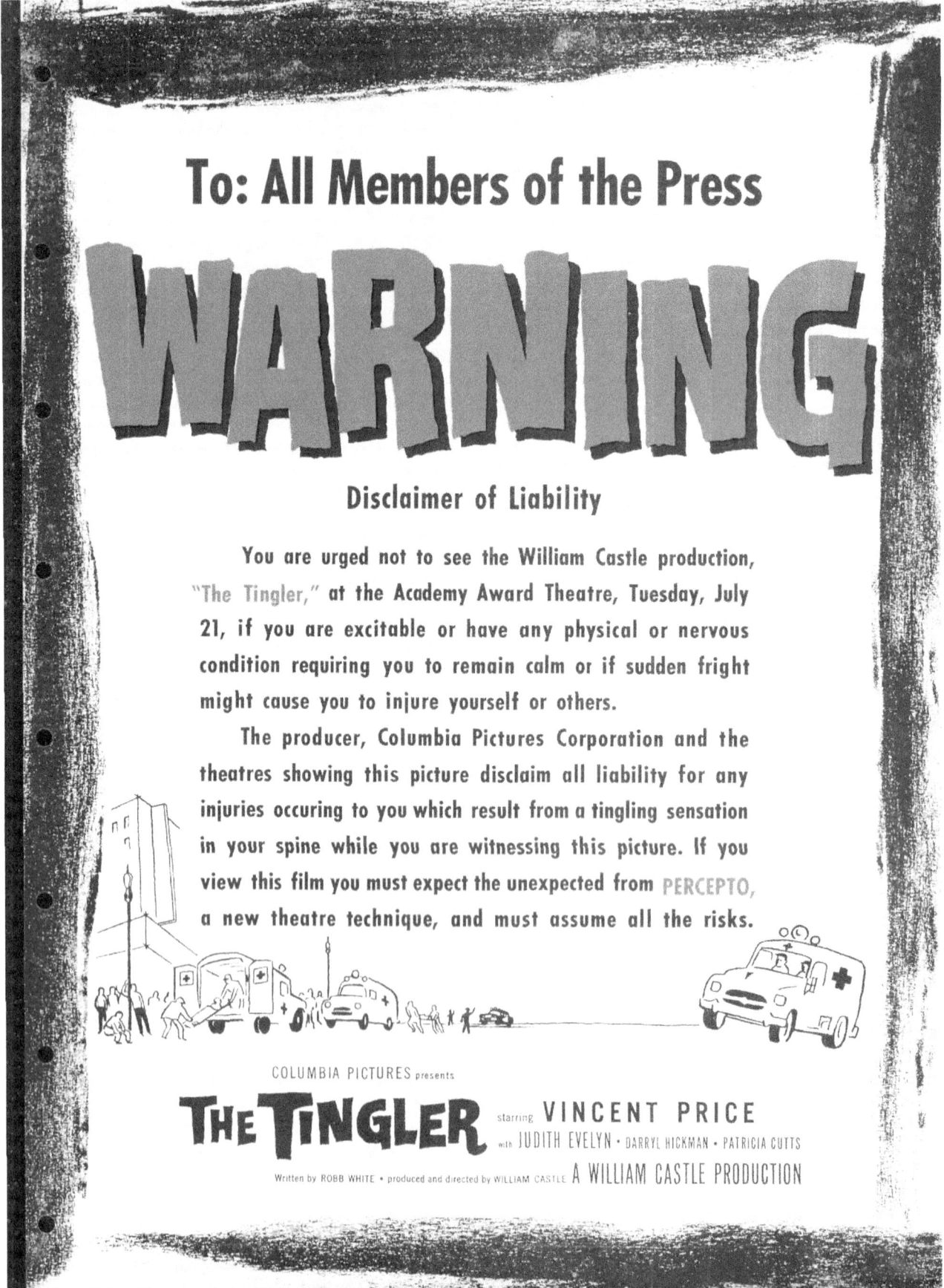

What self-respecting Cinemaville scribbler could back down from the challenge of a Tingler *press screening? A full-page ad from the July 13, 1959,* Variety.

Tingler, which began shooting in mid–May 1959. Another Vincent Price starrer, its gimmick (Percepto) involved battery-powered vibrator motors installed beneath some theater seats, giving audience members' tailbones "a strange tingling sensation." The fun fright flick was the first to feature Castle, addressing the audience in the pre-credits sequence. He told interviewer Bea Smith in 1961 that he appeared in this and other horror pics because he wanted to start "talking to the [audience], setting the mood of the film and get to be a part of them. It's all done tongue in cheek. What I'm really saying is: 'Hi. Welcome. Let's have some fun.'"

The Tingler had a midnight opening at Detroit's Broadway Capitol (now the Detroit Opera House), drawing a street-jamming mob of 5000 – plus some 100 policemen doing crowd control. Three thousand shudderbugs thronged the theater and took their seats (several hundred of them wired by Percepto developer Milt Rice) and screamed their way through the movie. It was still vibrating its way across the country in mid–January 1960 when filming commenced on Castle's *13 Ghosts*, where the gimmick was Illusion-O: Moviegoers were provided with Ghost-Viewers (cardboard eyeglasses, one transparent cellophane lens red and the other blue), and they had the option of watching the ghost scenes through the red lens and seeing the ghosts, or through the blue and eliminating them.

There is no god but Gimmick. And Bill Castle is his prophet.

—Castle, quoted in the *San Francisco Chronicle*

Castle wrote in *Step Right Up!* that he was in Hawaii with his wife and their daughters, sunning himself poolside at Honolulu's Kahala Hilton, when he read "Sardonicus" in *Playboy*. Castle may have read the story in Hawaii but it couldn't have been in *Playboy*, because *The Hollywood Reporter* announced on December 1, 1960, before the publication of the "Sardonicus" issue, that he had already acquired the film rights. So obviously Castle, and perhaps other producers, somehow got an advance peek. A rummage through 1960 trade papers shows just a single Hawaiian jaunt for Castle that year, an approximately two-week trip (beginning on May 27) to huddle with exhibitors about *13 Ghosts*' local openings. If Castle was correct about reading "Sardonicus" in Hawaii, and if his May trip was his one visit to Hawaii that year, then "Sardonicus" was on the moviemaker's radar nearly a full year before the start of production.[7]

As the story's Bohemian baron awaited his big movie break, Castle's next film was *Homicidal*, a thriller so indebted to Alfred Hitchcock's *Psycho* (1960) that it wouldn't be impossible for a casual fan to confuse the two.[8] *Homicidal* began production on November 1, 1960, with Castle doing a week of location filming in Ventura and Solvang. By this time, the Sultan of Selfsploitation had made *himself* so well-known, via his horror pictures, that Ventura kids haunted him for autographs. "I didn't have any idea people cared that much about who makes pictures," Castle declared with feigned modesty, as though he was not a card-holding Screen Actors Guild member, inescapable in his movies and their trailers, and even in person, in the theaters that *played* them! *Homicidal*'s gimmick was that, as the picture's high point of climactic horror loomed, the action stopped and a Castle voiceover advised audiences that anyone too frightened to stick it out now had their chance to leave the auditorium and get their money back.[9]

According to Robb White, the *Homicidal* plot was Castle's idea, and Castle worked on the script more than he (White) did. It wasn't until *Homicidal* was in production that White saw *Psycho* for the first time and was shocked to discover how much Castle had lifted from it. And with that, the Castle-White partnership quietly came to an end.[10]

As part of an international survey we would appreciate your answering this questionaire and returning it to us as soon as possible.

WILLIAM CASTLE PRODUCTIONS
1438 NORTH GOWER STREET
HOLLYWOOD 28, CALIFORNIA

HOLLYWOOD 2-3111

1. If a kind, sweet old lady backs her car into the side of your Cadillac, do you: (check one)

- Give her a hearty handshake?.. ☐
- Belt her right in the mouth?.... ☐
- Get drunk?............. ☐
- Kill her?............... ☐
- Call your insurance man?..... ☐

2. If your spouse (or other close friend) were unexpectedly to find you in a compromising situation, would you: (check one)

- Try to explain?.......... ☐
- Belt her (or him) right in the mouth?............. ☐
- Kill her (or him)?......... ☐
- Turn over a new leaf?...... ☐
- Proceed?............... ☐

3. If your boss calls you in on your birthday and says "Congratulations. You're fired!" would you: (check one)

- Treat it as a joke?......... ☐
- Belt him right in the mouth?... ☐
- Choke him?............. ☐
- Thank him?............. ☐
- Make a pass at his secretary?.. ☐

4. If the result of this test points to the possibility of your being potentially homicidal would you: (check one)

- Laugh?................ ☐
- Resent it?.............. ☐
- Kill the producer?......... ☐
- Go see "HOMICIDAL"?...... ☐
- Write a story about it?...... ☐

"HOMICIDAL" A WILLIAM CASTLE PRODUCTION.

begins shooting at Columbia, Tuesday, November 1.

A full-page Homicidal *ad from the October 27, 1960,* Variety. *It'd be fun to know how the Monster Kid subset of 2021 society fares with this questionnaire!*

Castle sometimes pretended to be mystified by his popularity among young people, as though Monster Kids' favorite flap-eared frightmeister hadn't joined the on-screen casts of his own movies and crammed himself down their throats.

> **William Castle to interviewer Linda May Strawn, 1973:**
>
> I got up to bat during the late '50s through the middle '60s, and every time I had a ball I struck a home run. I was a money machine. ...They were booking Castle pictures sight unseen. They wanted to know just when the next one was coming. I had no stars, so my name was above the titles and on the marquees. It was "William Castle Presents," and they booked my pictures a year in advance. All I had to do was deliver and I could do no wrong.

With White abandoning ship, Castle needed a new scenarist – and who better to adapt "Sardonicus" for the screen than that story's writer? On a leave of absence from *Playboy*, Russell flew to California some time in January 1961, certainly prior to the 25th when Hedda Hopper's column featured this news: "Bill Castle found another old-fashioned horror story which he'll produce titled *Mr. Sardonicus*. Ray Russell, editor of a national mag, is here writing the script."[11] "Coming to California to write the *Sardonicus* script was not Dad's first time in the Golden State," Amanda Russell recalls. She continues:

> Mom and Dad took a short trip to San Francisco in 1959.[12] They were guests in the home of S.I. Hayakawa [then an English professor at San Francisco State College], which Mom said was one of the great experiences of her life. They also had lunch with the newspaper columnist Herb Caen, "Mr. San Francisco." Dad told me that it was on this trip, while enjoying the beautiful climate and scenery, that he thought to himself, "I don't want to live in Chicago any more." He always hated the bitterly cold Chicago winters, so a big part of his reason for moving was the weather.
>
> He was ready to move on from his *Playboy* job to becoming a freelance writer full-time. I'm sure he already loved the idea of writing movies. The opportunity to write the *Sardonicus* script accelerated the process of moving to California, which we did. But even if that opportunity had not materialized when it did, he would have moved out here eventually anyway, to concentrate on writing novels and short stories. His first novel, *The Case Against Satan*, was written while we still lived in Chicago, but was not published until 1962, after we had relocated.

Dad did not retain the *Playboy* editor job after the move. He could never have performed the duties of executive editor remotely. Our first California home [1961-1966] was at 129 North Le Doux Road, Beverly Hills, around the corner from the famous Restaurant Row. But our parents rented that house; they wanted to *own* a home. In 1966, they bought a house on South Elm Drive, where I still live today.

An interesting January 4, 1961, column by Mike Connolly reveals that Castle bought "Sardonicus" with Jack Palance in mind to play the title role, Connolly adding, "Palance isn't signed yet but it looks good." Connolly presumably wrote that on January 3 – which was the day that English actor Guy Rolfe, the eventual Baron Sardonicus, flew from London to Hollywood to play a diabolical count in 20th Century-Fox's *Snow White and the Three Stooges*.

According to Marc, "Jack Palance *was* considered for the part of Sardonicus, but he would not have been as good as Guy Rolfe, despite the fact that he was more of a Middle European type than Rolfe." At first blush, the suggestion of Palance as the nefarious nobleman does seem slightly ridiculous, but scoffers should consider the fine job he did several years later, playing a certain Transylvanian count in producer-director Dan Curtis' telefilm *Dracula*.[13] In his intro to this book, Marc names other actors that he was told were contenders for the role of Baron Sardonicus.

A macabre yarn told in first-person point of view by protagonist Sir Robert Cargrave, "Sardonicus" was an excellent novella – Richard Matheson called it "one of the great horror stories written in the classical style" – but there needed to be more to it as a movie, especially a William Castle movie, than three characters and dialogue. Therefore, in writing the screenplay, Russell padded it with additional characters and incidents. Some of them were shopworn even by 20-year-old cinema standards, but perhaps this was at the behest of Castle, who may have relished his one chance to make a period horror picture, and knew that a certain amount of familiarity is no drawback in a genre piece; in fact, it can be part of its pleasure. Thus Sir Robert's journey to Gorslava calls to mind Renfield's trip to Castle Dracula in Reel One of *Dracula*; Sardonicus preys on peasant girls à la Karloff's Baron Gregor in *The Black Room* (1935); the baron has a disfigured henchman handle his dirty work, etc. Russell also gave the screen Sardonicus a mask to wear throughout most of his footage. In the *Playboy* story, the baron went without; he makes his initial appearance at the start of the third chapter, and right from the jump his grisly grin is on full display. As the story's Sir Robert recounted:

> [T]he gentleman before me was the victim of some terrible affliction that had caused his lips to be pulled perpetually apart from each other, baring his teeth in a continuous ghastly smile. …A pallor approaching phosphorescence completed his astonishing appearance.

The script included in this book, dated February 15, 1961, is presumably the draft submitted to Geoffrey M. Shurlock, administrator of the Motion Picture Production Code. (The handwritten notations in that script, incidentally, are Ray Russell's.) On February 17, just one day after receiving it, Shurlock put his reaction in a letter to Samuel Briskin, the v.p. in charge of Columbia's West Coast operations:

> This script is unacceptable under the requirements of the Production Code because of a definite suggestion of cannibalism. It seems quite clear that the young girls are brought to the Baron's castle to be killed and devoured.
>
> In view of this important basic Code problem, we will refrain from mentioning any details at the present time.
>
> Should you care to discuss this property we will place ourselves at your disposal.

Could Shurlock have seen a script different than the script in this book? It includes no hint *whatsoever* that the beauties imported to the castle by Krull are to be killed and eaten. (Admittedly we never do learn the fate of the fair girl selected by Sardonicus, but as for the runners-up, each of them receives a gold coin from a very friendly Krull on their way out.) Amanda Russell's reaction: She calls Shurlock's complaint "idiotic" and adds, "Despite the baron's sinister references to ghouls, he could never have devoured any of his beautiful female 'guests,' because he can only slurp thin stews and porridges through his teeth! Mr. Shurlock must not have paid close attention when reading the script."

Castle got on the horn with Shurlock to straighten things out, and on February 22, the minder of Hollywood moviemakers' manners put this memo into the Production Code files:

William Castle called today and indicated he had no intention of suggesting cannibalism in this script.

The undersigned [Shurlock] read to him the pertinent scenes, which we thought gave this flavor.

Mr. Castle stated he would re-write them and submit new pages of changes so as to remove this unacceptable reference.

Those new pages, dated February 22, were sent to Shurlock; and on the 28th, he addressed another letter to Samuel Briskin:

Dear Mr. Briskin:

We have read a number of revised pages dated February 22, 1961, for the proposed William Castle production *Mr. Sardonicus*, and are happy to note the changes and improvements made therein.

Please, however, bear in mind that it will be absolutely essential, in the finished picture, that there not be even an inference of cannibalism anywhere.

And yet references to ghouls as cannibals did make it to the screen in *Mr. Sardonicus*: During Castle's pre-credits appearance, he pulls out a pocket dictionary and giddily reads aloud the definition of ghoul ("an evil being who robs graves and feeds on corpses"); and over dinner at the castle, Baron Sardonicus tells Sir Robert that a ghoul is "a disgusting creature who opens graves and feeds on corpses." (That line is later heard a second time, as Sir Robert recalls it in a dream.) Apparently dialogue references to the dietary preferences of ghouls were okay by Shurlock, as long as no character expressing (or demonstrating!) those preferences appeared in the movie. As pointed out by reviewer Edith Lindeman (the *Richmond [Virginia] Times-Dispatch*), "Mr. Sardonicus never fell so low as to chomp on his pappa."

Castle must have been pleased with the script, and with Russell, because by late February, the trades were announcing that William Castle Productions had signed him to a multiple picture writing contract. On April 11, when the shooting of *Mr. Sardonicus* was in the home stretch, Russell revealed that one of his assignments was an adaptation of his novella "Sagittarius." The only movie that came out of this, however, was 1962's *Zotz!* (see the chapter "Ray Russell's Other Horrors").[14]

Meanwhile, just a few miles away, at 20th Century–Fox...

> **Count Oga** (Guy Rolfe), contemptuously eye-balling the Three Stooges: You're hardly what I would call prepossessing to the eye.
>
> **Curly-Joe** (Joe DeRita): *Thank* you, your honor!

The shooting of *Snow White and the Three Stooges* was proceeding, with Olympic champion figure skater Carol Heiss as Snow White and Edgar Barrier as her ailing father, the king – who from his deathbed chooses Count Oga (Rolfe) to be the girl's protector until she comes of age and ascends to the throne. Since Oga has a satanic beard and mustache, a leonine mop of hair that makes his ears look pointed, black raiments and a name that sounds like *ogre*, the viewer probably wonders if the king really wants to make this his Final Answer. Oga and the equally creepy queen (Patricia Medina) join forces to liquidate Snow White, but a trio of strolling players (The Three Stooges) takes the fugitive princess under their wing.

Oga is a fine swordsman and a master of the black arts, but he still comes up short in a climactic *Adventures of Robin Hood*–inspired swordfight with Prince Charming (Edson Stroll): In a textbook example of overkill, it's not enough for Oga to fall from the dizzying heights of the top of the castle, he must land in a cauldron of boiling oil!

Poor Guy Rolfe: After co-starring in *Snow White*, he proceeded to the dubbing room to discharge the last of his responsibilities to the picture and then, on the night of February 27, boarded a plane to make the cross-country (and then cross–Atlantic) journey home to Mother England ... a trip which, back then, probably took the better part of a 24-hour day. Then, just days later, his casting in *Sardonicus* was announced and he had to turn right back around.

Rolfe to Essay Title Role of *Sardonicus*

British actor Guy Rolfe has been cast by producer-director William Castle in title role of *Sardonicus*, Columbia release. Oscar Homolka, previously cast, also co-stars.

– *Variety*, March 10, 1961

According to the reviewer for England's Coventry Evening Telegraph, *"[Mr. Sardonicus'] acting honours are stolen by Oscar Homolka, a sinister, evil-looking, yet sympathetic figure as the baron's henchman," and* Variety *said that Homolka "turns in a highly effective job as the nobleman's jack-of-all-trades, mostly evil." But a* Miami News *critic merely quipped that Homolka "looks like Nikita Khrushchev with hair." (Courtesy Ronald V. Borst/ Hollywood Movie Posters)*

In the movie, the relationship between Baron and Baroness Sardonicus is born on the rocks, but in this publicity shot they're all smiles (and, inexplicably, no skull teeth!). Guy Rolfe was English, Audrey Dalton a daughter of Ireland. Except for William Castle, the entire cast may have been foreign-born. (Courtesy Ronald V. Borst/Hollywood Movie Posters)

Born just before the turn of the 20th century, Oscar Homolka was a stage and movie actor in his native Austria, until Hitler's ascension prompted him to get while the getting was good. He landed first in England, where one of his next pictures was Hitchcock's *Sabotage* (1936), as the London movie house owner turned terrorist who gives an unsuspecting young boy a time bomb which he takes aboard a bus (one of Hitchcock's most famous scenes). Borrowing Homolka from Gaumont-British, Paramount gave him his first American role, the top spot in the Technicolor *Ebb Tide* (1937), a South Seas adventure based on a Robert Louis Stevenson novella. Some reviewers thought that Homolka (as a disgraced German sea captain) and Barry Fitzgerald (as his drunken, roguish Cockney sidekick) did award-worthy work. But there'd be no movie stardom (or Oscars) for Oscar – although, as Uncle Chris in 1948's *I Remember Mama*, he did receive a Supporting Actor nomination. The Continental actor's legit debut in the States was in 1940's *Grey Farm*, a psychological horror piece with Homolka as a strangler ("a box office dodo" – *Variety*). For Homolka, playing Krull in *Mr. Sardonicus* was like going back to his early Hollywood days, when with his un-handsome mug and foreign accent he provided menace in *Seven Sinners* and *The Invisible Woman* (both 1940).

Unable to shoot *Mr. Sardonicus* in the story's Central Europe locale, Castle had to content himself by bringing Europe to Hollywood – actor-wise. That's why, according to a *Variety* item, he "filled eight out of the top ten roles in his production with actors from Europe, or newcomers having just recently arrived from the Continent. From England, Castle has brought co-stars Guy Rolfe and Ronald Lewis plus Mavis Neal. From Austria comes co-star Oscar Homolka; from Germany actresses Lorna Hanson, Erika Peters and Ilse Burkert. Annalena Lund, also featured, hails from Sweden." The blurb ended with Castle commenting, "It's the first time I've felt like a foreigner on my own set."[15]

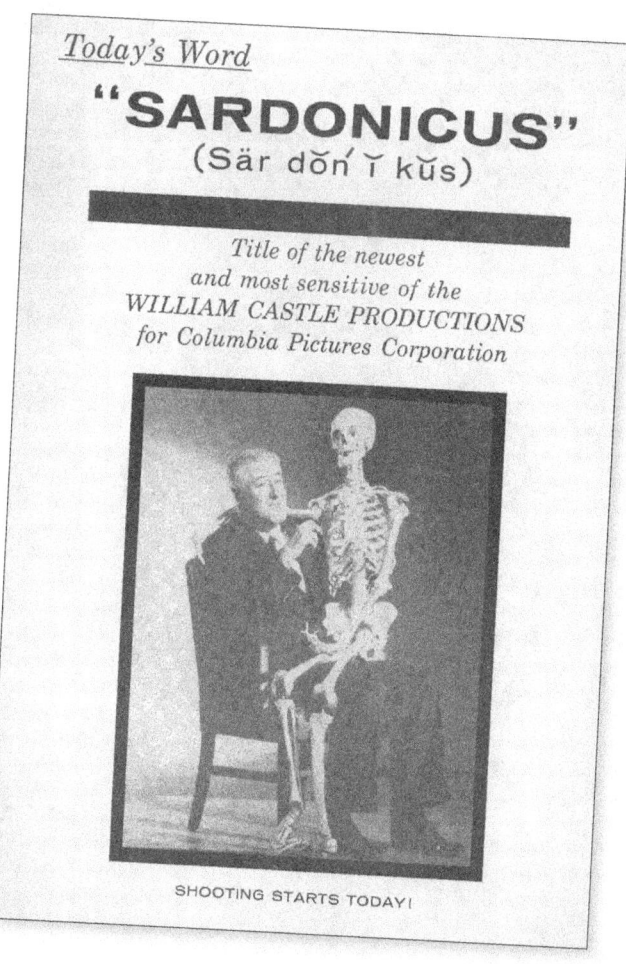

This full-page ad appeared on the back cover of the March 28, 1961, Variety.

The SardoniCast

The filming of *Mr. Sardonicus*, scheduled for 13 days, was slated to begin on Tuesday, March 28, 1961, according to a 17-page breakdown that was prepared in advance of production. (A copy was very generously provided to me by collector Jon Jashni.) I will use this breakdown to describe the shooting, even though there's the possibility that plans changed, i.e., perhaps not everything was shot the way it's laid out in this document. *Mr. Sardonicus* was an independent (William Castle Productions), shot at Columbia for Columbia release. Ray Russell no doubt headed home to Chicago after finishing his script in mid–February, but he returned to the Gower Gulch studio before the picture started shooting, and Marc Russell believes that he was on the set during the entire filming. His wife Ada was there also, but Marc suspects that her stay in California was short, perhaps just a few days; "If she had been absent from Chicago longer than that, I think I would remember."

For the first two days, actors and crew were scheduled to convene on Stage 4 to shoot Peasant Cottage interiors (living room, the father's bedroom, Marek and Elenka's bedroom) and exteriors for the flashback sequence. The script calls Marek "Young Sardonicus" throughout these scenes, but to avoid reader confusion, this book will call him Marek. This book will also point out that, even *before* Marek got a gander at Decomposed Dad and his features froze in a hideous grin, he looked a little too long in the tooth to be called *Young* Sardonicus. Guy Rolfe was then a hair shy of 50, almost twice the age of German actress Erika Peters (*Monstrosity, House of the Damned*), who plays his money-mad missus.

One wonders if Vladimir Sokoloff, featured early in the 12-minute flashback as Marek's father, counted Gorslavian when he estimated that he had played 35 nationalities in the course of his half-century acting career. A nationality he played just twice: Russian ... even though he *was* Russian-born.

In his time, Sokoloff (born in 1889) "dined out" quite a bit on stories told to him by his acting teacher Stanislavski, and had his own tales of his days at the Moscow Art Theatre, his Max Reinhardt association and more. In 1922, he shifted to the German stage, and 11 years later to France. Warner Brothers brought him to Hollywood to act in their movies, starting with *The Life of Emile Zola* (1937) in which he played the writer's painter-friend Paul Cezanne. He made his Broadway bow as Robespierre in the Mercury Theatre's *Danton's Death* (1938).

Vladimir Sokoloff (seen here in a caricature) came to Hollywood in the mid–30s, and filmland insiders predicted that he would soon change his mouthful of a moniker to something more American. But Vladimir Sokoloff he remained, in movies both major and minor.

Sokoloff was still in harness in the 1950s but alas, the man whose name was once spoken by theatrical folk with as much reverence as when they spoke of Reinhardt, was now being seen in support in such films as *Monster from Green Hell, I Was a Teenage Werewolf, Beyond the Time Barrier* ... and *Mr. Sardonicus*. Frail as he neared the end of an illness-plagued life, the 72-year-old trekked to Argentina for *Taras Bulba* (1962) and refused to be doubled in a riding scene – and the horse threw him. Two broken ribs and five days of hospitalization later, he again insisted on doing his own riding. In February 1962, Sokoloff died of a stroke in his 8624 Holloway Drive, West Hollywood, home.

You don't pull the mask off that old Lone Ranger / And you don't mess around with Baron Sardonicus. Pictured: Annalena Lund, Guy Rolfe. (Courtesy Ronald V. Borst/ Hollywood Movie Posters)

Oscar Homolka gives the impression that he's enjoying himself as an actor as he delivers his humorous lines; it's the closest thing to a touch of fun in the movie.

Activity was to shift to Stage 12 on Thursday the 30th, the first part of the day devoted to the Cellar Chamber scene where Baron Sardonicus, on one of his "feelin' single" nights, scrutinizes the five peasant girls submitted for his approval by Krull. The girls Sardonicus calls "dark," "saucy" and "buxom" do not speak and are therefore probably extras; the one he calls "slender" is Ilse Burkert from Germany;[16] and the one he calls "fair" is Annalena Lund from Sweden, making her American picture bow.[17] Lund's character, living almost a half-century before Lon Chaney's *The Phantom of the Opera* (1925), doesn't know enough not to remove the baron's mask; we don't see Sardonicus' face at this point, but we do hear her "No! No! No!" screams, loud enough to scare every cat in the castle.[18] As mentioned above, there's no indication that Sardonicus will kill and devour her; one *Sardonicus* publicity blurb says that "she must spend a night of terror" with him.

March 30 was Oscar Homolka's first day on the picture, and he went from playing an amusing, avuncular Krull (putting the peasant girls at their ease) in the first half of the day, to hanging Anna the servant girl (Lorna Hanson) up by her thumbs and applying a leech to her ankle in the second. Between Homolka's performance and the work of the makeup man, the actor does justice to Ray Russell's script description of Krull:

> He is lumpish, uncouth; unpleasant to behold. He lacks an eye, and the empty socket is imperfectly sewn into a jagged, stitch-crossed scar. He is somewhat Neanderthal in appearance – short but powerfully built, with a sloping forehead and stubbled, prognathous jaw. His voice is rough, thick, deep-pitched. A menacing type, he can sometimes break into flashes of ghoulish humor, then suddenly cool into a compact mass of smouldering evil.

Krull's omnipresence around the castle also provides Sir Robert with a reason *not* to paste Sardonicus one in the nose and spirit the baroness away, at the first evidence of her husband's fiendishness.

"Of all the kinds of masks Castle could have selected, that he chose a blank white mask cannot be underplayed. ...[I]n the context of Mr. Sardonicus itself it makes perfect sense: from the Noh mask of Japanese theatrical traditions to that of Michael Myers in the Halloween series, the blank mask offers a space bereft of meaning, a receptacle or canvas ready for inscription." – Alexandra Heller-Nicholas in the book ReFocus: The Films of William Castle. (Courtesy Ronald V. Borst/Hollywood Movie Posters)

[When wearing a mask,] the man disappears, and a creature of mythic proportions replaces him: some demon or divinity, a terrible intelligence.– Clive Barker

Another "first" for the Cellar Chamber scene: It was the first time during production that Guy Rolfe wore his mask. Emmy-winning makeup artist Michael Blake watched *Mr. Sardonicus* at my request so that he could weigh in on the Sardonicus makeup and the mask. Regarding the latter, he says that it was possibly made from what he calls "a John Doe mold" but then opined that it looks just enough like Guy Rolfe that he believes that it was cast from an impression of Rolfe's face. To Blake it appears to be made of hard rubber or plastic (he leans toward plastic), and probably has some Vaseline or glycerin on it, to catch the lights and make it look more realistic and/or interesting. Blake says that the brows look like hand-laid hair; he points out that the lips were painted, and he detected black liner around the eyeholes. In his script, Russell wrote that the mask "should roughly resemble the actor playing Sardonicus, although the mouth is drawn downward like that of a character from Greek tragedy." Suggestion #1 was taken, Suggestion #2 not.

As noted above, the latter part of the day was devoted to the Anna's Room scene in which Krull threatens the disobedient servant with leeches. In multiple shots, we can see that she's hanging from the ceiling by her thumbs (that's *one* way to insure a Punishment Poll thumbs-up vote!) but in at least one publicity shot (see page 74), she's simply clinging to the ropes with her hands. A surprising touch: When she finally cries out, "I'll tell you! I'll tell you!," she directs the lines not to Krull but into the camera.

Continued on page 178

Backstage on Mr. Sardonicus

The Mr. Sardonicus team poses with their star: Right to left, William Castle, Ray Russell, Guy Rolfe and associate producer Dona Holloway. It appears that Columbia distributed no photos of Rolfe in his skull-teeth appliance but this one. (Courtesy Ronald V. Borst/Hollywood Movie Posters)

Ronald Lewis, William Castle and Guy Rolfe on a break.

Ronald Lewis, Audrey Dalton and Oscar Homolka behind the scenes.

Castle with his arm around d.p. Burnett Guffey.

Guy Rolfe was tubercular and had just one lung, but he signed up to play a role (Sardonicus) that required him to wear a mask over his nose and mouth. And sometimes a skull-teeth makeup appliance over his nose and mouth. And sometimes both at once. And he smoked. And yet he lived to almost 92! Pictured: Audrey Dalton, William Castle, Rolfe, Ronald Lewis.

In *Step Right Up!*, Castle recalled that the leech victim was male – a hard-to-understand boner, since even a bad memory and the passage of a few years ought not to replace lovely Lorna with a guy in *anybody's* mind:

> Another little goodie was the leeches. One of Sardonicus' victims, while being tortured, had to be covered with the dreadful little monsters. Always one for reality, I got a bottle filled with the real thing — long, slimy creatures. The day the scene was shot, the victim refused to have the leeches put on his body. Demonstrating their harmlessness, I put several leeches on my own chest. "See, it's nothing," I told the actor. "They're perfectly harmless." When they started to suck my blood and I couldn't pull them off, I quickly changed my mind. They weren't as much fun as I thought. I postponed the scene until artificial leeches could be made.

An aside: Simply pulling a leech off one's skin, as Castle claims he did, is exactly the wrong way to do it. And yet in the movie, when Sir Robert, a *doctor*, undertakes to remove some from Anna's face, that's what he does, yanking them off like Band-Aids.

On Friday, March 31, the end of the first week of filming, it was back to Stage 4 for the two cemetery scenes – one with a "Sunset Effect" (Marek, his father Henryk and the gravedigger talking about ghouls), the other a "Moonlight Effect" (Marek venturing out into the murk of a foggy night to violate Dad's grave). The latter is well-done, especially photographically. Marek, burdened by shovel and lantern, strides through ground fog to the gravesite, tracked by d.p. Burnett Guffey's camera; and once he's on the working end of that shovel, the camera gets both down-into-the-grave shots and up-*out*-of-the-grave shots. Guffey had quite a respectable list of credits on his 1950s-60s résumé (*Homicidal* and *Mr. Sardonicus* notwithstanding!), including *The Harder They Fall* (1956), *Birdman of Alcatraz* (1962), *King Rat* (1965) (he was Oscar-nominated for all three), *From Here to Eternity* (1953) and *Bonnie and Clyde* (1967) (Oscar wins).

> And so that night, Sir Robert, I became a profaner of the dead … a robber of graves … a *ghoul* … !
>
> — Baron Sardonicus

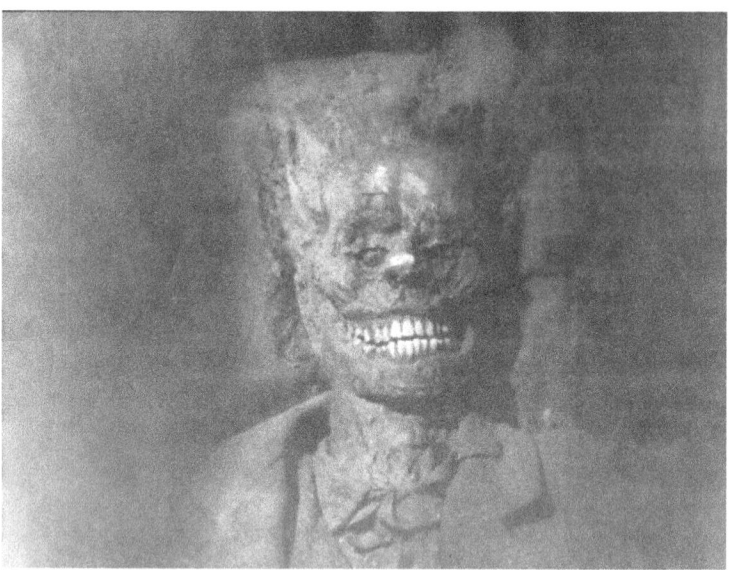

Daddy's death's-head grins up at Marek from the desecrated coffin. When it's seen in the movie, the handheld camera shot is skittish, creating the impression that even the cameraman got a nasty jolt. P.S.: Ol' Poppa Henryk rates a shout-out from the Guinness Record folks for fastest skeletonizing!

Particularly striking are the shots of the decomposed Henryk. These are presumably Marek's point-of-view shots as Guffey's un–Steadicam convulsively quakes, as Marek must be doing, as it focuses on the crumbly face and pearly whites. Then, adhering to an instruction in Russell's script, Guffey is careful to keep Marek's face off-camera or in deep shadow for the rest of this scene.

Mix in Von Dexter's creepy score (his fourth and last for Castle) and the insert shots of the night sky (one with scudding clouds, the other with the moon showing), and the cemetery scene stands up as one of the best in all of Castle's horrors[19] – certainly better than *Macabre*'s cemetery scenes, meant to be scary but dull enough for sleeping.

> [*Mr. Sardonicus*] succeeds nicely at the atmospheric level, and though Castle is not long on "shock," there are still some adroit moments of this type. The grave excavation, for one. – Pit. in *Variety*

As effective as the grave-robbing scene is, let it also be said that it would have been better if shot outdoors. Exteriors in indoorsy pictures "give the film some air" – and *Mr. Sardonicus* could have used some air. All the exteriors (Sir Robert at the railroad station, the cemetery scenes, the scenes at Sardonicus' castle gate, etc.) are interiors, and about as obvious as the supposed "exteriors" in any of that era's low-budget TV shows. Little by little, these scenes give the whole movie the feel of "made for TV."

Imagine an alternate universe version of Mr. Sardonicus *where Marek digs up Dad's coffin, sees the face (and suffers the consequences), searches the pockets for the lottery ticket – and comes up empty. Wouldn't that have been a kick in the teeth! (Courtesy Ronald V. Borst/Hollywood Movie Posters)*

Medical guru Sir Ronald didn't expect to ply his trade at the castle, but just moments after coming through the door he finds himself peeling leeches off the servant girl's face. He'll soon know that if these walls could talk, they'd scream. (Courtesy Ronald V. Borst/Hollywood Movie Posters)

Was any *real* historical figure the inspiration for Baron Sardonicus? Certainly not – although a man buried with a winning lottery ticket is based in fact, according to Amanda Russell:

My father's novella "Sardonicus" was inspired by a true story told by my grandmother, my mother's mother. It happened in a rural area of Poland where her ancestors came from: Generations ago, a man was buried with a winning lottery ticket in his pocket, and his widow guarded the grave at night so no one would dig him up. The man was either someone on our mom's side of the family, or someone the family heard about. On the set of *Mr. Sardonicus*, Dad was interviewed by a German reporter for Düsseldorf's *Rheinische Post*, and he said that his own grandfather was buried with a winning lottery ticket. He also added, "But of course we didn't dig him up." Dad was tweaking the true story.[20]

Amanda is more honest than the writer of a September 1961 *Mr. Sardonicus* publicity squib, who reported that William Castle had just arrived in Cologne, Germany, to begin filming trailers for the movie. The story continued, "Castle's Columbia release … is the story of the legendary Baron Sardonicus whose history is Native to the Cologne area. The producer will film the trailers at the Baron Sardonicus castle, and at other of the city's landmarks."

The first week of production was scheduled to end with the shooting of two more very brief quote-unquote exteriors: Sir Robert seen by lantern-light in the fog at the rail of the sailing ship, en route to Gorslava, and Krull out on the road in a mule-drawn cart, collecting the dogs necessary for Sir Robert's research.

On Monday, April 3, it was back to Stage 12, where they would remain until the 11th. The day was to begin with Sir Robert's first entrance into the torch-lit castle and his shocking discovery of Anna the servant girl, tethered to a chair, leeches on her face. One of the *Mr. Sardonicus* publicity items, probably as reality-challenged as most of the rest, described a fun incident on the set:

During the filming of one terrifying scene of William Castle's *Sardonicus*, Ronald Lewis discovers Lorna Hanson locked in a room with her face covered with leeches. Oscar Homolka … is the man responsible for the dire deed and during one "take," Lewis turns to him and asks:

"Why did you do such a terrible thing to this poor girl?"

Homolka's ad lib reply endeared him to Castle and broke up the cast and crew.

"Because I heard her say something nice about Alfred Hitchcock on a Bill Castle set!"

We can surely place more trust in the account of Hollywood columnist Harrison Carroll, a visitor to the *Sardonicus* set on the day this scene was put on film. Carroll began his story by mentioning the "scarred red socket" created by makeup men for Homolka, and quoting Castle as saying, "I believe [*Mr. Sardonicus*] will be a classic horror picture. Worthy of comparison to *Dr. Jekyll and Mr. Hyde*, *The Phantom of the Opera*, *The Hunchback of Notre Dame* and the first *Dracula*. Only it will have a modern psychological trend. The horror in it actually could happen."

Carroll wrote that the leeches seen in the water-filled jar were real, the ones on Hanson's face plastic and rubber. "Some of them are hollow. If you squeeze them, a red, bloodlike substance squirts out."

"They look and act like the real thing," Castle said proudly.

Carroll continued:

[Castle] summons a special effects man, takes one of the imitation leeches out of a box, suddenly presses it to my wrist. It clings tightly to the flesh.

After peeling the nasty thing off, I ask, "Where do you get real leeches?"

"A place in Rochester, New York, grows them," he replies. "They sometimes are used in research on blood diseases of animals. We bought five dozen at 75 cents each."

I look at Castle.

"Do you ever have bad dreams?"

"Yes," he laughs, "but, if I can get a plot, to me they are good dreams."

The rest of the day was spent on the two salon scenes, first the one in which Sir Robert, newly arrived at the castle, reunites with Maude. A minor blooper here: Russell's "Sardonicus" was set in the mid–1800s and he peppered the story with references to events of that general time period: the writing of the opera *Ernani* (1844), actor William Macready's farewell appearance as Macbeth (1851) and the invention of the first hypodermic needle (1853). Russell's *Mr. Sardonicus* script is set in "the late 1800's," per page 1, and he has Maude enthusing about the works of Arthur Conan Doyle ("a most fascinating writer"), who *was* then prominent. But Russell still allowed the hypodermic needle to be called new.[21]

Making things worse: Someone connected with *Mr. Sardonicus* (God knows who) later got even more date-specific, superimposing **London 1880** on the screen at the start of William Castle's pre-credits sequence, and this balls *every*thing up: In 1880, the hypodermic wasn't new and Conan Doyle, not long out of his teens, was completely unheard-of!

In the movie, Maude is composed throughout the scene but in the script, Sir Robert's line "There have been – no others" (no other women in his post–Maude life) brings tears to her eyes; and the scene ends with Maude, alone in the salon, tearing up again and covering her face with her hands.

The gown that Maude wears in the scene (see photo on next page) was talked-up in a Columbia publicity blurb: Insured by the studio for $4500, the "very old and valuable" garment was made in Germany in 1892 for the Graffin von Seyffertitz of Dresden. When I passed this tidbit of information along to Audrey Dalton, she found it fascinating and told me

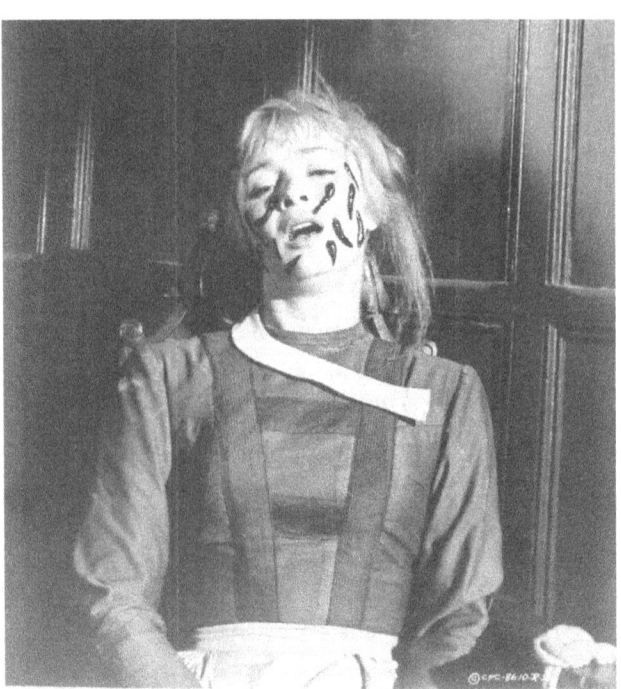

Burnett Guffey's appreciative camera gives us front-row, up-close looks at each of the film's horrors, from Decomposing Dad and the unmasked Sardonicus, to Krull's eye, the knife point pressing on Maude's cheek and the leech woman (Lorna Hanson). Indianapolis Star: "[I]t seems that a large group of the populace really goes for ghoulishness, and them – they'll just love this." *(Courtesy Ronald V. Borst/Hollywood Movie Posters)*

One of Audrey Dalton's Mr. Sardonicus *gowns was described (probably falsely) by a publicist as "completely hand-sewn of Irish crochet and hand–Battenberg. Columbia purchased the gown from the costumers, Berman's, who had located it during an auction of the contents of an old Pasadena mansion."*

that she remembered the dress as heavy but "ever so gorgeous." But then I did some Googling, and found that "Graffin von Seyffertitz" yields no result other than this *Mr. Sardonicus* blurb! So the whole yarn smells like yet another whopper.

The sixth day of production, April 4, was set aside for shooting short scenes and other odds'n'ends for various parts of the picture. It was to begin with a shot of Krull escorting Sir Robert upstairs, the camera crane rising with the men as they pass the empty picture frames. Krull sounds like he's busting with admiration for his master as he stops and tells Sir Robert, "In such frames, ordinary men would honor the portraits of their forefathers. But the baron has disowned his forefathers in one magnificent gesture!"

With that, the men resume climbing the stairs, Krull leading the way *and* repeatedly turning his head to give Sir Robert dirty looks; each time, it's accompanied on the soundtrack by an eerie keyboard chord (Novachord or Hammond organ). Homolka's twice-repeated stink eye, and the music track's funny reaction to them, are about as close as the movie ever gets to a playful moment. But in the big picture, *Ham*-olka's performance is good for the movie, and the actor rates his top billing. "Oscar Homolka's over-the-top performance is wonderful," opined music expert John Morgan. "Like Lugosi, Atwill and Laughton before him, his acting gave the film an entertaining twist." Another admirer of his work, back in the day, was the *Oakland Tribune* reviewer (December 11, 1961): "Only Oscar Homolka as a one-eyed, evil man-of-all-trades sneaking about the mountain castle even begins to suggest that any thought of acting had crossed his mind."

In *The House That Hammer Built* #24, Guy Rolfe told interviewer Wayne Kinsey that when he signed to do *Mr. Sardonicus*, *he* had top billing. Rolfe later learned that Castle had offered Homolka the henchman role, but Homolka turned it down "because I had the [top] billing. I said I had great admiration for Oscar so let him have the billing ... and that caused quite a sensation, because nobody in America had apparently done anything like that before, passing up top billing [*laughs*]. And Oscar was charming to me from then on. He was a great character."

In our 1999 *Fangoria* interview, Audrey Dalton told me, "Oscar Homolka came up with *all kinds* of wonderful things to do with the character that absolutely would break Bill Castle apart because it was just ... *funny* ... *right* ... and added so much to the scenes." Perhaps it was partly Homolka's hijinks that prompted Castle to write in *Step Right Up!*, "The sheer joy of making *Mr. Sardonicus* made it one of my favorite films." When I quoted that to Audrey, she agreed about the fun factor: "He's right, it was great fun. And it had a lot of [horrific] *meat* to it – dreaming up that plot, and building that atmosphere of foreboding in the scenes. It was just great."

Scenes set in the corridor outside Sir Robert's room were also on the April 4 To-Do list, along with closeups of Krull and Anna (shot against black velvet) for Sir Robert's dream sequence. (Lorna Hanson is seen twice in his dream, once with a face-full of leeches, once without.) The black velvet shots of Sardonicus, Maude and the railroad stationmaster seen during the dream were scheduled to be shot on subsequent days.

Ronald Lewis sat inside a coach mock-up for the scene in which Sir Robert rides to the castle. When he looks out the window, we see the process plate footage of dead trees used in *Son of Frankenstein*'s (1939) opening-reel train scene. (Across the top of this page and the next, a series of overlapped frame grabs provides a good look at the miniature trees and the background; many thanks to Fred Rappaport and Mike Bannon.) Next all the Maude's Boudoir footage was to be shot, including the scene in which the baron enters to exhort her to use her "charms" to convince Sir Robert to do the right thing. "Do not worry, I am not a man who is affectionate in the morning hours," Sardonicus says as he enters, subtly raising the question: Has their marriage been consummated? The fact that he says she need not worry about him ... at *this* time of day ... implies that, unlike the Maude of the novel, the movie Maude is *not* an unkissed bride. This said, Sardonicus reveals in the torture chamber scene that the baroness has been a wife to him "in name only"; and later he closes the chapter on their marriage by annulling it himself, in a note stating that she has been "no wife to me."

On a very trivial, couldn't-*be*-more-trivial note: Sardonicus writes the abovementioned note to his wife, and a second one to Sir Robert, with his right hand. Then, just moments later, he writes **BEGONE** on the fireplace wall with his left. He's right-handed whenever he pours wine. In the flashbacks, a southpaw Marek nails shut his father's coffin, uses a writing implement and unlocks a money box. He uses a shovel right-handed in the movie and lefty in a publicity still (look at this book's cover). Guy Rolfe must have been ambidextrous to the point where everything worked out the same with either hand.

GUY ROLFE'S NEW VOICE

ALTHOUGH British actor Guy Rolfe is reputed to have one of the finest speaking voices in films, the tight-fitting face mask he wears during most of his starring role in William Castle's Columbia Pictures "Sardonicus" necessitated some electronic wizardry on the part of sound man James Flaster to enable Rolfe to be understood.

Guy's normal voice would have been completely unintelligible through the plastic mask, so Flaster rigged up a transmitter and midget microphone that were hidden under Rolfe's shirt. Rolfe's voice was then picked up to sound as if it were coming from deep inside him, which is exactly the way producer-director Castle intended it in the first place.

Rolfe plays the title role of a man who is unable to move his jaw and has had to learn to speak an entirely different way.

A Columbia publicity item that made its way into some newspapers. Guy Rolfe's voice sounds so clear throughout the movie that we're calling b.s. on this.

Ronald Lewis put in a full day on April 5 as all shooting was done on the "Sir Robert's Chamber" set, including footage of the physician in experimental research mode, making scientific advances one "dead" dog at a time. Four dogs on the set meant that there also had to be a dog handler, a veterinarian and an SPCA man. On April 6, every "Sardonicus' Room" scene would be put on film, beginning with a shot of the baron, back to the camera, slurping his bowl of mush.

A zoom lens was required for a closeup shot of Sardonicus' mask, hanging on the baron's bedpost; the zoomed-in shot pulls out to show the baron face-down in bed. Next: Sir Robert's massage treatment of the baron, a scene involving stacks of white towels and a basin of steaming water. One of *Sardonicus*' least believable publicity blurbs began by mentioning the "business acumen" of actress Erika Peters (who played Marek's wife Elenka) and continued:

> While reading the script, Erika noted that in several scenes involving facial treatments for the evil Sardonicus, a great many towels were going to be used. In fact, some 600 of them. So businesswoman Peters, who owns a Laundromat in Los Angeles, made a deal with Castle for the towel-washing concession during the filming of the picture.

(Actually, a grand total of *two* towels are used in the scene.)

More nonsense from the Columbia publicity gristmill: Sir Robert perspires profusely during the massage marathon, so presumably this is the scene that prompted the blurb "Sweating It Out Poses No Problem":

Sir Ronald, aware that his methods have failed, wants to throw in the towel. But the baron knows how to force him to continue. (Courtesy Ronald V. Borst/Hollywood Movie Posters)

> With temperatures soaring to over 100 degrees..., British actor Ronald Lewis had no trouble acting out one scene in the macabre film.
>
> The script called by Lewis ... to break out in a nervous sweat....
>
> "I needed direction for the scene," laughed Lewis, "but my sweat glands didn't!"

William Castle decided to go for baroque with Mr. Sardonicus: period setting, ancient castle, a Phantom-like masked fiend, fog and the whole rest of the Gothic horror hit parade. Here's the baron, up to even less good than usual, luring Sir Ronald to the torture chamber. (Courtesy Ronald V. Borst/Hollywood Movie Posters)

Newspaper readers who saw this item during the summer of 1961 might have swallowed it – but *Mr. Sardonicus* was made in the spring, during a drizzly SoCal cool spell. April 6, when this scene would have been shot, was a day of scattered drizzle and an anticipated high of 68 degrees.

In the script, the massage treatment scene begins with Ray Russell's instruction that Sardonicus should remove his coat and shirt, "baring a handsome torso." (Sardonicus also strips to the waist in the novella, "displaying a trunk strong and of good musculature, but with the same near-phosphorescent pallor of his face.") But in the movie, only the coat is shed; perhaps Guy Rolfe didn't pack the gear. "He was not well, I remember. He was terribly thin, he was ill," Audrey Dalton told me. (Read about Rolfe's career, and his health woes, in Laura Wagner's chapter; begin on page 209.)

Rolfe told *House That Hammer Built*'s Wayne Kinsey that he "took a bit of a liberty" with Ronald Lewis on the *Sardonicus* set: "I had his name painted on the back of his chair as **ROLAND LOUIS**. He was very annoyed about that because it was only the third time he'd had his name on a chair on set. He eventually got the painter to alter it for him. I thought it was funny and I laughed, but he wasn't terribly amused [*laughs*]! I had a lot of fun making that."

"I was recently surprised while doing a little reading-up on Ronald Lewis," Dalton told me. "He was perfectly charming and professional on the set when we worked together. I didn't know his career later fell apart, his rough treatment of women or his bankruptcy, presumably leading to his suicide. What terrible years he had."

On the next two days, Friday the 7th and Monday the 10th, the Torture Chamber and Padlocked Room sequences were filmed. Again a crane was used, the camera keeping pace with Sardonicus and Sir Robert as they descend stairs toward the torture chamber door. Next: the dramatic scene with Sir Robert on the rack, Maude secured to a chair and Krull reluctantly touching her cheek with the business end of a surgical knife. It's in this scene that viewers get their first hint that the worm (Krull) may eventually turn and be the baron's undoing. When the brutish servant questions Sardonicus' order to disfigure Maude, the arrogant baron makes him aware of the possible consequences of his *in*action:

You well know what happens to people who raise objections to my acts. You know what happened the single time you questioned my authority, many years ago. Or have you forgotten that once you had *two* eyes?

Even madmen like the baron ought to know that once you've disfigured an underling, once you've put the –scar in O-scar (Homolka), it's probably best not to poke that bear. Watching this scene, savvy Monster Kids will suspect that Krull may indeed be a "man of all work" — but not *this* kind of work (cutting the face of a woman) – and that Sardonicus' trash talk may come back to bite him. This was how Karloff went from zero to hero in *The Raven* (1935), to name just one example.

In the chair, Maude wears one of her usual all-concealing outfits, complete with high collar, and throughout the scene she holds a brave face while looking at danger – but on the *Mr. Sardonicus* posters is artwork of Maude in the chair, wearing a low-cut, cleavage-revealing dress, a strap falling off one shoulder, and squirming in such a way as to reveal a lot of bare leg. (While on the subject of the movie's posters: They depict Sardonicus as a caped, top-hatted all-black silhouette and shadow, a bit of art calling to mind Jack the Ripper or Mr. Hyde – but certainly not Sardonicus. Far from being a night prowler as the artwork conveys, the self-ennobled noble is actually quite the shut-in.)

A set anecdote well-distributed by Columbia's publicity department, Grain of Salt division:

> One day when Castle's pretty secretary, Marjorie Wintner, who's been with him through all of his macabre film ventures and never blinked an eye, walked on the set of *Mr. Sardonicus* at Columbia and saw star Guy Rolfe for the first time in his terrifying, facial-distorting makeup for the title role, she became faint and had to leave the stage. She returned only after Rolfe had removed his shocking visage.

When Rolfe removes his mask in the torture chamber scene, it was the first time during production that his skull-teeth appliance was filmed.[22] Michael Blake has examined a still and some frame grabs of Rolfe in his horror makeup, and watched the movie, and he postulates that what we see on Rolfe's face is a one-piece foam rubber appliance, the top edge just under the actor's eyes, the lower edge hidden from sight under his jawline. Blake says that if he had applied it, he would have put glue on Rolfe's chin, cheekbones, jawline, upper lip, the bridge of his nose and the tip of his nose. Once it was glued down, the appliance would then be covered with makeup, blending into Rolfe's skin so that the edges become invisible.

In the movie, we first see the appliance when Elenka lights the candle in the Peasant Cottage bed-

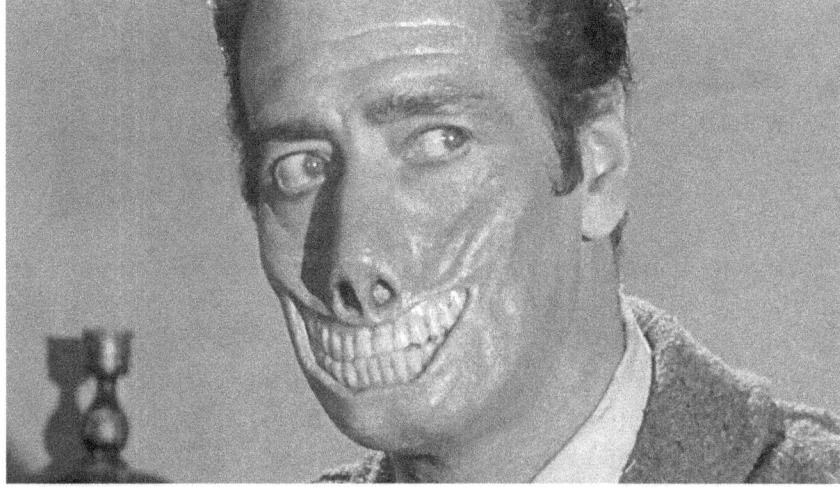

We get our three glimpses of the baron's skull teeth in the peasant cottage, torture chamber and padlocked room scenes.

room. Watching that scene, Blake was surprised to notice that, through one of the appliance's nostrils, the real nose of Rolfe is plainly visible. The actor's nose should have been covered with black makeup so that it could not be seen through the opening.

Marc Russell says, "Quite a few years after the

fact, Dad told me that Maurice Seiderman was the makeup artist. When Dad was chatting with Seiderman on the set, Seiderman mentioned that he had worked on *Citizen Kane* [1941] – he was responsible for the great old-age makeups in that movie. Dad was not even sure this was true until I confirmed it to him!"

William Castle wrote in *Step Right Up!*:

Creating the grinning face was a problem. In order for the mask to appear realistic, Guy Rolfe ... was fitted five times. His mask had to conform to the contours of his mouth, yet appear three times the normal size. Rolfe also had to be able to speak with it on. Finally we achieved the perfect grin — not humorous, but horrible. Hours were lost in shooting because Rolfe could not tolerate wearing the mask for more than an hour at a time.

The moviemakers next worked on the Padlocked Room set, where the furnishings included the body of the baron's father in an upright coffin. (This coffin is much nicer than the one he was buried in. Even the father looks much nicer!) Sardonicus' skull teeth are seen for the third and last time in this scene, as he sits roped to the chair in preparation for Sir Robert's injection and his "cure by shock."

Scheduled as the last shot of the day: Sardonicus tearing wallpaper off a mirror and getting his first

The baron's cure puts a whole new face on things at Sardonicus' castle. But he isn't out of the woods yet. (Courtesy Ronald V. Borst/Hollywood Movie Posters)

look at his restored face. In the movie he stares at himself as if in disbelief, then grimly strides away; the script describes a more emotional reaction (see the script, and/or this book's "Script-to-Screen Changes" chapter for details). After the baron has marched off, Krull, drawn by curiosity, approaches the mirror and gets what is presumably his first look at himself since the sun set on his stereoscopic days, and hangs his head in anguish. Our second indication that Sardonicus' comeuppance is coming up-ance.

Tuesday, April 11, found cast members on a new Stage 4 set: the castle gate exterior. With the fog machine set to **MAX**, the moviemakers first shot the scene of Sir Robert arriving by coach, then the final-reel scene of Sir Robert, Maude and Anna about to *leave* by coach. The best thing about these two brief scenes; indeed, one of the best things about the movie: In the background, we can see Sardonicus' medieval castle and, true to Ray Russell's directive in his script, "Somehow, because of the placement of the windows and portcullis, it bears a faint, almost 'subliminal' resemblance to a giant, grinning skull."[23]

Next to be shot: on the railroad station waiting room set, Sir Robert's conversation with the stationmaster (Charles H. Radilac), whose smile turns upside down at the mention of Baron Sardonicus.[24] Watching this scene, what Monster Kid doesn't flash back to *Dracula* and the innkeeper (Michael Visaroff) who has kittens when Renfield name-drops Count Dracula? The stationmaster tries to warn Sir Rob-

"Not like this! Not in the dark!*": Krull peers through the hinged door viewer to see why the boss is turning the Padlocked Room into the Panic Room. (Courtesy Ronald V. Borst/Hollywood Movie Posters)*

ert but it falls on deaf ears, the way the innkeeper's warning failed to deter Renfield; the stationmaster then crosses himself the way the innkeeper's wife did. Attention, blooper fans: When Sir Robert and the stationmaster enter the waiting room from outside, camera and cameraman are reflected in a sheet of glass on the left side of the screen.

Next they shot on the hospital anteroom set. At one point, Sir Robert opens his gold pocket watch and peers in at a small daguerreotype of Maude (in her "Graffin von Seyffertitz of Dresden" dress), and we hear her echo-chamber voice run through his mind: "But my father forbids our marriage, Robert. He says you will never amount to anything. I must marry a man of substance, he says. A certain wealthy widower." That last sentence, in combination with Maude–Sir Robert dialogue in the second salon scene, gives us the whole scoop on the Sardonicus-Maude union: The baron blackmailed Maude's father and forced a marriage with Maude (whom he had never met), obviously with the goal of using *her* to get the upper hand over Sir Robert. Astonishingly clever, these foreigners!

> listen, said the master of the castle, and you will learn how monstrous a man can become
>
> – subhead on the first page of "Sardonicus" in *Playboy*

But give this devil his due: Set aside Sardonicus gouging out Krull's eye, raping pretty peasants, bedecking servant girls with leeches, etc., and he's quite a soigné and highly polished figure. And danged if he ain't got the "masterly manner" thing down pat. We can't help but wonder how Marek Toleslawski could have pulled himself up by his clodhopper-straps to *these* lofty heights, and also wonder what Henry Higgins molded the common clay of this simple farmer into Baron Sardonicus. The baron could regally roll his Rs with the best of 'em at *any* ritzy round-up ... were it not for his killer smile.

(The novella Sardonicus was *not* a baron and spoke with difficulty, almost incapable of uttering b and v sounds. *His* rise from the lower to upper classes is somewhat more believable in the novella than in the movie: We read that even as a lad, he was "interested in improving his lot through the learning he found in books.")

How small is Gorslava? The railroad station has a large hanging **GORSLAVA** *sign. Can this mean that it's the only railroad station in Gorslava?*

It's also worth a quick mention that, unlike the Sardonicus of the movie who marries Maude just to sink his hooks into Sir Robert, the Sardonicus of the novel actually *was* smitten with her. He even describes to Sir Robert his love-at-first-sight reaction when he spotted her from a distance in Paris. But in case this made any reader the least bit sympathetic to his plight, he then announces that if Sir Robert fails, he (Sardonicus) will start banging Maude like a screen door in a cyclone, instantly re-wrapping himself in the cloak of villainy.

Seen as the hospital's head nurse is English-born Mavis Neal. In 1965, she went from actress to back-of-the-camera: She became an administrative assistant in ABC-TV's daytime network programming department, and then in 1969 its associate director. Resigning from that position in 1971, she went back to acting with a bit of help from her husband, casting director Tom Palmer, who appears to have found spots for her in several of "his" shows (*Cannon, Dan August, Barnaby Jones*, maybe more).

Mr. Sardonicus' Day 12, April 12, Stage 12: The troupe tackled the dining hall scenes. First, the moment when Sir Robert, newly arrived at the castle, tells Maude, "But I am very anxious to meet the baron face—" ... and before he can get out the rest, there's a cut to a shot zooming in on the faceless (masked), dressed-for-dinner Sardonicus. It's a great "horror character entrance," spoiled only by a musical stinger that sounds like something from a TV cop show. Then the dinner table scene, with Sardonicus pouring himself "just a little brandy." (In the script, he drinks "a little Tokay" — Bela Lugosi's social lu-

Starvation ... what a way to go. But the baron's sins were as black as the inside of a weskit pocket in a coffin at midnight, so viewers relish the moment.

bricant of choice.)

For Sir Robert's dream sequence, the black velvet shots of Sardonicus and Maude were photographed. Then the unforgettable closing scene of Krull telling Sardonicus that he missed Sir Robert at the railroad station – and withholding the tidbit that the baron, within himself, has the power to open his mouth. (We scratch our heads wondering why Sir Robert's charade has *worsened* Sardonicus' condition, depriving him of his hard-earned ability to speak and to slurp up stews and porridges.) Sardonicus once said that he found "bitter irony" in the idea of re-naming himself after the Latin term for the grimace on the faces of lockjaw victims, *risus sardonicus*; and now in the movie's closing minutes, there's the *ultimate* irony of Fate shuffling the cards and giving the abused Krull the power of life and death over the baron.

It's amusing that Sardonicus, so long cut off from normal interaction with men and women, so long denied access to the haunts of man, gets his handsome face back but has no urge to rejoin the human race, no "I'm going to Disneyland!" impulse. Instead, his first priority is to tie on the feedbag; and by "feedbag," the baron means turning his dining hall table into a Sirloin Stockade all-you-can-eat buffet ... for one. But his feast falls flat when his mouth remains closed tighter than a scared clam.

In another of the movie's high points, Sardonicus slumps in a chair at the head of that table, perhaps figuring out (on the fingers of one hand) how many days he'll last without food and drink, and doesn't notice that Krull, emboldened by the certainty that the countdown to his master's extinction has begun, cops an uninvited squat in the chair on the other end, and proceeds to dig in. Soon Sardonicus is watching enviously and Krull, showing no emotion, is *watching* him watch. The movie alternates between tighter and tighter closeups of the two, Krull eating and drinking, the baron eyeballing Krull and trying to pull his mouth open. Soon we're down to shots of just Krull's mouth and nose and just Sardonicus' eyes and nose; on the track is one of the better Von Dexter cues and the sound of Krull's munching, which is nearly as revolting as the baron's stew-slurping. Leaping to his feet, Sardonicus frantically tries to *force* food and drink into his mouth, to no avail,

Krull still observing with the placid attitude of a guy watching an object of amusement. His impassivity would be infuriating to anyone in the baron's fix. The camera's on a crane, backing away from the approaching Sardonicus and rising, as he staggers from the table to the staircase, clutching the balusters to brace himself as he weeps. Krull, in the blurry distant background, has turned around in his chair and is savoring *this* delicious moment also.

Krull is the picture of unconcern, ignoring the baron's crisis, eating with his hands as the anguished baron stares – and starves. The scene is reminiscent of the *Sabotage* dinner scene where Homolka does the same thing to his wife Sylvia Sidney. Responsible for the bomb-on-the-bus death of her young brother just hours earlier, Homolka now sits on the far side of the table from her, again the picture of unconcern, clueless-ly ignoring her deep distress, eating with his hands and voicing banal complaints about the food, as Sidney struggles to keep a lid on her emotions – and her hatred. It's a stand-up-and-cheer moment when she ends the grotesque stare-off with a carving knife.[25] Check out our tribute to *Mr. Sardonicus*' dining table scene on pages 190 and 191.

Mr. Sardonicus production wrapped on Thursday the 13th of April, a work day that began on Stage 4's Exterior Garden set. The scene starts with Sardonicus telling Sir Robert, "I thought perhaps you might care to walk in my garden before breakfast" – a comment crying out for a "That's a *joke*, right?" rejoinder, as the place is all weeds, and spiders have worked diligently in every corner. "Wolfbane, mandrake root, hemlock, deadly nightshade – they are *all* here," says Sardonicus, like that's a *good* thing.[26] Guy Rolfe briefly wears the skull-teeth appliance in this scene, but this time it was probably affixed with no great care, because we only see it dimly and distantly in the baron's upside-down reflection in the garden arbor pool. The last sets on the last day: Queens College Hospital interiors, including the dispensary where Sir Robert massages the little girl's leg. In a movie about paralysis, a movie that makes a big deal about hypodermic needles, it might be interesting to mention the uncredited actress playing the girl's mother: Constance Cavendish was a ballerina until circa 1946, when a doctor using the wrong hypodermic gave her an injection that left her paralyzed from the waist down for almost two years (and ended her professional dancing career). Cavendish acted on radio (sometimes playing small boys) and stage, and started playing minor parts in movies in the late '40s with *The Paradine Case* and *That Forsyte Woman*.

Still un-filmed after principal photography wrapped: Castle's appearance as the movie's "host," and many insert shots. On the production breakdown, the lengthy list of needed inserts includes the Queens College Hospital plaque, the watch open to show Maude's daguerreotype, various letters and envelopes, Henryk's winning lottery ticket (7707), the list of lottery winners, and a hand pulling the ticket out of the weskit pocket.

A lottery ticket with English-language writing was made (and it still exists, among Marc Russell's possessions; see photo below).

According-ing to Amanda, "They must have made this English version first, but someone, probably my dad, thought it would look more authentic in Polish. So a Polish one was also made. My dad must have phoned one of our relatives or friends in Chicago to get the Polish wording."

The list of lottery winners seen in the movie is in Polish, but again, an English-language version was also made; this too is now owned by Marc. It has a **National Lottery Gorslava** heading, and the fifth name on the list is Wilhelm Schloss – an in-joke variant on William Castle's real name. The produc-

In Truffaut/Hitchcock, François Truffaut's book-length interview with Alfred Hitchcock, the French director included a two-page spread of sequential frame grabs from a scene in Sabotage (1936): Oscar Homolka, a bomb-planting terrorist, sits at his kitchen table awaiting dinner, unaware that his wife Sylvia Sidney is borderline hysterical because Homolka's newest bomb killed her younger brother. He has an uncaring attitude, speaks with a studied calm and grotesquely eats with his hands, further agitating her. In Mr. Sardonicus, Castle may have copied Hitchcock and Sabotage – in fact, going to the extreme of casting Homolka! And so, in that same collegial spirit of intellectual piracy, this book will copy frame-grabber Truffaut:

tion breakdown also features a list of stock shots that the moviemakers needed to locate and incorporate. A random selection: London street at night with fog (for the Castle intro), a ship on the English Channel and a European train (Sir Robert's journey to Gorslava), clouds rolling away from the moon (for the cemetery scene).

Preceding the start of the first hospital scene, we see stock footage of turn-of-the-century London street activity, previously seen in 20th Century-Fox's *The Ghost and Mrs. Muir* (1947). And notice how *Mr. Sardonicus* took the fullest advantage of it: In the *Mrs. Muir* footage, one pedestrian (played by an extra) is slightly prominent. Seen from the back, he wears a hat and ulster coat and carries what looks like a soft leather briefcase. Then there's a dissolve to *Mr. Sardonicus*' first Queens College Hospital interior, which begins with the camera focused on the back of an *identically costumed extra* as he ambles, bag in hand, down a hospital corridor. Thanks to editing room magic, we get the impression that this extra walked in off the *Ghost and Mrs. Muir* street and into *Mr. Sardonicus*' hospital, and makes us

Play it again, Guy: While the English-based actor was in Hollywood to do Mr. Sardonicus, *he got in another creepy credit: the mad concert pianist Vladimir Vicek in an episode of NBC's* Thriller.

think that Castle & Co. staged that very elaborate street exterior.

You'd think that Guy Rolfe, Sardonicus himself, would know that the takeaway from his newest picture was to keep your mitts out of people's coffins, no matter *how* much you want what's in there. But less than two weeks after finishing *Sardonicus*, the actor was again ankle-deep in fog on a cemetery set, and opening a coffin, this time at Universal where he starred in the *Thriller* TV episode "The Terror in Teakwood." In the opening minutes, a *Sardonicus*-like story seems to be building, with Rolfe and cemetery caretaker Reggie Nalder invading a crypt, and Rolfe taking *something* from the coffin of its occupant. (In the fog and darkness, Rolfe and Nalder could easily pass for Rolfe and Oscar Homolka; Nalder even sounds like Homolka.)

And again as in *Mr. Sardonicus*, Rolfe has an unhappy wife (Hazel Court) who invites a former flame (Charles Aidman) into the story. Vladimir Sokoloff even shows up in the episode. Based on one of the weirder *Weird Tales* stories, it began shooting on April 24 – and played on TV on May 16![27]

> Chicago has become a city of two seasons—hellish summer followed immediately by hellish winter. No spring, no fall.
>
> — Ray Russell, 1964

Climate Change (of address): As mentioned above, the experience of writing *Mr. Sardonicus* in clement California prompted Russell to move to the Golden State sooner than later. In the last week of April 1961, about two weeks after the movie wrapped, his wife and children were on a train leaving Chicago for LaLaLand, with Ray waiting for them in the rented house on North Le Doux Road when they arrived.[28] (Not until 1966, shortly before moving out of that house, did the Russells learn that another writer had once resided there: William Faulkner.)

In mid-May, just a few weeks after the Russells had made North Le Doux their new home, the Hollywood trades reported that American International Pictures had signed Ray to write three screenplays. The first would be based on his story *X* (this became 1963's *X—The Man with the X-Ray Eyes*), and it would be followed by an adaptation of Jules Verne's novel *Off on a Comet*. (*Off on a Comet* was never made.) On a higher plane, it was also publicized that Russell was writing a comedy script for Tony Curtis' Curtleigh Co., for Universal release. Starting out with the title *Exit 41* and then becoming *The Soft Sell*, it was to have top-lined Curtis unless his schedule forced the casting of another star.[29] In May 1961, Ballantine Books announced that, as a tie-in with the fall release of *Mr. Sardonicus*, they would publish "Sardonicus" in a paperback titled *Sardonicus & Other Stories*.[30] (The others were Russell's Gothic novellas "Sagittarius" and "Sanguinarius.") There was also a September 1961 announcement that in the spring of '62, his first novel *The Feast of St. Michael* (later re-titled *The Case Against Satan*) would be published.

Amanda Russell: "After we moved to California, he did all his writing at home. Once in a while, he'd drive to the beach in Santa Monica with a notebook, find a bench, and write there." In a whimsical *Variety* article, Russell interviewed him*self*, the Chicago transplant admitting he had taken to the California lifestyle. You need to know, before reading this excerpt, that Russell was a bearded man of formidable girth:

> **Q:** To the charge that you have "gone Hollywood," how do you plead?
>
> **Russell:** Guilty. I attend opening nights at the Huntington Hartford Theatre, drive a white convertible, am on a low calorie diet, and have even been known to sign autograph books for people who've mistaken me for Peter Ustinov.
>
> **Q:** What name do you sign?
>
> **Russell:** Sebastian Cabot.

Back to William Castle – and the whirlwind life of the producer of popular movies: At this point, with *Mr. Sardonicus* in the can, Castle's To-Do List included (a) putting the finishing touches on it, and coming up with a gimmick; (b) getting behind the upcoming June release of his previous picture *Homicidal*, including many personal appearances; (c) prepping his next picture, *Zotz!*, and (d) lining up his post–*Zotz!* projects. With all this on his plate, he didn't need a problem with *Mr. Sardonicus* – but there *was* one. He wrote in *Step Right Up!*:

> Columbia had seen the final cut of the picture and demanded that I reshoot the final scene, which they cautioned would be unacceptable to audiences. In the scene in question, Sardonicus, unable to eat or drink because of his frozen grin, goes insane as he slowly and agonizingly dies. Columbia wanted a more palatable ending and insisted I let Mr. Sardonicus live. I refused adamantly, and just as adamantly they demanded another ending.
>
> During the stalemate, I suddenly realized that Columbia had unknowingly given me the gimmick for the picture. I would have two endings — Columbia's and mine — and let the audience decide for themselves the fate of Mr. Sardonicus.

Activator Booth

Available at your Columbia Exchange is a "Punishment Poll Activator Booth Kit" containing:
- Three lithographed "Activator Booth" sheets for mounting on a simple wood frame, to make the booth with a minimum of trouble.
- Set of do-it-yourself directions, outlining the way to make the booth, which is shown at right, below.

With this material, all that is needed in addition is an extension cord and light to be placed inside the booth.

The Activator Booth should be set up in a prominent place in the outer lobby, well in advance of playdate. During your engagement of "Mr. Sardonicus," move the booth to a spot where patrons, waiting to be admitted, can use it to activate their own Punishment Poll cards.

The following are suggestions to help carry on this Castle-style boxoffice showmanship:
- Use a simple flasher attachment on the light inside the booth, to add to the effectiveness of the gimmick. The William Castle lobby record is to be played continually to increase the effectiveness of the lobby promotion.
- Be sure to post the starting time of your picture, and the time of the Punishment Polls, so that audiences know whether or not they have long to wait before they can be admitted.
- During the polling, do not raise the house lights.
- Atop, or near, your Activator Booth, place a tally system so that the "Thumbs-up, thumbs-down" voting can be recorded after each "poll."
- Plant the Activator Booth stories, elsewhere on this page, and try for photo coverage of a pretty girl making use of the lobby display to activate her Punishment Poll card.

From the Mr. Sardonicus *pressbook: a list of Activator Booth instructions and suggestions.*

My new gimmick was the punishment poll and a special gadget, the Activator Booth. Arriving at the theater, patrons were given a card with a hand imprinted — four fingers closed into a fist, the thumb pointing upward. "Mercy" was printed atop the raised thumb. When the card was turned upside-down, the thumb now pointing downward, the printing now read, "No Mercy." By exposing the card to the Activator Booth set up in the theater lobbies, the luminous thumb glowed in the dark. [Read more about the Activator Booth in the *Mr. Sardonicus* pressbook excerpt above.]

Did Columbia's rejection of his finale *really* give Castle the Punishment Poll idea? Maybe; but that's not what he told the *Newark* (New Jersey) *Evening News'* Bea Smith in mid–October 1961 when *Mr. Sardonicus* was playing at Proctor's Theater in that city. "[I]t was a woman in the lobby of a Los Angeles theater who gave me the idea for my latest gimmick, bless her," Castle said. "She suggested I let

194

The beastly baron tears at Maude's clothes; is it any wonder that audiences, cast in the role of Roman emperor, voted "No Mercy"? Look at the Audrey Dalton image on the Mr. Sardonicus *ads (domestic and foreign) and you'll see that the top part came from this still.*

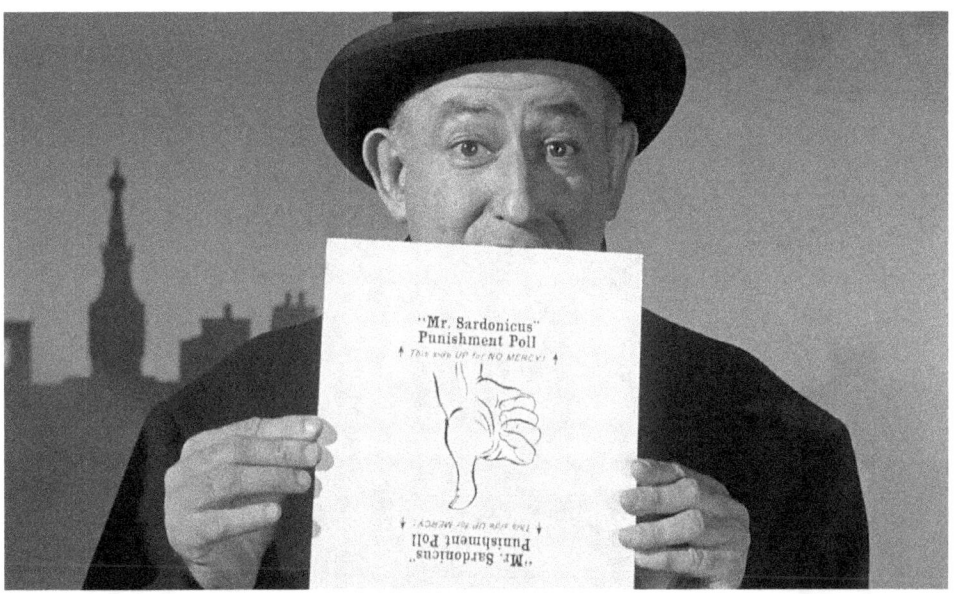

Punishment Poll. The former was scripted by Russell (it's in his February 15 script), the latter by who knows?

The pre-credits sequence begins with a stock shot of Big Ben at night and that troublesome **LONDON 1880** superimposition. After some more stock, we see a serious-looking Castle walking through the fog on an interior set representing a Thames-side thoroughfare. He's supposed to be on the Embankment on the south side of the river, opposite the Houses of Parliament and Big Ben. He stops and talks to himself as he struggles to light his signature cigar, then looks into the camera and starts addressing the audience directly; he seems quite delighted with himself as he gives his name as William Castle.

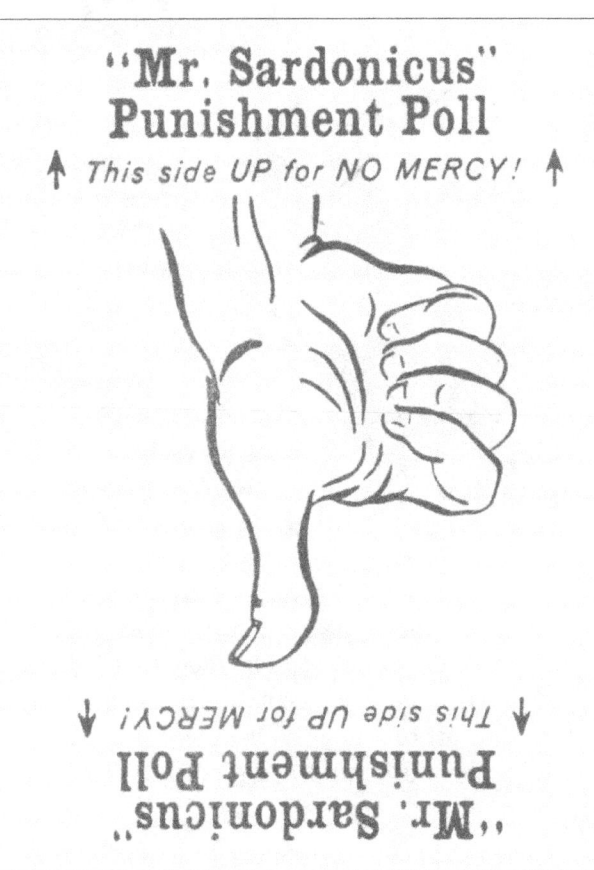

With William Castle in charge, 1961 moviegoers could expect -- and got -- the mother of all "rigged elections"!

"Oh, it's good to see you again, my homicidal friends," he tells the audience, an in-joke allusion to *Homicidal*.[31] His eyes sparkling with the gleam of movie madness, the P.T. Barnum of horrordom plays unashamedly to the galleries as he says that he's in London (apparently someone thought the **LONDON 1880** superimposition would not suffice alone); he advises viewers that this new picture will be something different, old-fashioned; and he merrily reads from his little dictionary the definition of *ghoul*, which includes the reference to cannibalism which Castle promised censor Geoffrey Shurlock would not be mentioned. He ends his first appearance in the movie by saying,

> I hope you enjoy it [*Mr. Sardonicus*], and I hope your nightmares are nice ones. So nice to have met you again.

the audience vote on how they want my pictures to end." (In that same interview, Castle also told Smith one of his most shocking lies: that his *Psycho* ripoff *Homicidal* was finished two years *before* the release of *Psycho* but held up by the censors!)

Now that a *Sardonicus* gimmick had been devised, it was time for Castle to step before the cameras. He appears in the movie twice, once in the pre-credits sequence and again in the last reel to conduct the

... but for part of that closeup, his lip movements do not match the words. Lip-readers who can tell us what he originally said, before looping a new line over it, are encouraged to report to the Classic Horror Film Board (use Google to find us) and break the news. Also filmed on that meager Embankment set: Castle's second appearance in the movie, telling audience members how the Punishment Poll works, counting the Mercy–No Mercy votes ("Seventeen …

Homicidal *and* The Terror of the Tongs *comprised the "double horror" program at the London Pavilion in 1961. Some patrons attended in ghoulish makeup, and several of them put on an act in the lobby.*

carry the three ... ") and then proclaiming that, per the viewers' wishes, Sardonicus will be made to suffer and suffer ... and suffer.

Richard Kahn, a Columbia publicist in the days when Castle nested there, recalled the director's performance in the Punishment Poll sequence for documentary filmmaker Jeffrey Schwarz: "He's enjoying every minute of his screen time. If Bill could have been in 90 minutes of his 90-minute movie, he would have!"

"Everything that [Castle] did, I think was geared to get a reaction," according to Fred Olen Ray, a "talking head" on Schwarz's made-for-DVD doc *Taking the "Punishment Poll."* "The movie wasn't a movie, it was more than a movie. It was sort of like an experience or an event."

As mentioned above, Castle also went out into the field that spring and summer on behalf of *Homicidal*.

On June 6, he flew to Minneapolis on the first leg of a five-city personal appearance tour; in July, he was in Cincinnati, Cleveland and Philadelphia (and probably 22 other cities I don't know about), and in August, he was off to Europe to beat the drum there.[32] He said in the aforementioned *Newark Evening News* interview:

> My way of communicating with the public is not only to talk to them from the screen but to meet them in movie houses. I sell popcorn, usher people up and down the aisles, gab to them on a buddy-buddy, first-name basis, get their honest opinions of what they want on the screen.[33]

San Francisco–based *Variety* columnist William Steif was unimpressed with the idea of moviemakers pressing the flesh with their audiences, and wrote on June 12:

Used to be actors and actresses made the circuit plugging their films — now it's the producers. For instance, Jerry Bresler's due June 19 for *Gidget Goes Hawaiian*, William Castle June 20 for *Homicidal* and Carl Foreman June 26 for *Guns of Navarone*. Such timing, and such thread-worn gimmickry, are liable to draw yawns from some segments of the press.

(It seems unlikely that theater appearances by Messrs. Bresler and Foreman added to the toil of whatever municipal department is tasked with preventing overflow audiences from standing in the aisles.)

In mid-September, after a confab of circuit executives, theater division managers and Columbia sales execs, *Mr. Sardonicus*' exploitation gimmick, the Punishment Poll, was revealed. Castle wrote in *Step Right Up!*,

> Just before the final scene, the picture stopped and my image came onscreen, asking the audience how they felt about the fate of Mr. Sardonicus. Should he be punished – or not? Thumbs down meant death; thumbs up, life. My image onscreen then began to count the voting. (The theater managers actually did the count.) Invariably, the audience's verdict was thumbs down. It's always amazed me how bloodthirsty audiences are.

Outside theaters showing *Mr. Sardonicus*, said Castle, were loudspeakers luring patrons with this recorded message:

> Have you ever envied the thrill-hungry Roman crowds in the Circus Maximus who, with a wave of the thumb, could make life or death decisions that sealed the fate of many a gladiator?
>
> The fate of that ghoulish character Sardonicus is in your tender little hands.
>
> You have the opportunity of literally deciding the monstrous fiend's fate.

Actually, they didn't. Contrary to what Castle wrote in *Step Right Up!* ...

> [J]ust in case the audience voted for mercy, we had the other ending. But it rarely, if ever, was used.

... there *was* no happy ending for the barbaric baron. Some spoil-sport reviewers let their readers know this. *Miami News* columnist Herb Kelly wrote on November 22, 1961, "There's no optional ending for the movie"; the *Oakland Tribune*'s Theresa Loeb Cone revealed (December 11, 1961), "Sly producer William Castle only made one ending for the picture"; Minneapolis' *Star-Tribune* described the voting process but then added, "It doesn't make any difference. There's only one ending, a miserable one for Mr. S."; according to *The Hollywood Reporter*'s Lawrence H. Lipskin (October 13, 1961), "Castle, normally intent on the horror at hand, has his tongue in cheek. (After all, there's only one ending in the projector!)"

> It was a heartless crowd at the show we caught. ...Almost everyone turned thumbs down on the villain.
>
> – *Miami News* columnist Herb Kelly

For years, Monster Kids wondered if the alternate ending would ever turn up; it ought to have always been plenty obvious to them that the picture had just the one finish, because all in one scene, Castle raises the issue ("Has Mr. Sardonicus been punished enough?"); explains how to vote; counts the votes; and instantly announces, "Hah! No mercy! So be it! You have given the verdict." And the *Mr. Sardonicus* pressbook, telling exhibitors how to run the Punishment Poll, says that on-screen, Castle will solemnly announce that the audience verdict is "'thumbs down,' which it invariably will be...."[34]

Will a *drive-in print* of *Mr. Sardonicus* ever turn up? In the pressbook, drive-in managers were advised to put Activator Booths near their concession stands, and told that the on-screen Castle would ask patrons to hold their Punishment Poll cards out their car windows.

Castle also talked about the Punishment Poll in *Sardonicus*' trailer, a very lengthy (over three and a half minutes) teaser in which camera-lovin' Castle is seen and/or heard for 4/7ths of the running time, leaving only about 90 seconds for clips from the picture. Amusingly, it starts with Castle (and that damn cigar) in profile and silhouette, evoking the Hitchcock profile-silhouette seen by TV viewers every week on *Alfred Hitchcock Presents*. "The screen's NO. 1 shock expert" talks and talks, introduces the clips, and then returns with a Punishment Poll card to explain how theater audience members can vote. Sardonicus appears in some of the clips but with his face partly or completely hidden (see photos on next page); Castle says that this was done because he felt that some trailer viewers might be "adversely af-

Top: a Phantom of the Opera *(1925) ad from which Lon Chaney's face was obliterated to whet the curiosity of potential ticket-buyers.* Below: *Mr. Sardonicus' trailer tried the same ploy.*

fected" by the sight. This calls to mind the way that Lon Chaney's made-up *Phantom of the Opera* face was "blanked out" on promotional photos, lobby cards and programs in 1925, to keep public anticipation for the picture on high; see photo on preceding page. Could the absence of Skull-Teeth Sardonicus shots in the trailer have been Castle's idea? He'd already compared *Mr. Sardonicus* to *Phantom* when talking with set visitor Harrison Carroll.[35]

In mid–October 1961, Castle the Eternal Showman was off on a *Mr. Sardonicus* p.a. tour. Like the baron, he was all smiles at theaters in New York (his birthplace), introduced by disc jockey-TV personality Fred Robbins. The movie got a *full-page* **STARTS TODAY** ad in the Wednesday, October 18, *New York Daily News*, listing not only the scores of theaters at which it would play, but also the places where Castle would make his appearances that day (the RKO Newark at 4 p.m., the RKO Madison at 7:30 p.m. and the RKO Flushing at 9 p.m.); there were more New York p.a.s in the days to come. The co-feature in that area was *Five Golden Hours* with Ernie Kovacs and Cyd Charisse, but in other parts of the country, its running mate was the fantasy-adventure *Valley of the Dragons*, supposedly based on a Jules Verne story. *Dragons* was directed by Edward Bernds, the Columbia sound recordist who, in the early '40s, watched as dialogue coach Castle was mocked by other crew members.

Mr. Sardonicus was not yet released when Marc Russell's dad brought him to a Columbia projection room where it was about to be screened; the ten-year-old next saw it in its first week of release at the Wiltern, a big Wilshire Blvd. theater where it was paired with *Valley of the Dragons*. "Even at age ten, I could tell that *Valley of the Dragons* was a crummy movie," Marc recalls. "It contained more stock footage than any movie I have ever seen. Even at that age, I recognized the stock footage and felt cheated."

Two denizens of the online Classic Horror Film Board, old enough that they saw *Mr. Sardonicus* first-run, had thumb fun voting on the baron's fate, and described the experience online. According to Rick Pruitt,

My theater [the LeRose Theatre, Jeffersonville, Indiana] ran out of Punishment Poll cards just before I entered, dang it! My friends all got them and evidently most of the crowd did. At the time, I believed that there were indeed two endings (though I had nagging suspicions that I was being had). At Poll time, I begged everyone around me to vote for "Mercy" because I assumed that, if there was only one ending, then that was gonna be "No Mercy." I knew that Castle wasn't really counting from the screen, but I was holding out childish hope that somebody was hiding behind the curtain somewhere, actually counting. I was gullible, yes, but more than that, I was just hopeful. I remember that everyone was anxious to hold their vote high and make sure it counted.

And Bill Littman posted, "A lot of us held the Punishment Poll cards sideways just to see what would happen; and there was this one fool who Frisbee-ed the card at the screen because he thought it was too small for Castle to see."

In 1999, Audrey Dalton told me that she had completely forgotten about *Mr. Sardonicus*' gimmick

> until I saw it again a few years ago. My husband Rod and I were in Atlanta for several months in '91 and '92, and a museum there was showing a series of horror pictures. That was one of them, and we went to see it. And I had forgotten all about the Punishment Poll. It was sort of a gimmick, wasn't it? It's a terrible interruption in the picture [*laughs*]! [*TW: But it wasn't on the level, since you never filmed a "happy ending" for* Sardonicus.] Of course not [*laughs*]! It was just sort of silly.

Theater managers were also encouraged by the pressbook to dust off a number of hoary attention-grabbing gimmicks: bathe the theater lobby in a green light, have a nurse hand out smelling salts, and of course…

> Send a man dressed in elegant 19th century costume and wearing a mask through the busy downtown streets of your situation. Have him carry on his back the following sign: "I Am 'Mr. Sardonicus,' Man of Mystery. If You Want to Learn My Evil Secret, See Mr. Sardonicus, State Theatre Now."

"I would rather have a child see *Mr. Sardonicus* than any pictures on sex and dope," Castle told interviewer Bea Smith. "Children are easily impressed. And don't they thrive on grotesque masks and costumes on Halloween. That's part of their heritage."

Movie critics in 1961, especially the ones writing for the trades, tended to vote thumbs-up for the picture, and some graded Castle's acting right along with that of its stars. *The New York Post* wrote that he "pulls a Hitchcock" and added, "Castle is better looking than Hitch, but not quite as irresistibly hammy. Give him time." *The Hollywood Citizen-News*: "One of the most amusing aspects to [Castle's] films … is the injection of his own dramatic histrionics somewhere in his pictures. Last night's 'ham' caused the party next to me to let loose with some rather explosive expletives – probably just as well Castle couldn't hear them." *The Boston Globe*: "There have been gossip-column rumors that Producer William Castle has been adopting several Alfred Hitchcock mannerisms and methods. But Castle, in introducing [*Sardonicus*] and making comments on it – as 'Hitch' does on TV programs – can never quite reach the unctuous delight in horror attained by the master."

It was a few years before *Mr. Sardonicus* made the passage to England, and not all of it reached the screen there. So much was cut, in fact, that Londoner Michael Freeman, a fan who obviously took his fright flicks seriously, wrote this lengthy letter, published in the July 1965 *Films and Filming*:

> Any ideas that the censor is becoming more liberal will be immediately dispelled on seeing *Mr. Sardonicus*…. Admittedly, William Castle isn't my favorite director, but his work (and this 1961 production is one of his best) deserves to be seen. One censor has decided otherwise and has produced a positively gruesome piece of mutilation. William Castle's opening introduction has been cut because he is about to say that "a ghoul is a creature that opens graves and feeds on the dead." This statement has wisely been cut in case it could corrupt anyone. The same goes for a similar statement later in the film made by Guy Rolfe. Then the censor starts on the visual side of the film. A shot of a tortured maid has been cut because she has (horrors) several leeches on her face! (*The African Queen* has Bogart positively smothered in leeches, but, of course, the circumstances were more acceptable.) When Guy Rolfe opens his father's grave, a shot (and an important one, plotwise) of the corpse's face is cut. Yet a similar shot was allowed in

Anna the servant girl, victim of Krull's (Oscar Homolka) ongoing abuse, was played by Lorna Hanson. The leech scene was one of several that English censors snipped, according to an annoyed Films and Filming *reader.*

The Premature Burial. The most important scene, in which Sardonicus' wife sees his face, has also been cut. (Not so the unmasking scene of *House of Wax* and Chaney's *Phantom of the Opera*.) This makes nonsense of the plot's ramblings about his deformed face and we don't see it until just before Sardonicus is cured. Then, it happens so off-handedly that any possible terror evoked by his deformity is lost. In fact, this scene brought derisive laughter from the audience, who were unprepared for it.

Now, the amusing thing is not just that it has been cut to such an extent that an "A" certificate could easily have been given, but that Ray Russell's novella, which his screenplay follows almost exactly, is available in paperback form to anyone who wants to read the lowdown on ghouls. When I was at school, dog-eared copies of "Sardonicus" were circulated among the First Formers. Yet the film adaptation is not only barred to them, it is barred to adults in anything other than an abridged version.

Count me in, alongside Freeman, as someone who considers *Mr. Sardonicus* one of Castle's best. (Ditto *Starlog* editor Dave McDonnell, who recently blogged, "The very thought of *Mr. Sardonicus* makes me smile.") But either 1961 audiences disagreed, or Castle was going to the well too often, because horror movie–wise, *Sardonicus* appears to have been his first box office disappointment. Surely the movie made a respectable showing at ticket windows, but by '61 Castle was used to seeing the titles of his chillers on each year's top-grossers list, and *Mr. Sardonicus* did not make the cut. And it followed on the heels of *Homicidal*, which as of September 1961 was heading for a $3,000,000 gross – his *biggest* grosser. At the end of '61, Castle proudly told columnist Sheilah Graham that *Homicidal* would earn $5,000,000. Perhaps *Mr. Sardonicus*' smaller numbers were what prompted Castle to also tell Graham, "I started the horror cycle and I've ended it with *Mr. Sardonicus*." (A bulletin from the Fact-Check Dept.: Castle did not start the horror cycle; and post–*Sardonicus*, after a couple of comedies and the unwatchable *13 Frightened Girls* [1963], Castle went right back *into* the goosebump business.)

***

Some might say that *Mr. Sardonicus* lays on the daubs of melodrama a little thickly, while others will find it delightfully old-fashioned and unrestrained. It certainly does observe all rules of Classic Horror Film etiquette – a hero (knighted, no less) with gallantry to spare, a heroine aswoon, a title character ranking with the more pitiless figures in the deep roster of drive-in depravity, all spouting their dialogue with relish. And all of this in the service of Ray Russell's imaginative premise. (Perhaps the only misstep: castle sets that are overlit and *then* some. I don't know what I'd want less, Sardonicus' face or his monthly candle and torch bills.)

With *Mr. Sardonicus*, William Castle proved that he could be a contender not just in the world of seat buzzers, audience plants and phony lobby nurses, but as a director of old-school period thrillers. And Ray Russell, who could have papered his walls with rejection slips before finally making his first magazine sale, demonstrated with his very first screenplay that he was ready for the Hollywood prime time.

Mr. Sardonicus (1961)
Columbia
William Castle Productions
89 minutes
Associate Producer: Dona Holloway
Produced and Directed by William Castle
Screenplay: Ray Russell, from his novella "Sardonicus"
Photography: Burnett Guffey
Music: Von Dexter
Art Director: Cary Odell
Editor: Edwin Bryant
Set Decorator: James M. Crowe
Makeup Supervisor: Ben Lane
Assistant Director: R. Robert Rosenbaum
Sound Supervisor: Charles J. Rice
Sound: James Z. Flaster

Variety "Film Assignments," April 4, 1961:
Assistant Director: Leslie Gorall
Script Supervisor: Eylla Jacobus
Camera Operator: Andrew McIntyre
Assistant Cameraman: Arnold Rich
Still Photographer: Homer Van Pelt
Sound Recordist: Joe Finochio
Mike Man: Doug Grant
Cable Man: Jim Tilcher
Grips: Walter Meins, Emmet Dambacher
Gaffer: Howard Robertson

Best Boy: Henry Stevens
Assistant Art Director: Philip Jefferies
Props: Harry Hopkins, Jeff Stanton
Lead Man: Jim Meehan
Costume Designer: Pat Barto
Costumers: Jack Angel, Iva Walters
According to Ray Russell:
Makeup: Maurice Seiderman

Cast
Oscar Homolka (*Krull*)
Ronald Lewis (*Sir Robert Cargrave*)
Audrey Dalton (*Maude*)
And
Guy Rolfe (*Marek Toleslawski aka Baron Sardonicus*)
Vladimir Sokoloff (*Henryk Toleslawski*)
Erika Peters (*Elenka Toleslawski*)
Lorna Hanson (*Anna*)
William Castle (*Himself*)

Unbilled:
James Forrest (*Dr. Geoffery Wainwright*)
Constance Cavendish (*Mrs. Higgins*)
Tina Woodward (*Mrs. Higgins' Girl*)
Mavis Neal (*Head Nurse*)
Charles H. Radilac (*Station Master*)
Albert d'Arno (*Gatekeeper*)
Annalena Lund (*First Girl*)
Ilse Burkert (*Second Girl*)
Franz Roehn (*Gravedigger*)
David Janti (*Janku*)

STORY

(Not for Publication) A famous British doctor, Sir Robert Cargrave, is called to a medieval Central Europe castle by Maude, his former love, to treat her husband, Baron Sardonicus, who wears a mask to hide his face, now paralyzed and resembling a grinning skull. This condition resulted when Sardonicus had ghoulishly profaned his father's grave to obtain a fortune-winning lottery ticket. Robert employs a psychological trick to free Sardonicus of his affliction. In gratitude, Sardonicus signs an annulment of his marriage to Maude and permits her to leave with Robert. The doctor tells Krull, the Baron's sinister servant, what else must be done but Krull deliberately ignores the advice. Torn by his ghoulish memory, Sardonicus suddenly discovers his jaws are now locked tight … he can no longer speak, eat or drink.

Script-to-Screen Changes

by Tom Weaver

Some of the more interesting differences between the *Mr. Sardonicus* script and the movie are listed on the next several pages.

Sardonicus' script calls for master of scare-emonies William Castle to stand on a dark, foggy London street as he makes his opening remarks in the pre-credits sequence. Through the miracle of stock footage and rear projection, the movie more picturesquely places him on the Embankment, with landmark buildings visible in the background. A ship's horn is repeatedly heard. The script indicates that he should wear a high silk hat but in the movie he sports a homburg.

Sir Robert works his massage magic at Kings College Hospital, according to the script. That's an actual London facility, opened in 1840. In the movie, we find Sir Robert laboring at Queens College Hospital, a name with no real-life London counterpart. Probably a wise change. "Queens College Hospital" does sound like a place you'd find in New York.

"Sardonicus" was set in Bohemia, and so was the script – at first. Perhaps to avoid giving offense to viewers hailing from Bohemia, someone must have ordered the deletion of the script's two dialogue references to that region. It's replaced the first time by Central Europe and the second time by Gorslava. What *was* Bohemia is now the Czech Republic.

Sir Robert is met at the railroad station by Krull, who keeps his horse-drawn coach at a leisurely trot while transporting Sir Robert to the castle. But in the script, the coach plunges wildly down a rocky winding road, reminiscent of Renfield's coach ride to Castle Dracula in the 1931 *Dracula*. Sir Robert, like Renfield, is jostled by the rough ride.

Seen first in the salon, Maude is reading a magazine which, according to the script, should be *The Illustrated London News*. That was, and is, the name of an actual English newspaper — the world's first illustrated newspaper, launched in 1842. Columbia probably didn't want to bother to ask their permission to depict a copy, and the on-screen magazine is titled *London Pictorial*.

Sir Robert sits in his hip bath tub washing himself and singing the English folk song "The Foggy, Foggy Dew" – in the *movie*. The *script* has him singing "Tit-Willow" from Gilbert and Sullivan's comic opera *The Mikado*. *The Mikado* premiered in 1885 and (again) *Mr. Sardonicus* is set in 1880, when (I presume) the song didn't yet exist.

Maybe a different song was chosen for Sir Robert to croon because Columbia would have had to shell out a few bucks to the Gilbert and Sullivan estate for the use of "Tit-Willow." Or maybe someone thought that a naked man singing about a little Tom-tit which he calls Dicky Bird, might set young audience members laughing. Probably a few older ones too.

Scandalous!: Krull is even rougher with women in the script than in the movie. He not only strings Anna up and threatens her with leeches, he also slaps her face.

Six is the number of lovely, shapely peasant girls that the baron has to choose from *in the script*. But in the movie, there are only five. In a cellar chamber, Sardonicus selects the fair girl, and orders Krull to pay the others and dismiss them. Krull and the four girls are just outside the closed cellar chamber door when the fair girl unmasks Sardonicus and screams, "No! No! No!" She has more to say in the script:

The beat goes on for Maude, who's learned that life with the baron is a three-ring circus: engagement ring, wedding ring, suffering. (Courtesy Ronald V. Borst/Hollywood Movie Posters)

No! Oh my God! Oh Merciful God in Heaven! No...no...NO!!

Presumably Sardonicus regularly presides over these mini-beauty pageants, and you'd think that word would spread among the local girls that he's a must to avoid. And yet we get the impression that there's never been a night when Krull had trouble getting enough girls.

Sometimes – not often, but *sometimes*, Maude shows some spirit in scenes opposite her husband, and she stands up to him the best she can when he makes his unexpected early-morning appearance in her boudoir. She's not the least bit sassy in the script version of that scene, where she shudders when she remembers the screaming girl from the night before, and is obviously frightened throughout the conversation. In the script, the scene ends with Sardonicus throwing her to the floor where she weeps uncontrollably.

Seen at the start of *Mr. Sardonicus'* flashback sequence is the Gorslava gravedigger – a hunchback in the script, straight-backed in the movie. Franz Roehn, who plays the role, talks about having actually seen ghouls prowl at night and open graves. In the script, the gravedigger adds one more detail:

GRAVEDIGGER: [A]nd we have heard them.

YOUNG SARDONICUS: Heard them?

GRAVEDIGGER: Feeding!

Script: Sardonicus, narrating the flashback, says that the *weeks* that followed his father's death were hard. **Movie:** He instead says *months*, not weeks, probably because someone realized that it would take more than weeks for the father's soon-to-be-unearthed body to decompose to the necessary level of gruesomeness.

Script: Marek unearths and opens his father's coffin while the moon is behind clouds, and begins searching the weskit pockets for the lottery ticket; when the clouds roll away and the sky brightens, he sees the horrifying face for the first time. **Movie:** Marek (and we) see the face the instant the coffin lid is raised.

Select a favorite: This book's copy of the *Mr. Sardonicus* script features *two* versions of the scene where Marek returns from the cemetery to his cottage. In the first version, he is calm and can speak and even kisses Elenka. In the second version, he is weeping and cannot speak, as in the movie.

Screaming Elenka is the first to see the title character's rictus grin, by the light of a candle in her cottage bedroom – and movie audiences also got *their* first look at it in that suspenseful scene. In the *script*, she lights the candle, turns to "us" (looks right into the camera) and begins screaming; then the flashbacks end and we return to the garden arbor and get our first look at Baron Sardonicus' scarifying kisser, in an extreme closeup, as he finishes telling Sir Robert his backstory.

Sardonicus is even more of a fright in the script: In addition to his ghastly teeth-baring grin, his eyelids are "hideously pulled down."

Several *Mr. Sardonicus* scenes provide good looks at the rictus grin. We first see it by the light of Elenka's candle in the cottage bedroom scene that ends the flashback portion of the picture. *In the script*, we do *not* see it then, but immediately afterwards: After Sardonicus finishes telling his backstory, the script calls for a return to the garden arbor and an extreme closeup shot of the unmasked baron.

During the scene where Sir Robert treats Sardonicus with hot towels and massage, the script dictates that viewers see the horrific face multiple times. But in this scene in the movie, when he's mask-less, we only see him from behind. Somebody – maybe Ray Russell – must have decided that viewers shouldn't see Sardonicus' choppers *that* often, and so we don't glimpse them even once during this scene.

Sardonicus, anxious to undergo some of Sir Robert's untested treatments, offers to pay the physician. In the script, he starts at 1000 crowns and, when Sir Robert resists, he ups the ante to 5000 crowns and then 10,000. On film, Sardonicus is looser with a crown, starting at 10,000 and then 20,000 and 30,000.

Seeking to force Sir Robert to continue the search for a rictus remedy, the baron threatens to let Krull disfigure Maude, who is trapped in a torture chamber chair. Outraged, Sir Robert attacks him, but Krull bludgeons him into unconsciousness. When he awakens, we blurrily see what he sees: Sardonicus, Krull and a stoic-looking Maude. In the script, the Sir Robert's Point-of-View Shot shows us Sardonicus, then Krull, then

> the lower part of the iron chair with Maude's ankles firmly manacled. Now the CAMERA PANS slowly up her body, building

Suspense builds as the baron offers Maude the key to the padlocked room. "If you like the horribly ghoulish, terrifying and the macabre, [Mr. Sardonicus] has its moments."—New York Daily News

> suspense. Just before we see her face:
> CLOSEUP ROBERT
> apprehensive. A very BRIEF SHOT.
> CLOSEUP MAUDE
> still held in the iron collar. Her face is tear-stained – but unharmed.

Say *what*??: In the script, Sir Robert tells Maude that to fix the baron's face, he'll require "equipment and *materia medica* from far-off places." The movie saves viewers a trip to the dictionary: Sir Robert says he needs "drugs and equipment from far-off places." How far-off is far-off? At this point, screenwriter Russell called for a shot of a map of the world, circa late 1800s, with the camera panning from Bohemia to South America; and superimposed over the pan, stock footage of a machete-wielding South American native "chopping off pieces of a tropical vine or 'climber.'"

Sir Robert refers in the script to poison darts used by "South American savages." The movie, politically correct before its time, upgrades them to "South American natives."

Salon scene #2: The script calls for Maude, seated at a spinet, to play "something serene and stately, perhaps the 'Moonlight Sonata.'" What we hear in the movie is not "Moonlight Sonata" or any other tune that my corps of musicologists (John Morgan, Scott MacQueen, David Schecter) could identify. Morgan opined, "Sounds like some ditty Columbia's house arranger put together," while MacQueen called it "cookie cutter romantic twaddle with some odd harmonies – modern chords – with a melody not unlike the main title of *House on Haunted Hill*. That makes me think it's an original composition by Von Dexter."

Sardonicus gives Maude the key to the padlocked upstairs room and instructs her to open it. In the script, there's a bit more build-up: The baron adds, "There is someone in that room..."

> Maude: "Someone? There? Who?"
>
> Sardonicus: "A good and almost saintly man who may be able to convince Sir Robert he should perform the treatment."

The evil baron is referring to his father's decayed body.

Strychnos toxifera is injected into the baron while the camera provides a closeup of hypo wielder Sir Robert. Writer Russell was more imaginative:

> Against a bare wall, the flickering candle casts the gigantic, wavering shadows of Robert and Sardonicus in the chair. In silhouette, we see Robert bring the needle close to Sardonicus' face and plunge it into the flesh. Sardonicus stiffens visibly in the chair.

And when Sardonicus begins screaming about being in the dark, it's Sir Robert in the script who opens the Judas window in the door (lighting up the face of the dead father) – this was presumably part of his "shock treatment." In the movie, Krull opens the window.

Sardonicus, his face restored to normalcy, hurries out into the hall and up to a huge papered-over mirror. He tears at the paper and takes a long look at the reflected image of his handsome-again countenance. Then, glaring as if angry, he

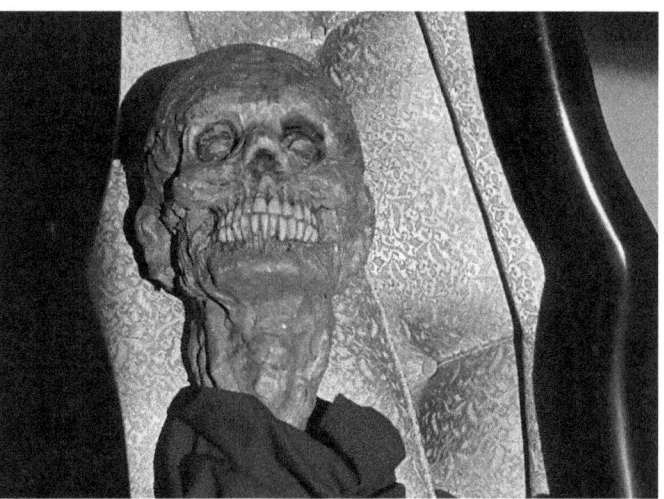

Make (a) Room for Daddy. Sardonicus does just that. Then he padlocks it.

stomps away. In the script, his reaction is quite different: "Whimpering sounds of joy issue from his closed mouth. Tears form in his eyes and run down his face." But these emotions don't last: "Then, he gains control of himself and some of the old arrogance and coldness return."

Shambling up to the mirror after Sardonicus has finished admiring himself, Krull gets what might be his first-ever look at his one-eyed hideousness – and then hangs his head in anguish. It's a great moment, and it's not in the script. I'd love to know who thought to add it. Set visitor Russell? William Castle? Perhaps Oscar Homolka? It certainly helps set the stage for Krull's betrayal of his master.

State your price!: In a note to Sir Robert, Sardonicus tells the physician to name his fee. Sir Robert crumples up the paper and says, "No, baron, you owe me nothing." In the script, this is followed by what *would* have been the movie's Stand Up and Cheer moment: Sir Robert continues, "But *I* owe *you* much. In payment for forcing Maude into marriage ... for terrorizing her ... for threatening to mutilate her ... for your unfeeling cruelty and rapacity ... I owe you *this*!" And with that, Sir Robert uncorks a punch that knocks Sardonicus to the floor.

The punch *must* have been filmed: In the *Mr. Sardonicus* still of Guy Rolfe standing by the wall on which he's written **BEGONE**, there's a bit of "blood" on one corner of the actor's mouth. (See the last page of this book.)

Seated inside the coach as it leaves the castle in the final reel: Sir Robert, Maude and Anna. But in the script, Sir Robert *drives* the coach, while the ladies converse inside:

> Anna: Oh, I'm so happy you let me come with you, Baroness!
>
> Maude: I couldn't let you stay there, Anna ... and you must not call me Baroness any more, or I shall be very angry!

Stricken by fear (and perhaps self-pity) now that he can no longer ingest food and drink, the movie Sardonicus staggers to the staircase and leans against its side, his head hanging low. In the *script*, the camera gives us a bird's-eye view of the action (accentuating his new status as a "defeated giant") as he leans against a *wall* and, with his head *upturned*, continues to claw at his mouth. This is followed by a cut to EXT. GATE OF CASTLE – NIGHT, a closeup of the **S** on the gate with the castle in the background. Out of the **S**, the end title looms.

"Accept this token of my censure and detestation!" I said.

From the January 1961 Playboy *that featured Russell's novelette "Sardonicus," here's an illustration depicting the tale's one feel-good moment: Preparing to leave Castle Sardonicus with Maude, Sir Robert sets aside his "apostle of science" mantel and gives the deep-dyed villain a parting shot – in the mouth! The script also called for Sir Robert to lay one on him, but that footage didn't make it into the movie.*

Meet the Sardonicuses

Guy Rolfe

By Laura Wagner

Strange are the ways of the movie world. In his native England, actor Guy Rolfe got the romantic roles that his good looks, lean 6'4" frame and suavity called for. But Hollywood took one look and could see only Villain. "I have what you call honest blue eyes and British directors instruct damsels to swoon when I take them in my bony arms," he told columnist Clement D. Jones. "[But in the U.S.], for some perverse reason, you see evil in my angelic English face. This I find difficult to understand, but I shall take your money and go home and resume my heroic romancing." For Hollywood companies, Rolfe played the fanatical rebel leader in *King of the Khyber Rifles* (1953) opposite Tyrone Power, and not-so-noble nobles in historical yarns that ranged from MGM's magnificent *Ivanhoe* (1952) to *Snow White and the Three Stooges* (1961). Notoriety came in 1961 via his role as one of shock cinema's top monarchs of menace, Mr. Sardonicus, the sadistic baron with the face that was half-human, half-skeleton.

He was born Arthur Edwin Rolfe in Hendon, in the London borough of Barnet, England, on December 27, 1911. He had a brother Thomas (1907-1936) and a sister Edith (1916-2017), the latter nicknamed "Queen." Brought up in Kilburn, London, they attended Christ Church School. The family subsequently moved to Charles Crescent, Harrow, and Ferring, Crescent. According to Rolfe's early publicity, he lived on a farm, but his niece Jane Culver ("Queen"'s daughter) said that this is untrue. "In Berkshire, my great-grandparents had an old pub, The Boot," Jane said. Guy's father Tom worked in the pub and then as a London Transport busman.

Rolfe left school at 15; some sources say he did so to pursue full-time his passion for motorcycle and car racing, often building his own vehicles from scraps. Jane remarked, "Having experienced Guy's driving when he lived high up on a mountain in Spain, the 'racing driver' could well be true!" But Rolfe spoke about that part of his life very casually in a *House That Hammer Built* interview by Wayne Kinsey: He said that he got into auto racing "only because some

Guy and his sister Edith (nicknamed "Queen") in 1935. (Courtesy Jane Culver)

A young Guy when he worked as a policeman. (Courtesy Jane Culver)

friends of mine owned a garage and they were always putting peculiar cars together and I used to drive them for them at Greenford dirt track. It was saloon car racing and it was tremendous fun, but I was never serious about it."

Since Guy also loved the circus and was handy with his fists, he worked in the boxing booth with three other men at a nearby fairground. Years later, Guy said in an interview with the *Worthing Gazette*'s Peter Dean, "We had to take on all comers. If they beat us, they won 10c, and we got the sack." He laughingly told Wayne Kinsey that spectators "used to throw pennies in the ring if we were any good. I got about ten bob a week." Traveling with the circus for a year, Guy went undefeated. But when a bone in his nose got pushed across to the other side of his face, he decided to seek different employment. Subsequent jobs included clown, greengrocer, policeman (where he also boxed as a light-heavy champion) and newspaper reporter. While working at the grocery Sainsbury's, he almost lost a finger in a bacon-slicer; co-workers got him medical help and the digit was reattached. He discovered acting in a "fit-up" company (i.e., "we build our own sets") in rural Ireland run by the renowned actor-manager Anew McMaster.

"One of [McMaster's] favorite parts was Othello," Rolfe told the *Reading Evening Post*'s Roy Martin, "and on most nights he would just black his face. But once in a while he would strip to the waist and make up his whole torso — and you knew on those nights you had better be on your toes! He gave some of the greatest performances I have ever seen in little country halls before a handful of people."

In 1936, Rolfe became an assistant stage manager for a Dublin acting company and played small roles. He became so identified with the Emerald Isle that he was often mistaken for an Irishman.

Circa 1937, Rolfe began working in films in England, commencing with uncredited parts in *Knight Without Armour* and *Dinner at the Ritz*. He was a stand-in for Michael Redgrave in various films, notably Alfred Hitchcock's *The Lady Vanishes*. Around this same time, 1938, he was briefly wed to Paula Phillips. They divorced when she decided to move to New Zealand.

Although adventurous and a risk-taker, the 6'4" Rolfe had chronic tuberculosis and was quite sickly. In 1938, he temporarily set aside his career and took the first of many rest periods. This illness was the reason he was not in World War II. (His older brother Tom died of tuberculosis at the age of 29 in 1936.) In 1940, after listening to Rolfe's lungs, a doctor warned him, "You must give up acting. It's the worst job you could have chosen." Rolfe ignored this advice.

He went back to Ireland for a six-week Shakespearean engagement—and stayed. Rolfe acted at the Gate Theatre in *Spring Tide, The Last of Mrs. Cheyney, The Case of the Frightened Lady et al*. A veteran of Glasgow Unity Theatre productions, Scottish actress Jane Aird (born Jane Kerr MacDonald in 1910) was also in the company. She later became the second Mrs. Rolfe.

Guy and Aird joined the Savoy Players at the Grand Opera House in Belfast. The productions were directed by Frederick Tripp, and the troupe consisted of such actors as Basil Lord, Norman Chidgey, Anna Turner, Michael Bilton, Jean Hamilton, Patricia Stewart, Maurice Maxwell and Catherine Salkeld.

Starting in 1941, the Savoy Players acted in a number of diverse productions: *Just Married, Distinguished Gathering* ("[Rolfe] is obviously an artist of experience, and his stage presence is good"—*Belfast News-Letter*), *When Knights Were Bold, Peg o' My*

In England, the cinema's Guy Rolfe was a heartthrob. Hollywood thought otherwise.

Heart, The Letter, Dangerous Corner, Good Men Sleep at Home, Private Lives, The Shining Hour, French Without Tears, Almost a Honeymoon, The Blue Goose, Rain, Springtime for Henry, Easy Virtue, Wuthering Heights* (Guy as Heathcliff and Aird as Catherine; the *Northern Whig* reviewer called it Rolfe's "greatest performance yet"), *It Pays to Advertise, Rebecca, Indoor Fireworks, Gaslight, Marry at Leisure, Maria Marten, or The Murder in the Red Barn, The First Year, What Every Woman Knows, No Time for Comedy, I Killed the Count, Flat to Let, Lovers' Leap, Murder Without Crime, Camille, The Little Foxes, And So to Bed, Lady Windermere's Fan, Too Young to Marry* and more. But such activity wore on Rolfe's health, and he took several breaks. He was firmly dedicated to acting, and didn't mind being uncomfortable for the sake of his art. The *Belfast Telegraph*'s K.A. Fritz wrote of the Savoy Players:

Nearly all have learned acting the hard way, for they have gone through the ardors of touring the small towns of Britain, playing on damp and clammy boards of countless theatres, large and small. Not one of them would trade that experience for all the gold in the Bank of England. For out of their experiences, out of those days and nights, has grown their deep-seated love of the theatre.

These players, all of them, are now firmly a very part of Belfast, so thoroughly a part of the entertainment life of the city that they are known and beloved by thousands of servicemen of all the Allied Nations. Few members of the entertainment world anywhere are doing more than they are doing right here.

But it was too much for Rolfe. After a night when he collapsed on stage, he spent 18 months in the hospital. "It was the finest thing that could have happened to me," he told *The Daily Mirror*. "It taught me how much in life one tends to take for granted."

In 1945, in England, the Rolfes joined the Overture Repertory Players headed by Victor Platt at the New Connaught Theatre. *On the Spot, Children to Bless You, Someone at the Door, The Breadwinner, The Blue Goose, The Wind and the Rain, There's Always Tomorrow* and *Hay Fever* were some of the plays on their schedule. The following year, Rolfe acted with Frances Day in *Evangeline*, a musical version of *Nymph Errant*; also in the cast were Sebastian Cabot and Jon Pertwee.

Nineteen forty-seven brought Guy Rolfe a movie contract with the J. Arthur Rank Organisation. His first for the company was the set-in-Ireland *Hungry Hill* (1947), where he played a miner. That year, he also had uncredited roles in *Odd Man Out, Meet Me at Dawn* and *The Life and Adventures of Nicholas Nickleby*.

Guy as the menacing Sepulchre Hawkes in Uncle Silas *(1947). Walking encyclopedia William K. Everson wrote that this thriller, "with its full-blooded style and marvelous sets, lighting and camerawork, ... is something of a classic of filmic Grand Guignol."*

In the latter, he portrayed Mr. Folair, whom Charles Dickens described in his source novel as "pretty well known among his fellow-actors as a man who delighted in mischief" and "by no means scrupulous." John Dighton's adaptation cut most of his character out of the story.

Uncle Silas, Rolfe's last released film of 1947, was based on J. Sheridan Le Fanu's 1864 Gothic novel of a teenage heiress becoming the ward of her duplicitous and greedy uncle. A suspense classic, it starred 18-year-old Jean Simmons as Caroline (changed from Maud in the book), Derrick De Marney as Uncle Silas, Katina Paxinou as the terrifying Madame de la Rougierre and Derek Bond as the romantic Lord Richard Ilbury.

One of the novel's *dramatis personae* is a miller named Dickon "Pegtop" Hawkes, a disagreeable character from his "swarthy, sullen face" down to his wooden leg. He abuses his daughter Meg. "Pegtop" is a major character in the novel, but the movie's scripter Ben Travers diminishes his importance to the story, while also changing his first name to Sepulchre (i.e., a tomb or burial place), his occupation to gamekeeper and his daughter to a young son; Travers also made Hawkes a mute. Even with his limited screen time, a surly Rolfe makes a vivid impression. He's the powerful henchman of old, frail, diabolical Uncle Silas, intimidating from his first scene where he backhands his own son, to his last scene where he brawls with Bond. (Bond ends the fight by clubbing him with a pistol.) *Uncle Silas* has production trimmings worthy of a David Lean Dickens adaptation and, at the center of its plot, a deep-dyed fiend whose black deeds would be the envy of a Karloff or a Tod Slaughter.[1]

Guy was cast in the thriller *Snowbound* (1948) with Robert Newton, about a search for Nazi treasures in the Alps. But in July '47 when the start of production was looming, he had to be replaced because of illness.

In a December 1947 *Kinematograph Weekly*, British film producer Sydney Box made his predictions for the ten British Stars of Tomorrow. Dirk Bogarde topped the list, which also included Margaret Leighton and Christopher Lee; Rolfe came in at number nine. Box wrote, "Guy Rolfe, six feet four and not unlike Gregory Peck, gets his first big chance opposite Phyllis Calvert in *Broken Journey* [1948]." Rolfe had just completed *Broken Journey* and *Easy Money*, the former produced by Box, the latter produced and co-written by him.

At the end of 1947, Rolfe was spending a "quiet Christmas in his small Hertfordshire country cottage" (*Kilmarnock Herald and North Ayrshire Gazette*) with wife Jane (who was taking a break from appearing in a play). He had recently converted two tiny cottages into one bigger one. As a Christmas gift, he wanted "the other three-acre meadow at the bottom of ours." Transforming smaller cottages into larger ones and then selling them was a hobby he would continue to pursue, sometimes with his actor friend John Justin (of the Korda *Thief of Bagdad* fame).

Broken Journey brought Rolfe to the attention of critics and moviegoers, although it did not do well at the box office. An ensemble piece, it featured a group of excellent actors: Phyllis Calvert, James Donald, Margot Grahame, Francis L. Sullivan, Raymond Huntley *et al*. The story of a plane forced down on a mountain glacier near the Swiss Alps and the efforts of the crew and passengers to survive, it was inspired by a real-life 1946 incident. In the movie, the plane's mild-mannered but no-nonsense pilot (Rolfe) proves to be one of the more efficient, practical characters. The *Sunday Mirror* called it "a tense, dramatic, well-acted comedy-thriller which moves slowly, but excitingly, and is brilliantly photographed," and counted Rolfe among those whose performances "clearly earmark them as future Big Names."

In September '48, at the Lyric Hammersmith in London, Rolfe was featured with André Morell and Peter Hammond in *An English Summer: A Play of the Battle of Britain*, where he portrayed the leader of a fighting squadron. Written by actor Ronald Adam (who fought in the real-life battle), it was a well-received and critically acclaimed production.

For the BBC, Rolfe and Sonia Dresdel starred as the combative acting couple in *The Guardsman* (1948). That same year, Rolfe had a small part in the film *Saraband for Dead Lovers* with Stewart Granger. Granger was the actor who, according to the press, had the career Rolfe should have had.

"In recent months the name of a new British screen discovery has been creeping into press reviews," wrote the *Waterford Standard*. "The name is Guy Rolfe, and in a new film called *Portrait from Life* [1949], the owner takes a big step on the road to stardom." Although billed third after Mai Zetterling and Robert Beatty, Rolfe got his first lead in *Portrait from Life*: He was a British Army major who becomes intrigued by a painting of a young girl and tries to locate her among the Jewish refugees in the camps for displaced persons in post–World War II Germany. Rolfe's low-key and smooth manner, coupled with his resonate speaking voice, pegged him as one of the most important new romantic leads in British films. The *Sunday Mirror* called him a "long, rangy character who reminds one irresistibly of Gary Cooper." *Portrait from Life* was imported to the U.S. and renamed *Lost Daughter*; Marjory Adams of the *Boston Globe* was not bowled over by the movie but she considered Guy "big, attractive and likable."

Fools Rush In (1949), a "light-as-a-bubble comedy" (*Banbury Guardian*), was based on Kenneth Horne's 1946 West End play. It centers on Pamela Dickson's (Sally Ann Howes) decision to postpone her wedding the morning of because she wants to be sure the marriage will succeed. Reuniting with her father Paul (Rolfe), 16 years after his divorce from her mother (Nora Swinburne), adds to her doubts about matrimony. Rolfe effortlessly glides through the hectic proceedings with an adroit handling of the material, making "an unusually suave long-lost father" (*Derby Daily Telegraph*). He has an amusing mock-seduction scene with Patricia Raine (as Pamela's friend Millicent), and he teaches her a lesson: "That's to spare your blushes," he purrs, as he shuts off the lights.

"Feminine adolescents will admire the performance of Guy Rolfe as a handsome wolf in sheep's clothing," wrote the *Crewe Chronicle*. The *Hull Daily Mail* was adamant that his performance would assure him of a "high place among Britain's stars."

A cartoon image of Rolfe from the February 23, 1950, edition of England's Daily Mirror.

The Spider and the Fly (1949), the story of a master thief matching wits with a police official, is inarguably one of Guy's career highlights. The first half is devoted to the efforts of staid Paris police chief (Eric Portman) to catch slick, over-confident safecracker Rolfe, and eventually drawing this "fly" into his police "web." The second half is set during World War I: The policeman, now a counter-intelligence agent, needs to steal documents from the German legation in Switzerland, realizes that the job Takes a Thief, and recruits the imprisoned Rolfe. The *Coventry Evening Telegraph* called Rolfe "imperturbably sardonic" in the film, while Molly Hobman of the *Bradford Observer* weighed in with: "Guy Rolfe, tall, lean and nonchalant, springs into prominence by his performance as the crook whose relationship with the policeman is the best thing in the picture."

The Reluctant Widow (1950), Rolfe's next assignment, was more in keeping with the interests of his growing female fan base. An adaptation of Georgette Heyer's Regency romance novel, set in England during the Napoleonic Wars, it has just about everything: deathbed marriages, French spies, British traitors, secret documents, smugglers and swordfights. Jean Kent, a governess, takes the wrong carriage and ends up at the home of a dying British aristocrat whose cousin implores her to marry the soon-to-be-deceased. A bit convoluted at times, the film is saved by its tongue-in-cheek approach and the performances: Rolfe and Kent are a splendid screen couple. He makes a very romantic, dashing Lord Carlyon, and his duel with Julian Dallas (aka Scott Forbes) is a corker.

Top-billed Rolfe took a back seat to child actor Jeremy Spenser in *Prelude to Fame* (1950), the story of an English philosopher (Rolfe) seeing an uncanny talent for musical orchestration in a 12-year-old boy. A wealthy woman's obsessive interest pushes the boy to study and perform, and this almost leads to tragedy.

Rolfe had been working constantly in pictures for six months when he was offered the anthology *Trio* (1950), its segments "The Verger," "Mr. Know-All" and "The Sanatorium" based on W. Somerset Maugham short stories. Guy was to appear in the latter as the notorious womanizer Major George Templeton, who falls in love with fellow TB patient Evie Bishop (Jean Simmons). It would have been an excellent role for him, ideal for his romantic image, but it was not to be: He bowed out when he himself had

Jean Kent and Rolfe on the cover of the May 13, 1950, Picture Show *magazine.*

to enter a Swiss sanatorium in February 1950 because of a flare-up of tuberculosis, and Michael Rennie took his place in *Trio*. A fan sent Rolfe a silver chain with a St. Christopher charm attached, writing in her note, "If you wear this, you will certainly get well." Rolfe wore it while being interviewed by the *Daily Mirror*'s Donald Zec just before he left for the sanatorium: "This, and the suit I'm wearing is all I shall be taking with me," he said. "I guess that's all I shall need." The Rank Organisation took care of his weekly sanatorium charges, plus specialist and treatment fees. As well, they paid Rolfe six weeks full salary (he was making £8000 a year), and the rest of the time he was on half-salary. "I am deeply grateful to [Arthur Rank]," Rolfe stated. His wife Jane wanted to go to Switzerland with him, but

Rolfe vetoed the idea. "This is one job I must tackle alone. I'll be back before people realize it."

Rolfe was supposed to spend six months away, but it wasn't until late October that he was able to return to work. In between projects, he would rest on his farm. "I used to be an actor who did a little farming," he said. "Now, I'm a farmer who does a little acting."

Rolfe's niece Jane Culver remarked,

> Guy was not a frequent visitor when I was growing up; he obviously travelled a lot. Although his career didn't recover that well after his illness, he still made some movies and also loved acting in the theater! He was always very generous, providing my nana and granddad with a home until my nana's death in 1962 when Guy and Jane moved to Spain. He was extremely well-read, and was interested in everything. He had a fantastic sense of humor and loved to tell his tales.... Guy loved animals and was always adopting waifs and strays.

Rolfe and Margaret Johnston starred in the Irish play *The Chuckeyhead Story* by Paul Vincent Carroll. It was a "rambling, undisciplined, engaging and diverting comedy," according to the *Birmingham Daily Gazette*'s Brian Harvey, who thought Rolfe "a little over-casual at times: his performance makes me see imaginary cameras when he strikes a pose and hear imaginary voices shouting 'Cut' when he has no pose to strike."

In January '51, Rolfe did Margaret Luce's play *Harvest Time* at the "Q" Theatre. He also trod the boards that year in *The Silent Inn* and *Intent to Murder*. And there was a return to movie screens in director Terence Fisher's B murder mystery *Home to Danger* (1951)—a comedown after his earlier films. Still, he acquitted himself nicely as a genial novelist aiding a lady (Rona Anderson) marked for murder by persons unknown. After a slow start, *Home to Danger* picks up the pace and comes to a roaring conclusion. Anderson told historian Brian McFarlane, "Guy was a strange, very saturnine man who used to play vingt-et-un for money—and always used to win—while we were sitting around on the set. I was rather dubious about him, but one day I had a scene where I had to ride a horse, but the thing went out of control. I couldn't make it stop.... The next thing I knew, I was lying in the mud and who should be picking me up and wrapping me in his camel-hair coat but Guy Rolfe, so I changed my opinion of him after that."

Again at the "Q" Theatre, Rolfe was seen in Ian Stuart Black's *We Must Kill Toni* (1951), a comedy thriller about brothers who are dispossessed from their estate when their cousin Toni (Eileen Moore) comes of age. Should they murder her? Or should one of them marry her? Decisions, decisions! Rolfe and his friend John Justin play the brothers. *The Stage* liked their "contrasted methods," adding, "[T]heir comedy, lined with a slight touch of the sinister, is most effective."

Rolfe's first Hollywood movie, *Ivanhoe* (1952), was filmed at MGM British Studios in Borehamwood, Hertfordshire. Following in the footsteps of the esteemed Claude Rains in *The Adventures of Robin Hood* (1938), Rolfe received special "And" billing for playing the treacherous Prince John, who rules in place of his missing brother King Richard the Lionheart—and knows more about his sibling's disappearance than he lets on. The gallant Wilfred of Ivanhoe (Robert Taylor) learns that Richard is being ransomed by Leopold of Austria, and sets out to raise the money. (MGM first envisioned *Ivanhoe* as a vehicle for Taylor as far back as 1937!) This Technicolor adventure has its share of romance, jousting, fencing and an exciting mace and chain–battle axe fight between Taylor and George Sanders. Wearing the expression of a man who lives on lemons, his voice oozing menace, the spidery Rolfe makes his presence felt throughout, notably as he presides over the trial at which "witch" Elizabeth Taylor is sentenced to be burned at the stake. His imposing performance impressed many. This was a different Guy Rolfe from the one British audiences knew, his deep voice, so dreamy in England, now barbed and malicious. *Ivanhoe* was a Best Picture Oscar nominee and the second highest-grossing movie of 1952.

While Rolfe was busy with *Ivanhoe*, his wife Jane Aird was making her first feature film, *Hunted* (1952), starring Dirk Bogarde. "I haven't filmed before because we always thought one film actor in the family was enough," she told the *Sunday Mirror*'s Dick Richards. "Besides, after I married, I was too lazy to do much." She was also busy taking care of her husband, who still was not in the best of health. During her short film career, Jane appeared in the genre offerings *The Quatermass Xperiment/The Creeping Unknown*, *X the Unknown*, *Quatermass 2/Enemy from Space* and *The Day the Earth Caught Fire*. She acted only once on screen with her husband: 1954's *Dance Little Lady*.

In Universal's The Veils of Bagdad *(1953), Guy was given his typical role in an American film—that of a villain.*

Surely on the strength of his work in *Ivanhoe*, Rolfe was off to Hollywood to play the "shrewd and coldly intellectual" (*Whitstable Times and Herne Bay Herald*) Ned Seymour in MGM's *Young Bess* (1953). The movie chronicles the childhood and early life of Elizabeth I (Jean Simmons) and her romance with Thomas Seymour (Stewart Granger). Brothers Rolfe and Granger have a contentious relationship and there is a rivalry between them. Ned's machinations with wife Anne (shifty-eyed Kathleen Byron) cause many problems for Thomas. Interestingly, in real life, the situation was reversed: Thomas was jealous and resentful of Ned's position as Lord Protector of England for their nephew, nine-year-old King Edward. Be that as it may, *Young Bess* is a romantic picture, half fact, half fiction and *all* Hollywood, and Rolfe is at his nasty best bringing a little malice to court intrigues.

Asked about Hollywood, Rolfe remarked, "I like to go there for a few months a year, but live there? Never." He stressed to the *Reading Evening Post*'s Roy Martin that he was never a part of the English colony. "To me, people like Ronald Colman with their clipped speech seemed to have become almost a caricature of themselves, but I was very friendly with George Sanders, an actor I particularly admired."

Universal's *The Veils of Bagdad* (1953) was a typically colorful Middle Eastern adventure story, set in the bandit-plagued Ottoman Empire of the 16th century. On the plus side, it had a little something extra in the way of acting and its fights (involving wrestlers, acrobats and swordfights). George Sherman's direction gave some zip to the story of the Pasha of Bagdad (Leon Askin) and his right-hand man Kasseim (Rolfe), hoarding gold to unite the hill tribes against the Ottoman Sultan. Out to thwart this plan, Antar (Victor Mature) pretends to help Kasseim while romancing his wife Rosanna (Virginia Field). Also in on the action is a dancing girl (Mari Blanchard) with revenge on her mind. Dissatisfied married couple Rolfe and Field bring a sense of fun to their bickering; he calls her a "whining wench" while she questions his manhood more than once. The two, with their flawless British accents, lend class to the production. Kasseim soon becomes infatuated with the dancing girl and brings delight to the line, "She looks like a wild, untouched gazelle of the hills"—dialogue that would sound silly coming from other actors. Unfortunately, movies such as this garner very little respect. "It is something of a surprise to see English actor Guy Rolfe in this piece of hokum," wrote the *Dalkeith Advertiser*. *The Province*'s Les Wedman, in his column "At the Movies," added, "Guy Rolfe is disguised behind a beard in this. Quite a talented fellow, Mr. Rolfe can be grateful that few of his fans will recognize him." If they did, they would have been satisfied by his "gaunt, slightly sinister charm" (*Londonderry Sentinel*).

Back in England, Rolfe acted at the "Q" in the productions *Birthday Honours* (1953) and *The Queen's Husband* (1953), and then he was back to stirring up hill tribes in another Hollywood production: *King of the Khyber Rifles* (1953). Beyond the title and a few basics, the color–CinemaScope production had little connection with the novel by Talbot Mundy, set during World War I (and previously filmed by Fox with a WWI setting as *The Black Watch*, 1929). This remake is set at a remote British Army fort in 1857 India as Captain Alan King (Tyrone Power), a half-caste officer, trains the native cavalry, the Khyber Rifles. Rolfe plays a rebel leader on the verge of getting his country's hill people to rise up against British rule. And, as it happens, he is King's foster brother.

Power, in a return to the type of dashing-heroic role that made him a star, arrives at Rolfe's stronghold claiming to have deserted and expressing the wish

King of the Khyber Rifles (Tyrone Power) with Karram Khan (Rolfe), his "outrageously evil" (New York Times) foster brother.

to join the rebel forces—when he's actually there to watch for an opportunity to slay Rolfe. (Rolfe: "I never thought to see my brother again—except in battle.") Their early encounters are tense as the canny Rolfe suspects the real reason that Power is switching sides. Power takes the fight to Rolfe in the final reel: His soldiers battle Rolfe's men while, in Rolfe's tent, Power and Rolfe have a lengthy, very un–Hollywood fight: Wrestling on the floor over a pistol and then a knife, it's a grueling minute and a half of hard-breathing close-quarters suspense. During their battle, according to the Fox publicity mill, Power wrenched an elbow and Rolfe sustained a cut on his upper arm.[2]

Khyber Rifles is an action-packed adventure fable and quite entertaining. Power is a bit too old for his character but he is excellent nevertheless, and works well with leading lady Terry Moore, as the fort commander's daughter who loves him, mixed blood and all. (Audrey Dalton, later to play Baroness Sardonicus, unsuccessfully tested for the role.) The critics saved their highest praise for the Technicolor photography of the other-worldly Lone Pine locations where much of the movie was made, but Rolfe got his share of their attention:

> Guy Rolfe, the lean and hungry-looking British actor who makes so dire a villain, is the picturesque chieftain and a very convincing one, too. — Boyd Martin, *Courier Journal*

> Guy Rolfe is a magnificent rebel leader baring as handsome a set of teeth as Hollywood can boast. — Jane Corby, *Brooklyn Daily Eagle*

> Guy Rolfe makes the flesh creep. — *Kinematograph Weekly*

> [Rolfe] makes a fine villain, long, lean, black-bearded and dripping nastiness. He impressed us as a better man than Mr. Power... — Annie Oakley, *Windsor Star*

"We went up into the High Sierras for that," Rolfe told Peter Dean. "Thousands of feet above sea level and in a temperature of 120 degrees. I was playing Ty's half-brother [sic], there were plenty of fights and I did my own stunts. I felt wonderful."

After doing the play *Nine Days' Wonder* (1953), Rolfe starred in the British B *Operation Diplomat* (1953) as a doctor kidnapped to perform an operation on a mysterious patient. Its director John Guillermin later became known for his action films (*Guns at Batasi*, *The Blue Max*, *The Bridge at Remagen*, *Skyjacked*, *The Towering Inferno*, more). *Film Comment* described *Operation Diplomat* as "perhaps the first example of prime Guillermin ... a 70-minute programmer so tautly directed that every image counts, every detail matters, every actor's movement feels perfectly timed—a true gem." *Kinematograph Weekly* wrote that Rolfe "acts with dignity and energy."

In December 1953, *The Film Daily* put out their annual call to newspaper critics and reviewers and television and radio commentators to determine the best in motion pictures for the preceding year. *Courier-Journal* critic Boyd Martin selected some of the usual suspects: Frank Sinatra and Deborah Kerr for Best Actor and Actress for *From Here to Eternity*; Gloria Grahame for Best Supporting Actress for *The Bad and the Beautiful*. But for Best Supporting Actor, he wrote, "Guy Rolfe for his performance as the decadent King in *Ivanhoe* or even for his equally sterling performance in *Young Bess*."

In 1954, Rolfe had two movie offers in the U.S., *The Court Jester* (as another wicked king) and *The Egyptian*, but he had to turn them down; his health would not permit it. It was announced in March that "part-time invalid" Rolfe would soon check into

London's Brompton Hospital to have his left lung removed. He remarked to the *Belfast Telegraph,*

> I am tired of being forgotten, re-discovered, and then, just as the good parts come rolling in again, packed off for another year or 18 months' treatment.
>
> This sort of hide-and-seek life has disrupted my career three times—in 1938 and 1943, and in 1950.
>
> The doctor restricts me these days to four months' work a year, but it is not a very satisfactory way of building up a career.
>
> My latest picture was *Dance Little Lady* with Mai Zetterling. I was allowed to make it only on condition that I lived at a clinic all the time.
>
> It's rather like being a prisoner on ticket of leave, and I've had about enough of it. This lung has been nothing but trouble to me, and I cannot be any worse off without it.
>
> By the autumn, I hope to be not only out and about again, but fit enough to take on a film part, at home or in Hollywood.

In his youth, Rolfe had physically active interests. Now, he settled into painting oils and watercolors, and making pottery. "To create something imaginative from a hunk of wet clay appeals to me immensely," he stated.

In November 1955, Rolfe went in front of movie cameras for a supporting part in the comedy *It's Never Too Late*. By now, he and Rank had parted ways; *It's Never Too Late* was his first under contract to Associated British Picture Corporation. Phyllis Calvert plays a housewife and mother who writes a book amid her chaotic life. To her surprise, it is accepted by publisher Rolfe. Since her family takes her for granted, she leaves them to go to Hollywood to work on the screenplay of the movie adaptation. The urbane Rolfe has a small role but he is smooth and has one of the film's few sympathetic parts as his character falls in love with the married Calvert.

Based on a Barré Lyndon play, the *ITV Play of the Week* episode "They Came by Night" (1956) found Rolfe helping Scotland Yard by infiltrating a gang to recover a ruby. In the film noir *You Can't Escape* (1956), creepy Peter Darwin (Robert Urquhart) accidently kills his pregnant ex-girlfriend Claire (Elizabeth Kentish). His fiancée Kay (Noelle Middleton) reluctantly helps him dispose of the body. Dr. David Anstruther (Rolfe), Claire's foster brother, wants to solve the mystery of her disappearance. When Anstruther also falls for Kay, Darwin frames him. Urquhart has the most interesting male role in the film, with Rolfe his usual stalwart and romantic self, standing by the girl.

In February 1957, Rolfe did the play *The Widower* with Peggy Sinclair and Daniel Massey (son of Raymond) at the Connaught Theatre. "Guy Rolfe, an actor with a strange, compelling power about him, strolls through the role of the millionaire with a hard-won serenity," wrote the *Worthing Gazette*. "He possesses tremendous authority and his personality is such that he has only to flick an eyelid to steal the audience's wavering attention away from the other players."

Associated British production chief Robert Clark bought the screen rights to Alistair MacLean's best-selling debut novel *HMS Ulysses* for £30,000. R.C. Sherriff was set to write the screenplay and Rolfe was to play one of the leads. The project stalled.

In April '57, Mr. and Mrs. Rolfe starred in Noël Coward's *Blithe Spirit* at Belfast's Grand Opera House. Film-wise, a "smooth and disarming" (*Kinematograph Weekly*) Rolfe joined Roland Culver and Eunice Gayson in the comedy *Light Fingers* (1957). Culver's Humphrey Levenham thinks his wife Rose (Gayson) is a thief and has Dennis Payne (Rolfe) watch her—but it turns out that Payne is the crook. *Kinematograph Weekly* listed as its points of interest a "novel and funny story, popular players [and a] sly woman's angle." Rolfe ended the year with an episode of TV's *Hour of Mystery*.

"Tall, dark and handsome ... a hackneyed description perhaps, but it fits Guy Rolfe admirably," an Associated British ad for Rolfe read in 1958. "Since his first picture ... Guy's six-foot-four-inch frame and dark velvet voice have unwound the heartstrings of many a female admirer. Country lover, artist in oils, Rolfe prefers the quiet life ... though still remaining a well-known figure about town."

That year, Rolfe acted in Britain and Ireland in the plays *The Silent Inn* and *The Rainmaker* (with Yolande Donlan) and as narrator for the Cavalcade of St. John. On TV, he reunited with Jean Kent for *BBC Sunday-Night Theatre*'s "The Sulky Fire." Also on the small screen, he starred in *Murder in Mind*. His only motion picture in '58 was the comedy *Girls at Sea*, where he captained a boat that had some females stowed away. American Anne Kimbell played one of

Rolfe as the padre in the critically acclaimed war movie Yesterday's Enemy *(1959).*

the ladies with whom Rolfe falls in love.

For six episodes, between June 1 and July 6, 1959, Rolfe starred with Barbara Murray and pal John Justin in the BBC's *The Widow of Bath*. Scottish author Margot Bennett adapted her own 1952 novel for the series. A murder mystery, it is now considered lost.

In 1959, Rolfe appeared in one of his most critically acclaimed movies. *Yesterday's Enemy* was based on a BBC teleplay (by Peter R. Newman) from the previous year. Hammer Films claimed that this was to World War II what *Journey's End* was to the Great War. Stanley Baker stars as a captain trying to lead the remnants of a British brigade through Burmese jungle swamps and back to their regiment. In a small village, he orders the shooting of two Burmese civilians to get information from a third. The film was controversial because it depicted the British as capable of war crimes. *Yesterday's Enemy* was made at Shepperton Studios in Shepperton, Surrey. Production designer Bernard Robinson converted a stage into a Burmese village with bamboo huts, jungle and livestock. There's no music, just the sounds of the jungle and the men. *Variety*'s Rich pointed out that Rolfe "has a tricky task as the padre who himself is confused as to what is really right in war-time," but Rolfe comes through with one of his best screen performances. Exhausted by his experiences, but strong in his faith, the padre has a heartbreaking moment near the end when he leads his fellow prisoners in prayer. Director Val Guest regarded the picture as one of his favorites.

Hammer's *The Stranglers of Bombay* (1959) was a Terence Fisher–directed "historical horror"—in Strangloscope! In 1829 India, Captain Harry Lewis (Rolfe) of the British East India Company battles the Thuggee cult of Kali, savages who strangle and steal in the name of their goddess. At first the movie endeavors to provide a sort of history lesson about this purportedly real-life cult, but that soon gives way to exploitation thrills and a whole lot of violence: hands are cut off (and thrown through a window), eyes are burned out, bodies branded, and a king cobra and a mongoose fight to the death, in the impatient era when they didn't wait for you to be dead to put you on a funeral pyre. Rolfe stands as four-square as Tyrone Power did when *he* was King of the Khyber Rifles and *Rolfe* was India's #1 native agitator; all the murder and mayhem doesn't turn a hair of Rolfe's wavy and luxurious black mane. *Variety*'s reviewer commended Hammer for having recently set horror aside and "deciding to grow up," and hailed Rolfe's "very good performance."

For British television, Rolfe acted in *Interpol Calling* and *ITV Television Playhouse*. Filmed in Italy, *Revak the Rebel* (1960) was an NBC pilot for a 90-minute TV series to be called *The Barbarians*. The story was adapted from the novel *The Barbarians* by F. Van Wyck Mason and cost the network $750,000, then an unheard-of sum. When it did not sell, it was shown theatrically overseas, sometimes as *Revak the Barbarian* and *The Barbarians*.

A breathy Jack Palance plays Revak, an Iberian prince from the fictional Penda Island, who is enslaved with his people by the Carthage army led by the ruthless Kainus (Rolfe). Revak and his sister Creoda (Melody O'Brian) are taken aboard Kainus' ship. While Revak is tied to the mast, Kainus orders Creoda, "Dance! Beat time for this fair-skinned wildcat. Stand back so I can observe her artistry. Now entertain us, princess, before *I* entertain you." She pretends to dance, secretly pulling a knife from her cleavage and slashing Kainus' cheek. "You'll dance better without your claws, tigress," he growls after the knife is taken from her. "Dance now, or I'll place your brother's head at your feet!" As she does her carefully choreographed dance, Kainus eyes her lasciviously. "Come, princess, we shall dance alone,"

Patricia Medina and Rolfe have fun as a pair of ignoble nobles in Snow White and the Three Stooges *(1961).*

he whispers, pulling her toward his cabin. Creoda wants nothing of Kainus' long, lean frame and after dramatically bidding her brother goodbye, she takes a swan dive off the ship to her death. "She'd been a driveling nuisance, anyway," Kainus remarks disdainfully. Revak swears revenge against the people of Carthage in general and Kainus in particular.

Revak the Rebel showcases Rolfe's expertise at playing scoundrels. With his angular face partly covered with a drooping mustache and beard, his lanky body in period costumes, and his malevolent voice dripping venom with every syllable, he is fabulously evil.

"Guy Rolfe, who could be John Carradine's brother, is sneering, leering perfection as the magician," wrote the *Los Angeles Times'* Charles Stinson of Guy's turn as Count Oga in the Hollywood-made *Snow White and the Three Stooges* (1961). It's a film "ranging from broad comedy and sly humour to mild horror and enthralling romance" (*Hammersmith & Shepherds Bush Gazette*)—and not as bad as its reputation suggests. The Stooges (Moe Howard, Larry Fine, Joe DeRita) largely dispense with their knockabout humor and do some modest acting as they save Snow White (ice-skating champ Carol Heiss) and Prince Charming (Edson Stroll) from the beautiful but evil queen (Patricia Medina) and her creepy confederate Count Oga. "For an interesting piece of acting, of which one can nearly always be found in the worst movies," wrote Louis Cook of the *Detroit Free Press*, "Guy Rolfe has a neatly understated part as the wicked queen's sorcerer." Rolfe is also a good sport, getting kicked in the shins and pushed over. In one of the picture's best scenes, he mixes a potion for the queen to turn into an old witch. Rolfe and Medina's chanting and romping are delightful.

Rolfe went from the Stooges at 20th Century–Fox to shockmaster William Castle at Columbia, playing the title role in the producer-director's *Mr. Sardonicus*. A period chiller, it's set in Central Europe where, by horror film tradition, nothing is sacred to the local lord (Rolfe wearing an expressionless mask), a baron who abuses his servants (his one-eyed henchman Oscar Homolka is Exhibit A) and preys on peasant girls. As for the face under the mask, viewers expect the worst after learning that his castle is as devoid of mirrors as Count Dracula's. The baron waves his freak flag cruelly and high for almost 90 minutes before Castle appears on-screen to tell audiences that they must decide his fate in the upcoming final reel. *Mr. Sardonicus* wrapped but Rolfe stayed in the ghoul groove, remaining in Hollywood to star in an episode of Boris Karloff's anthology series *Thriller* ("The Terror in Teakwood"; for details, see page 192).

Mr. Sardonicus was Rolfe's last leading role in a feature until the 1980s. Why, after so many years as a stalwart of the British film community? According to the *Daily Herald*'s Ann Buchanan, British film companies shied away from him because his health—or lack thereof—made him a bad insurance risk. "Of course, I'd like to work in British films, but all that matters to me is that I *can* go on acting," he told her. "You grow philosophical when you're lying in bed."

"I'm thinking of selling up here, and going over to California for good," he said. His wife didn't like the idea one bit. "I agree with her, for Guy is everybody's idea of the perfect Englishman," wrote Buchanan. "His piercing blue eyes, perfect manners and beautiful voice make you think of cricket on the village green, the whir of a lawnmower on a Sunday afternoon—and chivalry. Why *should* we export this delicious home product to America?"

In September '62, he starred in the play *The Merry-Go-Round*. *The Stage* said, "Mr. Rolfe's timing, dry delivery, and skilled use of tone and glance never flagged, whether he was at his lectern or in his

Christine Kaufmann and Rolfe on the Taras Bulba *(1962) set.*

Prince Grigory (Rolfe) threatens to cut off Andrei Bulba's (Tony Curtis) hand in Taras Bulba *(1962).*

screams: His hand is chopped off by the angry Taras. Taras and his remaining army escape. Many years later, the Cossacks get their revenge by trapping the Polish army in their own city, where there's soon famine and disease. Taras' son Andrei (Tony Curtis) sneaks into the city to rescue the woman he loves, Natalia (the future Mrs. Curtis, Christine Kaufmann), but is caught and brought before Prince Grigory. Andrei comes close to losing a hand, but the prince reconsiders: Grigory promises to release Natalia in exchange for food held by the Cossacks. Rolfe is only in two sections of the film, but he makes the most of it with his regal and commanding bearing. Rolfe told Wayne Kinsey that *Taras Bulba* was shot in Argentina, where he and actor Sam Wanamaker took a house in the village of San Lorenzo and had a great time riding to the set on horses every morning.

Rolfe added that his *Taras Bulba* stunt double was the best horseman in that part of Argentina and "made me look absolutely marvelous." He could have used the guy again on *The Fall of the Roman Empire* (1964), for which he was signed to play a character named Marius. "I had a riding accident at the beginning of that film," he told Kinsey. "I got thrown from my horse and lost the part I was going to play."

In the British-made comedy-mystery *The Alphabet Murders* (1965), Belgian detective Hercule Poirot (Tony Randall) investigates a series of murders based on the initials of the victims. Rolfe portrays shady, womanizing psychiatrist Duncan Doncaster, who is treating schizophrenic Amanda Beatrice Cross (Anita Ekberg). His role was not substantial, but he made his mark and, importantly to him, he was working.

home. He was beautifully partnered [with] Elizabeth Hunt...."

Rolfe had a blink-and-you-miss-him role in *King of Kings* (1961, as Caiaphas) and a much better one in Harold Hecht Productions' *Taras Bulba* (1962), a 16th-century tale in which the title character (Yul Brynner) and his Cossacks help Prince Grigory's (Rolfe) Polish Army defeat the Turks for possession of the Ukraine. At a victory banquet, Grigory double-crosses the Cossacks by ambushing and killing them. The prince's gloating soon turns to anguished

From 1967 onward, Rolfe was seen mostly on the small screen, guesting on *The Saint, The Revenue Men, Love Story, Armchair Theatre, The Champions, Mogul, The Avengers, Department S, Churchill's People, Space: 1999* and *Secret Army.* Although he resumed moviemaking in the 1970s, the parts were again few and small (*Land Raiders, Nicholas and Alexandra, And Now*

Shady psychiatrist Duncan Doncaster (Rolfe) romances Amanda (Anita Ekberg) in The Alphabet Murders *(1965).*

Guy Rolfe and Hilary Mason in Dolls *(1986), the first of Rolfe's six pictures for exploitation movie producer Charles Band.*

the Screaming Starts!, Bloodline).

Beginning in the late '50s, he and Jane had a home in Marbella, Spain, where they "lived in solidary splendour at the end of a mountain path in one of the most beautiful settings on the coast" (David Wynne-Morgan of *The Tatler*). The climate was beneficial to Guy's health. "We had a wonderful time there," Rolfe told Roy Martin of the *Reading Evening Post*. "We were the first foreigners to settle in the area which was then totally unspoiled and the locals accepted us completely. Everything was about 200 years behind the times which suited me perfectly!" On their 50 acres of land, the couple cultivated fruit trees and tended sheep—and Rolfe claimed to keep in "vocal trim" by reciting Shakespeare to them. "They really seem to listen to you which is more than you can say for some people!"

On May 26, 1979, Rolfe's devoted wife Jane died in London at the age of 68. She had stayed by his side and took care of him through his many years of ill health. With her passing, Rolfe moved to London, and was dismayed at how dirty the city had become. "A lot of its elegance has gone and I really miss that, but culturally it is still a very exciting place and I enjoy living within ten minutes' walk of everything. I think you should either live in the heart of a city or totally away from it—there's nothing worse than the suburbs."

In 1981, Rolfe went back to acting in *Kessler*, a BBC miniseries about the hunt for a former Gestapo officer, now a war criminal (Clifford Rose). Guy portrayed Paraguayan aristocrat Don Julian Yqueras, a Nazi sympathizer loosely based on Juan Perón, president of Argentina, and Alfredo Stroessner, president of Paraguay.

In 1983, he did the plays *The Hollow* and *Tales from Hollywood* (playing Thomas Mann); he starred as the renowned detective in the movie *Sherlock Holmes in The Case of Marcel Duchamp* (1984); had a fleeting part in *The Bride* (1985); acted on BBC Radio Four's play "A Change of Frequency" (1985); was the title character in the bizarre short *Visiting Mr. Beak* (1987); did the miniseries *The Dark Angel* (1989); and portrayed the emperor on the filmed-in-France TV series *Crossbow* (1988-89). He continued to take periodic breaks between roles.

Producer Charles Band's *Dolls*, a "horrific parable on the value of innocence" (*The Kerryman/Corkman*), began filming in 1985 in the Rome, Lazio, Italy, movie studio once owned by producer Dino De Laurentiis. Rolfe, who portrayed dollmaker Gabriel Hartwicke, was cast due to the fact that its director Stuart (*Re-Animator*) Gordon was a big fan of his performance in *Mr. Sardonicus*. The actress who played his wife Hilary, Hilary Mason, was best known to genre fans as the blind psychic in Nicolas Roeg's *Don't Look Now* (1973), another Gordon favorite.

Six people take shelter from a storm at the Hartwickes' dark, out-of-the-way home. The dollmaker and his wife seem like kindly souls, especially to little Judy Bower (Carrie Lorraine) and child-like Ralph (Stephen Lee). But the dolls that fill many of the rooms have a life of their own, and they target the four other travelers. Second-billed Rolfe has one of his best roles as the soft-spoken Gabriel, complete with perfect manners and unkempt white hair (he bleached it for the movie). "*Dolls*' greatest pleasure is the presence of Guy Rolfe as the dollmaker-sorcerer," wrote Michael H. Price of the *Fort Worth*

To younger generations of horror movie fans, Rolfe is known for his role as puppet master Andre Toulon in the Puppet Master series. Here he is with his puppet Blade in Puppet Master III: Toulon's Revenge *(1991).*

Star-Telegram. "Now resembling a late-in-life Boris Karloff, Rolfe serves *Dolls* with a playfully droll turn that tips the film's balance—from a fans-only entry to more generally enjoyable fare." According to the *Kerryman/Corkman*, "An excellent cast, some marvelous special effects, imaginative camera angles, a generous helping of super black humour and, above all, stylish direction by Stuart Gordon make this a classic little chiller."

By 1990, Rolfe was back living in semi-retirement in Spain with his third wife (since 1992), actress Margaret Allworthy (who played on stage with him in *The Hollow*). His friend and agent Vincent Shaw told *The Stage*, "Guy is so happy in Spain that it would take a fascinating part and a positively hypnotic fee to lure him back. He is one of the most enduring British stage and film stars of them all and I'm sure the public would love to see him again. He has a great following in this country." For whatever reason, offers did not pour in.

In 1989, *Dolls* producer Charles Band made the straight-to-video *Puppetmaster*, with title character André Toulon played by German-accented William Hickey. It begins at the Bodega Bay Inn, California, 1939, with puppeteer Toulon hiding his living puppets in a chest behind a wall so that approaching Nazi spies cannot learn his secret. (Using an ancient Egyptian spell, he transferred souls into the puppets, bringing them to life.) As the Nazis break in, Toulon shoots himself. We flash forward to the Bodega Bay Inn in 1989: A group of psychics is brought together by a friend who has found the puppets. What results is typical slasher fun with the puppets Blade, Tunneler, Jester, Leech Woman and Pinhead (animated by visual effects supervisor David Allen) stealing the show.

In *Puppet Master II* (1990), the puppets open Toulon's grave and pour a strange liquid on his rotting corpse, reanimating *him*. (Actor Steve Welles plays the resurrected puppet master, but looks more like the Invisible Man wrapped in bandages, dark glasses, coat and hat.) The victims this time are paranormal investigators, including Carolyn (Elizabeth Maclellan), who Toulon believes is his wife Elsa reincarnated. Pretty soon, he pisses off the puppets (including a new one, Torch) and they turn on him.

Puppet Master III: Toulon's Revenge (1991), arguably the best of the series, introduces Guy Rolfe as the puppet master. A prequel, it has a different tone than the previous films: The puppets (including the new Six Shooter cowboy) and André Toulon are shown in a more sympathetic light. Although in the first film Toulon killed himself in 1939, this film starts in 1941 Berlin. The Nazis are attempting to reanimate dead soldiers to make a zombie army. Toulon comes to Major Kraus' (Richard Lynch) attention when he makes the mistake of satirizing Hitler in his puppet show. The Gestapo want Toulon's formula. When Toulon's wife Elsa is killed, the puppet master plots his revenge ("No mercy, my friends. *No mercy*," he snarls to his puppets), and the mayhem begins.

True, this is a straight-to-video exploitation slasher, but the ever-professional Rolfe gives it his all and brings a dignity to the character. His scenes with Sarah Douglas (as Elsa) are sweet and show a gentle human side to Toulon. Rolfe is also able to convey a tender rapport with the various puppets, speaking to them in an affectionate manner. But when a scene calls for it, as when he pledges to avenge his wife, Rolfe's voice changes to a horrifying whisper, as he subtly but effectively shows Toulon's murderous side. It is no wonder that most fans of the series remember Rolfe as *the* one and only puppet master.

In *Puppet Master 4* (1993) and *Puppet Master 5* (1994), Rolfe barely does anything. He shows up here and there to tell the puppets "I am with you" and to advise the new puppet master Rick Myers (Gordon Currie). *Puppet Master 5* was supposed to

Guy and his dog Bitsy at his last home in Torrox, Spain, in 1993. (Photo courtesy of Jane Culver)

end the series, and it did for a while.

In 1998, the Rolfes moved back to the United Kingdom, residing in Benhall Green Suffolk. "I saw a lot more of Guy when he moved back to the U.K.," his niece Jane said. "He maintained his love of life and was always up for something new. Guy was always the optimist, hoping that another part would come up even when he was in his early nineties."

Rolfe was not included in 1998's *Curse of the Puppet Master*. Instead, George Peck portrays Dr. Magrew, a new puppet master who has some strange ideas on how to use his puppets. The following year's *Retro Puppet Master* brought back Rolfe as Toulon, but only in a framing story. He appears in the pre-credits sequence, set in 1944 as he and his puppets hide out from the Nazis and the rain near the Swiss border. Rolfe reassures his friends that they are almost to freedom, and lightly jokes with them. His mind then flashes back to 1902 Paris, when as a young puppeteer he learned the secret of bringing life to his puppets, how he met Elsa, and how three demons attempted to take away his power. (For some reason, the actor playing the young André Toulon is the very blond, very effeminate, and very French Greg Sestero.) After this main narrative ends, Rolfe returns to wrap up, quietly telling his friends that the rain has stopped and they should be in Switzerland by lunchtime. "Safe at last," he says with a smile, the camera lingering on his face. His voice is a little weak, but his acting talent is still sharp and full of emotion. Asked about the Puppet Master movies by Wayne Kinsey, Rolfe laughed, "They were great fun … but they were terrible films."[3]

The 91-year-old Rolfe passed away of natural causes at Ipswich General Hospital in Ipswich, Suffolk, England. He is buried at St. Mary Churchyard in Benhall, Suffolk Coastal District, Suffolk.

Near the end of his life, Rolfe remarked, "I think actors are a very lucky lot—in a world in which most people are doing jobs they don't like, they are doing what they love and getting well paid for it."

Audrey Dalton

by Laura Wagner

I could do without a career. I hope I never have to, because I love acting. But I could never do without a family.

—Audrey Dalton, 1962

Audrey Dalton was born in Glasnevin, Dublin, Ireland, on January 21, 1934, the third of five children of Emmet Dalton and Alice Shannon;[1] she was preceded by Emmet Michael and Sybil, and followed by Richard and Nuala. Emmet Dalton (1898-1978) led an eventful life: During the first World War, he fought in the British Army with the Royal Dublin Fusiliers, going from a commissioned second lieutenant when he joined up, to captain. Awarded the Military Cross, he was often referred to as "The Boy Hero of Ginchy." He was a major general in the Dublin Brigade of the Irish Republican Army in the Irish Civil War. Dalton was also a good friend of Irish revolutionary Michael Collins, and was with him in 1922 when he was ambushed and killed in Cork. (Read more about him in the 2016 book *Emmet Dalton: Somme Soldier, Irish General, Film Pioneer* by Sean Boyne.)

Audrey's interest in acting started early: "I was probably five years old [*laughs*]—I just *allllways* wanted to be an actress, as long as I can remember. Probably from just being in theaters. Irish people generally are more theater-going than in a lot of places. I wanted it right from the beginning. I did the usual, school plays. I attended the Convent of the Sacred Heart School and while there played Antigone in one of the school plays when I was 13!"

Emmet Dalton moved to London in 1941 and became a sales agent for Paramount Pictures. In 1947, he became Hollywood producer Samuel Goldwyn's personal representative in Britain. In December 1949, the rest of his family joined him in London, and Audrey finished high school there.

At 17, Audrey auditioned at the Royal Academy of Dramatic Art (RADA). "They didn't accept anyone 'til 18, so I had a few months in a preparatory academy that they ran. I was at the Royal Academy until I came to the U.S., which was a little under two years later."

In 1952, Dalton was appearing in a RADA play when a Paramount executive in London saw her and asked her to screen-test for an upcoming Hollywood movie, *The Girls of Pleasure Island*. Dalton and two other aspiring British actresses, Joan Elan and Dorothy Bromiley, landed *Pleasure Island*'s three ingénue leads. ("The Irish papers kicked up quite a fuss over my selection as a typical English girl," Audrey told columnist Florabel Muir.) In March '52, the ladies left London and, after a few days' stopover in New York City, continued on to California, where *Girls of Pleasure Island* filming began in late May. The movie was based on William Maier's 1949 novel *Pleasure*

Audrey Dalton, Joan Elan and Dorothy Bromiley on the set of The Girls of Pleasure Island *(1953) with their director F. Hugh Herbert.*

Island (a fictional South Pacific island), adapted and directed by F. Hugh Herbert. After 20 days of shooting, Herbert fell ill and was hospitalized. First assistant director Alvin Ganzer finished *Pleasure Island* and received a co-director credit.

Dalton, Elan and Bromiley play the naïve, sheltered teenage daughters of the island's British administrator Leo Genn. They get their first glimpse of young men when 1500 Marines arrive to build an airstrip. These men haven't seen a woman in 18 months, and hilarity ensues. Dalton, who "bestows

her gentleness" (*East Kent Gazette*) on lieutenant Don Taylor, comes across well, especially in a quiet, sweet scene with Genn, talking about how much they both love the island. Jimmie Fidler predicted in his column that Dalton was "headed for the top rung in movie fame. She has beauty, and what's equally as important, acting ability."

Paramount went all-out publicizing the trio (called "New Paramount Personalities" during the end credits), and they became a *Life* magazine cover story (July 28, 1952): Inside, was a photographic essay by John Engstead, with the gals demonstrating "first an English conception of what American girls are like—sultry, giggling, fervidly leave-taking, jitterbugging; then America's conception of English girls—demure, tea-drinking, shuddering at the idea of a goodnight kiss, dancing with straight backs at a good yard's distance from their escorts." *Life* quoted an unnamed Paramount editor who remarked, "The Bromiley dame is a pixie, Dalton is ladylike, but the third one is hard to dig." The three girls and a pair of *Pleasure Island* actors, Don Taylor and Richard Shannon, were scheduled to go to Korea to entertain U.S. troops in battle zones and hospitals, but at the last minute Bromiley got appendicitis and couldn't travel. Paramount substituted one of their "Golden Circle" contract players, Kathryn Grant, to take her place. Dalton told Tom Weaver,

> Kathryn Grant was fine and fit in well. That Korea trip was an incredible experience. Flights were long in those days before jets: We flew from Burbank to Travis Air Force Base [in Solano County, California] at night and the next morning we flew to Wake Island or Guam, I can't remember which, for refueling. The next

Above: The Girls of Pleasure Island, with their guys: Don Taylor, Audrey, Gene Barry, Joan Elan, Dorothy Bromiley and Peter Baldwin.

Left: This ad appeared in the May 4, 1953, Variety.

day we took off for Tokyo, where we stayed at the famous Imperial Hotel, Frank Lloyd Wright's "earthquake-proof" hotel. A couple of days there and then on to Seoul. All our travel was on MATS [Military Air Transport Service] planes—backs against the sides of the plane and small, upright seats.

In South Korea, we traveled from one base to another every day in an Army truck—always in a convoy of other trucks. The Army treated us so well, serving us their best food. Each night, *The Girls of Pleasure Island* was shown to a huge audience. After the film, we three girls put on a short skit wearing our beautiful Edith Head ballgowns. The rain was pretty much constant, so as we walked from the truck to the room where the film had been shown, we thought it was funny as we slipped around holding those tulle creations out of the mud and puddles. Inside, we'd sit on the edge of the stage and chat with the guys. Paramount had arranged for us to take a note from anyone who wanted us to send a message home for them. The studio collected the names and addresses and mailed the messages home.

When we were close to the border, [actor] Don Taylor and I were flown in the general's bubble helicopter up to the front where the fighting was actually going on. The two of us were greeted like you can't imagine and just talked and posed for pictures with the guys. This whole experience is something I will never forget.

Dalton was the only one of the three girls to continue with a long-term Paramount contract. "Serenely beautiful, dark-haired, with gray-green eyes, she is 18, intelligent and Irish. Looks like a winner," wrote *Photoplay*. Her first assignment was a loan-out to 20th Century-Fox for *My Cousin Rachel* (1952), an adaptation of Daphne du Maurier's then-new Gothic novel, with Olivia de Havilland in the title role and Richard Burton making his American film bow. Director Henry Koster told Louella Parsons that he requested Dalton because "I saw her on the screen and I think she has great possibilities as a coming actress." The young master of a mansion on England's Cornish coast, Philip Ashley (Burton) tortures himself over his enigmatic cousin Rachel (he can't

Dalton is flanked by Hollywood veteran Olivia de Havilland and Hollywood first-timer Richard Burton on the My Cousin Rachel *(1952) set.*

decide whether she murdered his beloved guardian or not). The *Boston Globe* wrote that Dalton gave a "sweet and warm characterization as the girl who wishes Philip would love her instead of Rachel...." In one scene with Burton, Audrey displays gutsy resolve, as she confronts him about his hopeless fixation on de Havilland.

Dalton said of her second movie job,

I was working at a different studio and with a director, Henry Koster, I didn't know—I don't recall if I'd ever even met him. To my astonishment, he greeted me as a professional, something I wasn't sure of myself, and we dove right into the scene being shot, effortlessly. He spoke quietly to me about that first scene, and others that followed during the filming, with a rehearsal run-through and off we went. He accepted my interpretation and our work together on the film went smoothly from there on. He came across to me as being confident, deeply involved and knowledgeable about his work. Henry Koster was probably the quietest and most low-key director I ever worked with.

Burton and de Havilland appeared to get along well when they were working, but off-camera on the set she retired to her dressing room and he stayed on the set, yakking away to the crew and with [English actor] Ronald Squire, who had become a great friend.

The two of them spent their time reminiscing about work and other actors in London, laughing uproariously and shooing me away when they felt the story they were telling was too risqué for my young ears (I was 18). My scenes with Burton were magic for me, he was never condescending and I always felt at ease. The scenes practically played themselves. I knew of his reputation as a serious and dedicated actor and couldn't believe my good fortune to be working with him.

Working with Burton and de Havilland in our scenes together was different. The atmosphere was a little uptight as the quiet de Havilland made clear the scene was hers, as she measured up to Burton. They were so different from each other. He was all noise and banter, fun and bluster, and oh, that voice! I was so impressed to be working with him on his first Hollywood film and he seemed to know how shy and overwhelmed I was. He went out of his way to try to draw me out and talk to me when we weren't shooting.

De Havilland was always courteous to me and professional and I continued to be in awe of her. She had such control of her work and never displayed any nervousness. The crew's respect for her apparent.

My Cousin Rachel was also the first of many times in my career where I had to ride a horse, and sidesaddle at that. I don't think my fear showed! In spite of all the Westerns I did later, I continued to be very wary and scared around horses.

Reporters were struck by Audrey's resemblance to Joan Bennett, and some readers wrote to movie magazines asking if she was Bennett's daughter. This caused further confusion when Bennett's real-life daughter, Melinda Markey, had a small part in Dalton's next.

Later in 1952, Dalton was loaned out again to Fox to play Annette, daughter of Richard and Julia Sturges (Clifton Webb and Barbara Stanwyck), in *Titanic* (she beat out Terry Moore and Margaret O'Brien for the role). Based on one of *the* major news events of the 20th century, the sinking of the British luxury liner, director Jean Negulesco's film bases a lot of its Oscar-winning story (pre-iceberg) on the wealthy Sturges family: Richard and Julia's marriage

In February 2019, Australian writer-broadcaster Clive James, reminiscing about his teenage years in the 1950s, wrote in The Guardian *about seeing* Titanic *for the first time: "The greatest filmed version ever of the tragic story, [it] featured a young lady who left both Grace [Kelly] and Debbie [Reynolds] in the dust. Her name was Audrey Dalton and I instantly realized that my lack of physical resemblance to the shyly smiling Robert Wagner was an irredeemable tragedy."*

is in trouble, and Annette falls for another passenger, handsome young college student Gifford Rogers (Robert Wagner). But the latter couple's romance is "suddenly split asunder" (*Spokane Chronicle*) when the "unsinkable" *Titanic* fails to live up to its hype and, as the closing narrator puts it, "passes from the British Registry." Regarding her on-screen parents, Dalton told journalist Nick Thomas in a 2016 interview that Webb "was very funny with a sharp wit," and Stanwyck "a dream—the ultimate pro, always prepared and ready to help."[2]

There is a certain similarity, Dalton noted, between the fictional characters in her *Titanic* and the 1997 megahit directed by James Cameron: "The family that was 'dysfunctional,' so to speak, the love affair with the young man and so on. Even the opening sequence of the family arriving at the boat, the flurry of the passengers and everything, was just so similar to the beginning of [the 1953] *Titanic*. ...I thought the dialogue in the new one was just inane.

Drum Beat *(1954)* stars Marisa Pavan, Alan Ladd and Audrey Dalton.

But it's a fascinating picture, no question. And what a success! Of course, now people say about me, 'She was in the original *Titanic*,' and I have to stress the *in*, not the *on*!" she laughs.

On January 1, 1953, teenage Audrey and UCLA student James Brown, 22, wed in Los Altos, California. They kept the marriage a secret until that May. Brown later became an assistant director.

Finally making a second movie for her home studio Paramount, Dalton joined the cast of the Bob Hope comedy *Casanova's Big Night* (1954). "Joan [Fontaine] was very effervescent and a great match for Bob Hope. They just traded barbs all the time and laughed and joked," Audrey told interviewer Rick Armstrong in 2016. "It was fun. On the set, he always had the same group of small-part players with him. He knew all these people and would make sure that they were included somewhere in his movie so they always had a job. He took care of people. He was very, very sweet. In fact, when I first came [to Hollywood], I was 18 and on my own. He had a son and a daughter, who were a little younger than me by a couple of years. On Sunday evenings, he would sometimes take me to dinner with his wife. They would come pick me up and take me to dinner because they figured I needed a little looking after. He and Dolores were kindness itself."

Casanova's Big Night is one of Hope's funniest films. Dalton has little to do except look gorgeous playing the lady that Hope, masquerading as the great lover Casanova, has been paid to romance, to test her virtue as her marriage to Robert Hutton looms. She wore a dress made of genuine Honiton lace that belonged to one of the last czarinas, a granddaughter of Queen Victoria. "The dress cost over $1000 and weighed 56 pounds! And I'm presuming the $1000 was what Paramount paid when they purchased it for their wardrobe department," Dalton said. "Studios had huge wardrobe collections in those days."

In October 1953, Dalton and Richard Allan (from 1953's *Niagara*) won first place for Best Newcomers in *Photoplay*'s "Choose Your Stars" awards. The ceremony took place at the Rodeo Room of the Beverly

Confession, called The Deadliest Sin in the U.S., did smash box office overseas. Variety: "Miss Dalton is extremely attractive in appearance, and able in carrying out her part of the plot."

Hills Hotel, with Barbara Stanwyck acting as emcee. According to Dalton, she was "very pregnant" at the event; and that same month, she gave birth to her first child, daughter Tara—just weeks after the filming of *Casanova's Big Night*! Apparently, most people involved with the production had no idea of her condition. (Dalton points out: "The costumes helped.")

"Why should people know?" she remarked at the time. "The wardrobe people knew, but nobody else did until I told them." A few months later, she reflected on her career for interviewer Philip K. Scheuer: "More has happened to me in the past two years than I'd ever dreamed possible. ...I have made four pictures, toured Korea and the United States, married and had a baby.

"I had wanted to act on the stage and was very determined never to do films. It's amazing what happens when you're offered a film contract!" Dalton today says that at that time, she liked the fact that she could work for perhaps a week on a TV episode, perhaps four weeks on a film, "and then be off for a while to take care of and have time with my family. This is why I never did a TV series and why after I had children I did not go away on location—except maybe to London or Dublin, where I had family."

After leaving Paramount, Dalton's first film as a freelancer began shooting in early June '54: She was leading lady to Alan Ladd in the Western *Drum Beat* (1954), made by Warner Bros. and Ladd's company Jaguar Productions. Delmer Daves wrote and directed the story of renegade Modocs threatening to break a peace treaty in the Oregon-California territory. Location shooting took place in Sedona, Arizona, where the cast "sweat[ed] it out in the 115-degree heat" (*Star Press*). *Miami Daily News* reviewer Herb Kelly ribbed Ladd, claiming he "shows some real tenderness in his love scenes with Audrey Dalton. Instead of the robot-like smooching he usually does, he's more hep ... especially in a night scene in the woods with Miss Dalton." As an Eastern girl smitten with Ladd, Dalton gave her customary lady-like portrayal; Marisa Pavan, as an Indian girl also in love with Ladd, has a more colorful and active role in the proceedings.

In 2016, Dalton remembered Ladd as "wonderful to work with—very professional. He was very quiet off the set, very much a gentleman. I knew his family in Los Angeles. My father had known Alan because they were both into racehorses. When I came here [to California], Alan was asked to keep an eye on me. He took me into his family. He had a daughter who was a student at UCLA and she and I became good friends. We're still friends."

She was signed by MGM for *The Prodigal*, a $5,000,000 "wannabe epic" based on the Bible story of the Prodigal Son; it was adapted by Samuel James Larsen, a cerebral palsy sufferer who lived in a hospital and typed with a pencil in his mouth. Lana Turner starred as the temptress Samarra and Edmund Purdom played the title role, with Dalton as Purdom's shy betrothed. *Modern Screen* summed this one up pretty well: "Wait till you dig Lana in those bugle beads! She is a real-life goddess for whom young men willingly dive into a pit of fire. And when Edmund Purdom spots her, he says goodbye Poppa (Walter Hampden) farewell Ruth (Audrey Dalton) hail Samarra (that's Lana) I'm your slave." Unfortunately, the movie gave Audrey very little to do.

Right after *The Prodigal* wrapped, Dalton went to England for writer-director Ken Hughes' *Confession* (1955), a "punchy" (*Banbury Guardian*) crime thriller involving a bank heist, murder in a confessional, and a family torn apart by a more modern Prodigal Son (Sydney Chaplin). Dalton makes a good showing as Chaplin's "charming and ingratiating sister" (*Kinematograph Weekly*) whose slow realization that he's a crook and murderer causes her much anguish (or, as the *Birmingham Daily Gazette* says, "[She] goes all broody"). Dalton followed this with the John Payne Korean War movie *Hold Back the Night* (1956): In flashbacks, she's seen as Kitty, a Melbourne girl to whom Payne is attracted out of loneliness (and vice versa). She only had a couple of scenes, but even in her limited screen time, she gives a moving performance as she tells Payne about her husband (she's unsure whether he is dead or a prisoner of war). "Because John Payne wanted me to play Kitty, I was paid very well indeed for a small part," Audrey recalled. "Never knew why. Never met him before or since!"

In May 1956, Dalton appeared in her first TV drama, *The 20th Century-Fox Hour*'s "The Empty Room," as Carey, a girl determined to prevent the reunion of her father (Patric Knowles) and mother (Virginia Field), who ran out on him many years before. An unimpressed *Variety* reviewer re-dubbed it "Stella-Dallas-on-the-Thames" and had no use for any of the characters, including Dalton's "babbling, idiotic" Carey.

With science fiction and horror pictures all the rage, Dalton signed on to make *The Monster That Challenged the World* (1957) with Tim Holt. "It was presented to me at a time when I wasn't working.

Dalton (seen here with Rod Taylor) had a modest-sized role in Separate Tables *(1958), but what a movie and what a cast to be a part of!*

And I *always* like to work! I was never discriminating with a capital D. I just wanted to *work*, I *enjoyed* working. I've always felt with those science fiction things that just that one little nugget of 'well, it could be true' kind of gets you [*laughs*]! So, it was fun." *Monster* was based on just that kind of true-life "nugget": A Mojave Desert lake bed, dry for decades, had recently flooded, hatching as many as 4,000,000 long-buried eggs, and soon the newly formed lake was teeming with fresh-water shrimp. *Monster*'s screenplay made the eggs prehistoric, and the late-blooming mollusks inside grow to the size of small trucks and terrorize California's Salton Sea area. Dalton, playing a scientist's secretary at a Navy base, has a dramatic scene in which she emotionally unloads on hero Holt about the recent death of her pilot husband.

Dalton had started at the top, acting with such stars as Olivia de Havilland, Richard Burton, Barbara Stanwyck and Alan Ladd. Asked by Tom Weaver if she felt *Monster* was a step down, she replied, "Of course it was. But I was also *just* pregnant, and I knew I wasn't going to be able to work much longer—in those days, once you were pregnant, you couldn't work. So I thought, 'Well, let me get another one under my belt while I can!'"

At the end of '56, she appeared in an episode of *Lux Video Theatre*, "Michael and Mary," with Patric Knowles (this time as her husband). Audrey did not return to acting until the following summer and fall, when she did two more *Lux Video Theatre*s ("Barren Harvest" and "Judge Not"), two *Bob Cummings Shows* ("Bob Hires a Maid" and "Bob the Gunslinger") and a *Men of Annapolis* ("Look Alike").

In between, she filmed two 1958 movies, *Thundering Jets* and *Separate Tables*. The former, shot on location at Edwards Air Force Base, had her as secretary Susan, girlfriend of USAF Flight Test School captain Rex Reason. Resentful and "broody" over being assigned as an instructor for novice test pilots, Reason makes everyone's life miserable, Dalton included. Dalton was ostensibly Reason's leading lady, but it's her scenes with the charming Buck Class (as Major Mike Geron) that sparkle.

She had a smaller part in director Delbert Mann's dramatic *Separate Tables*, based on two Terence Rattigan one-act plays and set in an English hotel. The stars were Deborah Kerr, Rita Hayworth, Burt Lancaster and Gladys Cooper, plus David Niven and Wendy Hiller, both of whom won Oscars for their performances in this Best Picture nominee. Dalton, portraying Rod Taylor's love interest, is not really involved in the main storyline of Niven's revelation that he has lied about his military career.

In 1958, Dalton's small-screen credits included two *Wagon Trains* ("The John Wilbot Story" and "The Liam Fitzmorgan Story"), *The Millionaire* ("Millionaire Ellen Curry"), *Bat Masterson* ("The Treasure of Worry Hill") and *Man with a Camera* ("Two Strings of Pearls"). Her next film, the post–Civil War Western *Lone Texan* (1959), starred Willard Parker as Clint Banister, who returns to his Texas hometown and is considered a turncoat because he served in the Union Army. He finds the town overrun by lawlessness—overseen by his own brother, Greg (Grant Williams). Dalton has one of her best roles as a feisty gal who doesn't know how she feels about Clint's return. Her part is more energetic than usual as she stands up to the bad guys, slaps them and fights one of them off when he attempts to rape her. When her father is gunned down, Dalton takes matters (and a pistol) into her own hands and confronts his killer.

Back in the old sod, Ireland, Ardmore Studios in Bray, County Wicklow, Ireland, opened in April 1958, founded by Audrey's father Emmet Dalton; Emmet and Louis Elliman then became its managing directors. Among the movies shot or partially shot at Ardmore: *Shake Hands with the Devil* (1959), *Dementia 13* (1963), *The Spy Who Came in from the Cold* (1965), *The Lion in Winter* (1968)—and the Audrey

Dalton–starring *This Other Eden* (1959). Produced by Emmet, the movie tells of a statue of a local IRA hero, Jack Carberry, being erected in the Irish village of Ballymorgan. The residents pretend Carberry was a saint, but know differently. Conor Heaphy (Norman Rodway), who wants to become a priest, learns that he is Carberry's illegitimate son and, angered by the hypocritical lies told about Carberry, blows up the statue. Audrey plays his friend Maire McRoarty, who is the object of Crispin Brown's (Leslie Phillips) affection. Nine days of location shooting took place in the County Wicklow and Dublin areas.

"The idea behind it was to showcase the Abbey Players," Audrey told interviewer Jim Rosin. "[My father] wanted to make a film of the play *This Other Eden* and he asked if I would star in it. So I went back and co-starred with Leslie Phillips, Milo O'Shea and members of the Abbey Players. Much of the crew that worked on the film were Irish who had been doing films in England. They were delighted to return home. So was I. It was a wonderful experience. I brought my three children and was able to visit with family and friends."

As for Ardmore Studios, Audrey told Tom Weaver, "I know it went through hard times a couple of times. In Britain, J. Arthur Rank had a monopoly on distribution, Rank owned all the British theaters and would only release his own productions. Other producers could make films but then have no theaters to release them to. The fight went on for years. Rank eventually lost the fight, but too late for my dad."

Dalton finished off 1959 with guest shots on *Disneyland* ("The Griswold Murder"), *Wagon Train* ("The

Studio portrait of the pretty-as-a-picture Audrey Dalton.

Jose Maria Moran Story") and *Bat Masterson* ("To the Manner Born"). Her TV activity picked up in the early 1960s as she guested on *King of Diamonds* (an episode partially shot in Paris and London), *Dante*, *The Aquanauts*, *The Tab Hunter Show*, *Acapulco*, *National Velvet*, *Lock Up*, *Michael Shayne*, *Bringing Up Buddy*, *Whispering Smith*, *The Investigators*, *Perry Mason*, *Checkmate*, *Bonanza* (one of her favorites, as she played a bad girl), *Kraft Mystery Theater* (as a secretary who schemes with her boss Louis Hayward to kill his wife, Signe Hasso—who is plotting to kill *him*!), *Ripcord*, *Gunsmoke*, *Death Valley Days*, *Wide*

Country, The Dakotas, Temple Houston, Dr. Kildare and *I'm Dickens, He's Fenster*. During this TV whirlwind, Dalton was seen frequently on *Wagon Train*— six episodes between 1958 and 1964.

> I used to do one every season, and one season they even squeezed me into *two*. There was that [rule] that you couldn't do two in the same season, because people were going to confuse you with your other role. Ward Bond *liked* me—I mean, in the nicest way. It was because I was Irish. He had this thing about Ireland.
>
> *Thriller* was the same thing as *Wagon Train*, I kept getting invited back. When they liked you on a series, you'd get invited back. It was like a stock company, and every year you'd come back. Alan Caillou, Abraham Sofaer, a whole bunch of people would keep showing up on *Thriller*, and you'd renew acquaintance and get to work together again.

Dalton recalled the Boris Karloff-hosted horror anthology series *Thriller* as "a *great* show" that provided her with some of her best parts. Her first, Season 1's "The Prediction," was also Karloff's first as a cast member in the story itself; he was a stage mentalist who suddenly *does* have second sight, she was his daughter. Just ten episodes later, in "Hay-Fork and Bill-Hook," *she* was the one with second sight: Playing the wife of a Scotland Yard detective, she has inexplicable "visions" in a Welsh village steeped in witchcraft. In Season 2, Dalton excelled at cold-bloodedness in "The Hollow Watcher," a one-of-a-kind mix of murder drama, sexual tension and backwoods horror, set in a North Carolina hamlet whose folklore includes an avenging, demon-possessed scarecrow. Dalton, the Irish mail order bride of a local yokel (Warren Oates), is actually a money-mad colleen partnered with her *real* husband (Sean McClory) on a globe-trotting murder tour. Dalton recalled, "Oooh, that was grand! That was a little 'different' part for me, too, which was nice. Now and then I played [meanies] ... but they were the exception. I was always the nice girl, the ingénue—which was fine, which was...the way I *was* [laughs]! So it

Los Angeles Times *movie reviewer Charles Stinson on* Mr. Sardonicus: *"Rolfe, Lewis and Miss Dalton are all accomplished artists and deserve an adult film. Miss Dalton ... ought to be doing much more film work of a much higher calibre." (Courtesy Ronald V. Borst/Hollywood Movie Posters)*

was fun to have something with a little more meat to it, and to be given free rein. [Director William Claxton] let me run with it, which was fun. That hadn't happened before."

As if three *Thriller*s in 15 months wasn't enough to please the Monster Kids in her fanbase, Dalton also joined the cast of the fright flick *Mr. Sardonicus* (1961). Nineteenth-century Europe was the backdrop for this bleak horror tale, with Guy Rolfe as a farmer without a farthing, reduced to digging up his father's coffin to retrieve a winning lottery ticket accidentally buried within. The sight of Dad's skeletal face is so shocking that the farmer's own face takes on the same lip-less, toothy grin. Now wealthy enough to re-dub himself "Baron Sardonicus," he forces Dalton to marry him in order to compel her former beau, London physician Ronald Lewis, to find a medical means of restoring his good looks. Horror producer-showman-huckster William Castle's gimmick for this production: Just minutes from the end, Castle (playing himself) asks audience members if Sardonicus should receive mercy or no mercy. This of course gave viewers the idea that the theater projectionist had two different finales and would then project the chosen one; but Castle knew that every audience would vote to give Sardonicus the works, and therefore a "mercy" ending was never filmed!

"Every time my acting career seems to be on the way up, I have another baby," Dalton remarked in 1962. By this time, she had four, Tara (born 1953), Victoria (1955), James (1957) and Richard (1959). In her 2016 interview with Nick Thomas, she said with a chuckle, "What's interesting is that many websites today have given me a fifth child! He even has a birth date and a name—Adrian. Needless to say, my children have made great fun of it and ask why I never told them about their lost brother!"

Dalton made her last two films in the mid–1960s. For *Kitten with a Whip* (1964), she phoned in her performance—literally! In her one scene, she phones her husband (John Forsythe) at their home and tells him she will return the next day, unaware that he has entangled himself with bad girl Ann-Margret.

Much better was the Western *The Bounty Killer* (1965). Filmed in only ten days on a low budget, it featured a wonderfully warm-hearted Dalton as saloon girl Carole Ridgeway—who sings "Go Away Old Man and Leave Me Alone," dubbed by Harlene Stein. (Dalton wants *Bounty Killer* fans to know that she was *directed* to sing it at an "agonizing slow pace"!) She falls for the naïve Willie Duggan (Dan Duryea) and they plan a future together. Then Willie's friend (Fuzzy Knight) is slain, and the lust for vengeance makes Willie a killer. *The Bounty Killer* received notice for the small role played by Western pioneer G.M. "Broncho Billy" Anderson (his last film), but for Dalton fans it contains one of her most heartfelt performances. Audrey also recalled with a laugh that producer Alex Gordon "made me feel like a star—even though I was over the hill by the time I did that."

Then it was back to TV in episodes of *Voyage to the Bottom of the Sea, Laredo, The Big Valley, Insight, The Girl from U.N.C.L.E., Dragnet 1967* and *Family Affair* plus the telefilm *Me and Benjy* (1967). She remembered her *Wild Wild West* ("The Night of the Golden Cobra," in which she plays maharajah Boris Karloff's daughter) as "*great* because I got to walk two cheetahs on a leash! That was fun, and so were the exotic costumes." She ended her acting career with a trio of *Police Woman* episodes in 1974, 1975 and '78.

After 24 years together, Audrey and James Brown divorced in July 1977. On July 20, 1979, she wed an aerospace engineer, and that union continues to this day. She is popular as a guest at nostalgia conventions and autograph shows. Asked why she drifted away from acting, Dalton replied, "It sort of drifted away from *me*. It happens. You have to *really* have staying power, and I *didn't*, I guess. I was involved with family, and I just let it drift. If I had it to do over again, I wouldn't. But I *did*. One goes on."

As for life today (2021), she enthuses, "I love being on the ocean and have sailed for over 50 years. Racing boats with my husband is one of my great pleasures. I have been so fortunate, all my life, to be able to continue on. Wherever 'on' takes me."

The Sound of Smilence

David Schecter Analyzes Composer Von Dexter's *Mr. Sardonicus* Score

Von Dexter's *Mr. Sardonicus* score is unlike his soundtracks for the previous William Castle films *House on Haunted Hill, The Tingler* and *13 Ghosts*. Those scores were a little gimmicky and emphasized shock hits; the deliberate pace of *Mr. Sardonicus* demanded more traditional and conventional music from the composer. Although the movie's score has some short action cues, it's mostly low-key, befitting the atmospheric period piece. There are a few interesting instrumental choices, but because they are used throughout the picture, they don't stand out too much, instead serving to contribute to an oppressive audio accompaniment that covers the film like a coating of gray musical paint. The lugubrious score adds an overriding sense of doom and despair to the story, with a number of shock hits added for variety and to keep theater patrons awake. Atmosphere definitely predominates over thrills and chills. Although there's little action in the movie and the script is rather talky, music still plays a large role in the production. Fortunately, it never conflicts with the dialogue, often matching the depressing natures of the film's two villains. The combination of the downbeat dialogue and the bleak score results in anything but a happy motion picture, but it does contribute to the story's overall dreariness. That might be considered one of the movie's strong points.

Dexter's writing centers around a few instrumental choices that are fairly consistent through the score. There are many passages for low, somber strings, as opposed to the high, shrieking ones often employed in horror movies, or at least post–*Psycho* ones. Pizzicato (plucked) strings are sometimes used for various effects, but that's certainly not unexpected in a suspense film. Solo woodwinds (including a lot of clarinet) are omnipresent, and although more than one woodwind is heard at the same time, they usually play the same lines. Whether this was due to budgetary restrictions limiting the number of players, or perhaps Dexter's decision to score the

The author of this chapter, musicologist David Schecter, with Mr. Sardonicus *star Audrey Dalton (right) and Julie Adams in 2012.*

film in a simpler manner, is left to speculation, if one feels the need to speculate about such non-vital matters. The composer often combines the low strings with high woodwinds, and seldom the other way around. This helps create an unsettling sound over a portentous foundation.

There are few full-orchestral action pieces, not surprising considering there aren't many visual sequences to demand such accompaniment. Outside of those and some shock hits, the brass is often quiet or muted, playing non-melodic passages that add to the oppressive atmosphere. Tympani and other percussion seldom make an appearance outside of those louder passages, and the score often resembles chamber music more than fully symphonic. This befits the overall feeling of the picture, which is intimate and claustrophobic rather than of one of great scope.

The music keeps pace with the visuals, not attempting to nudge the action a little faster, something film music is able to accomplish. Instead, the score plods along with the determined unraveling of the plot, which is not a criticism. Dexter obviously wanted to write very appropriate music for the picture, as opposed to allowing his contributions to unnecessarily stand out. When movies are subtly scored, as happened here, most filmgoers probably don't even notice the music at all (although there are also many cineastes who don't notice music even when it's outrageously doled out). Dexter's underscore supports the general mood of the story, rather than trying to capture too many visual moments outside of those required shock hits. This conservative ap-

Von Dexter (LaVon Hawley Dexter Urbanski) was born December 9, 1912, in Aurora, Illinois. While still at school, he began his musical career, performing on saxophone in Chicago night clubs and bars. After receiving a music degree from the University of Southern California, he became West Coast music director for NBC and he worked on a number of programs. These included *The Penny Singleton Show* (under the name Von Urbanski), *Dangerous Assignment* (he was musical director, conductor and composer), *Who in the World*, *Rheingold Theatre* and Ralph Edwards' *This Is Your Life*.

"Von Dexter & His Orchestra" released *Music from **This Is Your Life*** (aka *The Ralph Edwards Album*) in 1958 on the Imperial record label. It featured standards such as "Makin' Whoopee," "Pennies from Heaven," "Who Will Shoe Your Pretty Little Foot" and "Cheerful Little Earful." Dexter wrote religious songs with Foster Carling, a short work called *How to Shop, Look and Listen Before You Buy That Piano*, and a 285-page book, *Commando for Christ*.

The composer reportedly suffered a hand condition that made it difficult for him to write music, and after moving to Iowa with his wife Catherine, he ran the Video Music Co. publishing company. Von Dexter died of lymphoma in Reinbeck, Iowa, on February 4, 1996. By then, according to his widow, Dexter had thrown out all of his manuscripts and recordings. The composer did not care much for his film music.

Despite some claims that Dexter was the same person as Alexander Lazslo, they were different people.

proach makes his work harder to appreciate than in his other horror outings, where the music often called attention to itself. *Mr. Sardonicus*' score belongs in the background, and there it mostly stays, sustaining the oppressive atmosphere. Without the music, the movie would have been dreadfully boring; the sequences that weren't scored bear testament to this. The music is probably not supposed to be heard so much as felt or experienced.

Dexter employs vibraphone and piano to conjure many things, most having to do with nefarious goings-on at the castle. The electrically powered vibraphone is probably the single aspect of the score that sets it apart from many others, and it's often used to call attention to both the damaged face and the damaged soul of Sardonicus. Vibe had long been employed in the movies for spooky musical effects, but it was rare when it played such a prominent role throughout the entirety of a score. The metallic instrument resembles a xylophone, only with long resonating tubes descending from the tone bars. Its motor can be operated at various speeds, and it has a damper/sustain pedal to alter the amount of oscillating reverb you desire. It can create some of the more haunting and mysterious sounds in an orchestra, although when the motor isn't on and the sustain is damped, it can be mistaken for a xylophone. Dexter also uses the instrument as a transitional device, something it excels at due to its pulsing sound, which suggests motion. By turning the motor up

Sir Ronald carries a torch for Maude, and he gets burned: lured into Baron Sardonicus' web.

high and using the sustain, the reverb-y tones intermingle, creating a sort of moving sonic boundary the way a wipe or dissolve affects a transition point from a visual perspective.

The film's score has a few other minor orchestral embellishments, but for the most part, it's a very consistent instrumental creation, its main purpose being to reinforce the oppressive atmosphere inside the Sardonicus castle where the bulk of the story takes place.

Mr. Sardonicus opens with a horror fanfare during the Columbia logo to inform you that this film will deliver the terrifying goods, even if most of those goods turn out to be that same old frozen smile again and again. After William Castle's talky prologue, the beginning of the "Main Title" is obscured by a thunder crash, which probably didn't make the composer very happy. If he'd been asked, he could have easily created a musical sound effect to accompany the lightning bolt and accompanying crash. But having the introduction to your opening creation obscured by noise is not what most composers want to hear. As the credits wavy-wipe from one card to the next, vibraphone shimmers mimic those transitions with correspondingly wavy sounds. The moody "Main Title" is fairly low-key, with woodwinds and organ predominating, and little brass after the opening measures. Not exactly what you'd expect from a "shocker," but given the minimal number of actual shocks in the picture, it's definitely a representative introduction. The cue's melody serves as a sort of "love theme" between Sir Robert and Maude, even though there's precious little love to be seen or heard in the movie. This piece could almost be a Henry Mancini tune if it had been orchestrated differently.

Neither the prologue nor the epilogue were scored, allowing us to focus on Castle rambling about his Punishment Poll, as the movie's bookends were supposed to convince theater patrons that he was talking to them and the projectionist. Unfortunately, having him stand in front of a watery backdrop with fog horns sounding in the distance quickly destroys that illusion unless you're watching the movie while on a boat. These talky bits might have benefited from some subtle underscore, perhaps a bit of "movie theater" music playing quietly in the background, like when the ads want you to visit the concession stand. As it is, these narrative sequences are rather lifeless and probably take viewers out of the movie.

A gentle folk melody signifies 1880s London, the tune standing out from the darkness that subsequently colors the majority of the score. There's also a rare, upbeat musical moment, heard after strings and woodwinds depict a young girl unable to move her leg. Vibraphone signals the beginning of her attempt, with tinkling celesta and strings celebrating her success. Along with the girl's crying, it helps create a poignant sequence that would have been difficult to achieve without such suitable musical accompaniment.

As Sir Robert notices the writing on the hand-delivered letter, the love theme plays on clarinet, then piano. Vibraphone enters as he notices the S (for Sardonicus) seal, and even though the melody continues, it is now spookily colored by that electric instrument, a clever use of orchestration in an otherwise simple musical sequence.

A foreboding full-orchestral transition highlights Sir Robert's boat-and-train trip to Central Europe, the composition letting us know that his life is about to change, and not for the better. When he arrives at the Gorslava railroad station and utters the name "Sardonicus" to the stationmaster, a subdued musical hit emphasizes the negative reaction he receives. Low strings and somber woodwinds provide the dour atmosphere, a musical approach that will cover most of the remainder of the movie. Krull's arrival at the station brings forth low piano sounds that offer a solid hint that he's as horrible on the inside as his deformed face makes him on the outside.

String harmonics, piano and other instrumental devices add to the foreboding atmosphere of the carriage ride to the Sardonicus castle, with the love theme adding an eerie touch to Sir Robert re-reading Maude's letter. Vibraphone shimmers again act as a transition device as the carriage reaches the castle, along with string harmonics and muted brass.

Another "hit"—this one of moderate shock value—accompanies the image of leeches on the face of Anna the servant girl. This musical impact is somewhat restrained because a bigger "hit" is being saved for later. Dexter obviously didn't just score as he went along, but he tried to be true to both the overall dramatic structure and also the pace of the script. He knew that if you kept hitting people over the head with similar musical jolts, they would become less effective over time. Therefore, he dispenses his musical shocks in discriminating portions. And since you can never have enough vibraphone in this movie, the percussion instrument again makes its presence felt as Sir Robert removes the slimy little bloodsuckers.

The baron pours himself a little wine at dinner – a waste of good booze, since he can't drink, and the mask has no mouth opening anyway! (Conversely, the novella Sardonicus drinks too much *at dinner.) Love the Gooney Bird–like carvings atop the chair. (Courtesy Ronald V. Borst/Hollywood Movie Posters)*

When Sir Robert meets Maude, their love theme is nowhere to be heard, as a romantic mood might hint at a happy ending for them, and the movie remains pessimistic about this until the very end. Even when the theme appears in the picture, it's never buoyant or uplifting, a wise dramatic choice. The couple's talky scene plays without music, even when they discuss their love lives. Granted, there's lots of exposition that needs to be imparted—including the absence of romance in their lives since their relationship ended—but Dexter's refusal to emphasize their present feelings keeps us from feeling confident that they might someday be reunited. The mostly joyless music heard throughout the film befits the joyless Sardonicus marriage, as well as the lack of love in Sir Robert's life, the misery suffered by Anna, and the absence of humanity in both Sardonicus and Krull. One is unlikely to find a more unhappy grouping of human beings in any single castle! Another minor shock hit occurs—this time on piano—when Krull interrupts the meeting between Sir Robert and Maude. Its effectiveness is due in part to the "shock" being delivered by an instrument different from the earlier ones. Again, Dexter is holding off on the full auditory wallop. Low strings and rumbling piano highlight Krull leading Sir Robert through the castle, with vibraphone and string harmonics conjuring the picture frames without portraits.

No music plays when Krull appears with the baron's bowl of stew, nor does any music accentuate the padlocked door. Dexter might have done this to give the viewer a break from the music, or perhaps he didn't have the time or inclination to score every second within the castle, as the continuous oppressiveness felt in almost every sequence could have certainly been treated similarly. A silhouette of the baron slurping down his food continues the slow, downbeat music, rather than switching to something shocking or more intense. Dexter was obviously trying to keep the score as restrained as possible, and considering that William Castle produced and directed the picture, it's pleasantly surprising that the composer's score did not end up too outlandish or gimmicky. One wonders whether there might have been any discussions between the two men regarding how realistically the movie should be musically accentuated.

When Sir Robert finally meets Sardonicus face to mask, the brassy shock hit is an interesting one, as it's in two parts, the second one accompanying a zoom on the baron's obscured visage. Extended low notes play as Sardonicus talks, the nondescript music offering no clue as to what's behind his mask or in his heart. There's a single vibraphone hit when Sir Robert looks at the mask. It's an interesting touch, because at the time we don't even see him noticing it—we learn about it a few seconds later, when Sardonicus mentions it.

Even in the scene with Krull (Oscar Homolka) and the peasant girls, Baron Sardonicus' S is seen above the background doorway, fulfilling Ray Russell's script instruction that it recur in the movie as a symbol: "[It] should be designed with an eye to massiveness, baroque evil, overpowering dark majesty."

There's another shock hit as Anna is strung up to be tortured, but again it's a musically suppressed jolt—sliding rather than with a sudden impact. It's almost as if Dexter created all his shock hits beforehand, doling them out in various ways so he wouldn't repeat himself or abuse the privilege of making the audience jump. As Krull again threatens Anna with leeches, the music creates an unpleasant sonic background that includes cymbal crashes to add to the horror. And like almost everything else in the picture, even the "party" with the young beauties is anything but cheerful, the grim underscore making Krull's upbeat speech seem even more deceitful. When one of the women sees Sardonicus' face, Dexter provides another multi-note hit to emphasize the event.

Sir Robert's nightmare is awash with vibraphone, small brassy hits and mysterious woodwinds barely hinting at the love theme, the vibe again recreating the passage of time through its undulating sound. While Maude sleeps, the love theme is slightly hinted at by clarinet, and when the scene switches to Sardonicus' bedroom, vibraphone accentuates his mask. Vibe is also used to emphasize the missing mirrors in the castle, further serving its role as representing the baron's physical and mental state.

As Sardonicus recounts his horrific tale to Sir Robert via flashback, the vibraphone again serves as a transitional device to take us back in time, a responsibility that harps have handled in many a motion picture. One odd moment in the score occurs when Marek nails shut his father's coffin, the music being cheerier than it has any right to be. Piano and clarinet then help conjure the moment when Marek realizes he can't find the winning lottery ticket.

In the cemetery scene, there's an excellent use of building orchestration and dynamics with piano, winds, brass and organ as Marek digs deeper to try to

Disciple of science Sir Robert must conduct his medical research under Krull's watchful eye (singular).

reach his father's grave. It may be the most effective use of music in the entire score, as it really elevates the sense of dread and horror. Dexter probably enjoyed having an extended action sequence where the music could be front and center rather than merely offering subtle dramatic support. There's another nice touch when the music stops so we can hear the creaking of the casket being pried open. The composer provides a powerful brassy shock when Marek sees the hideous grin on his father's face, with further brassy blasts sounding alongside piano as he runs away. This is all the more potent because the composer didn't offer too many competing shock hits during earlier moments when they could have been employed.

Quiet winds and strings and possibly organ accompany Marek returning to the grave to retrieve the ticket, a visually effective sequence because he's shown in shadow. Dexter refrains from scoring the action here, instead covering the mood, deciding not to offer any musical clue that something horrible has happened to Marek. After providing an aural jolt on a shot of the corpse, the music builds tension and atmosphere to prepare us for the next shock: When his wife sees his ghastly new face, the composer provides another orchestral blast, powerful enough to compete with her subsequent screams.

Shrill woodwinds, organ and strings augment Sir Robert beginning his medical treatment on Sardonicus, with slow tympani suggesting the passage of time; low strings ultimately reveal the futility of the attempt. As the baron leads Sir Robert to the torture chamber, quiet strings and winds set the stage for the brassy shock revealing Maude roped to the chair. Had Dexter built up the tension beforehand, the ultimate reveal wouldn't have been quite so surprising, although a bit of vibe as they enter the chamber does offer a hint of foreshadowing. When Krull is identified as the "surgeon" to alter Maude's face, vibraphone emphasizes his evilness, and the same instrument is again enlisted when Sardonicus reveals his face. Dexter gets another opportunity to write some action music when Sir Robert attacks the baron, but the excitement is short-lived: The tympani player has just a few moments to pound his drums before the good doctor is clubbed on the head and knocked out.

Vibraphone shimmers accompany Sir Robert awakening on the rack, and the percussion instrument is called upon again when the doctor writes to London for some medical equipment. We then hear the earlier gentle folk melody, which transitions the film to the London hospital. Harp and xylophone (or else unreverbed vibe) add subtle touches to match the weird medical supplies seen in the montage. This is the first break from the downbeat music in quite some time, and it helps create some contrast before the story returns to Gorslava. Pizzicato strings and more xylophone tell us that the supplies have now arrived at the castle, these instrumental choices setting this particular sequence apart from the rest of the movie. When one of the research dogs is presumed dead, low strings, vibraphone and piano mix in various ways to continue the mood of doom and gloom.

Ray Russell's "Sardonicus" came to the screen as Mr. Sardonicus – but why Mr. Sardonicus *rather than* Baron Sardonicus? Mr. takes the toothy terrornaut off the Royal Register and he lands with a thud amidst such movie Mr.s as Belvedere, Blandings, Deeds, Chicken, Limpet, Magoo and Mom. (Courtesy Ronald V. Borst/Hollywood Movie Posters)

Even when Maude plays a pretty melody on the spinet for Sir Robert, there's still much sadness to the piece, something the film characters actually mention. No matter what, this movie was simply not going to provide the viewers with much of a break from the solemnity. As the couple converses, there's a welcome section without underscore, probably to allow some exposition out without competition from any music.

A piano note and low pizzicato strings are heard before Sardonicus invites Maude to enter the padlocked room, whereupon a hushed brassy crescendo leads to the door being closed behind her. The musical silence inside the darkened room continues for about 40 seconds and is an effective prelude to the brass-and-piano shock hit that accompanies the grinning skull of the father.

Harp, vibraphone, winds and brass accompany the injection of the "cure" into Sardonicus, a new musical sound that helps the audience believe that a different type of cure is being attempted. When Sardonicus is forced to look at his father's face in the dark, the powerful music ends with a vibraphone shimmer, but it's somewhat buried under his screams.

This was probably the best approach to take on the soundtrack, as screaming is an important component of the movie, shock being both the initial cause of his affliction as well as his cure. After his supposed recovery, there's nothing very celebratory in the music, as the same dark instrumentation of low strings, vibraphone and winds is heard when his face is restored. Perhaps this was done to offer a clue as to the movie's final outcome. Had Dexter written more upbeat music here, it might have made us feel sadder for Sardonicus at the end. And since he's still a pretty repugnant character even after he's supposedly been cured, it would have been a mistake to paint him in any kind of positive musical light.

There's an interesting zithery effect as Sardonicus prepares to put his seal on the letter to his wife. It's odd that the composer would offer something new from an instrumental standpoint this late in the picture, especially as he had the opportunity to use it at the beginning of the film when Sir Robert noticed the same sealing wax on Maude's letter. Some warm strings are only mildly hopeful as Maude receives the letter that annuls her marriage, and quiet woodwinds and low strings sound as she and Sir Robert (and Anna) leave by carriage. There's nothing particularly triumphant about the ending, and Dexter

"I missed them – the train had already left!": Krull has fiendish fun delivering a fatal dose of Fake News to his malevolent master. (Courtesy Ronald V. Borst/Hollywood Movie Posters)

wisely carried his bleak musical approach right up to the end of the movie. When Sir Robert tells Krull that Sardonicus can heal himself, the music is anything but positive, telegraphing that the Punishment Poll is not going to turn out very well for the baron. And when Krull grasps that he will now have the upper hand on his master by not informing him that his affliction is all in his mind, a vibraphone shimmer tells us all we need to know.

After the Punishment Poll break, a mixture of low and high woodwinds offers contrast rather than harmony, with brass foretelling Sardonicus' miserable future. Piano and vibraphone are heard as Krull feasts, leading to a fortissimo full-orchestral ending that is suitably harsh and pessimistic. It's the composer's way of letting us know that Sardonicus will never figure out that his ailment is psychosomatic. There was never a "mercy ending"; if there *had* been, some of the earlier scenes likely would have been scored quite differently.

Von Dexter is to be applauded for a musical score that has no noticeable missteps, and is true to the picture's dramatic intents from beginning to end.

Mr. Sardonicus Reviews

Newsday (October 12, 1961): [A]udiences probably will enjoy the horrifying histrionics of *Mr. Sardonicus*, wherein its leering villain, Guy Rolfe, and his obliging henchman, a one-eyed Oscar Homolka, make things unpleasant for Ronald Lewis and Audrey Dalton in a medieval castle far removed from civilization. So go and have yourselves a happy, terror-filled time.

The Hollywood Reporter (October 13, 1961, Lawrence H. Lipskin): The Castle touch, which has been consistently turned even ghouls into gold via the gimmick, should once more prove potent with this one. He's the only one in the film who kids the proceedings, the true principals [Homolka, Lewis, Dalton, Rolfe] playing with appropriate gravity their respective roles as servile assistant ghoul, surgeon, wife and "Mr. Sardonicus," the fiend with the fixed grin. ...Eerie lighting and properly funereal atmosphere enhance thrill content for horror fanciers.

Film Daily (October 18, 1961): Good picture, good gimmick, and it should add up to good box office, enough to make exhibitors smile as they count their money. But not too much of a smile now, mind you. Remember what happened to the Baron.

New York Times (October 19, 1961, Howard Thompson): [D]irector-producer William Castle ... is not Edgar Allan Poe [and *Mr. Sardonicus* is] painful proof....

Variety (October 25, 1961, Pit.): It may ... leave some craving for more blood and old-fashioned spookery than the producer has chosen to lens this time. Those who dig the shock-for-shock's-sake approach are apt to feel a little cheated, because Castle has woven the tale of *Mr. Sardonicus* with rather more intelligence than is usually accorded the genre, and the moments aimed at making audiences recoil are well-spaced and story-integrated with relative plausibility.

Credit for the more reasoned delineation must be shared with Ray Russell....

Indianapolis Star (October 26, 1961, Lynn Hopper): Guy Rolfe and Oscar Homolka turn in performances worthy of a more pretentious film. ...This is the sort of film that lovers of sweetness and light need not bother with.

Detroit Free Press (October 28, 1961, Ron Martin): [*Mr. Sardonicus*] is another in a series of the ventures of Producer William Castle, the poor man's Alfred Hitchcock. ...You will be wise to vote thumbs up [in the Punishment Poll]. That way, you will not prolong the suffering ... either of Sardonicus or yourself.

Boston Globe (November 2, 1961, M.L.A.): [T]here's considerable manufactured terror in [*Mr. Sardonicus*], and the cast is of higher caliber than in previous Castle productions. What with Oscar Homolka as an ugly but occasionally comic servant, tall, cold Guy Rolfe in the title role ... *Mr. Sardonicus* is a better-than-expected fright film. ...It's all fun for the kiddies and elders who enjoy this kind of entertainment.

Star Tribune (Minneapolis) (November 13, 1961, Will Jones): I wouldn't say *Mr. Sardonicus* is the scariest horror movie I've ever seen, but it's certainly the most revolting. ...William Castle [is] the sick man's Alfred Hitchcock.

El Paso Herald Post (November 17, 1961): *Mr. Sardonicus* is macabre to the final flicker.

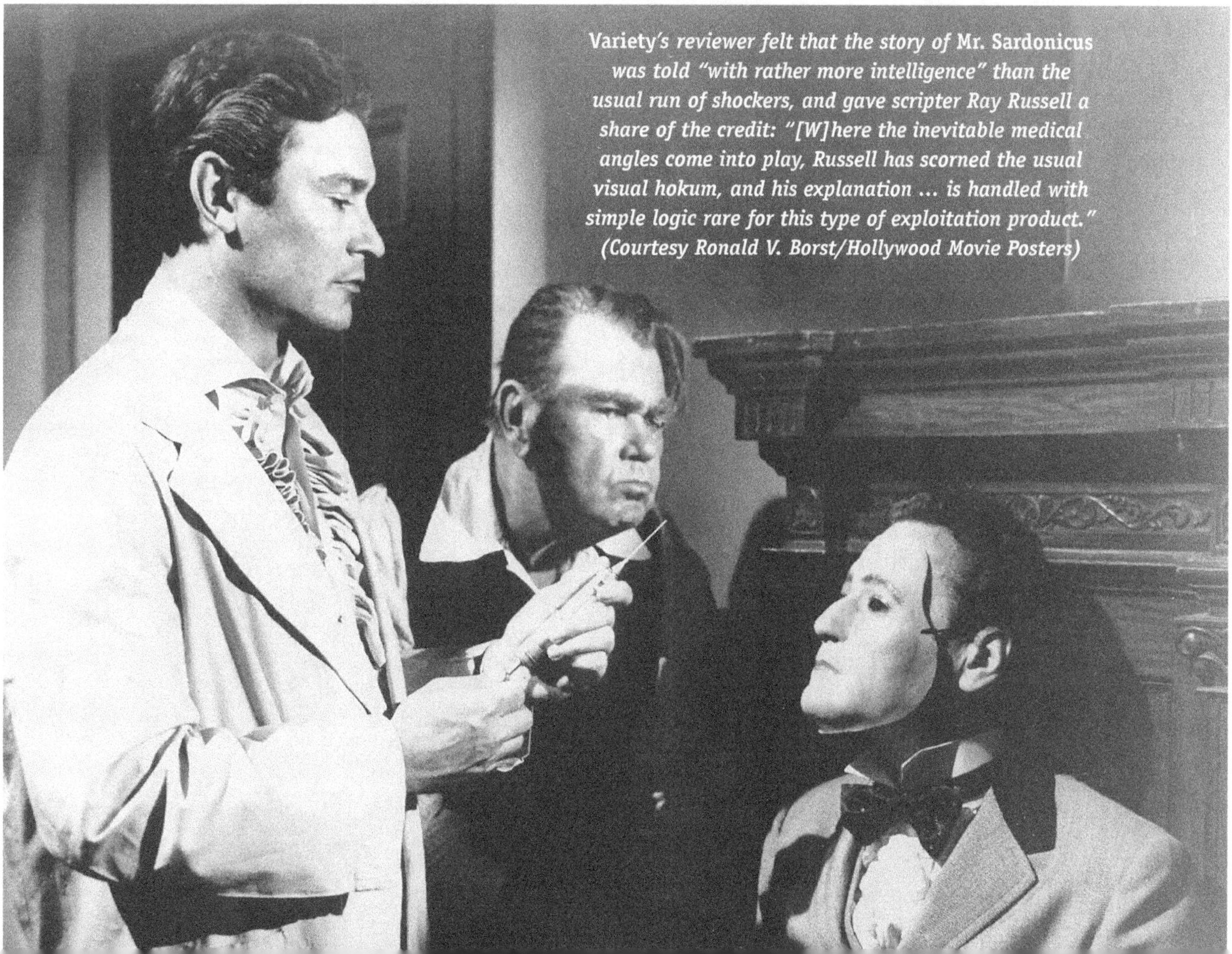

Variety's reviewer felt that the story of Mr. Sardonicus was told "with rather more intelligence" than the usual run of shockers, and gave scripter Ray Russell a share of the credit: "[W]here the inevitable medical angles come into play, Russell has scorned the usual visual hokum, and his explanation ... is handled with simple logic rare for this type of exploitation product." (Courtesy Ronald V. Borst/Hollywood Movie Posters)

Miami News (November 18, 1961, Herb Kelly): If we're going to sit through a suspense chiller we want it done right. Like barren trees with gnarled limbs and crooked trunks, soupy fog and murky countryside. Also there must be spooky shadows and nobody must laugh. Sneers, yes, but no laughter.

These are the ingredients of *Mr. Sardonicus*, a sort of intellectual horror movie....

It's scary, but done on a fairly high plane.

The Tablet (Brooklyn) (November 18, 1961): [T]his William Castle chiller relies more heavily upon revolting sight effect than upon shock by situation. Why an actor of Oscar Homolka's ability should be asked to indulge such macabre effects as empty eye-sockets is beyond reasonable understanding. But then, so is the story, or what passes. ...Designed strictly for the jolt-and-bolt crowd, this is not even up to Castle's usual standard.

Miami Herald (November 18, 1961, George Bourke): There is somewhat less gore and unreasonable goose-pimpling in this one than is the norm for Castle's sanguine sagas – but the more conservative treatment is a plus not a minus.

Richmond (Virginia) *Times-Dispatch* (December 2, 1961, Edith Lindeman): [Behind Sardonicus' mask] is the most horrendous hunk of makeup since Lon Chaney the Elder appeared as the Hunchback of Notre Dame.

San Francisco Examiner (December 4, 1961, Dick Nolan): The audience ... gets to vote on whether the turkey, *Mr. Sardonicus*, ends by punishing the villain or showing him mercy. The first audience, if you care, voted thumbs down.... Now let's hold a vote on the producer.

Los Angeles Times (December 8, 1961, Charles Stinson; the review is titled "Sardonicus Can't Do a Thing with His Face"): There have been rumors that Mr. Castle is leaving the horror business. Can this be his last creation? Dare we hope?

[T]his one, compared to his others, is almost bearable. His direction is still slow and uninventive – an occasional quickie shot of skull or a decaying face is still his primitive concept of the ultimate in

An entertainingly written Sardonicus *review from the* Fort Worth Star Telegram *(November 16, 1961).*

'Mr. Sardonicus' Pays

Brooks Runs Up Ballot But Castle Not Undercut

BY ELSTON BROOKS

Gad, decisions, decisions!

Now we know how Truman felt about Korea, how Stengel felt about all those pinch hitters, how Hedda felt about which hat for Tuesday...

WILLIAM CASTLE

There we were, minding our own goose bumps in the Hollywood Theater while watching a ghoulish thing called "Mr. Sardonicus," when suddenly our old friend William Castle appeared on screen.

Castle is the hammy producer who usually comes through town every time he thinks up a new gimmick for one of his horror epics. He has buzzed our seat with electricity in "The Tingler," given us a heart attack insurance policy in "Macabre" and even clanked a skeleton across the theater rafters in "The House on Haunted Hill."

But this time he was presenting himself on celluloid in his own picture.

"It's up to you—you make the decision," Castle smiled, interrupting our next swipe into the popcorn box. "The picture could end now, but if you think 'Mr. Sardonicus' should have more punishment merely hold up your ballot with the printed thumb pointed down..."

• • •

VIEWERS GIVE THUMB DOWN TO REVIEWER

"Aw, Bill," we said aloud, forgetting he was just on the screen. "We came to the movies to relax, not make decisions." A mother and her small child eyed us and moved away.

"Or," Castle continued, "if you're the weak-hearted type and think he's had enough, display your ballot with the thumb pointed up."

Awwhatheheck, we figured, this cat Sardonicus has had enough troubles for the last 90 minutes. After he had buried his father he discovered the old man had tucked a winning lottery ticket into the vest he was buried in. So Sardonicus goes grave robbing, and he is so shook up when he sees dad's skeletal remains, his face freezes in such a horrible mess that he has to wear a mask.

"That's where he got his name," Castle was intoning from the screen. "Sardonicus is the Latin term for the death grimace on the face of lockjaw victims."

"You coulda fooled us, Bill," we found ourself saying. "When you hopped on the title of 'Homicidal' after Hitchcock hit with 'Psycho,' we figured you registered 'Sardonicus' because 'Spartacus' was big at the boxoffice."

We chuckled at our cleverness, and two more people moved away from us, muttering.

"Hold your ballots high so I can count them," Castle's image was saying.

We started to hold our ballot with the thumb down and scowl like Charles Laughton sitting in one of those Roman balconies. After all, Sardonicus did grow wolfbane and hemlock in his garden.

• • •

LIKE DAD, YOU'RE A NOWHERE CHICKEN

And how about that scene where he hung the upstairs maid by her thumbs and stuck leeches on her face? Yeah, how about that, buddy! That don't sound like no nice guy next door that you'd want marrying your daughter!

We looked frantically at the small ballot that had been handed each patron as he walked into the theater. Time was running out. The suspense music from "The $64,000 Question" was running through our brain.

"Save him! Save him!" we breathed aloud—and triumphantly held up our ballot. The thumb was pointing upward. We felt good all over.

Someone was tapping us on the shoulder. "Uh, man, like you're stickin' that card up so I can't see, man," said the patron behind us who was wearing a spiked motorcycle jacket. "Like, how about coolin' it?"

When we turned around we saw we were the only idiot in the theater holding up a ballot.

"Let's see, now," said Castle on the screen, "that makes 453, subtract 2, and we have the verdict. It's thumbs down! More punishment for 'Mr. Sardonicus.'"

Castle left the screen and the movie came back for five minutes more.

It's been that way with us ever since Nixon.

suspense. But the script by Ray Russell ... is gratifyingly tighter and less rambling than the scenarios of earlier Castle efforts.

...Oscar Homolka hobbled around in a beamingly lowbrow burlesque style. He didn't take the film seriously at all. Good for him.

...The audience voted overwhelmingly to punish the Baron with a case of lockjaw. I made a motion to sentence the Baron to an eternity of playing in William Castle's horror films. I was ruled out of order. Cruel and inhuman treatment, they said.

Hollywood Citizen-News (December 8, 1961, Nadine M. Edwards): In the acting department, Ronald Lewis as the doctor gives a highly creditable performance, the film's best; Oscar Homolka is commendable as the baron's wicked cohort; and Audrey Dalton gives a capable portrayal as the lovely wife. And Guy Rolfe as the masked Sardonicus lends effective support to the picture's dramatic worth.

Oakland (California) *Tribune* (December 11, 1961, Theresa Loeb Cone): If ever a story creaked with silly dialogue, wooden performances and phony fright, that is Mr. Castle's *Mr. Sardonicus*. ...The percentage of moviegoers who stay to see the end ... must be in direct ratio to a special kind of endurance which this reviewer unfortunately lacks.

Films and Filming (England): It has taken this film several years to reach us, and now it is slipped in apologetically to take its place in the outer suburbs....

...There is little humour except of the unconscious variety. I think this is more the fault of Ray Russell.... He deliberately set out to recreate a Gothic novelette, and where he scored a qualified success on paper with his cleverly imitative prose, in his screenplay he was loth [*sic*] to discard his stylised treatment. The result is that the dialogue is stilted and the cast is uneasy. Guy Rolfe and Audrey Dalton particularly seem awkward. What could have been a good film, based, as so many horror films are not, on a dramatically defensible premise, collapses into a sadly substandard melodrama.

Castle of Frankenstein: Lurid but compelling horror tale.... ...Incredible but made easier to swallow by spoofing approach of director William Castle.

Coventry Evening Telegraph (April 27, 1965): William Castle ... is often outrageous in the manner in which he plays to the gallery in his horror films, but he has taken a serious line with *Mr. Sardonicus*.... [I[t is a pity that Ray Russell's script ... should be the weakest point of the film. [Rolfe and Dalton] have an awkward time with their lines.

Starlog editor Dave McDonnell, reviewing the Sony Pictures DVD box set *William Castle* (2009): "[*Mr. Sardonicus* is] a mouthwatering delicious dark fantasy – with an ending that's simply the best of this set's eight films. [The set's other flicks included *The Tingler*, *Homicidal* and *Strait-Jacket*.]

> ★ MR. SARDONICUS (Yorkshire ITV, 8.0). Oscar Homolka, Ronald Lewis. A man, paralysed in the face for years, threatens a surgeon. *TENSE, but sometimes difficult to keep a straight face.*

Ray Russell's Other Horrors

by Tom Weaver

The Premature Burial (AIP, 1962)

Screenplay: Charles Beaumont and Ray Russell; Suggested by the Story by Edgar Allan Poe; Produced and Directed by Roger Corman; Photography: Floyd Crosby (Pathe Color); Music: Ronald Stein. **Cast:** Ray Milland, Hazel Court, Richard Ney, Heather Angel, Alan Napier, John Dierkes, Dick Miller.

After Ray Russell wrote his first screenplay *Mr. Sardonicus* in early 1961, he was almost immediately offered more scripting jobs: At various points throughout that year, the Hollywood trades announced that he had been signed to write for William Castle (*Zotz!*, *Sagittarius* and *The Spitting Image*), AIP (*X* [aka *X—The Man with the X-Ray Eyes*] and *Off on a Comet*) and others. But when the second Russell-scripted movie went into production in the fall of '61, it was one that apparently had *never* once been mentioned in Russell squibs until after the screenplay was completed: *The Premature Burial*, based on Edgar Allan Poe's short story.

Perhaps producer-director Roger Corman had Russell and Charles Beaumont write it on the down-low because he intended to make it not for AIP, where his "Poe cycle" began with *House of Usher* (1960) and *Pit and the Pendulum* (1961), but for Pathe Labs, then intent on starting their own distribution company. AIP president James H. Nicholson and his v.p. Samuel Z. Arkoff didn't think much of the idea of Corman and Poe going AWOL so they surreptitiously sank their hooks into the project, and then showed up unannounced at Producers Studio on the first shooting day: Both wearing sunbeam smiles, they told Corman that his well-laid plans had gone awry and that he was again working for AIP.

The protagonist of the 1844 story was a typical Poe worry wart, very talkatively consumed by the thought that his undertakers may do a rush job. Then he falls asleep in a cramped berth on a boat, wakes up forgetting where he is, thinks he's in a coffin and has a fit of screaming meemies; fortuitously, this gets the phobia out of his system. In a *Famous Monsters* #25 article (mostly a reprint from the British mag *Science Fantasy*), Russell said that when he and Beaumont were hired to adapt "Premature Burial," they beelined to their bookcases to re-read it:

> "Within the Coffin I Lie... *ALIVE!*"

> We were in for a shock, but not the sort one usually expects to receive from a Poe yarn — for, unlike the stories that formed the bases of the two earlier AIP Poe films..., this story was not really a story at all; more like a formal essay on the disadvantages and general undesirability of being buried alive.

> And so we had to build the whole structure from the ground up — plot, characters and dialogue — while retaining the essential elements of Poe's piece; namely, the obsessive terror of premature burial.[1]

Beaumont and Russell's protagonist (Ray Milland in "the Vincent Price part") has money, a posh home on the English moors and a flame-haired bride-to-be (Hazel Court) young enough to be a daughter. That's the good news. But he also has the fear that his father was buried alive, and the knack of being Johnny on the Spot whenever anything happens that could rattle a guy with a fear of coffins.[2]

Could someone be *making* these things happen

in order to bedevil Milland? Perhaps so, and Heather Angel as Milland's sourpuss sister would very much like viewers to think it's her. (A quarter century earlier, at Paramount, a young and beautiful Angel played Phyllis opposite young and beautiful Milland's Bulldog Drummond.)

Corman was surely eager to make a hit movie during his holiday from AIP and there's a good chance that it was his idea that the *Premature Burial* script should be full of plot leftovers from *House of Usher* and *Pit and the Pendulum*; why tamper with success? Mark Damon gets a chilly reception at the House of Usher when he appears there looking for his sweetheart; John Kerr (*Pit and the Pendulum*) has an equally frosty time getting his foot in the door of the castle where his sister mysteriously died, and *Premature Burial* begins with Hazel Court finding an **UNWELCOME** mat on Milland's doorstep when she shows up in search of her M.I.A. fiancé. Premature burials also figured into the plots of *Usher* and *Pit*, Milland has a weird (but brightly colored) dream in the *Usher* tradition, etc. *Premature*'s surprise ending exposes Court as the money-minded perpetrator of all the monkey business ... although by 1962 it probably wasn't much of a surprise, the twist of a wife or husband driving a spouse to madness and/or death having been used in *Gaslight, Diabolique, House on Haunted Hill, The Screaming Skull, The Tingler* – and also *Pit and the Pendulum*! Even the *Thriller* TV episode "The Premature Burial," shot in August 1961 and aired a month before Corman's movie started shooting, made the cataleptic man's new bride the villain of the piece. Of course, Ray Russell was no stranger to stories in which men are traumatized by finding a shocking surprise inside a coffin.

Variety noticed the re-use of tried and true story elements ("Roger Corman seems to have run thin in imagination on this third trip to the same literary well") but horror movie fans didn't seem to care: A few months after *Premature Burial* hits theaters, AIP had to start refusing bookings (a first for the company) because the number of playdates accepted had exhausted the print supply. (Perhaps taking a page from William Castle's book, Corman made a two-week swing of the country ballyhooing the picture.) In June 1962, AIP sales chief Leon P. Blender crowed that, with a total gross of more than $1,250,000 in the domestic market, *Premature Burial* was on its way to becoming one of the company's all-time top grossers. At the beginning of '63, *Variety*'s list of the big rental pictures of '62 included these four horror

Marc Russell:

The screenplay was a collaboration with Charles Beaumont, who was a close personal friend of Dad's. I can't tell you how many Beaumont stories were in *Playboy,* but it was a large number, and I think almost all were in the period when Dad was the executive editor. I have a fairly good memory of Beaumont visiting the house many times, and the whole family visited him and his wife and four children at *their* house in North Hollywood once, around 1963. Beaumont also accompanied me and Dad to movies a couple of times in the early '60s. Beaumont died at age 38 after about three years of serious deterioration. The last time I saw him was about three years before he died. As I understand it, by the time of his death, he looked like a very old man. The exact cause was never definitely determined.

The Premature Burial turned out to be the only one of the Roger Corman Poe films to star someone other than Vincent Price. Having the doctor character [played by Richard Ney] bear the same name as a character in *The Maltese Falcon* – Miles Archer – was Beaumont's idea, but don't ask me why. I was on the set during the filming of the wedding reception scene, when Guy Carrell [Milland] becomes upset by the piano music.

movies (in descending order): *What Ever Happened to Baby Jane?, Tales of Terror, The Premature Burial* and *The Innocents*. Two years later, the low-budget black-and-white *The Curse of the Living Corpse*, another horse-and-buggy era chiller, was practically a remake of the Beaumont-Russell *Premature Burial*: A wealthy cataleptic, betrayed by members of his greedy family after his "death," comes back with a vengeance (pun intended).

Ray Russell also wrote in *Science Fantasy* that in an early script draft, he and Beaumont "tried to get in more of the Poe original. Considerations of length made it necessary to jettison several scenes but perhaps [*Science Fantasy*] readers would be interested in reading the following sequence which did not reach the screen. They will recognize it as being derived directly from Poe." (Read it in *Famous Monsters*

#25, pages 24-28.)

In the 1990 *New York Times* article "The High Art of Horror Films Can Cut Deep Into the Psyche," Caryn James wrote that, as a child, she saw drive-in horror movies with family members. But *The Premature Burial*

> was more frightening than anyone had expected. When Ray Milland, buried while he was merely in a coma, woke up and started gasping for air and struggling to push the lid off his coffin, my cousin jumped in the front seat with his father, and my aunt climbed in back with me. We hadn't even done that during *Psycho*.
>
> ...The day after seeing it, I could still hear the slow, eerie melody of "Sweet Molly Malone" ... which haunted the film's soundtrack.... "They sang this really scary song," I told my mother, who replied in the most commonsensical tone on earth, "How can it be scary? It's a song about fish." It was then that I knew anything could be frightening on film, and then that I knew you had to be there.

Zotz! (Columbia, 1962)

Screenplay: Ray Russell; Based on the Novel by Walter Karig; Produced and Directed by William Castle; Photography: Gordon Avil; Music: Bernard Green. **Cast:** Tom Poston, Julia Meade, Jim Backus, Fred Clark, Cecil Kellaway, Zeme North, Margaret Dumont, Mike Mazurki.

Some of the theaters playing The Premature Burial *had a front-of-house exhibit that included a tuxedo-clad mannequin in an open coffin. Posing with it in this photo is Ray Russell's wife's cousin John Stefanski.*

By 1961, William Castle's track record of success with gimmick horror movies had brought him a great deal of attention and presumably an even greater deal of money. But the King of Shockers' *next* shock was his announcement that he would follow *Mr. Sardonicus* with a Disney-type movie! "[*Zotz!* is] about an absent-minded professor, and [Walt] Disney says it's a great follow-up to his [*The Absent Minded Professor*, 1961]," Castle told interviewer Bea Smith. "I'm varying my productions, you see, trying to keep up with my audiences' tastes and wants."

Tom Poston stars as Jonathan Jones, a specimen of *nerdus maximus*, subsisting on a diet of wheat germ and sauerkraut juice, and making his living as a professor of Ancient Eastern Languages at a California college. His niece Zeme North's boyfriend is in Yukranistan on an archaeological expedition; he mails her a coin discovered in the hand of an idol in temple ruins. A relic of some ancient civilization, the coin has supernatural powers: Its bearer merely needs to point at another person to cause sudden pain. By speaking the sacred name of the god Zotz, the bearer makes him move in slow motion. And by doing both at once, he causes the person's death. Poston tries to demonstrate the coin's power at a cocktail party at the home of college dean Cecil Kellaway: Unaware that he hasn't brought the coin, he releases a cage-full of white mice. Unfazed by Poston's pointing and "Zotz!"-ing, they scatter throughout the room and cause *mouss* hysteria.

Poston realizes that the power of the coin can also destroy ships, tanks and planes, so he flies to Washington D.C. to offer it to the Pentagon. Officers there, including Fred Clark, peg him as a kook and give him the runaround. But Poston's pitch has been overheard by a window washer who's really a Russian spy, and the Reds soon have Poston in their clutches. Ultimately he outwits his Commie captors, but in the fracas, the magic coin drops through a storm drain grate and may never be recovered.

Zotz! is based on a same-name novel by Walter Karig, a Navy captain and workaholic writer (he even wrote under female names). Published in 1947, it was a whimsical wartime tale of a fellow trying to bust through bureaucratic red tape and get to President Roosevelt, in order to sell the prez on the idea of sending him to Germany and put the "Zotz!" on Hitler and his cronies. Karig did not live to see the only movie ever made from one of his novels; he died in 1956.

Full-page ad from the November 28, 1962, Variety.

"After a few decades of owning a copy of the book, I finally read the novel *Zotz!*" says Marc Russell.

> It was amusing, but kind of hard to get through. It was similar to an old screwball comedy movie, with funny dialogue and lengthy misunderstandings, etc. But a *huge* amount of the book involves Prof. Jones making his way through multiple levels of government and military offices, trying to explain his magical powers. It just went on for too long. I think the movie was an improvement, for the most part.

Ray Russell updated Karig's novel at Columbia in the fall of 1961. Either he knew how to please the boss (William Castle), or Castle made some scripting suggestions, because there are some extraneous scenes that bear the Castle stamp; for example, Zeme North and her date Jimmy Hawkins at a drive-in watching Castle's *Homicidal*. Production began in late November 1961 and extended into early 1962; extensive interior and exterior shooting was done at L.A.'s Occidental College. Tom Poston was a popular TV comedian (he was one of Steve Allen's "second bananas") and game show panelist, co-star Julia Meade a TV pitch woman; the *New York Daily News* reviewer wrote that in *Zotz!*, both Poston and Meade "seem eager to return to the 21-inch screen." In the Pentagon part of the movie, Louis Nye, another one of Steverino's second bananas, has a cameo as a death ray inventor. Also briefly seen: Albert Grazer, a pudgy, bald-pated Bank of California employee, cast as a Russian pilot because he was the mirror image of Soviet honcho Nikita Khrushchev! And Jim Backus returns to the William Castle fold as a college professor competing with Poston for a promotion; after playing the bitter, pugnacious sheriff in Castle's *Macabre* (1958), Backus is back to buffoonery here.

The *Harrison's Reports* reviewer rated *Zotz!* as "Poor" and described the screening where he saw it: "As you enter the projection room, you're 'paid off' with a half-dollar size wooden amulet.... [Castle's movie adds up] to the sum total of his story symbol, the worthless coin." Ouch! *The New York Post* called Castle's way with comedy "distinctly heavy-handed" and Robert Salmaggi urged *New York Herald Tribune* readers, "Skip this one—zotz good advice." On the flip side of the coin (sorry), *The Hollywood Reporter* called *Zotz!* "a superior film to Castle's previous productions." In June 1962, Columbia sales vice-president Rube Jackter reported that the movie was shaping up as Castle's biggest grosser to date.

The day before production began, *Zotz!*'s associate producer Dona Holloway was one of three "mystery challengers" on an episode of TV's *To Tell the Truth* (with Tom Poston among the celebrities trying to pick out "the *real* Dona Holloway). When the movie went into release, she made a personal appearance tour carrying more than $50,000 worth of ancient coins for exhibition. (Armed security officers accompanied her.) Columbia announced that more than five million Zotz coin replicas would be distributed in theaters showing the film.

Marc Russell:

I visited the set of this zany comedy and saw the filming of the scene on the roof of a building when the Russian spy [Carl Don] fires his gun at Tom Poston, who is able to slow down the action by shouting "Zotz!" and thereby sidestep the bullet. I saw the movie at the time and then again, many years later. The second time, I did not enjoy it as much as my 11-year-old self did, but it is still fun. And most of the actors are good, especially reliable old Cecil Kellaway [as the college dean], as well as Margaret Dumont [the dean's wife], long after her Marx Brothers days. *Zotz!* might be the only Columbia movie in which the Columbia logo (the lady with the torch) *speaks*. At least I am not aware of any others. She speaks at both the beginning and end of the movie.

Indeed she does: During the opening COLUMBIA logo, William Castle (seated in a director's chair at the feet of the Torch Lady) points at her and says "Zotz!" – and the Torch Lady casually turns her head and asks, "Zotz? What's zot?" At the end, she tells the audience, "Zotz all!" Castle's unexpected side trip into comedy continued with his next picture, an English-made 1963 remake of *The Old Dark House*, again with Poston. But not long after that, he was back at the helm of full-fledged horror pictures (*Strait-Jacket* and *The Night Walker*, both 1964), just where Monster Kids wanted him.

Zotz! was the second and last Castle-Ray Russell collaboration. Two other movies that Russell reportedly signed to write for Castle, *Sagittarius* and *The Spitting Image*, fell by the wayside.

The Zotz! coin – cleaned by Amanda Russell with water, a mild spray cleaner and cotton swabs for purposes of photography, thank you very much. It's bronze-colored plastic, an inch and a half in diameter. The symbol design is raised. She also has a silver-tone metal Zotz! tie clip that must have been given to her dad at some point.

X
(aka *X—The Man with the X-Ray Eyes*) (AIP, 1963)

Screenplay: Robert Dillon and Ray Russell; Story: Ray Russell; Produced and Directed by Roger Corman; Photography: Floyd Crosby (Pathécolor); Music: Les Baxter. Cast: Ray Milland, Diana van der Vlis, Harold J. Stone, John Hoyt, Don Rickles.

Ophthalmologist: My dear friend, only the gods see everything.

Ray Milland.

Ray Milland, unidentified woman, Don Rickles.

AIP president James H. Nicholson, Ray Milland, producer-director Roger Corman and unidentified man on the X set.

Dr. Xavier: My dear doctor, I'm closing *in* on the gods.

Less than four minutes "into" *X*, our protagonist Dr. James Xavier has made that audacious, irreverent comment, and put the mother of all whammies on himself. He must never have been a science fiction movie fan, or he'd know the fate of mortal men who dare to emulate God.

Frustrated by his awareness of how little Man *really* sees of the world around him, Dr. Xavier (Ray Milland) develops a compound that gives his test animals see-through vision. But he ignores the wisdom of Abraham Lincoln, who famously said "A man who experiments upon himself has a fool for a guinea pig" (or something similar), and begins eye-dropping the mixture into his own peepers. The longer he uses it, the better it works: Initially he can see through people's clothes, then clear through to their innards. Before long, he's counting on the cumulative X effect to enable him to explore the mysteries of Creation. The story takes an *Invisible Man* turn when his colleague Dr. Brant (Harold J. Stone) wonders about the compound's effect upon the brain and wants Xavier to find a way back.

On the lam from the law after recklessly killing Brant, Xavier goes underground: Wearing either a large blindfold or dark glasses, he becomes a seamy carnival sideshow's Mr. Mentalo, and then a "healer" who diagnoses the medical conditions of ailing indigents. In Las Vegas, he makes a killing with his ability to see through blackjack cards, but with his growing arrogance (megalomania?) he arouses suspicion and is back on the run. Once he gets a look at the center of the universe, and the eye that sees us all (God), Xavier is overcome with anguish. In a revival tent, a Bible-quoting fire-and-brimstone preacher exhorts him: "If thine eye offends thee, pluck it out!" The crowd takes up the "Pluck it out!" chant and the crazed Xavier gouges out his eyes.

According to Roger Corman, the movie's origins date back to a lunch date with AIP president James H. Nicholson, who had dreamed up yet another great title—*X—The Man with the X-Ray Eyes*—and now wanted a movie to go with it. Over the next few days, they threw ideas around, including (according to Corman's autobiography) "a jazz musician on weird drugs, a criminal who uses X-ray vision for robberies. They seemed like dead-end stories." With a story involving drugs, he also worried about censors giving *him* the evil eye. Once Corman realized that the central character must be a medical researcher, the writing of a script was assigned to Ray Russell. This was announced in the *Hollywood Reporter* of May 11, 1961—nearly two full years before the picture began shooting. *X* may have been Russell's first script after *Mr. Sardonicus*, pre-dating even *The Premature Burial*.

According to Marc and Amanda, Ray's final draft is very much like the eventual movie, but for some reason, screenwriter Robert Dillon was then engaged to revise and/or add material – and Dillon even gets top billing over Russell in the on-screen writing credits. Marc says that Ray and Dillon wrote consecutively, not shoulder to shoulder; "Dad definitely did not actually collaborate with Robert Dillon. I don't think he even met him. Dillon made no radical changes to the basic story."

I own a no-cover, no-date copy of what I assume was *the* final draft, or close *to* it – a script that presumably includes Robert Dillon's contributions, whatever they may have been – and there are a few spots where it's interestingly different from the movie. Preparing to put some X-fluid in a lab monkey's eyes, Xavier dons two pairs of gloves and uses tongs to get the vial out of a lead box marked DANGER…RADIOACTIVE MATERIAL. Right from the first time that he tests the X-fluid on himself, his eyes "seem to glow with a light of their own"; later in this script, one of Xavier's carnival co-workers describes his eyes as "shining like a fire burning through windows in his skull." Xavier operates on the little girl with his surgical mask covering his eyes. The carnival is not on a pier but on the outskirts of a desert town; Xavier's co-workers there are not the ordinary folks we see in the movie but a Dwarf, a Thin Man, a Fat Woman, etc. Unable to cope with his all-seeing eyes, a shaky Xavier uses a hammer to break the lenses of his dark glasses and then puts pieces of lead in the frames, which makes things more tolerable for him. At the end, as Xavier staggers toward the revival meeting tent, he becomes consumed by an urge to "truly see" and upturns the entire bottle of X-fluid into his eyes, which causes him to scream. Now when he looks downward, he sees layer after layer of the Earth, "[f]irst the crust and then the red hot lava and then the boiling white interior." Standing before the preacher, he says, "I – come – to – tell you – what I see—" and then, looking upward (i.e., into the heavens), he describes "great darknesses … as far off as time itself – and they are coming … coming to destroy all our world. Larger than the

PAGE 3

RAY MILLAND HOPES FOR ANOTHER "OSCAR"

It was a dedicated and inspired Ray Milland who appeared daily at the famed Republic Studios in the Studio City section of Los Angeles to star in the title role of American International's "X."

At the end of a long, hard day of gruelling work before the cameras and under the guidance of producer-director Roger Corman, Milland was a tired but happy man.

As Dr. James Xavier, the doctor who gives himself X-ray eyes, the Academy Award-winning veteran actor had, in terms of script, the most arduous and longest role of his spectacular career. For, in all but six scenes, Milland was in front of the cameras and is the principal part of the thrilling and suspenseful action of this contemporary science fiction tale. Now let's let the Oscar star tell about "X" in his own words:

"After over thirty years as an actor and with well over one hundred motion picture roles behind me," Milland says, it looks like I've finally found my biggest and most important role in terms of acting demands and in terms of content.

"My role as Dr. Xavier is every bit as taxing as the one for which I was honored in 'The Lost Weekend.' If my efforts come to fruition, perhaps 'X' will give me another crack at that elusive Oscar inasmuch as it's the role and the story which must be combined with acting to come up with the magic ingredient which results in the honor.

"There's many a fine actor in Hollywood who has the talent to win an Oscar but who never quite came up with the role in which to properly display his ability. I was fortunate to have had a chance with that fine film 'The Lost Weekend' and I believe that 'X' is another such vehicle.

"I've always had a scientific bent, with a particular fondness for the sicence of astronomy and the wonders of the universe opened to man by powerful telescopes. Until recently I had my own telescope which enabled me to reach outward beyond the narrow confines of my eyesight to view the stars and planets of the heavens in all their glory.

"I also was privileged to be one of the first non-scientists permitted to look through the fantastic 200-inch lens of the giant Mt. Palomar telescope. Now, at long last, I have been given an opportunity through my part in 'X' to recreate and verbalize some of the feelings of wonder I have always felt about the universe and man's role in it.

"It's a funny thing, too, with all the diverse roles I've had throughout my acting career that this is the first time I've ever portrayed a doctor or a scientist. The closest I've ever come before was one role as a psychiatrist.

"Now, with 'X,' I have a role such as I might have dreamed of for myself after reaching for the stars with my telescope or after that breath-taking night on Mt. Palomar.

"I firmly believe that 'X' is one of the finest scripts I've ever read. Most important is that, while it must be classified as science fiction, it also is a story which might actually have happened just yesterday, or which might even be happening today, or which quite possibly can happen tomorrow or the next day.

"My Dr. Xavier is a real and wonderful person, much like that of the thousands of dedicated men who daily give their lives and their beings to help their fellow man. Dr. Xavier is a brilliant doctor who, in his endless striving to improve his healing powers in the true tradition of doctors and scientists, seeks to improve upon the limited and imperfect mechanical devices which assist them in their work.

"It is quite conceivable in this atomic age, with its electron microscopes and other modern miracles, that the strange experiment which gives Dr. Xavier his X-ray vision could become an actuality. There is no reason why man cannot some day give his own limited and imperfect optical instrument the fantastic powers which he has given to his microscopes and telescopes.

"The discovery of such a technique, as in the story of 'X,' conceivably could result in the frustrations, uncertainties, terrors, dangers and obsessions which gripped Dr. Xavier. My character in 'The Lost Weekend' was obsessed by his craving for alcohol, but there is an added terrifying dimension for my fictional obsession in 'X' — a scientists's natural craving for perfection, for greater learning, for probing into the great mysteries of the universe.

"I felt this as we put this great human story on film. I trust that I have been able to convey this as well as I was able to depict the desperate hunger for alcohol in 'The Lost Weekend.' You will be the judge."

AGONIZING MOMENT

Ray Milland discovers that his new power of X-Ray vision has gotten out of hand in dramatic scene from AIP'S "X." Don Rickles, comedian who co-stars in dramatic role.

A legit interview or a publicist's concoction? X-Ray Milland shares his thoughts on X.

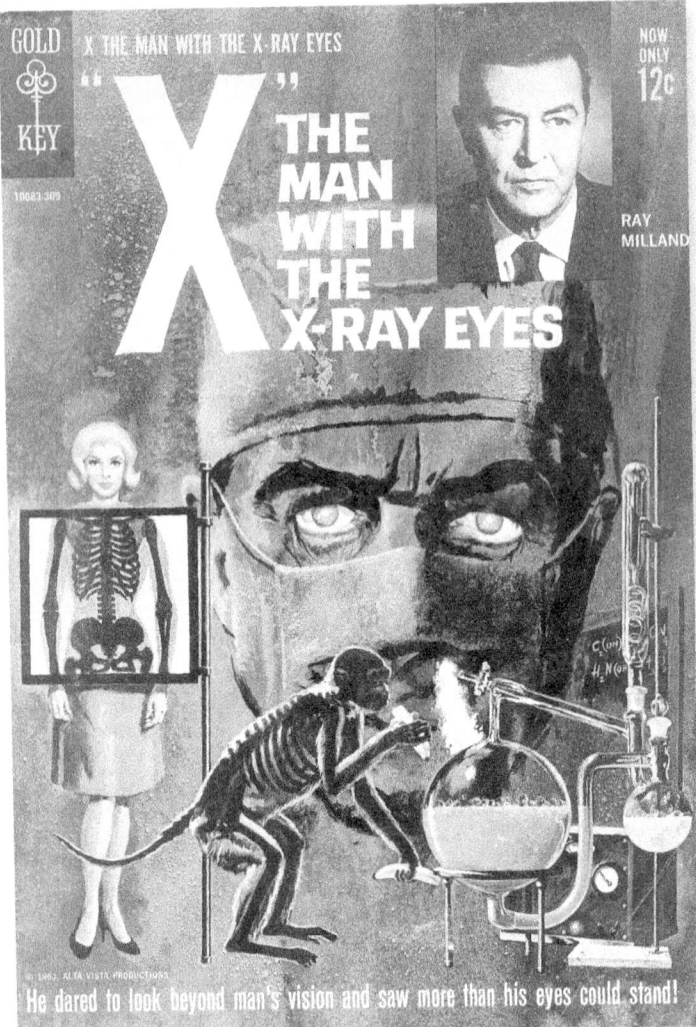

The Gold Key comic book tie-in gave its young readers, on the last page, a look at the eye of God—but spared them an image of Xavier with empty eye sockets.

stars – than galaxies of stars, they're coming..." The script calls for this to be seen on-screen, and also "a giant eye – an eye of the universe..." (God's eye).

Writing a script in which you call for awe-inspiring effects is one thing, but putting those effects on film is quite another ... in fact, borderline-impossible on a low budget. Corman knew audiences would feel cheated if they never got to see what Xavier sees, so many weird point-of-view shots were created via a combination of distortion lenses and optical work. The footage is disappointing, even confusing: More and more as the movie progresses, it's not the point of view of a man who can see everything, but the point of view of a man who can see practically *nothing*; if he sees the world like that, he's as good as blind.[3] The implication that looking upon God's face – even just His eye – will drive men mad, and even make a lab monkey turn up its toes, is creepy in a vaguely Lovecraftian way (as is Xavier's description of "great darknesses" coming to destroy our world). Les Baxter's score is equally eerie, with passages that sound like they were written for a haunted house movie.

Milland is excellent and that's a big plus since, except for a minute or two of exterior carnival activity, he's in every scene of the movie; it starts with an extreme closeup of his face and eyes, and ends with a closeup of his eye-less face. *X*'s three-week schedule must have taxed the 56-year-old actor, who undoubtedly needed to be on set every hour of every day. The trailer narrator calls it Milland's "most challenging role since his Academy Award-winning *Lost Weekend*," which might actually be true. The picture world-premiered in July 1963 at the International Science Fiction Film Festival in Trieste, Italy, where it won the Silver Spaceship award for the year's best English-language SF film. I'd like to think it won because it *was* among the year's best, but perhaps it won because the festival had attracted only two celebrities, AIP's James Nicholson and his European rep, and the festival organizers thought it would be showmanly to have someone (Nicholson) actually *accept* an award. That same month, Ray Russell reportedly wrote a piece about *X* for the British magazine *New Worlds*. Months later when *X* opened in Omaha, AIP sent Peter Lorre, of all people, to thump the tub for it.

At one point in the mid-1990s, *X* remakes were reportedly in the works at *three* companies, Sony Pictures, Warner Brothers and DreamWorks-Orion, the latter with Tim Burton attached. In 1999, 81-year-old Samuel Z. Arkoff was working on a remake, according to an unreliable source (Sam himself); in 2008, Joe Dante-Nigel Kneale; in 2009, MGM.

When it came to Ray Russell, AIP talked a good game: In 1961, they claimed to have a multiple-picture deal with him, and that he was scripting their *Off on a Comet*. A year later, they said, he was writing *Genghis Khan*, a $4,500,000 70mm Technirama-Technicolor spectacle for Chrlstmas 1963 roadshowing. Then in 1968, AIP announced signing him to adapt H.P. Lovecraft's 1929 novella *The Dunwich Horror*.[4]

But after all these exciting announcements, the *real* AIP-Russell box score is less impressive: AIP ultimately produced only *one* of the movies they'd signed him to write, *X*.

The Horror of It All
(20th Century-Fox, 1964)

Screenplay: Ray Russell; Associate Producer: Margia Dean; Executive Producer: Robert L. Lippert; Directed by Terence Fisher; Photography: Arthur Lavis; Music: Douglas Gamley. **Cast:** Pat Boone, Erica Rogers, Dennis Price, Valentine Dyall, Jack Bligh, Archie Duncan, Erik Chitty.

You ring the doorbell of a spooky-looking, middle-of-nowhere English mansion and a gunshot rings out, invisible hands open the creaking door, and a disembodied voice bids you enter. Do you go in? Yes, but only if you're the lead character in a horror comedy, because otherwise there'd *be* no horror comedy.

Pat Boone fills that slot in the English-made *The Horror of It All*, at first glance a throwback to footlight melodramas such as *The Cat and the Canary* – but as it progresses, it becomes more and more remindful of Universal director James Whale's darkly comic classic *The Old Dark House* (1932). There's an explanation for this.

"The screenplay of *The Horror of It All* had an unusual genesis," Marc Russell reveals. "After *Mr. Sardonicus* and *Zotz!*, Dad wrote a screenplay for William Castle's next picture, the 1963 remake of *The Old Dark House*. Castle paid him for it, but was not satisfied with it, so the script that was filmed was another one, written by Robert Dillon. Dad then made a few minor changes to his own script, gave it a new title, and it was soon filmed in England."

According to the August 14, 1963, *Variety*: "Ray Russell ... has written an original satire, *The Horror of It All* (for [producer] Robert Lippert), which spoofs the entire film genre and reprises all the gimmicks employed in such films the past 50 years." One wonders if Russell told Lippert that it was formerly an *Old Dark House* script rejected by Castle; I might not have; what would *you* have done? By October 7, 1963, when *Horror of It All* went into production at Shepperton Studios, Castle's *Old Dark House* had been completed and was on the verge of release. *The Horror of It All* came out in the late summer of 1964. Truth be told, neither scare comedy is particularly scary or particularly funny. But *Horror of It All* has plenty of funny music, reminding viewers that it's *meant* to be.

Boone, an American encyclopedia salesman, arrives at the house in search of his intended, pretty Erica Rogers. But maybe he'll have second thoughts

once he gets a load of her family. Her uncle Valentine Dyall is a macabre character who "speaks in Lugosi-like tones" (*Variety*); her cousin Dennis Price, formerly a stage actor, is a bit of a nut. Dyall's elderly brother Jack Bligh, an inventor, has been stuck in the house so long, he doesn't know that all his inventions (an electric light bulb, record player, etc.) have already been invented. Archie Duncan, a mad, powerful brute kept in a locked room, was once captured by headhunters and now thinks *everyone* is a headhunter. Then there's Andrée Melly as Natalia: Her entrance is accompanied by a loud musical stinger, as well it might, as she looks as vampiric and "thirsty" as she did when she played one of the title characters in *The Brides of Dracula* three years prior. Price tells Boone, "Natalia drinks very little ... except at night," one of the first of *many* lines driving home the vampire connection. From the Faint Praise Dept.: Melly *is* the best thing in the picture.

"[This] house – my ancestral home – is known throughout the countryside as a house of horror," says Dyall. The place lives up to its reputation when a series of murders brings to mind the old gag "Where

Former "Bride of Dracula" Andrée Melly as the Vampira-like Goth ghoul in The Horror of It All.

there's a will ... I want to be in it." ("All this probably seemed amusing on paper." – *Variety* again.)

Russell changed his Castle-commissioned *Old Dark House* script, but not enough, as any fan of the vintage Universal movie can easily spot some of the corresponding characters here. The most obvious: a bedridden grandfather with a womanly voice, confined to his sickbed. Dennis Price even talks about gin! (Ironically enough, there's almost *nothing* in the Castle *Old Dark House* that would make viewers flash back to the '32 version.) Once *The Horror of It All* goes the whodunit route, things get less derivative of *Old Dark House*, and there are a few fun final-reel twists that compensate for some of the familiar material that came before. And ... could this be a Ray Russell in-joke? ... at one point, the ancient paterfamilias of this strange family is in bed reading *The Financial Times*; but as the scene ends, we see that he's got a copy of *Playboy* secreted inside the newspaper. Presumably it's the fiction that Grandpa likes!

The Horror of It All was the first film by veteran quickie producer Robert L. Lippert's newest production company, formed to make pictures in England for worldwide 20th Century-Fox distribution. The prolific company's later titles included *Witchcraft*, *The Earth Dies Screaming* and *Curse of the Fly*. According to Tony Dalton's book *Terence Fisher—Master of Gothic Cinema*, director Fisher agreed to make *Horror of It All* during a low point in his career and later regretted it; Dalton wrote, "There are some films he rarely mentioned but this was one he really did not want to talk about at all." Apparently even English distributors were leery of the movie: It was released in the U.S. two years before it played in England.

[W]hen we – as quite often happens with a comedy – were shooting [*The Horror of It All*], we all thought it was hilarious, and then the finished version wasn't very funny. – Andrée Melly in an interview with *Little Shoppe of Horrors*' Oscar Martinez

Not a lot of unforeseeable stuff happens in movies that spoof oldtime genres like the Spooky Mystery. But at least one *Horror of It All* viewer did find something in it that he didn't expect – and that viewer was Ray Russell. "Dad definitely did not write the title song that Pat Boone sings in the scene in the old inventor's laboratory," says Marc Russell. "When he saw the movie and Pat Boone started singing, it came as a complete surprise to him!"

(For the record: "The Horror of It All," music and lyrics, were written by Boone himself.)

Chamber of Horrors (Warner Brothers, 1966)

Screenplay: Stephen Kandel; Story: Ray Russell and Stephen Kandel; Associate Producer: Jim Barnett; Produced and Directed by Hy Averback; Photography: Richard Kline (Technicolor); Music: William Lava. **Cast:** Patrick O'Neal, Cesare Danova, Wilfrid Hyde-White, Laura Devon, Patrice Wymore.

TV spin-offs of popular movies – weekly series taking advantage of the proven appeal of established big-screen favorites – sure sounds like a winning strategy. So why *isn't* it? In the 1950s, the movie mills began checking their theatrical backlogs for TV-worthy titles, but right from the start, the series were seldom the hoped-for hits: *The Thin Man, Broken Arrow, Casablanca, Bus Stop*. Some have dropped down the Memory Hole almost completely: *My Sister Eileen, Min and Bill, Mr. Smith Goes to Washington, Going My Way, Harry's Girls* (based on *Les Girls*), *How to Marry a Millionaire, The Greatest Show on Earth* and more.

In 1958, Warner Brothers planned a 3-D double-bill reissue of *House of Wax* (1953) and *Phantom of the Rue Morgue* (1954) and at the same time considered bringing a *House of Wax* series to TV. The initial segment was to have been produced by Harry Tatelman and scripted by Nelson (*The Haunting*) Gidding. This went nowhere. But the idea was revived in 1964, a year when small-screen viewers were getting weekly doses of such movie-to-TV crossovers as *Peyton Place, Flipper, 12 O'Clock High, Voyage to the Bottom of the Sea, No Time for Sergeants, The Virginian, The Farmer's Daughter* et al. Presumably encouraged by the success of *some* of these titles, a jaw-dropping number of additional movie-based series were proposed for the coming season. From MGM came announcements of *Meet Me in St. Louis, Please Don't Eat the Daisies* and *Boom Town*; from Screen Gems, *Gidget, The Wackiest Ship in the Army* and *Diamond Head*; from Universal, *Tammy* and *Ma and Pa Kettle*; from 20th Century–Fox, *The Long, Hot Summer* and *The Legend of Jesse James,* and from Warners, *Dial M for Murder, Mister Roberts* ... and *House of Wax*. From the October 19, 1964, *Variety*:

Ray Russell Plots WB's *Wax* TV Pilot

Ray Russell had been signed to pen the pilot script of Warner Bros.' *House of Wax*, being made for ABC-TV for next season. Richard Bluel is producer.

Warners made a theatrical pic of same title in 3-dimension 13 years ago [*sic*], Vincent Price and Phyllis Kirk toplining.

After this, little or nothing more was heard for over a year. Then in December 1965 came word that Hy Averback would produce and direct Warners' hour-long *House of Wax* pilot, which he was currently casting.

Ray Russell and Stephen Kandel are credited with writing the story, Kandel the teleplay. But did Russell ever actually set pen to paper? We may never know. For this title, Marc and Amanda Russell have found nothing in their collection of their dad's scripts. And in our 2004 interview, Kandel (hired after Russell had come and gone) maintained that he can't remember meeting Russell or seeing anything written by Russell. He said that as he prepared to write the teleplay, "I never heard anything more than a few offhand references to earlier groundwork. For all I know, [Russell] wrote a complete teleplay; if so, I didn't see it. *I* got a memo, a lot of verbal chitchat, a screening of *House of Wax*, a walk through the sets and away I went." It's conceivable that Russell had been a consultant, brought in for brainstorming sessions, and proposed enough usable ideas to rate a screen credit. To make things even more confusing, at least one Warners press release credits Kandel and writer-producer Jim Barnett with the screenplay. Perhaps Russell's only published comment on this project: In 1970 as Movie Nerd-dom buzzed with excitement over the announcement of the rediscovery of a print of the 1933 "lost film" *Mystery of the Wax Museum* (the earlier version of *House of Wax*), Russell wrote a letter to *Variety* saying that in 1964, when he was involved with the *House of Wax* TV pilot, he asked to see *Mystery*—and that very afternoon he found himself in a WB projection room watching "a perfect print ... in beautiful color"!

The shooting of the pilot (set in 1880 Baltimore) began not on January 5, 1966, as planned but on the 24th, perhaps because the casting process took longer than expected. Eventually the pilot's stars (who presumably would have become the series' stars) were in place: Cesare Danova and Wilfrid Hyde-White as full-time operators of a wax museum and part-time criminologists. They are assisted in both their vocation and their avocation by Pepe, a dwarf played by Mexican film and nitery performer Tun Tun. *Variety* columnist Army Archerd mentioned that Michael Dunn was considered for the latter part. A month later, Archerd reported that in this pilot, Hyde-White was called upon to use a gun for the first time in his career. "It's quite a gory series," the actor commented.

One would assume that when the pilot was finished, ABC decision-makers liked what they saw, because by early March, there were reports that in the fall, the network's Friday night prime-time lineup would consist of *The Time Tunnel* (7:30 to 8:30), *The Milton Berle Show* (8:30 to 9:30), a half-hour comedy (9:30 to 10) and *House of Wax*. Then Army Archerd (*again*) weighed in with this surprising item:

> Warners is so hot on its *House of Wax* pilot, a feature will follow whether the tv'er sells or not. The vidversion was made with ABC cooperation, passed censorship here, but somebody someplace got cold feet — temporarily? It's figured an added 35 minutes will make a bigscreen version ...

Sure enough, *House of Wax* failed to go to series – but, unlike many flunked pilots, it did not simply pass out of existence. At a time when the average pilot cost between $200,000 and $400,000, its production costs had soared to close to $650,000. That was too big a wad to blow, so yet *more* scenes were scripted and shot, stretching the pilot to feature length so that it could be released theatrically. In one of the new scenes, set in a bawdy house, Tony Curtis has a cameo as a gambler. I can't imagine why, but Curtis' cameo prompted other actors to volunteer to make quick appearances, among them Otto Preminger; but by the time these offers came in, the picture had wrapped. Incidentally, that same bawdy house scene features entertainers played by Barbro Hedstrom and Annazette, a couple of Hollywood Playboy Club bunnies. Ray Russell would have approved!

In the opening scene of the movie, *Chamber of Horrors*, a mad blue-blood, Patrick O'Neal, forces a clergyman to perform the wedding ceremony for him and his bride, a young beauty O'Neal strangled with her own hair. With the help of Danova and Hyde-White, police apprehend O'Neal and he is sentenced – but en route to prison by train, he chops off his own shackled hand and escapes. Throughout the rest of the story, *The Butcher of Baltimore* (the movie's tentative title at one point) replaces the missing hand with various weapons and begins settling scores.

In the pre-credits sequence, narrator William Conrad tells viewers that the movie's "four supreme fright points" will be preceded by a Fear Flasher (split-second inserts of blood-red film) and the Horror Horn (an electronic screeching noise). When I was a kid, New York's WNBC-TV repeatedly ran the movie, and every Fear Flasher and Horror Horn instead preceded a cement-splice and an abrupt jump to the beginning of the next scene, the local TV station's film editor apparently too squeamish to let the "carnage" be televised. Monster Kids in other parts of the country probably had the same experience. Truth be told, the violence was rather tame, but *Chamber of Horrors* does slip in several sick touches that make it a bit ahead of its time; Classic Horror Film Board moderator Gary Prange called the necrophiliac marriage set piece "one of the strongest film openings in 1960s horror cinema." The movie also has the advantage of having been made by a major studio, with large and impressive standing sets (seen in Technicolor) giving it the "look" of a movie and not a TV episode. Richard Kline photographed the pilot and the added scenes, and his work added to the impression of a pricey production.[5]

Only three of the TV series that bowed in the 1966-67 season were based on theatrical movies: *Shane*, *The Rounders* and *Tarzan*. Rejected: an aggregate $25,000,000 worth of pilots, including the movie-based *High Noon*, *From Here to Eternity*, *Marty*, *Three Coins in the Fountain*, *The Paleface*, *This Gun for Hire*, *Sunset Blvd.*, *East of Eden*, *The African Queen*, *Journey to the Center of the Earth*, *The Big Country* and probably more. As if a giant hand had turned a spigot, the flood of feature-to-series pilots was henceforth reduced to a trickle.

Read more of Stephen Kandel's memories of *Chamber of Horrors* in my book *Earth vs. the Sci-Fi Moviemakers* (McFarland, 2005).

> When Ray Russell was interviewed by Roger Anker for the March 1987 issue of *Starlog* magazine, he refused to talk about his film work on the grounds that it "lacks interest." He added, "My best scripts were never filmed. I wrote three adaptations of SF and fantasy classics for MGM: Olaf Stapledon's *Odd John*, Ibsen's *Peer Gynt* and an amalgam of two Washington Irving tales. 'Rip Van Winkle' and 'The Legend of Sleepy Hollow'— but they're still gathering dust." He also said that he had stopped writing screenplays a few years earlier, after he made what he called "a life decision": "I finally had to admit to myself that I'm not a team player, I'm a lone wolf, and all screen writing is collaboration, with producers, directors, story editors, stars, other writers. So, 1 quit cold turkey."

Two More Ray Russell Stories

Put Them All Together, They Spell Monster
(previously published in the 1966 book *The Little Lexicon of Love*)

It really is the last straw.

For some time now, the *bourgeoisie* have been catching up with every hip, inside, cultist fad to which I've taken a shine – and the minute they do, of course, it's no longer hip, inside, or cultist. It's square.

The latest thing they've spoiled is monsters. A love of movie monsters was once a very Camp thing, truly an exclusive club, and I was a charter member.

But not anymore. What with television's *The Munsters* and *The Addams Family*, and a newsstandful of monster magazines, it's all been spoiled. There are monster dolls, and monster statuettes, and monster masks ... there are even monster *cookies*.

I feel so bad about this that lately I've begun to have frustration dreams about the good old days when monsters were special, In. Had one last night, in fact. Want to hear about it? No!? Then go read another book! Anyway ...

I was in this theatre (in my pajamas, of course, bottom half only, let the Freudians make of that what they will), and a box of popcorn was in my hand. Among the other spectators, I recognized several friends of mine, an old flame, my dentist, my old flame's dentist, Elizabeth Taylor and John Quincy Adams, all in their pajamas, with the single exception of Liz – she was in the top half of mine. I doubt the significance of these details and pass them on only in the interests of documentation and good fellowship. A newsreel was in progress (I seem to remember something about Johnny Weissmuller being inaugurated President of the United States), but it was soon over and the main attraction smote the screen with an annihilating blast of neo – Stravinsky. The title was:

THE

And the subtitle:

stuff from outer space

My pulse quickened and my fingers clawed at the popcorn. ...

"I can't understand it."

The words were spoken by a young fellow with white shoe-polish in his hair and a fascinating network of greasepaint lines on his face. These told me he was Elderly and lent weight to the next utterance: "Never in my entire medical career have I encountered anything remotely like it."

The camera pulled away to reveal the body of a sumptuously-shaped starlet, horizontal on a white slab. I was keenly disappointed to see her dead, for she had been unusually active in the newspaper ads – veritably entwined in horror around the H of THE, baring her thighs and eyeballs with equal vigor, and displaying a healthy supply of pearly molars. However, I was too excited to quibble.

A gentleman with prognathous jaws and a belligerent manner asked, "What's the cause of death, Doc?"

The Doctor scratched his head, got a fingernailful of white shoe-polish, and replied softly. "Severe nausea, Lieutenant."

"Brought on by what?"

The Doctor's silence and tight-lipped headshake were eloquent. Eloquent or not, though, he had a line and, by Gadfrey, he was going to say it: "I ... don't ... know," he said. And added, "That's more in your department, isn't it – the police – rather than mine?"

It was the Lieutenant's big scene. He played it to the hilt, stalking back and forth, shoving his hands in and out of his pockets, and casting hostile glances alternately at the Doctor and at the camera. "If we only had something to *go* on!" he ranted. "*Any*thing," he whined. "Anything at all," he whimpered. "But there isn't a *thing*." A cogent line like this deserved expansion, and the Lieutenant was not a man to stint: "Not one single blessed *thing*!" Then, with a deprecating wave of his hand, he muttered, "Just these big fat globs of strange, unearthly type goo all over the body, that's all."

"Mmmnnnye-e-esss," said the Doctor (actorese for "Yes"). "But in those strange globs may lie the answer."

"Whaddaya talkin?" sneered the Lieutenant, growing more belligerent by the second.

"I suggest we get in touch with Bradstone."

"Who's that? I don't want no Federal men musclin' in on my precinct."

"Dr. Bradstone," explained the medico with withering condescension, "is the world's foremost authority on viscosimetry."

"Who? Ha?"

"Viscosimetry, Lieutenant, is the science of measuring viscosity."

"What's viscosity?"

The Doctor pointed to the body and the camera focused sharply on the strange, unearthly-type globs. "Goo," he said, solemnly.

And here, the Stravinsky got more neo than ever.

I chewed my popcorn furiously and stole a glance at Liz. She winked with abandon. "Goo," I said, solemnly, and winked back.

On the screen, one scene was melting into another with head-swimming speed. Starlets of diverse dimensions were to be seen going about such workaday pursuits as cooking, gardening, screwing rhinestones into their navels, etc., with such a remarkable degree of studied unconcern that I knew their dooms were sealed. And—sure enough—in each case, a towering shadow entered the picture, the theremin began its timorous wail, and the beauty in question looked over her shoulder, uttered Scream of Mortal Terror, Female, No. 84-B (Full-Throated), and was promptly gripped by severe nausea just at the fade-out.

Newspapers loomed upon the screen:

GOO STRIKES AGAIN!

STRANGE STUFF SLAYS SEXY SIREN!

And *Variety*, shocked at the death of a prominent girl vocalist, reported:

THRUSH HUSHED BY MUSH

"Things," said the Lieutenant, picking his nose with a matchstick, "are getting worse."

"You are not just a-clackin' your prognathous jaws, Buster," quipped a melon-bosomed blonde, undulating into range with a crackle of taffeta and flapping her well-greased eye-lids.

"Who are you?"

"Bradstone's the name: Dr. Brenda Bradstone. Girl Viscosimetrist."

"You mean *you're* the—"

"World's foremost authority?" She struck an attitude. "The same. Where is the latest victim?"

"Well, uh—"

"*One moment*." The new voice belonged to a young man with broad shoulders and a sincere tilt to his eyebrows who lumbered, profile first, into their midst. "Dr. Bradstone is not entirely correct, Lieutenant," he blathered. "Though possessing a certain proficiency in the field," and here he bowed low to the lady and sized up her ankles, "she is not the world's foremost authority."

"Who is, then, you're so smott?" asked Brenda.

"The author of *Viscosity in a Changing World, Viscosity for the Millions, How Viscous Are You?* and *Whither Viscosity?* of course. In short, myself."

"Then you're Dr. Quentin Conroy of the Institute for Viscosimetrical Research!"

"The same," said Conroy, striking an attitude.

"Well, Dr. Conroy," said Brenda, striking another attitude and strikes, also, the Lieutenant, whose hands had been roving, "just because your books have been selected by the Book-of-the-Month Club, reprinted in soft covers and serialized in *McCall's* doesn't necessarily make you a viscosimetrist's viscosimetrist. It may be news to you, but in the best viscosimetrical circles, you're considered a common vulgarizer and opportunist: in plain language, Dr. Conroy, a slob."

The Lieutenant, whose jaw had dropped at all this erudition and was now dangling indecorously from side to side, asked Brenda, "You want I should toss this bum out on his ear?"

"Dr. Conroy," replied Brenda, writhing with ambivalence and lamping her opponent's shoulder with something more than scientific interest, "is not a bum, lieutenant. A slob, yes. But not a bum. He may stay."

"Thank you," smirked Conroy, removing from his satchel a small device resembling a double-barreled rectal thermometer.

"What, pray, is that?" asked Brenda, haughtily. "A double-barreled rectal thermometer?"

"It is obvious, Dr. Bradstone," responded Conroy with cool decorum, "that you do not know a capillary viscometer from a hole in the ground."

Brenda sniffed huffily. "It that is a Thorpe and Rodger viscometer, or even a Wilhelm Ostwald viscometer, I'll eat it."

"It is neither," came the sharp riposte. "It is a Conroy viscometer. Now shake your ass and help me set up my equipment."

"Yes, sir," mumbled Brenda, submissively.

Having made the obeisance to the spirit of scientific discussion and also putting half the audience to sleep, the scene now shifted to the city room of a local newspaper. The screen was a riot of shirtsleeves, blue pencils, green eyeshades and cigarette smoke. The city editor, picking his nose with a blue pencil, was snarling at an unkempt but earnest young man. "Yurroutaya mind, Pfeiffer," he said. "Just because" – here he paused to suck a dram of coffee from a soggy container – "just because the first goo killing coincided with reports of a flying saucer sighted in the hills near town, and just because a few hundred nitwits say they've seen a weird monster fifty feet tall walkin' around, and just because a bunch of boobs swear they've been hearin' some strange, unearthly-type theremin music the last few days – *you* get the dim-bulb notion that these broads are bein' knocked off by a creature from outer space! Pfeiffer, you kill me. you know what I think? You really wanna know what I think?"

"What, boss?"

"Yurroutaya mind, Pfeiffer, that's what I think. Go get me another pint o' java."

The city editor, I noted, was cast from the same rugged mold as the police lieutenant: in fact, upon closer inspection, I discovered that he was played by the same actor, his busy hair covered with liquid latex to simulate a lumpy baldness. I admired this stroke of economy.

Pfeiffer, of course (if I may condense the action a bit here), took his story to the Lieutenant and was promptly catalogued as a troublesome illusionary. Conroy, however, overhearing the reporter's theory, got a faraway look in his eye and, loosening his Countess Mara, began to wade into his work with renewed bustle.

Two lap-dissolves and a theremin solo later, Conroy looked up fro his viscometer. His face was pale, his eyebrows knotted. "It's – incredible!" he said. "And yes – why should it be incredible? If, on our world, all living things have a basis of carbon, why then on other worlds may not life have a basis of something else? Silicon, or hydrogen, or – *this*?"

"Quentin," breathed Brenda quietly, looking soulfully into his hair-line (they had reached the First Name Stage while I wasn't looking), "what is it?"

"The stuff," said Conroy, "the horrible goo on the bodies..." He broke off, consulted his viscometer once more, then looked up again, nostrils akimbo. "Yes! Brenda, the monster that killed those poor girls, the monster that, even now, is roaming at large: that monster is a fifty-foot blob of – Vaseline!"

"*Vaseline*?!"

Conroy nodded grimly. "With hair."

"Yurroutaya mind," said the Lieutenant.

"But...but..." floundered Brenda, forgetting her lines, "but Vaseline is harmless..."

"Yes—Vaseline as *we* know it," Conroy agreed. "But what if it were endowed with *a superhuman intelligence beyond our ken*???"

"Yeah," said the Lieutenant, "but even so—"

"Lieutenant," Conroy said evenly, "picture it. What would *you* do if you saw a blob of Vaseline fifty feet high and all covered with hair coming at you?"

The Lieutenant's eyes grew glassy at the image; then he clapped his hand to his mouth and lurched straight for the washroom.

"It all fits together, Quentin," said Brenda, breathing heavily. "The severe nausea – the globs of goo – the flying saucer – the theremin music. But what is this monster's purpose in killing these girls? And why only girls?"

Conroy frowned. "I...don't...know," he said.

And suddenly, the monster was upon us. The screen was filled with hairy Vaseline – fifty feet of it, strolling oafishly down the road and humming to itself. John Quincy Adams clapped his hand to his mouth and was never seen again. My dentist climbed up the theatre wall. Liz clung to me for comfort. My popcorn, of course, went flying at the fight sight of the monster, and for a moment I was blinded by salt and falling kernels.

When my vision cleared, I saw to my horror that Brenda was in the coils of the unearthly-type creature and was giving the theremin some stiff competition in the wailing department. Next we saw Conroy, his viscometer awry, pointing wildly and yelling: "It's taking her toward the hills!"

"The hills!!" echoed Pfeiffer the reporter, materializing from behind a clothes-tree. "That's where the flying saucer was sighted!"

After some scratchy stock footage of Grant Withers and Onslow Stevens climbing in a couple of '35 Chevvies and barreling down the road, we got our first glimpse of the saucer. It was made of Limoges china, trimmed with blue. The monster oozed into the picture, lugging Brenda, whose struggles had grown noticeably lacking in sincerity. The armed services had apparently been summoned, for we were now treated to stirring shots of the U.S. infantry, the Polish cavalry, and the air force of an unidentified nation, all engaged in dust-raising activity of one sort or another, culminating in the detonation of the hydrogen bomb. Needless to say, these efforts left the monster unscathed. By the time Conroy and Pfeiffer arrived, it had miraculously released Brenda, however, and she ran toward her colleague.

"Brenda!" said Conroy. "You're all right! It let you go ... and you didn't get severe nausea ... What—"

Panting, Brenda said, "I found out everything. That theremin music – it's Morse code. The goo told me the whole story. He didn't want to kill those girls, they just got deathly ill at the sight of him. He was only looking for a mate. He's lonely."

"A mate?! But he's – that is – he doesn't have any – I mean –"

"You don't understand, Quentin. Look at my eyelids."

"They're ravishing."

"What else?"

"They're well-greased."

"Correct. *With Vaseline!*"

"You mean –"

"Exactly! All those other girls greased their eyelids with Vaseline, too. And the stuff from outer space was just looking for someone of his own kind!"

"Amazing!" Conroy embraced her. "You're wonderful, Brenda! A true scientist. Brenda, darling – will you marry me? Together, we will plumb new depths of viscosity!"

"Yurroutaya mind," said Brenda. "I'm going home with Pete."

"Pete??"

Brenda sighed ecstatically. "I can't pronounce his real name. I call him Pete because he's made of petroleum jelly – known to commercial vulgarizers like you as Vaseline."

"What? You're going back to his native planet with *him*?"

"Yes, isn't it wonderful? Talk about plumbing new depths of viscosity – man, he's *really viscous*! I'll be doing the cause of viscosimetry a great service. Besides," she added, with a libidinous growl, "I always was a sucker for tall, hairy guys."

Hand-in-pseudopod, Brenda and Pete walked toward the flying saucer as the music climbed to great heights. It was still neo, but this time it was more like Tchaikovsky than Stravinsky. Conroy took it like a man, blinked back a tear, packed his viscometer and walked slowly in the opposite direction.

The lights of the theater went up and I became suddenly aware of the coldness of the leather seat on which I was sitting. A sudden fear gripped me and I looked down to find it confirmed. Somehow, by the wizardry of dreams, I was now clad in only the tops – rather than the bottoms – of my pajamas. Furtively, I looked at Liz. *She* was wearing the bottoms. I found this turn of events charming and, as I left the theater with her, hand-in-pseudopod, I did not even try to understand the transference. That would require, I knew, a superhuman intelligence beyond my ken.

"The Devil Is a Tightwad"
(never before published)

Let's begin by assuming you write for money, like me. If you don't, read no further. Let's further assume that you're comparatively a novice but have at least two years of deadening, discouraging rejections behind you.

By now, your first stories have bounced like rubber balls from a dozen or more editors. They're dog-eared, dirty, clip-chewed, and so often folded, unfolded, and refolded that they're dangerously close to perforation at the creases.

Nobody wants them. You've exhausted all the likely markets. You've exhausted all the unlikely markets. You've revised them, re-typed them and sent them back again. Still nothing. Although they were once dear to your heart, you now regard them as turkeys. Zombies. Dead for a ducat, dead.

Enter Lucifer. As usual, he makes his appearance precisely at the moment of your darkest despair, your greatest weakness. He comes in the guise of a "little magazine."

He's a handsome devil: slick, smooth pages, shiny black type, tall straight columns. His offer is irresistible. He purrs that velvety word "publication." He draws voluptuous pictures of Your Name enshrined on a gleaming page under the title of your favorite manuscript.

As always, in transactions with this infernal gentleman, there's a catch. The catch is called No Payment.

"What of that?" you cry. The bait obscures the hook and, like Faust, you're ready to nibble. But hold on. Here's why:

The time is just a few years ago. The scene is a two-room apartment in Chicago. The apartment is occupied by a beautiful young actress, her newborn son, and a third party who is the husband and father of the first two. This fellow has had what is commonly called a checkered career: he's worked at an assortment of lackluster jobs; studied composition long enough to knock out a couple of copyrighted songs and half an opera; sung leads with an itinerant Gilbert-and-Sullivan troupe; played in reparatory theatre on the West Coast. At the time of our story he's making $55 a week in a mail-order house as a correspondent, and at night he's trying to write fiction on the kitchen table. Having had no success at this enterprise, he is a very discouraged, short-tempered, bitter young man: me.

(This present-tense, third-person stuff has served its purpose, so let's shift gears to the past-tense, first-person and stay there.) Along about this time that fellow with the cloven hooves made his appearance. Did I resist? Did I say *Retro me, Satanas*? Oh no, not I. I was weak. I gave in. I yielded to temptation and donated some of my rejects to a little magazine. They were printed. My ego swelled but my wallet remained slender. Lucifer laughed.

One of my well-traveled manuscripts, however, I was not eager to let go without payment. I still thought it was hot stuff and worth money. So, instead of giving it to the little magazine, I sent it to an agency for appraisal (a polite word meaning I wanted them to agree that it was hot stuff). Having already squandered $1.44 in postage on the story, their fee was cheap at the price.

But the agency did not think it was hot stuff. They told me, in two pages of closely typed matter, that it "completely lacked reality," had "no substance," was "absurd ... ridiculous ... unpopular ... flimsy ... impossible ... forced ... far-fetched ... strained..." and therefore, unmarketable.

With a sigh, I gave up all thought of payment and sent it to the little magazine. Having published several of my pieces that were inferior to this one, I was confident that they would snap it up.

Wrong again. It was rejected. "Not up to the standard of your earlier stuff," wrote the editor. Despair settled over me like a cold wet shroud.

But don't go away. The story isn't over. A market notice in *Writers' Digest* told me a new magazine was being launched. From the description of its needs, my oft-bounced brainchild seemed to stand a chance. Without any real hope, without even bothering to re-type the battered old warhorse, I wrapped it up for the fourteenth time and, next morning on my way to the mail order house, dropped in the mail box.

This time it did not return. Instead, I got a letter from the editor. They liked the story; would $100 be satisfactory? Satisfactory! For a 1700-word yarn that had been rejected by an agency, a contest, and eleven magazines (the last a non-payer), it was beyond satisfactory.

A few months later, *Esquire* bought another one and the avalanche had begun: an avalanche that led first, to the assistant editorship of a glossy house organ. Exactly one year after my first sale, I became Associate Editor of *Playboy* – a job I got principally on the strength of stories submitted to the publisher – stories which had been rejected anywhere from five to twenty times.

After several years as Associate Editor, I was promoted to my present position as the first Executive Editor of *Playboy*. We moved into a larger apartment; I got myself a coat with a fur collar and took to smoking long cigars. Every time I light one I give silent thanks to the little magazine editor for rejecting the story that led to it all. And, while trying unsuccessfully to blow smoke rings, I often think about some of the other drawbacks (besides no payment) of the little magazines. Which are: slow reports (anywhere from six months to two years, in my experience), a reluctance to answer their mail, and a general air of irresponsibility.

But the worst thing about them is that they tend to undermine the quality of your writing. No matter how conscientious you may be, it's hard to avoid that deadly attitude of, "Oh, what the hell, they'll print it as is – why should I bother to polish it?" The overstocked inventories and strict requirements of the top magazines are the best incentives to write stories so damned good they'll smash their way into print.

Let me anticipate the protests of little magazine editors by parenthetically acknowledging the good they do by providing outlets for scholarly works, experimental writing, specialized talents, etc. But any little magazine worth its salt pays something, however small. Those that pay nothing usually print only the dregs, have limited circulation, and collapse quickly. Thus, except for tickling the egos of the editors and print-starved writers, they serve no purpose: their writing is not of high quality and their small circulation makes them poor showcases. Poetry magazines are probably the exception. Even some of the very good ones cannot afford to pay, and at least one I know of won't even give you a gratis copy of the issue in which your poem appears!

The moral is obvious. Keep writing, keep learning, keep improving and, above all, keep mailing out those stories. But to paying markets only. Don't listen to that impecunious Prince of Darkness. Don't give them away.

Breaking the Fourth Wall and Opening Eyes: The Calling of a Castle Connoisseur Turned Film Archivist

by Rachel Del Gaudio

As latchkey kids, the content that my sister Sara and I gleefully devoured after we raced home from school was rarely censored. While the question of how well we turned out remains open for debate, this lack of censorship cultivated an unadulterated appreciation of horror films. One evening after being left home alone, I was indulging in my own movie marathon when I happened upon William Castle's *House on Haunted Hill*. My ten-year-old brain was so wrapped up in the film that the noise of my family returning mere minutes after the movie concluded sent me running to hide in a closet (I said that I *appreciated* horror films - not that I was anything closely resembling brave). Brave or not, the notion that films could have such an effect on a person determined what I wanted to dedicate my life towards.

Now a quarter-century later, as a film archivist at the Library of Congress, I strive to preserve and share some of the films that I debatably should not have been viewing at such a young age (no running to hide in closets – or vaults for that matter – involved). Working at a building that is partially built into a hill results in being inundated with questions as to what "we actually do there." It does not help that the building previously served as a Cold War–era bunker and overlooks a small town. While the bunker has been retrofitted and currently serves as the Library of Congress' Moving Image and Recorded Sound archives, locals still firmly believe in the more scandalous tales. When I report that instead of aliens and other government secrets, we actually house thousands of 16mm and 35mm film elements along with other archival material, they are skeptical. As if to ferret out the truth, I then get peppered with questions essentially requesting a list of the most impressive titles. "What is the oldest film in the collection?" "Do you have [insert prestigious title]?" Unless the inquirer is in the film business, they never ask about B-movies. Much less a horror B-movie – especially one that lacks a marquee-worthy cast. Yet these B-movies or otherwise forgotten-about mediums such as educational films, shorts and non–A list pictures are what comprises most of any film archive's collection.

At the Library of Congress Packard Campus in Culpeper, Virginia, we are lucky enough to have a beautiful movie theater which gets utilized year round. Around 160 movies are shown annually and most of those are from actual 35mm prints within the collection. As we have our own film laboratory, the LoC preserves and makes new prints of dozens of titles each year. These newly preserved films, as well as beloved classics (especially those that correspond with calendar events such as war anniversaries and Christmas), have comprised most of the calendars throughout the decade-plus that the theater has been open. However, like the locals' questions, horror B-movies have been mostly excluded from the programming.

Late in 2018, one of my longtime dreams finally came true. We screened *House on Haunted Hill* complete with our own twist on the Emergo process. The Packard Campus theater is new and pristine

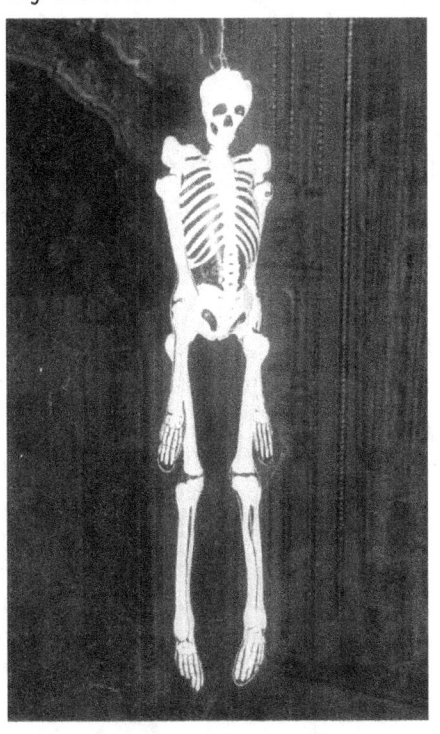

The inflatable House on Haunted Hill *skeleton that soared high in theaters filled with Monster Kids of all ages.*

Pictured: the 35mm print of Mr. Sardonicus *that went from the basement of a Lebanon, Pennsylvania, collector to a Library of Congress archive, where it's now rehoused in archival cans with new labels.*

enough that the projection booth does not have a raised opening to rig a skeleton on a pulley to hover above the audience like the original Emergo. Instead, projectionist David March and I utilized the organ pit to slowly raise a posable skeleton to stage level employing low, red lights to cast an eerie glow. While some audience members arrived anticipating *something*, their reaction proved that the slow lift from below the screen was a surprise. Thankfully, unlike when the film was originally released, there were no projectiles catapulted at the skeleton.

In the months following the skeleton's grand debut, two more William Castle films were screened. *Homicidal* was easier as the Fright Break gimmick is built into the movie, but I was back in action when we showed *Mr. Sardonicus*. Much to my demented delight, the film was programmed in December – just in time to remind everyone to plaster smiles on their faces during any forced holiday family gatherings. The LoC's original 35mm print was donated by the family of John Stegmoyer, a collector with a 35mm theater in his home in Lebanon, Pennsylvania. Side note: Mr. Stegmoyer's collection was kept in his basement, and myself and five co-workers did all the moving. All 982 films, trailers and television shows were hauled up a flight and a half of stairs *by hand* and loaded into a rented moving truck with the hot, late–June sun above. Archiving is *such* glamorous work!

The evening of the *Mr. Sardonicus* screening, I handed out copies of the Punishment Poll cards to a somewhat baffled audience. The film rolled, and as the time to vote approached, I proudly clutched my Punishment Poll card and straightened my arm to the sky like a child hoping to get chosen first. When I glanced around the theater, I realized that most members of the audience were hesitant to interact with a filmmaker who had been dead for over 40 years. *Weird.* The charismatic William Castle eventually cajoled the reluctant viewers and all votes were "counted." I cannot fault them for needing a push to become active participants in a film; this breaking-down of the fourth wall is not a common occurrence at the Packard Campus nor in films in general.

Films are constructed to be the ultimate escapism, and it can be jarring to suddenly be asked to become an active participant in one. In the heyday of Castle's gimmicks – from the mid–1950s through mid–1960s – audiences were being groomed by the filmmaker to expect the unexpected. In today's movie-gimmick–free world, the effect makes the audience feel juvenile. Nevertheless, that frivolity is exactly what I enjoy about *Mr. Sardonicus* and other Castle films. The inherent playfulness reminds me of being a kid and gluing myself to the television devouring old movies back when American Movie Classics lived up to its name. Then (and now), Castle's level of ballyhoo lured me deeper into the world of vintage films and made me yearn for a time when such unapologetic gimmicks were embraced and not shunned.

Castle's infectious energy and enthusiasm urge you to use your imagination and join Uncle Bill in embracing mayhem. Mayhem inasmuch as viewers enter the theater expecting a standard "scary sto-

An eerie image from 1905's The Hen That Laid the Golden Eggs.

ry," but get the added experience of show-stopping shocks — literal shocks in the case of *The Tingler*, and literal show-stops in the case of *Homicidal* and *Mr. Sardonicus*. Castle's specialty is taking a seemingly ordinary narrative, and then not only adding a gimmick but also allowing time for audiences to absorb and enjoy the twist. With films that separate themselves so far from the traditional Hollywood narrative, it is easy to see why viewers would exit theaters brimming with conversation. Each person who recommends or programs a William Castle film becomes a salesperson, just like the maestro of schlock - which is exactly what I was doing at the Library of Congress' Packard Campus that December evening: carrying on a little showmanship in an otherwise stodgy world.

John Goodman lovingly captured that showmanship spirit as Lawrence Woolsey in Joe Dante's *Matinee* (1993). While the film is essentially a love letter to William Castle (and movies in general), the relationship between horror filmmakers and their audiences is perfectly punctuated with two lines of dialogue. "The people who go like this [*he covers his eyes*] at the scary parts, they aren't getting the whole benefit. You gotta keep your eyes open." This impulse to obscure our vision from things that frighten us has existed throughout the history of motion pictures. Possibly *because* of this, horror and fantasy films have a very close relationship with eyes and the sight that accompanies them.

Pathé's *The Hen That Laid the Golden Eggs* (1905) features two large pairs of disembodied eyes closely watching the protagonist as he greedily fondles his gold. While those eyes represent paranoia, the eyes of monsters tend to be the first signifier that they are otherworldly and murderous creatures. The often-referenced shots of Bela Lugosi in *Dracula*'s (1931) title role utilize a light that specifically accentuates his menacing eyes. Likewise, the intense shot of Conrad Veidt's eyes opening in *The Cabinet of Dr. Caligari* (1920) indicates that he is a supernatural character that we should fear. In modern zombie films such as *28 Days Later* (2002) and *Dawn of the Dead* (2004), the first signal that normal life has ceased and the dead have reanimated are their inhuman eyes. Eyes have also been employed to unsettle audiences. The Pale Man in *Pan's Labyrinth* (2006) has a sightless head which is navigated by an eye on each palm. Possibly generating the most nightmare fuel of them all, *Un Chien Andalou* (1929) famously features an eyeball being sliced by a razor blade.

William Castle joins these prestigious filmmakers at the well-traveled intersection of Horror Film Alley and Sight Boulevard with *Mr. Sardonicus*. While the distorted smile of Baron Sardonicus has become the public's salient memory of the film, it is actually the eyes that play a larger part within the movie. From the titular character's mask and his abhorrence of mirrors, to the audience's visual ballot-casting, the film hinges on our relationship with eyes and the sight that goes with them.

The plot revolves around a man who went to great lengths to obtain a winning lottery ticket. Acquiring the ticket gave him wealth, a castle, servants and

The baronic lord of the land, and his lady. The mask hides this human gargoyle's face of horror, but he alerts the world (its Latin speakers, anyway) to his naked-gums-and-teeth look via his nom de ghoul, *Sardonicus.*

a new wife; seemingly everything traditional values state you must have to be happy. That is, everything but an attractive appearance. After being educated that grave robbing is the lowest deed a person can commit, seeking fortune and a better life, he stole from his own father's grave. The act robbed him of his good looks, as glimpsing the father's corpse left the grave robber with a physical reminder: a replica of the frightful death grin he saw in the coffin. This grimace serves as Sardonicus' personal scarlet letter for all the world to see and recoil from.

To hide his new skull-like look (naked teeth and gums), Sardonicus wears a mask. This mask covers everything but his eyes, limiting his worldview to what he can see through the small openings. These narrow slits are representative of how little we know about Sardonicus. As the only backstory we receive is through a story Sardonicus himself relates, the audience is only cognizant of what the man reveals about himself. While he never claims to be a hero, the picture he paints via a flashback illustrates how he faced bad circumstances and a demanding first wife. In Sardonicus' eyes, he is a victim, and he is determined to seek justice and revert his face back to normal so that he no longer has to hide behind a mask.

Just as the film was constructed to reveal the omnipresent grimace in dramatic fashion, the dialogue and characters' reactions reveal just how horrified the audience should be by the baron's distorted face. His statement "If you had my face, Sir Robert, your house would be devoid of mirrors too" underlines just how hideous we must expect his face to be. Coupled with the screams of the fair servant and the stationmaster's recoiling at the mere mention of the name Sardonicus, this signals the audience to judge him as ghastly before even seeing what lies behind the mask.

But this mask also symbolizes just how little Sardonicus sees, and therefore understands, of the world. While he has gone to an extraordinary extent to be educated in worldly and medical affairs, the baron lacks emotional maturity. The most telling example is his relationship with his second wife. Forced into a loveless marriage, the baroness makes no secret of her fear and revulsion of Sardonicus. While trying to persuade the doctor, Sir Robert, to bend to his demands and cure him, Sardonicus actually threatens to disfigure his wife's face in the hope that if she too were viewed as a monster, then perhaps she wouldn't bar her bedroom door against him. If he would open his eyes to more than his immediate surroundings, then perhaps he would be more empathetic. His heavily alluded-to rape of the fair village woman and any lack of acknowledgment of its brutishness illustrate his psychotic behavior which he fails to perceive.

The script also contains frequent references to sight and how important seeing and physical appearance are. From William Castle's prologue "it's good to see you again, my homicidal friends," the visual remains a constant thread throughout the film in even minor characters such as the gravedigger who mentions "my eyes are not what they were" when he comes upon Marek (the future Sardonicus) and his father in the graveyard. Furthermore, inanimate objects reflect this sentiment. A religious icon statue silently witnesses the grave robbing, and the castle's garden contains no lovely flowers for the occupants to gaze upon. Instead, the grounds are indicative of the horrors that can be found inside the castle: only weeds flourish. The titular character and his own description of the ordeal that has scarred him pick up that thread: "What I had not foreseen was that the face of my father, the muscles stretched by a terrible death rigor, would look directly and hideously upon me." His description of "a constant and soul-shattering smile" is beautifully poignant.

We veer further down Sight Boulevard just seven minutes into the film, in the form of Sir Robert's conversation with a fellow doctor about deadly poisons and their "useful[ness] in treating the ailments of the optic nerve." To the uninitiated, that line of dialogue almost feels like throwaway medical jargon but it actually forecasts the film's entire plot: Sir Robert can only alter how Sardonicus views his situation (which by extension remedies his ailment) with the threat of utilizing deadly poisons. Had not the pair been cleverly interrupted by their quest for that day's post, the entire crux of the story may have been laid out. *Insightful filmmaking indeed.* As explained by Sir Robert, he played Sardonicus' own sight against him, making certain that he saw ~~lab rats~~ "dead dogs" being removed from the makeshift laboratory. Once Sardonicus *saw* the evidence, he believed that the doctor had gone to great lengths to create the cure. This belief was just the placebo that Sardonicus needed to finally confront his past ghoulish act.

As is the nature of films, the audience's knowledge is limited to what it witnesses on screen and the film visits that visual theme via characters' internal struggles. Beyond the glaring example of Sardonicus is the servant Krull, who experiences a

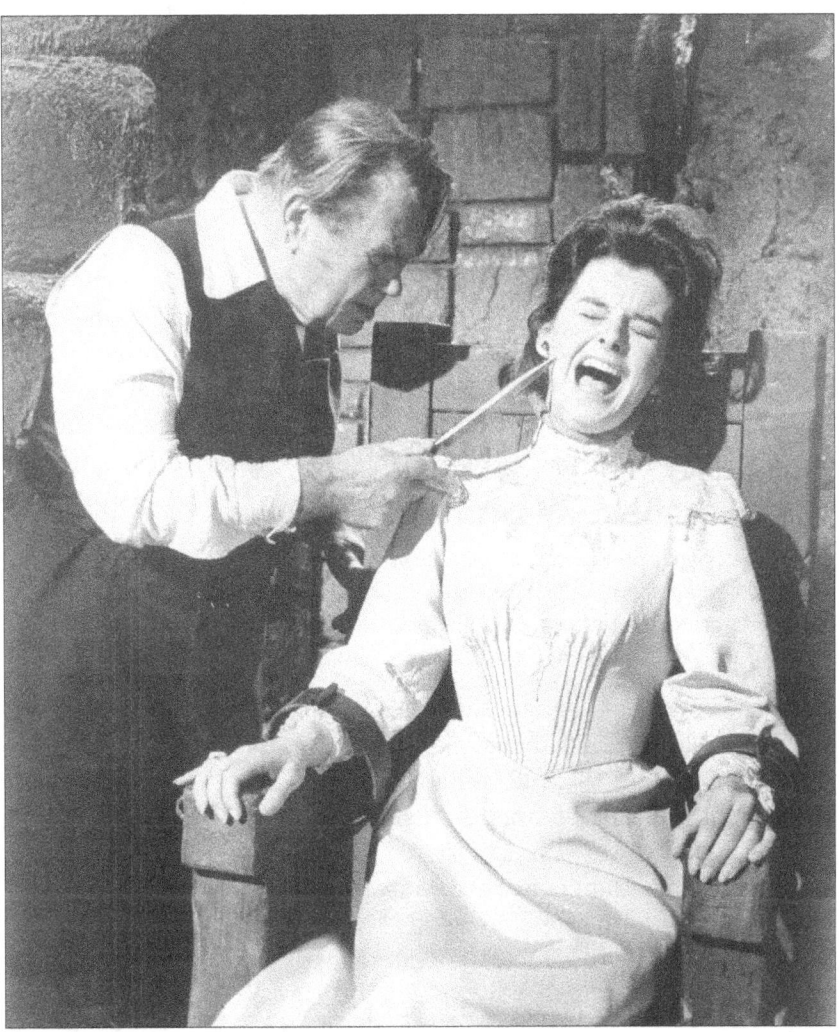

In any "castle of horrors"–type movie, it's nice to have a Krull around, a character to give the joint atmosphere. But Maude's mileage may differ. (Courtesy Ronald V. Borst/Hollywood Movie Posters).

transformation by the conclusion of the film. Krull is blind in one eye as a result from a punishment he received from Sardonicus. Along with this partial loss of vision, the injury also symbolically blinded him to how horrible his master had become. Krull follows his master's orders even when it means harming others. The one time Krull questions Sardonicus is when the baron demands Krull disfigure the baroness' face: "But she is so *beautiful*," Krull protests. It is not Sardonicus' faulty reasoning, nor the act of violence that has halted Krull, it is the threat to the loss of visual beauty.

When Sardonicus has been "cured" and a mirror is uncovered, Krull finally sees his reflection. In that moment, he realizes how blind he had been and sees how he too will be judged. When Krull glimpses his reflection, he figuratively regains his eyesight and his disposition changes from faithful servant to ambivalent companion.

Sir Robert finally conveys to Krull that the baron's cure must come from within himself. "Oh, I seeeeee," the henchman grins. But he's actually got one eye toward settling the score with Sardonicus.

After the results of the Punishment Poll are tallied and it has been decided that Sardonicus deserves further punishment, Krull refrains from sharing the insight he learned from Sir Robert about the placebo. Thanks to the power of information, Krull finally has the upper hand, a realization that he punctuates with the statement "I *see*!" Before addressing his distressed master, Krull tenderly rubs his scarred eye as he solidifies his decision to let Sardonicus suffer. As he enjoys the smorgasbord, Krull almost gleefully watches the baron's anguish of struggling against himself in an attempt to eat.

Just as the grimace on Sardonicus' face mocks those who can see, Castle stops the narrative and asks the audience to make visual votes to decide Sardonicus' fate. While serving as only a gimmick (no "happy ending" was ever made), the act of voting breaks the barrier between screen and audience, which in turn urges audience members to glance around the room themselves. Audience members cast their Punishment Poll votes based on what they witnesses with their own eyes. In turn, Castle (with much fanfare) tabulates the results with his vision. Castle requests that the viewers hold their ballots higher, so that viewers have longer to survey those around them. Friends and family learn something about the demeanor of fellow patrons – and perhaps discover that their loved ones are not as pious as they seem.

I hope that today's latchkey kids continue to get a chance to view these delightful B-movies and discover the visual and interactive experience that is William Castle. Who knows, it might help to give rise to a whole new generation of film archivists!

Good night, my Sardonic friends.

Krull kruel-ly sees to it that the baron gets no dinner ... just deserts.

Endnotes

Mr. Sardonicus Production History

1. Decades after they were written, Russell's "Captain Clark of the Space Patrol" stories were published in the first issue (Spring 1976) of *Odyssey*, a short-lived (only two issues) SF magazine. They also appeared in the Russell collection *The Devil's Mirror* (1980). "*The Devil's Mirror* has a large selection of some of his very best short stories … *and* 'Captain Clark,'" says Marc Russell. "Not all writers manage to get some of their childhood scribblings published!"

2. "Bill was the kind of guy crew members ribbed," Edward Bernds, a Columbia sound recordist at that time, told me regarding his co-worker Castle. "Like Rodney Dangerfield, he got no respect. Some guys seemed destined by nature to be the butt of jokes and ribs; Bill was one of 'em. His real name was Schloss – that's *castle* in German. And because the crew guys knew that Bill aspired to be a director, and an artistic one, they called him Orson Schloss.

   "Even some directors participated in the ribbing, some of which to my mind was downright cruel. Charlie Vidor started out at Columbia directing B-pictures. We were doing one that involved scenes of the crew of a German submarine. Bill Castle had been a stage actor, and Vidor demanded that he get a German sailor's uniform and play one of the parts. [The uniform was too small for Castle and he looked ridiculous in it.] Now, Charlie Vidor was a mean, vicious little bastard, and he rehearsed and harassed poor Bill until Bill was ready to weep, or walk out, or both.

   "Maybe what sustained Bill through those humiliating days at Columbia was his determination that one day he'd make it big, and that he did."

3. "He could lie faster than anybody I ever saw!" according to Robb White, Castle's moviemaking partner from 1957 to 1960. "We went to a meeting at Columbia one time and he told a horrendous lie. When we came out, I said, 'Bill, why did you tell a lie like that?' And he said, 'To keep in practice!' He was un-embarrassable, that guy."

4. There *was* no writer named Theo Durrant; in actuality, 12 mystery writers collaborated on *The Marble Forest*, each contributing one chapter, and the name "Theo Durrant" went on the cover as author. By 1950 when it was published, probably very few readers knew that there had once *been* a real-life Theo Durrant, an assistant Sunday School superintendent who committed a double-murder (two young women) in San Francisco a half-century earlier. The grisly killings were compared to the work of Jack the Ripper. By March 1958, Castle was announcing that his first follow-up to *Macabre* would be a movie about the maniacal Durrant, *The Girl in the Belfry*, to be scripted by one of *The Marble Forest*'s 12 authors, Lenore Offord; it was never made.

5. The Philadelphia coroner cited "sudden fright" as the possible cause of death when 25-year-old Albert Orsini turned up his toes in a Market Street theater during a Friday night, June 26, 1953, showing of *The Maze*. Then, a few days before Halloween 1956, nine-year-old Stewart Cohan succumbed to the terrors of United Artists' *The Creeping Unknown* in Chicago's Lake Theater. After a six-hour autopsy, the coroner's pathologist revealed, "[T]he boy died of a heart collapse after extraordinary tension while watching a movie."

6. The Emergo skeleton would slide out along the wire, that's all that would happen. But on TV's *This Is Your Life* (January 28, 1959), here's what William Castle *said* would happen: "[Emergo] is a new process, and what actually happens is, the ghosts and the skeletons leave the screen, and all the objects leave the screen and wander throughout the audience, go up to the balcony, roam around, meet the public, and go back into the screen."

7. Castle originally intended to make *Ghost Train*, an original film concept he had developed for his Columbia slate, just ahead of *Sardonicus*, but that proposed picture never left the station. *Variety* reported on January 19, 1961, that Castle "has dropped plans to film *Ghost Train*.… A property called [*The*] *Ghost Train* was filmed for Gaumont-British [in 1931], and J. Arthur Rank informed Castle he has plans to remake the film. Thus, Castle now moves ahead with *Mr. Sardonicus*.…" One wonders why Castle didn't just change the title and get right back on track. Incidentally, Rank then proceeded *not* to remake *The Ghost Train*.

8. James Brown confused *Psycho* and *Homicidal* during a 1969 appearance on TV's *Mike Douglas Show*—the Godfather of Soul even addressing a question about *Homicidal* to fellow guest Hitchcock! Hitch sidestepped it so easily and amusingly that one gets the feeling that this wasn't the first time it had happened.

9. Amusingly, Castle, the indefatigable ringmaster of horror movie mayhem, got a bad scare himself during a *Homicidal* test engagement in Youngstown, Ohio. Just a few minutes into the movie, there's a very bloody stabbing, strong stuff for 1961 – and once that scene played, according to Castle, "about 500 people got up and walked out. I thought we were sunk." But the theater manager told him that it was an exodus of patrons who had just finished seeing the movie from beginning to end, and had stayed over to enjoy the stabbing scene a *second* time!

10. White told me in our 1989 interview, "I just said I didn't want to work for him any more. I didn't like working for Bill. Just as soon as I wasn't putting my own money into these pictures any more, he got very bossy. Also, there had been the business about the *Homicidal* script, the way he ripped off *Psycho*. When I found that out, I told Bill I would never work for him again. ...I never saw Bill again after *Homicidal*."

11. *Mr. Sardonicus* is often called Russell's first script for Hollywood – but a teleplay may have preceded it. According to a May 1960 *Variety*, TV producer-director John Florea and writer Charles Beaumont had formed a TV production company to make a new series, *Out There*, and they were armed with 14 finished teleplays by Beaumont, Russell, Jerry Sohl, George Clayton Johnson, William F. Nolan, Ray Bradbury, John Tomerlin, Robert Bloch, Algernon Blackwood and Richard Matheson.

12. Marc Russell adds an amusing footnote: "Mom and Dad made the trip by train. Mom noticed that the train crew was being exceptionally nice to her, which puzzled her. When the train reached its destination, she learned that they thought she was Polly Bergen!"

13. It's possible that Kirk Douglas was once attracted to Russell's novella: Marc Russell recalls that, nine or ten years after the Castle movie, Ray was contacted by Douglas' agency: "Someone there had the great idea that 'Sardonicus' could make a good movie. They were apparently unaware that it had already been done!"

14. On December 28, 1961, *Variety* announced that Russell was set to script *The Spitting Image*, an original comedy that Castle was prepping, but the movie was not made. Well, at least Russell got *one* job (*Zotz!*) out of his multiple picture writing contract with Castle. Alex Gordon wrote in *Fangoria* that, while making *The Underwater City* at Columbia in 1961, "Castle promised me a producer job with his proposed new company to make films under his executive aegis. It turned out he merely wanted me to drive him home, which I would have been glad to do without all the hoopla."

Mask hysteria! Maude is horrorstruck at the sight of the baron's paralyzed pan. Actually, there's no such scene in the picture; we don't even know if Maude has ever seen her husband's incapable-of-kissing kisser. (Courtesy Ronald V. Borst/Hollywood Movie Posters)

15. *The New York Times*' Howard Thompson sneered at Castle and *Sardonicus* throughout his October 19, 1961, review; but if Castle and the movie were *that* bad, they shouldn't have been able to fool cocky bright-boy Thompson into writing that it was English-made. And yet that's just what Thompson did.

16. According to the *Mr. Sardonicus* publicity squib "Finds Little Love":

HOLLYWOOD – In her two Hollywood film roles, German actress Ilse Burkert has been on the losing end, romantically. In her first picture, *The Blue Angel* [1959], the pretty brunette lost out to Mai Britt over the affections of Curt Jurgens.

Now in William Castle's *Sardonicus*, Ilse remains out in the cold, when Annalena Lund is picked by star Guy Rolfe as his feminine companion.

"It is discouraging," muses the shapely Miss Burkert. "I always heard American men were so gallant. I guess it doesn't include scriptwriters."

17. Audience members voted on the fate of a movie character for the first time in *Mr. Sardonicus*—and for the *second* time in 1963 when they saw filmmaker Larry Buchanan's *Free, White and 21*, a Dallas-made courtroom drama based on a recent criminal assault case in that city. Frederick O'Neal starred as a black businessman on trial for allegedly raping a woman; after the judge charges the on-screen jury, the showing of the film would stop and movie theater audience members would cast their "guilty" or "not guilty" ballots. By a wild coincidence, the movie's other starring role—the woman charging rape—was played by Annalena Lund, Mr. Sardonicus' pick of the peasant girls!

18. Russell's script calls for Sir Robert, in his room, to faintly hear the girl's "<u>almost</u> inaudible ... last, despairing 'No!'" and to look "visibly disturbed." But in the movie, that bit is botched: We see Sir Robert while the sound of the anguished "No!"s, loud and clear as a bell, is reaching his room; and he reacts only by momentarily turning his head, then casually commencing to unpack his bag. The viewer gets the impression that Sir Robert, despite having just arrived, already knows that cries in the night are just part of the drill at the House of Sardonicus, and that he should simply ignore them!

19. One amusing/annoying thing about the scene: Marek, standing on the coffin lid, forces the coffin open by putting the point of his shovel near the edge of the lid and wiggling it. I'd love to know the scientific principle behind this feat.

20. On a trivial note: In the Cornell Woolrich story "Port Mortem," first published in *Black Mask* magazine in 1940, a winning sweepstakes ticket is retrieved from the pocket of an exhumed body. It has been dramatized for radio and TV series, including *Alfred Hitchcock Presents*.

"Maybe if a man looks ugly, he does ugly things," Bateman ruminated in The Raven *(1935). Mr. Sardonicus says there's no "maybe" about it. (Courtesy Ronald V. Borst/Hollywood Movie Posters)*

21. Even Maude, dippy about Conan Doyle, ought to have known about the hypodermic syringe: Sir Arthur's second Sherlock Holmes story "The Sign of Four" (1890) begins with a description of cocaine user Holmes plunging one into his arm and pressing the piston. While reading Chapter 6, Maude's eye might also have been caught by the passage in which Holmes recognizes the distortion on the face of a murder victim as "[a] Hippocratic smile, or '*risus sardonicus*,' as the old writers called it."

Could Ray Russell have first learned of *risus sardonicus* in "The Sign of Four," and made Maude a Conan Doyle fan as a tip of the hat?

22. That's an assumption on my part. Toward the end of the second day of shooting, March 29, the moviemakers shot the Peasant Cottage bedroom scene in which a whimpering Marek returns from the cemetery and Elenka lights a candle; this is followed in the movie by a three-second extreme closeup of Marek with the skull teeth. Surely they didn't put the appliance on Rolfe that day to get that four or five feet of film; surely they

waited until a day when he'd wear it in much longer scenes.

23. In Russell's novella, the rays of the moon transformed the castle façade: "[They threw] the castle into sudden, startling chiaroscuro, its windows fleetingly assuming the appearance of sightless though all-seeing orbs, its portcullis becoming for an instant a gaping mouth, its entire form striking the physical and the mental eye as would the sight of a giant skull."

24. Radilac hailed from Czechoslovakia, the part of the world where, roughly speaking, *Mr. Sardonicus* is set. According to a hard-to-Czech line in his 1972 *Variety* obit, he was a "film, stage and radio star" there.

25. Talking with interviewer François Truffaut, Hitchcock, the master of audience manipulation, said that in this scene, he wasn't trying to frighten viewers, he was trying to make them feel like killing a man – "and that's a good deal tougher."

26. From the Funny Coincidence Dept.: Almost 130 years after the 1880 setting of the story, and almost 50 after the making of the movie, scientists in Italy determined in 2009 that the toxic plant *hemlock water dropwort* makes facial muscles contract into a grimace or rictus. Poor Marek!: He went the long way around to get the affliction – guilt and shock over what he saw in Dad's grave that moon-bright midnight – and the long way around to have it cured; and now he lives on an estate where he can get it again, this time the old-fashioned way, just by walking in his own garden!

27. Nearly all of *Mr. Sardonicus*' stars were also in *Thrillers*. Vladimir Sokoloff was not only in "Teakwood" but also "Flowers of Evil." Audrey Dalton leading-ladied in "The Prediction," "Hay-Fork and Bill-Hook" and "The Hollow Watcher," while Oscar Homolka was the proprietor of the "Waxworks." Erika Peters is dispatched by skeleton hands at the start of "Prisoner in the Mirror."

28. Soon two *more* members of the Russell clan traded Chicago for the Hills of Beverly: Six months after the Ray Russell brood migrated west, Ray's dad (newly retired from the Chicago Transit Authority) and mom built a nest (well, actually an apartment) six blocks from Ray's new home.

Born in the 1800s he was; *homely as a mud fence he may have been. But Oscar Homolka went home every night to a nicelooking,* much *younger wife: stage-screen-TV actress Joan Tetzel. On Broadway, she was Nurse Ratched to Kirk Douglas' McMurphy in the original* One Flew Over the Cuckoo's Nest *(1963-64).*

29. According to Marc Russell, "That never-made 'comedy with Tony Curtis,' *Exit 41* aka *The Soft Sell* … that was just a cover story. You will never guess what it was really going to be, so I will tell you. It was going to be a nostalgic documentary about monster movies, consisting mostly of clips (some lengthy, some short) from the old classics, and also some more recent movies. Tony Curtis was going to be the host."

30. Amanda Russell points out that "Sardonicus" has appeared in nine English-language anthologies. "Most significant among these is *The Oxford Book of Gothic Tales*, Oxford University Press, 1992. Its inclusion in this anthology is an exceptional honor because Oxford University is the oldest university in the English-speaking world. Teaching existed in some form at Oxford as far back as 1096. Another noteworthy anthology is *The Century's Best Horror Fiction*; the two massive volumes feature one story published during each year of the 20th century as best story of that year. 'Sardonicus' was chosen as the best horror story of 1961."

31. Perhaps modern-day Monster Kids are getting only half that joke: In 1960, Henry Mancini and Johnny Mercer wrote the song "Moon River" for the movie *Breakfast at Tiffany's* (1961) and in one line, heard twice, the singer refers to "my huckleberry friend." In addition to referencing his other fright flick, could Castle's "my homicidal friends" have also been a nod to the mega-hit "Moon River"'s "my huckleberry friend"?

This is one for the "Be Careful What You Wish For" files: Janku (David Janti) brings his friends Marek and Elenka (Guy Rolfe and Erika Peters) news of the winning lottery ticket; Elenka nags Marek to exhume it; but she's not the one who comes up smiling.

32. The amount of overseas business done by Columbia movies in 1961 was a big improvement on the previous year, largely due to their hit *The Guns of Navarone*. But studio exec Mo Rothman also ascribed the overseas boom to the marketing of inexpensive but exploitable pictures such as *Homicidal*, and said that Castle's European tour played an important part in skyrocketing grosses wherever he visited. With his low-cost creep-shows, Castle had become quite a rainmaker for the company.

33. Amidst all this activity, Castle was one of a number of producers asked by a *Variety* writer, "What is your favorite motion picture out of all the pictures you've ever seen?" Castle's pick: 1930's *All Quiet on the Western Front*, which he first saw as a teen. "[W]hen it came out, I was young enough to be impressionable, and years later it still held up for me … it had an identification … a tremendous emotional impact … and movement." Castle's second choice: *Spellbound* (1945).

    You'd think that Castle, second to none in self-promotion, would have named one of his own pictures. But he left that to Alfred Hitchcock, who picked his 1943 suspenser *Shadow of a Doubt*.

34. There *was* a Castle movie with two different endings: On the day that *Macabre* wrapped, August 12, 1957, *The Hollywood Reporter* ran an item stating that he had two endings in the can to submit to exhibitors.

35. To the fans who have written that Castle was aping Hitchcock when he began starring in his own movies' trailers: a reminder that before Hitchcock did it for *Psycho*, Castle did it for *The Tingler*. Looks like Hitchcock took a page from *Castle's* book!

Guy Rolfe

1. In 1989, Rolfe was cast in a BBC three-part mini-series, *The Dark Angel*, an *Uncle Silas* adaptation starring Peter O'Toole. In this version, Guy portrayed Dr. Bryerly, Maud's father's physician friend, who mistrusts Uncle Silas.

2. *The New York Times'* Bosley Crowther praised the way *Khyber Rifles* took advantage of the new CinemaScope format, and perceptively surmised that the Power-Rolfe fight, with the combatants

"stretched out in a straining grapple on the floor" throughout, was done that way so that they'd fill theaters' new wide screens.

3. Archive footage of Rolfe from past *Puppet Master* films was used by producer Band in *Puppet Master: The Legacy* (2003), *Killjoy 3* (2010) and *Puppet Master: Blitzkrieg Massacre* (2018).

Audrey Dalton

1. Alice was said to have acted in the Irish move *Willy Reilly and His Colleen Bawn* (1920). "I did hear that rumor once before but unfortunately after my mother and father were dead," Audrey said. "I have no memory of any talk of it when I was growing up. I imagine if my mother was in it, it was probably as an extra or a small part for a gag. She would have been 19 or 20, before she married my dad. She never, ever expressed any interest in being an actor to my knowledge. My father was the famous one."

2. In 1954, *Screenland Plus TV-Land*'s Ruth Cummings Rowland asked Wagner what it was like working with Dalton: "Well, Audrey is quite different in personality from the others [I've acted with]. She has that English reserve. But once you know her, you find she has a very subtle, yet zingy sense of humor that sort of jolts you."

Russell's Other Horrors

1. *The Crime of Dr. Crespi* (1936), the screen's first feature version of "Premature Burial," barely nodded to the Poe tale. It had a contemporary hospital setting.

2. When Milland is bending Court's ear with a description of what it's like to be buried alive, it's dialogue adapted from the Poe story. Also derived from Poe is the mausoleum that Milland builds for himself, full of just-in-case escape hatches and hidden exits. But that's about *all* the headstart Poe gave to the screenwriters.

3. Marc Russell agrees that the X-ray effects are a letdown: "A few really do give the impression of seeing through solid objects, but many are just

Sardonicus made the cover of Famous Monsters—*as a Basil Gogos painting—in 1976.*

things out of focus with weird colors. It has also occurred to me that what Xavier has is not technically X-ray vision. It might more accurately be called CT-Scan vision."

4. Scripts for *Genghis Khan* and *The Dunwich Horror* were indeed written, says Marc Russell, but he doesn't think *Off on a Comet* was.

5. Actually, *Chamber of Horrors was* a rather pricey production. *Variety* reported that according to various sources, the final negative cost had topped a million. Director Joshua Logan happened to see some of the *Chamber of Horrors* dailies and he too was impressed, and subsequently sought out Kline to shoot his next picture, *Camelot* (1967). For *Camelot*, his first feature as cinematographer, Kline received an Oscar nomination

www.ingramcontent.com/pod-product-compliance
Lightning Source LLC
Chambersburg PA
CBHW082315230426
43667CB00034B/2751